Nebraska Symposium on Motivation 1983

Volume 31

University of Nebraska Press
Lincoln and London 1984

Nebraska Symposium on Motivation 1983

Theories of Schizophrenia and Psychosis

Richard A. Dienstbier

William D. Spaulding and James K. Cole

Rue L. Cromwell

P. H. Venables

Raymond A. Knight

Peter A. Magaro

Kurt Salzinger

Series Editor

Volume Editors

Professor of Psychiatry, Pediatrics, and Psychology
University of Rochester

Professor of Psychology
University of York

Associate Professor of Psychology
Brandeis University

Professor of Clinical Psychology
Ohio State University

Polytechnic Institute of New York and the New York State Psychiatric Institute

Charles J. Wallace   *Clinical Associate Professor of*
                           Psychology
                           University of California
                           at Los Angeles

Steven E. Boone   *Assistant Research Psychologist*
                           University of California
                           at Los Angeles

Keith H. Nuechterlein   *Assistant Professor of Psychiatry*
                           University of California
                           at Los Angeles

Herbert E. Spohn   *Director of Research*
                           The Menninger Foundation

Nebraska Symposium on
Motivation, 1983, is Volume 31
in the series on
CURRENT THEORY AND
RESEARCH IN MOTIVATION

Copyright 1984 by the University of Nebraska Press
International Standard Book Number 0-8032-4148-8 (Clothbound)
International Standard Book Number 0-8032-9145-0 (Paperbound)
All rights reserved
Manufactured in the United States of America

The paper in this book meets the guidelines for permanence and durability of the Committee on Production Guidelines for Book Longevity of the Council on Library Resources.

"The Library of Congress has cataloged this serial publication as follows:"
Nebraska Symposium on Motivation.
    Nebraska Symposium on Motivation. [Papers] v. [1]—1953—
    Lincoln, University of Nebraska Press.
        v. illus, diagrs. 22 cm. annual.
    Vol. 1 issued by the symposium under its earlier name: Current Theory and Research in Motivation.
    Symposia sponsored by the Dept. of Psychology of the University of Nebraska.
    1. Motivation (Psychology)

BF683.N4   159.4082   53-11655

    Library of Congress

Preface

*L*ike all volumes of the *Nebraska Symposium on Motivation* published since the early 1970s, this volume is devoted entirely to a single topic. It focuses on theory and research in schizophrenia and psychosis.

During the year past, it has been a pleasure to work with Professors Will Spaulding and James Cole, who shared responsibilities as volume editors of this volume. My thanks to both.

The Symposium series is supported largely by funds donated in the memory of Professor Harry K. Wolfe to the University of Nebraska Foundation by the late Professor Cora L. Friedline. This Symposium volume, like those of the recent past, is dedicated to the memory of Professor Wolfe, who brought psychology to the University of Nebraska. After studying with Professor Wilhelm Wundt, Professor Wolfe returned to this, his native state, to establish the first undergraduate laboratory of psychology in the nation. As a student at Nebraska, Professor Friedline studied psychology under Professor Wolfe. The editors are grateful to the late Professor Friedline for her bequest and to the officers of the University of Nebraska Foundation for their continued interest in and support of this series.

RICHARD A. DIENSTBIER
Series Editor

Contents

Introduction

*F*ew if any behavioral phenomena have proven so resistant to scientific understanding as those associated with insanity. For a full century now, this devastating affliction has been under the scrutiny of the biomedical, behavioral, and social sciences. Yet today it ranks as high as ever, with heart disease and cancer, as a public health menace.

The history of society's attempts at solutions to the problem of mental illness is marked by misplaced optimism and tragic irony. A century ago, the immensely successful biomedical sciences were seen as the certain source of future cures. The urban and rural communes and "moral therapy" that had appeared in the course of worldwide social reform were replaced by "mental hospitals." It was hoped that this transition would produce miraculous advances like those made against smallpox and other traditional scourges of humankind. Unfortunately, new etiological understandings and effective treatments did not come, and the hospital model brought back the horrible dehumanizing insane asylums of the eighteenth century.

History repeated itself in the 1950s and 1960s. The discovery of antipsychotic drugs, combined with the social activism of John F. Kennedy's "New Frontier," generated an expectation that institutionalized patients could be returned to their communities. However, antipsychotic drugs were found not to establish adequate functioning in most patients, and the national mental health center system proved ineffective in delivering services to those who needed them most. Instead of deinstitutionalization, a process of "trans-institutionalization" occurred. Large numbers of patients were discharged, but their "communities" became the streets of urban slums, where many now suffer as an economically, politically, and socially disenfranchised class.

Perhaps the principal reason for this strange history is the degree to which insanity has been addressed from limited and parochial points of view. A century ago religious and moralistic models were replaced by early allopathic biomedical models, primitive by today's standards. When no successful treatments were found, the medical professions reverted to even more primitive naturopathic models, represented by reliance on rest cures. This induced a reaction, led by Harry Stack Sullivan in the 1930s, which rejected the biomedical approach and called for new models based instead on psychoanalytic and socio-psychological principles. The introduction of psychotropic drugs has produced new advocates of exclusively allopathic models, but the tragic spectacle of trans-institutionalization has also generated new critics who call for solutions based on sociopsychological models and enlightened public policy.

Controversy continues. In some quarters, the most fundamental concepts in general use are held to be invalid or even harmful. The concept of "schizophrenia" is the best example. Introduced before the early allopathic models had fallen into disrepute, "schizophrenia" remains today the label most often applied to severely impaired mental patients. The most radical critics of the term argue that it is a pseudoscientific label, useful to capitalistic societies for repression of lower classes. Less radical critics point out that it has little reliability or validity as currently defined in the behavioral sciences. Defenders of the concept often argue that despite its limitations there seem to be no viable alternatives.

Fortunately, scientific progress in the last decade seems less hindered by these controversies than fifty years ago. Researchers today appear to be less parochial, less evangelical about their particular point of view, and more cognizant of the limitations and hazards of their terminologies. Perhaps for this we owe as much to Ludwig Wittgenstein, Thomas Kuhn, and Karl Popper as to any psychopathologist. Whatever the case, significant progress has occurred in scientific understanding of the behavioral phenomena that generate the controversies.

This volume of the *Nebraska Symposium on Motivation* brings together eight prominent scholars distinguished for their studies of phenomena associated with insanity. The volume is entitled "Theories of Schizophrenia and Psychosis," but that title does not imply endorsement of any contemporary or traditional version of the allopathic medical diagnosis of "schizophrenia." Indeed, each participant has his own view of how the concepts of schizophrenia and psychosis should be understood. The title is less representative but more practical than "Theories of behavioral phenomena which, for better or for worse, are usually associated with the allopathic-medical-diagnostic concept 'schizophrenia' and with the generic behavioral descriptor 'psychosis.'"

The hard lessons of the past are manifest in the contributions in this volume. Most important, there is no affiliation with particular psychopathological "schools of thought"—allopathic, naturopathoic, psychoanalytic, psychosocial. The participants have in common a commitment to empiricism, to the hypothetic-deductive method, and to carefully considered use of terminology. Each participant does have a unique focus of study within the range of phenomena which must be considered. However, the different foci yield views that are more complementary to each other than competitive.

The first six papers are the main contributions. The last two are discussions of the main contributions. The order of the papers reflects a hierarchical view of the phenomena associated with schizophrenia and psychosis. That view, in turn, represents an assumption that a full understanding of insanity must address human functioning at a multiplicity of levels of analysis—biological, psychological, and social. Thus the first paper, Rue L. Cromwell's, focuses on genetic processes. The second, by P. H. Venables, deals with physiological processes. In the third paper Raymond A. Knight considers relatively molecular cognitive processes, especially those involved with perceptual organization. The fourth paper, Peter A. Magaro's, focuses on more molar cognitive processes, including interactions between input and central processing modalities. The fifth paper, Kurt Salzinger's, emphasizes the importance of interactions between the whole organism and environmental configurations. In the sixth paper Charles Wallace and his coauthor apply cognitive and behavioral concepts to social skills training, probably the most promising new treatment modality for schizophrenic patients.

A hierarchical ordering is also evident in the way in which fundamental assumptions about psychopathology are addressed by each contributor. With the continuing controversies about "mental illness" in general and "schizophrenia" in particular, careful attention must be paid to philosophical and linguistic considerations in contemporary psychopathology research. Indeed, these issues must be thoroughly addressed at each level of analysis if true complementarity between levels is to be achieved. Professor Cromwell begins this hierarchical philosophical process by suggesting that before we consider the behavior of schizophrenics we should carefully consider our own conceptual behavior as psychopathologists. In the following contributions similar caveats reappear as increasingly molar analyses bring new perspectives on fundamental issues. This careful attention to the logical foundations of research by all the contributors augments the complementarity of their various points of view.

As this volume's discussants, Keith H. Nuechterlein and Herbert E. Spohn, expertly point out, there is much yet to learn, many questions and paradoxes yet to be resolved. Yet it seems clear that significant progress is being made toward a complete and practical understanding of insanity as a complex biological, psychological, and social phenomenon.

WILLIAM D. SPAULDING
AND JAMES K. COLE

Preemptive Thinking and Schizophrenia Research

Rue L. Cromwell

University of Rochester

*A*student I sent to England on a postdoctoral fellowship was struck to see that water pipes leading into houses were often aboveground. With each severe cold spell many of them froze and burst. On one such freezing day he saw a plumber repairing one of these pipes and walked over. "Sir!" he said, "may I ask you a question?" "Why is it," my colleague asked, "that the water pipes are not underground and inside the walls to protect them from the weather?"

The plumber was stunned. He looked at the American in patronizing disbelief. "Why, that's obvious," he said. "If they were underground, you couldn't get at them to fix them when they froze."

George A. Kelly (1955), in his theory of personal constructs, made the point that we all look at and deal with the world through such constructs. They organize our input. We cannot escape them. Our constructs are like cages. We can choose to change cages or even invent cages to look at cages, but we must have them to anticipate and deal with our life encounters. If our constructs (or cages) fall short, we experience *anxiety*—as Kelly would say, we are caught with our constructs down.

The British plumber was not anxious. He had his construct (or cage) well in place. From our own cages, we might label his construct "chronic aboveground plumbing."

More recently the daughter of a British plumber succumbed to mental illness and was hospitalized. The distraught father sat down with the psychiatrist and clinical psychologist to try to allay his own apprehension. "Tell me," he said, "why is it that you diagnose my daughter as schizophrenic? It does not explain how it all came about. It does not indicate a way to cure it or prevent it. It does not even tell you whether the outcome will be good or bad."

The psychiatrist and psychologist were stunned. They looked at the plumber in patronizing disbelief. "Why," one said, as the other nodded, "that's obvious."

So ends the parable. History has shown that when facts do not persuade, parables are often useful.

Overview and Goal

Here I shall attempt to show that the conceptual behavior of researchers and clinicians obstructs progress in understanding schizophrenia. Many essential issues will be covered, sometimes necessarily in a sparse manner; thus this is an argument, not an elaborative review. In the section to follow, I shall discuss aspects of scientific definition. These aspects apply generally rather than to schizophrenia research alone. In particular, I shall discuss the ways new information is assimilated by clinicians and researchers and consider whether these ways yield progress. Then, I shall look at the status of current schizophrenic definition, giving special attention to some "thorns in the side" of those who struggle with the concept. Next I shall describe strategies for studying schizophrenia, with occasional examples. These strategies to understand schizophrenia affect the evolution of its definition, and, unfortunately, the current definition affects strategies. At the end of this section, I shall enumerate some of the foibles in interpreting data from some of the more recently used strategies. Finally, having argued that both definition and strategies fall short, I hope the reader will contemplate the importance of creating new strategies. One new strategy, involving schizophrenic-related variants, is provided as an aid to this contemplation.

SCIENTIFIC DEFINITIONS AND THEIR VICISSITUDES

A common view holds that the reason for lack of progress in understanding, curing, and preventing schizophrenia lies in our continued failure to identify—or have the technology to identify—the relevant variables. That is true; and if it were the complete answer, we could continue the rush of what we are already doing in investigative research. But there is more to it than that. A major thesis of this chapter is that at present an overriding obstacle is not the elusive nature of schizophrenia but the conceptual behavior of the scientists who study it. In other words, we are obstructing the very progress we wish to achieve.

In this section I shall discuss some aspects of the conceptual behavior of *psychopathologists*, not of schizophrenics, in terms of guidelines general to all science. These aspects include definitional clarity, definitional utility, reification of less-than-adequate constructs, data domain for defining criteria, and conceptual processing of new observations.

Definitional Clarity

In 1927 Percy Bridgman published *The Logic of Modern Physics*. Many have felt that this book revolutionized not only physics but science in general (see also Jensen 1960, 1970). In it Bridgman introduced the notion of "operational definition." He argued that the definition of a scientific construct should include the operations necessary to measure it. In the 1930s articles were published in psychology on the operational definition—by S. S. Stevens (1935a, 1935b), E. C. Tolman (1936), and J. R. Kantor (1938). Indeed, although the radical forms of operationism were modified, the notion did spread like wildfire, and scientists started to become more concerned about their philosophical roots and definitional problems.

As late as 1980 the notion of operational definition had its first influence upon the *Diagnostic and Statistical Manual of Mental Disorders* (3rd edition), often referred to as DSM-III (American Psychiatric Association, 1980). Why psychopathology researchers failed for more than fifty years to recognize this approach is a matter for scientific historians. Nevertheless, the advance was made, and at least some workers assumed this was the only or at least the major problem in need of solution.

Definitional Utility

Along with increased clarity through operational definitions, people like Bergman and Spence (1941) and Kelly (1955) also emphasized the utility criterion—what and how well the operationally defined concept predicts. Utility for prediction is separate from clarity through operational definition.

One way to illustrate this distinction is through a current view concerning diagnostic classification (Cromwell, Strauss, & Blashfield,

1975). Diagnostic constructs are invented from four classes of data—the ABCDs (Cromwell, 1976) if you will. Diagnoses are operationally defined in terms of (a) historical/etiological events and/or (b) currently observable events (e.g., symptoms). As a separate step, the utility of each diagnostic construct is determined in terms of (c) what treatments, preventions, or other interventions (or absence thereof) lead to (d) what outcome (prognosis). The adequacy of a diagnostic construct depends upon how well these two criteria, clarity and utility, are met. Workers like J. S. Strauss and Carpenter (1972) have shown how our formal nosology falls short in this respect.

Reification of Less-Than-Adequate Constructs

If schizophrenia or any other construct had absolutely no utility, it would probably be discarded forthwith. Schizophrenia, as we know it, is a construct of positive though minimal utility. It is not completely useless and invalid—it works for us. It helps us classify (and sometimes segregate) about 1% of the population who, usually by early adulthood, have come to behave in ways that meet our operational definition. Although no claim can be made about prevention or cure, certain pharmaco-, socio-, and psychotherapies have been recognized as retardants to this psychotic process for certain people. With this minimal utility (partial reinforcement), scientific constructs, like other linguistic constructions, tend to stay in place and become "real." Consequently, constructs like schizophrenia take on a life of their own and, though unintended, preempt alternative constructions.

So, in spite of the advances in operational criteria, as the beginning parable suggests much is yet to be desired. At least some of the shortcoming resides in the ability of the clinician-scientist to set aside old constructions (e.g., defining criteria) so as to invent and explore potentially more useful ones.

Construing New Observations

When faced with new observations—whether about schizophrenia or about other aspects of life experience—the thinking of people, including scientists, differs. Kelly (1955) described three alternatives in such construing: preemptive, constellatory (i.e., subordinative), and propositional. These do not represent personality types; all of us shift from one to another as we deal with new information. Which mode one chooses affects whether definitions evolve to meet the dual criteria in better and better fashion. Which mode one chooses can fairly easily be inferred from one's comments and questions in response to new information.

Preemptive thinking occurs when a person relegates information to a state of equivalence to what is already in his conceptual structure. In so doing, his conceptual structure is allowed to remain unchanged. In the process of accomplishing this operation, the individual may ask a question such as "How does this (new observation) relate back to . . . (be it to schizophrenia or some other concept)?" An assertion that the preemptive operation has been achieved is exemplified in the classic "nothing but" response or some variation thereof: "This (new observation) is nothing but . . . (say, schizophrenia as per current criteria)." Or, "In spite of the new measure you have devised, what you are looking at is . . . (schizophrenia)." In other words, the preexisting conceptual system of the individual, whether he or she sits at a clinical conference table or in a scientific colloquium, remains unmodified. The new information will be buried and likely forgotten, since the preexisting criteria still seem sufficient and continue to be salient.

The conceptual tool for linking the new information preemptively to the preexisting conceptual system can be simply expressed in terms of the equality sign ($=$) or a form of the verb "to be." The new information *is* (equivalent to) . . . (just another manifestation of schizophrenia) and nothing more.

Subordinative thinking occurs when a person views new information as representing a new and separate category within a preestablished hierarchical system. Alternatively, it may be a subclassification of a preexisting construct. The elements and dimensions of the hierarchical system remain unchanged except for the "extra room" that must be provided to incorporate this information as new and separate. The subordinative operation may be reflected by a comment like "Isn't it possible that this is a new manifestation of . . . (schizophrenia) that you have described?" Or "The syndrome you describe from your measures is certainly a type of . . . (psychosis in general)." A generalized and ultimate form of subordination is to reduce all new observations according to their convergence upon preexisting basic dimensions used in the culture or language system. For example, in studies of semantic differential (Osgood, 1957) extended numbers of terms are reduced to good/bad, active/passive, and so on, without concern for either individual characteristics of the terms being subordinated or individual differences in how people use a given term.

Subordinative thinking in diagnosis or other nosological work inevitably demands a concern for specificity: "But is what you are describing specific to . . . (schizophrenia)?" If it is not, one must either find some other way to subordinate the new observation clearly or else cast it aside as not useful information. I shall return to the issue of "specificity" later.

The conceptual tools for subordinating new information may be expressed in such forms as the verb "to have," descriptions of belonging, or the format of the traditional dictionary definition. "The (new information) is an aspect (or type) of (schizophrenia or other broader construct) which . . ."

Subordination is a necessary tool serving the human predisposition toward territoriality. We need to know what belongs to what and whose turf is whose.

Propositional thinking occurs when a person considers new information as a way to reformulate existing conceptual structure. It may be used as a replacement (or substantial redefinition) of an existing concept. It may be used as a way to link two or more concepts that were hitherto viewed as independent. In accomplishing this operation one's questions and comments are of yet a different sort: "Will this (new observation) predict outcome better than (any dimension or diagnostic classification we now use)?" "Does this offer a better way to classify individuals and predict who will benefit from . . . (a given treatment) than (any categories or dimensions we now have)?" "Does it provide new leads to link etiological (historical) data to current pathology?" "Is it possible that this (new information) could be standardized as a new dimension to supersede or replace (schizophrenia)?"

The tools of propositional thinking must be described by a broader range of symbols, such as inequality signs, "if-then" statements, and more complex algorithms.

Once the new information meets the test of validity (predictive utility) in a more favorable way than previous concepts, then, rather than its being subordinated, a new or reformulated construct is proposed. In consequence, a pandoric array of new questions arises. Waves of uncertainty and reconsideration are introduced. How does this new concept (or new information that modifies the definition of an old concept) relate to all the other proximal concepts in the conceptual structure? These new questions must be answered before the uncertainty is reduced. As propositional thinking continues and new questions are faced, this state of uncertainty (and subsequent inquiry) becomes a continuing, dynamic process for the predominantly propositional thinker. Especially for us clinicians, who have to make practical decisions, this dynamic process and its uncertainty are irksome compared with a comfortable static structure in our knowledge. Only the scientist in us takes delight.

In recent decades, physics and astronomy have illustrated how scientists have availed themselves of propositional thinking (and then new data) rather than subordinating or preempting new information. It is therefore not surprising that quantum theoreticians from physics (Oshins & McGoveran, 1980; Orlov, 1982) have introduced models of doubt states in human thinking and consciousness.

General Comment

When we consider together these vicissitudes in the conceptual behavior of those who study mental disorder, the emphasis of Meehl (1967) and Lykken (1968) in philosophy of science becomes clearer. In particular, they have argued that progress in science depends not so much upon the accumulation of knowledge de novo as upon the disconfirmation and reformulation of existing knowledge.

We can again see that the reification of existing constructs and their consequent preemption over new alternatives, while well intended, stand in the way of the search for a greater focus of convenience within a broader domain of data. As we construe new information about schizophrenia in the ways described, we are dealing not so much with formidable, elusive subject matter as with our own fear of giving up preemptive (and sometimes subordinative) thinking. To quote the notable philosopher and comic strip character Pogo, "We have met the enemy—and he is us!" (see Romano, 1977).

STATUS OF PRESENT
DEFINITIONS OF SCHIZOPHRENIA

This section addresses issues and problems specific to the defining of schizophrenia rather than to scientific definitions in general. It does not include a comparative examination of the current operational definitions of schizophrenia. This has been done adequately elsewhere (e.g., Klein, 1982), and few important differences seem to result.

Interobserver Reliability

The recent use of operational definition, as already described, has increased *interobserver reliability*. Two or more clinical observers can now view the same videotape or live interview and reach a higher level of agreement about diagnostic classification.

Diagnosing Early and Mild Forms of Disorder

Interobserver reliability drops when dealing with early and mild forms of disorder. For example, this problem was encountered in the University of Rochester Child and Family Study, which focused on young children of intact families where one parent had been hospitalized with a major psychiatric disorder. Since the rate of intact marriage is low among schizophrenic patients, we might expect that these intact families with young children would be associated with early and mild disorder. Indeed, when diagnoses of the hospitalized parent were independently done, agreement regarding schizophrenic versus affective disorder was only 52% (Romano, 1977).

Recognizing "Consequent" Effects

It has long been known that the course of schizophrenic disorder is confounded by treatment effects, by institutional, socially reactive, self-reactive, and other "consequent" effects. These effects overlay and obscure the disorder itself. Consequently, the genesis and course of the disorder cannot easily be studied in chronic, long-treated cases. Therefore the early and mild cases mentioned above are vitally important for investigation, even though diagnostic reliability is low.

Accommodating to Phasic Symptoms and Deficit

Symptoms come and go. In other words, they are phasic. A much overlooked fact is that a typical schizophrenic patient is not psychotic most of the time. Even in severe cases a stressful or exciting event, such as a fire on the ward or the patient's breaking an arm, has been known to cause remission of symptoms for hours or days. Also, an "incoherent" schizophrenic ordinarily has no difficulty inquiring how long it is until lunch. Any diagnostic procedure must accommodate to this phasic attribute; otherwise reliability is reduced by the nature of the disorder itself.

One phasic nature of deficit is exemplified in the following word association task where a patient, after a string of appropriate responses and then a mild disruption, spins off into a word salad.

Examiner:	Deep
Patient:	Like the ocean
Examiner:	Soft
Patient:	Soft like a piece of candy, soft.
Examiner:	Candy, did you say?
Patient:	Candy, Sealtest-good. Like a piece of candy. Sealtest-good-good-good. You know, the candy is soft like a baby. You give a baby the candy. The baby eats it. (Cromwell & Dokecki, 1968)

Another illustration was found in choice reaction time (Nideffer, Space, Cromwell, & Dwyer, Note 1). Subjects placed each forefinger on a key and looked into a box at two lights. If the right light went out, the right finger was lifted; if the left light went out, the left finger was lifted—as quickly as possible. When the trials are sorted according to speed of finger lift, the accuracy (lifting correct finger) at each speed level can be plotted. This speed-accuracy trade-off function is in Figure 1. Speed levels are grouped on the horizontal axis, and an index of accuracy is on the vertical axis. An essentially straight line is expected; the faster the response, the greater the likelihood of lifting the wrong finger. As may be seen, normals tend to conform to this function. Schizophrenics, on the other hand, show an inflection. During their faster trials schizophrenics are as fast *and* as accurate as normals; there is no significant difference. During the slower trials, however, schizophrenics show evidence of being periodically "out of contact." The slower response does not purchase the increased accuracy that normal subjects

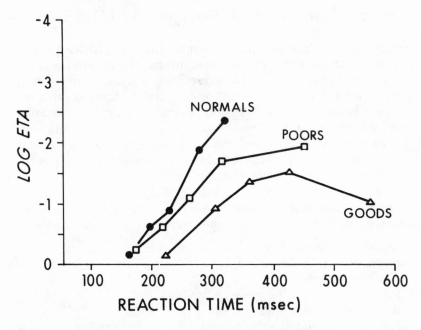

FIGURE 1. Trade-off function of speed (horizontal axis) and accuracy (vertical axis) in choice reaction time of good and poor premorbid and normal subjects. From Nideffer, Space, Cromwell, and Dwyer, Note 1.

obtain. Instead, the patients have a greater number of trials that are *both* slow *and* inaccurate. As may be seen, this is especially true for the good premorbid schizophrenic group. In signal detection terms, this means that the sensitivity of schizophrenics in this choice task cannot be described with a single index. Among fast trials their sensitivity is normal; among slow trials it is less than normal. Since these slow and inaccurate trials are scattered throughout the experiment, the deficit may be described as phasic.

With the use of the Kelly rep grid, Dingemans, Space, and Cromwell (1983) demonstrated the phasic deficit in yet another way. With the traditional Kelly procedure patients designated names of family and acquaintances according to role titles, such as in Table 1. Then, by distinguishing among triads of these names, the subjects provided a self-produced construct (construct/opposite dimension) for each of a series of triads. This is illustrated in Table 2. Following each elicitation of a construct/opposite dimension, all names of people

Table 1
List of Rep Grid Role Titles

1. Myself	12. A person who disliked me
2. My mother	13. A person for whom I feel sorry
3. My father	14. A person with whom I feel uncomfortable
4. My brother	15. The ideal female (undesignated personal concept)
5. My sister	16. A person I would like to know better
6. My spouse or present boy/girlfriend	17. A teacher I admired
7. A boy/girlfriend closest to me before my spouse	18. A teacher with an objectionable point of view
8. The ideal male (undesignated personal concept)	19. An employer I had during a period of stress
9. My best same-sexed friend	20. The most successful person I know
10. A disappointing same-sexed friend	21. The happiest person I know
11. My psychotherapist	22. The most ethical person I know

Source: Space and Cromwell (1978).

were rated on the dimension with a six-point scale. At the end of this series of computer-guided steps, a matrix of rating had been completed, one column for each of the twenty-two people rated, and one row for each of the twenty-two construct dimensions on which ratings were made.

In less than a week each subject repeated the ratings on the same constructs. This produced a second matrix. From these two matrixes an absolute difference matrix was computed for each subject. One such difference matrix, from a schizophrenic patient, is shown in Table 3. The differences from first to second ratings are arranged sequentially from left to right and from top to bottom. If the second set of ratings were identical to the first, all the cells would contain zeros. One hypothesis, strongly supported, was that schizophrenics, once disrupted—that is, having a higher discrepancy from test to retest on any given rating—would continue to be disrupted on immediately subsequent ratings, independent of the construct

Table 2

A Partial Rep Grid of a Schizophrenic Subject

Role Designees[a]

Construct-Opposite Pairs		Ted	Helen	Roy	Alvin	Catherine	Alice	Mary	Ideal Male	Carl	Jim	Dr. Rosenbloom
(+) Close to me	Far away	6	3	6	6	1	1	2	1	1	2	1
(+) Love	Hate	6	1	1	1	1	2	2	1	1	1	1
Used to love	(+) Unlove	6	1	1	1	1	2	2	1	1	1	1
(+) Good personality	Bad personality	2	6	1	1	1	1	1	1	1	1	1
(+) Party a lot	Unparty	1	6	1	2	2	2	2	1	1	1	4
(+) Help me	Unhelp me	6	1	1	1	1	2	2	1	1	1	1
(+) Sense of humor	Bad sense of humor	2	6	1	2	1	2	2	2	1	1	1
Kind	(+) Generous	1	1	1	1	1	1	1	1	6	6	6
(+) Help me	Don't help me	1	1	1	1	1	1	1	1	1	1	1
(+) Too good	Better	3	6	6	6	6	6	6	6	6	6	6
(+) Somebody to talk to	Untalk to	6	6	6	3	1	2	2	1	1	1	1

Source: Space and Cromwell (1978).

[a]Names are fictional

dimension used or the persons being rated. As may be seen in the schizophrenic patient's difference matrix in Table 3, several strings of large consecutive test-retest discrepancies (shown in bold type) occur, followed by recovery to reasonably reliable performance. Patients hospitalized with affective disorders had overall test-retest differences as great as those with schizophrenia, but only the schizophrenics had these episodes of consecutive disruption.

What do we learn from these studies? First, converging evidence is presented that phasic disturbance in schizophrenics indeed occurs. These events cannot always be gleaned from clinical interviews, or even from observation while the subject is performing a task. Second, looking at the word association, choice reaction time,

Preemptive Thinking and Schizophrenia Research

Table 3
Difference Matrix from Two Rep Grid Administrations

1	0	0	0	2	0	4	0	0	3	0	0	1	1	0	1	1	1	0	1	1	0
1	0	0	0	2	0	4	1	1	2	0	1	1	2	2	1	2	2	2	0	0	0
0	0	0	0	0	0	2	2	3	3	1	3	2	1	0	0	0	1	2	2	2	0
1	3	3	2	2	2	2	5	2	2	4	2	4	4	4	2	0	5	5	1	2	3
0	0	4	4	0	1	2	3	2	2	1	1	2	3	4	0	1	1	1	2	0	3
0	2	2	2	2	1	1	4	2	0	0	0	0	1	0	3	0	0	0	4	0	2
1	2	2	2	3	5	4	2	2	3	2	2	2	1	0	2	3	3	3	3	4	2
2	3	1	2	1	4	1	0	2	5	0	0	4	2	2	0	1	0	0	0	1	0
0	1	4	0	1	0	0	2	1	2	0	0	2	2	3	0	3	5	3	5	2	4
1	2	0	0	0	0	0	0	2	1	0	1	1	2	1	2	2	2	2	0	2	2
1	0	0	0	5	0	0	0	2	2	2	2	4	4	1	2	1	1	1	2	1	1
2	0	0	0	1	1	1	1	1	1	0	0	0	2	2	1	0	0	1	1	0	2
2	3	3	3	3	0	0	1	1	0	0	0	1	1	1	4	4	4	4	2	0	1
1	0	1	1	1	3	1	1	0	4	2	0	1	0	0	3	0	0	0	0	4	1
0	0	0	0	2	1	0	2	1	3	0	0	1	1	1	1	2	1	1	1	3	1
1	1	1	1	2	1	2	2	0	2	0	0	1	0	0	2	2	2	2	0	0	1
0	0	2	2	2	0	2	2	0	1	2	2	2	3	1	1	1	1	1	3	1	2
2	0	2	2	2	2	1	0	1	1	1	1	1	1	2	0	0	3	3	1	3	0
2	1	1	1	1	1	2	0	4	2	0	0	3	1	0	1	0	0	0	2	2	0
2	0	0	0	0	1	2	5	5	5	5	5	5	2	0	3	3	3	3	2	3	2
0	1	1	1	1	1	0	2	3	4	1	3	1	1	2	2	1	1	1	3	3	3
0	1	0	4	4	4	0	2	1	1	0	0	1	1	0	2	1	2	0	0	0	0

and rep grid findings together, it is clear that a void exists in understanding the correlates that account for this phasic (within-subject) change in performance, let alone understanding how to control or modify it. Between-subject and between-group comparisons have been our typical pursuit as psychopathologists. Third, the phasic nature of schizophrenia, whether we refer to the defining symptoms in the clinical interview or to these more subtle but easily demonstrated manifestations in the laboratory, contribute to the lowered test-retest reliability of any single-assessment session definition. Fourth, unless repeated sessions become part of standard diagnostic procedure, evaluating the severity of a schizophrenic disorder becomes a fanciful charade.

Retreating to Clinical Authority

The lines of categorization in our current symptom classification approaches, such as DSM-III, are drawn on the basis of clinical authority, not on the basis of factorial validity or other forms of validity. Some classifications are made on the basis of some knowledge of the degree of interrelation, cooccurrence, or similarity among elements within classes and the degree of independence or nonrelation among elements between classes. This prescribed degree of interrelation may be present within subjects, so that given characteristics are present in *all* who meet the criteria. Or it may be present across subjects, so that two individuals in the same diagnostic class need not have the same symptoms so long as each meets the minimum class criteria (see Sneath & Sokal, 1973, concerning nomothetic and polythetic classification).

Another approach, already designated in terms of ABCD interrelations, is to build classifications on the basis of elements (i.e., symptoms and/or historical events) that have in common the fact that *treatment decisions and outcome predictions are maximized*. In other words, homogeneity of diagnostic groups is sought only in terms of treatment-outcome effects rather than in terms of interrelation of the separate symptoms, historical factors, or both. Neither of these approaches, factorial validity or predictive validity, is at present adequate in schizophrenia research. Therefore, as a retreat, the stature of the clinician as expert or authority becomes important, not only to ratify the nosology but also often to screen subjects in given studies.

In this adherence to authority rather than evidence, the practice of psychodiagnosis shares common ground with traditional religious and mystical thinking. A well-known sociologic/anthropologic principle holds that the less a system of thought depends upon empirical substantiation, the greater the invocation of authority, superstition, and pageantry needed to substantiate and maintain it.

The Importance of Negative Symptoms

The negative symptoms of schizophrenia are more powerful in their predictive validity than the positive ones (Strauss, Carpenter, & Bartko, 1974). As I mentioned earlier, J. S. Strauss and Carpenter (1972) demonstrated that clinical symptoms, as used for defining schizophrenia, have little or no value in predicting outcome. More recently, however, a distinction has been emphasized between positive and negative symptoms. Positive symptoms refer to the observed presence of deviant behavior, such as delusion, hallucination, or thought disorder. Negative symptoms refer to absence of a behavior that would ordinarily exist in an individual who is functioning and coping well. Negative symptoms would include the absence of attention to personal appearance, self-support, developing and maintaining relationships with others, displaying sociosexual desire, and making the socially appropriate affective responses of laughter or sadness. These negative symptoms portend a less favorable outcome.

The positive and negative symptoms of schizophrenia act very differently from each other within the social fabric. Positive symptoms elicit such responses as "He is different. . . . disturbed . . . mentally ill. Is he dangerous? He needs help. He should be put away . . . taken care of." With negative symptoms the person tends first to be viewed not as sick or deviant but as lazy, unmotivated, or obstinate. The person begins to stay at home, fails to perform on a job or in school, centers his or her life around something like hi-fi or television, eats, sleeps, goes to the toilet, and seldom assumes even simple household chores. Family members tend to become angry rather than concerned. They find they have to support the person financially and clean up after him; they cannot rely on him for household responsibilities. The affected person provides no respite for family members by going out to visit friends or hunt for a job. The family members tend to let their frustration and anger be known. When they later recognize the positive symptoms of schizophrenic illness, they often assume that their negative attitude or retaliation (or that of each other) precipitated the mental illness. Guilt and blaming each other are typical results. Family therapy becomes important to resolve problems that are sometimes more evident than the schizophrenia itself. Meanwhile the schizophrenic patient's status indeed appears to be affected negatively by the family members' affective tone and communication deviance (e.g., Vaughn & Leff, 1976; Doane, West, Goldstein, Rodnick, & Jones, 1981).

Symptom Change during the Course of the Disorder

The current symptom classification approach does not take into consideration the *change* in how schizophrenia is manifested during the *temporal course* of the disorder. The premorbid ("high risk"), prodromal, acute, and chronic phases of disorder reveal themselves in different ways. Not only are the defining symptoms most characteristic of the late acute to chronic phase, but a time requirement is imposed to ensure that the symptoms are enduring. A schizophrenic must be schizophrenic for six months before he can be called schizophrenic and (in theory) treated as such. This time requirement is useful in distinguishing toxic effects, such as amphetamine psychosis and limited episodes of affective disorder, from process schizophrenia. On the other hand, if a clinician concludes that he is dealing with early stages of what will eventually meet the defining criteria of schizophrenia, he is not likely to wait to start treatment. Nor is he likely to make any dramatic change the day the criteria are met. In short, the practical clinical demands are not well met by the DSM-III temporal criteria, and the symptom criteria are aimed primarily at a limited period during the prolonged course of disorder.

Separating Primary from Secondary Symptoms

Primary symptoms are not distinguished from secondary symptoms in the current criteria. Primary symptoms are those that are necessary antecedents to the secondary symptoms. In addition to the temporal picture of the disorder, as I mentioned above, there is also a need to sort out the antecedent-consequent relations among the observable dimensions. Path analyses are useful in testing hypothetical models about the necessary antecedents to each consequent manifestation. However, the pioneer attempts by Bleuler (1911) to separate primary from secondary symptoms have not been adequately continued. Thus many or all of the defining criteria are likely to be secondary symptoms.

Restriction of the Data Domain

To the present, the definition of schizophrenia has been limited to what a person has revealed about himself in clinical interview (and possibly in psychological testing and ward observation). For example, in DSM-III the operational criteria for schizophrenia involve specified types of delusion, hallucination, and/or thought disorder. Historically, these events must have been observed for six months or more and must have been associated with a lowered level of functioning. This approach to diagnostic classification can be likened to the era in diagnosis of diabetes and specific infections when no laboratory procedures were available. Why, in the face of so many changes in clinical medicine, mental health clinicians have limited their potential diagnostic data to the clinical interview is another matter for historians. For decades schizophrenia has been known to manifest itself on levels other than verbal behavior. Many behavioral and psychophysiological laboratory findings have been reported since the 1930s; yet even their proponents have usually assumed that such findings are off limits as defining criteria for diagnosis. Thus their relevance to treatment decisions and outcome predictions have not been well examined.

Recently I suggested that eight decades' focus upon symptom classification is enough (Cromwell, 1982). This comment does not imply a blanket rejection of data from clinical interviews; it does, however, question the view that definitions of schizophrenia should forever be limited to that domain of data.

Concluding Comment on Schizophrenia Definition

The problems of definition in terms of symptom classification present a paradox. Even with the advances in interobserver agreement resulting from operational definition, the general psychometric status, the practical clinical utility, the scientific predictive utility, and the range of data bearing upon classification are grossly inadequate. To continue depending only on clinical interview data to define the problem area of schizophrenia appears to be a bankrupt approach.

Yet clinical symptoms cannot be forsaken. Just as with the symptoms derived from talking to a victim of diabetes or a staphylococcal infection, the interview-based understanding of the patient will always be necessary to evaluate the distress and human suffering, to assess the need for help both for the patient and for his family. On the other hand, again like diabetes and staphylococcal infection, the interview-based understandings are not necessarily the sacrosanct bases on which differential diagnoses, treatment decisions, and prognostic statements should forever stand.

TRADITIONAL STRATEGIES
FOR UNDERSTANDING SCHIZOPHRENIA

An inadequate classification construct has a bearing upon the strategies used to investigate schizophrenia, and the kinds of strategies used have a bearing upon any evolution in defining the problem. I once made the comment (Cromwell, 1982) that the construct of schizophrenia deserves a promotion—a promotion to a level of abstraction like the concept of perception. One can do research on perception without identifying a group of subjects who have perception and comparing them with controls who do not. Yet if you say you are a schizophrenia researcher, you are expected to begin a study by classifying subjects on the basis of an inadequate construct. The following strategies, commonly used to study schizophrenia, should therefore be examined in light of the weakness in the diagnostic construct itself.

The Correlate

The most common strategy has been to compare a schizophrenic group with one or more groups who are not schizophrenic. When differences between schizophrenics and other groups occur on variables other than the pathognomonic signs (i.e., defining criteria on which the schizophrenic group was constituted), these variables can be described as *correlates* of the presence/absence of schizophrenia or one or more of its "consequent" effects. In recent years more attention has been shown to demographic and clinical characteristics in group selection. Thus we have increasingly precise knowledge about a group defined with criteria not usefully chosen. This crude type of comparison has indeed led to some insights. For example, very little so far examined among biochemical variables (Kety, 1982) and practically everything examined so far among cognitive variables can be replicated as a schizophrenic/normal difference. At the 1976 Second Rochester International Conference on Schizophrenia, Snyder (1978) summarized the leading biochemical theory, involving dopamine, by saying that the evidence for it rested on the positive, but less than perfect, correlation between the treatment potency of drugs and their effectiveness as dopamine blockers. No difference in the brains or other body substances of schizophrenic patients had been identifiable and replicable. Recently, Haracz (1982), as well as Kety, has essentially repeated Snyder's earlier conclusion.

Among cognitive and behavioral variables (e.g., Shakow, 1963), it seems that one must move to peripheral ones such as visual acuity, pure tone threshold, and patellar reflex before differences between schizophrenics and normals become difficult to establish. Ironically, it is the lack of difference, or better still the superiority of schizo-phrenic performance over normals under specific conditions, that becomes the theoretically interesting finding. The big challenge now is to sort out which cognitive variable is the necessary antece-dent to which.

Psychophysiological variables seem to be second only to the cognitive variables in showing schizophrenia/normal differences, some being definitely affected by the "consequent" effects of medication. Among the remaining biological variables, position emissions tonography appears promising (Buchsbaum, Ingvar, Kessler, Waters, Capeletti, van Kammen, King, Johnson, Manning, Flynn, Mann, Bunney, & Sokoloff, 1982). Metabolic activity in schizophrenic subjects resting with closed eyes appears high in the visual cortex and low in the frontal area. But again, further progress appears dependent upon relating these metabolic correlates to cognitive deficit and treatment outcome variables rather than the crude diagnostic construct. This circumvention of the categorized diagnostic constructs has been beneficial in the study of blood platelet monoamine oxidase, where students without diagnosis but who scored at extremes on monoamine oxidase and evoked re-sponse differed in important indexes of personal adjustment (Buchsbaum, Murphy, Coursey, Lake, & Zeigler, 1978).

The Subtype

Another strategy has been to subclassify the schizophrenic group in order to make not just comparisons with normals but also subgroup comparisons. This movement was sparked by the two papers in 1964, one by Peter Venables and one by Julian Silverman. In these papers the within-group comparisons of length of hospitalization (acute-chronic dimension), premorbid adjustment (process-reactive dimension), and paranoid versus nonparanoid symptomatology were emphasized. Findings were inevitably more interesting when two schizophrenic subgroups differed from controls in opposite directions. Also, when schizophrenic subgroups produce less variance than either the control subjects or all schizophrenics combined, an advance has been made in group homogeneity.

Examples of these subgroup differences from our laboratory include variables of visual perception and memory. In simple visual size estimation, good premorbid and paranoid subjects underestimate, and poor premorbid and nonparanoid subjects overestimate. This has often been replicated (e.g., Davis, Cromwell, & Held, 1967; Neale & Cromwell, 1968; M. E. Strauss, Foureman, & Parwatikur, 1974; McCormick & Broekema, 1978; Asarnow, Cromwell, & Rennick, 1978; Asarnow & Mann, 1978) but is still not fully understood (e.g., see a contrary result by Magaro, 1969). In Muller-Lyer illusion good premorbid paranoid schizophrenics have substantially greater illusion than poor premorbid nonparanoids or normals (Cromwell, 1968; Kar, Note 2). In the same study, incidental recall was measured by recall of previously unmentioned distractor figures around the illusion stimulus. The recall was greater among good premorbid paranoid schizophrenics than normals and greater among normals than poor premorbid nonparanoid schizophrenics.

Other notable subgroup comparisons have been reported by Kety, Rosenthal, Wender, and Schulsinger (1968) on acute versus chronic schizophrenics. "Acute" and "chronic" are defined here in terms of symptoms rather than length of hospitalization. Converging evidence from their studies indicates that the biological relatives of chronic (process) schizophrenics have increased probability of schizophrenia, whereas the biological relatives of acute (reactive) schizophrenics have increased probability less of schizophrenia than of affective disorder. As the criteria distinguishing schizophrenic and affective psychosis change, these distinctions between schizophrenic subtypes and also between schizophrenia and affective disorder must be interpreted cautiously. Especially the reactive schizophrenic group contains members now more often classified as affectively or schizoaffectively disordered.

Effects upon Conceptual Structure

The major problem of schizophrenia can potentially be assumed to be a breakdown in *conceptual structure*. Conceptual structure refers to the way an individual organizes and stores life experience. The breakdown may be hypothesized to have biological antecedents, for example, relating to defects in the way the brain processes information. Or it may be hypothesized to be primarily environmental in origin, with biological factors playing only an incidental predisposing role. In other words, schizophrenia is viewed in this instance primarily as a software problem. This latter hypothesis is well illustrated by recent work on *communication deviance* and *expressed affective tone* (Vaughn & Leff, 1976; Doane, West, Goldstein, Rodnick, & Jones, 1981). In this respect conceptual structure is studied not directly but in terms of how interaction and emotional expressions from family members and others impinge upon the status of the person.

A more direct study of conceptual structure is the aforementioned research by Dingemans, Space, and Cromwell (1983) with the Kelly (1955) rep grid (see also Space & Cromwell, 1978). In addition to identifying the phasic deficit, already described, these authors also identified methodological problems in the study of conceptual structure. Enduring conceptual structure of the schizophrenic patient cannot be studied—via rep grid or other technique—without separating out the "noise" introduced during the "disattention" epochs.

Earliest Deficit in Processing Sequence

The search for the *earliest stage in the processing of a single stimulus* where a deficit clearly occurs in schizophrenia is another current strategy. One example of this strategy has been the examination of temporal sensory integration by Spaulding, Rosenzweig, Huntzinger, Cromwell, Briggs, and Hayes (1980). A set of dots, such as that in Figure 2, is followed by another set, such as that in Figure 3, and the interval between the two presentations is varied. If the second presentation occurs before the first one decays from iconic memory, the dots can be integrated and reported as a number, as in Figure 4. This experiment was to determine whether the iconic decay (and integration) functions of schizophrenics varied from those of normal controls. Results, shown in Figure 5, indicated a smooth decay function with no notable differences among any of the groups tested. These results are valuable because they indicate that the breakdown in processing stimuli either comes later in the sequence of processing events or else requires distracting stimulation not examined here (see also Knight, Sherer, & Shapiro, 1977).

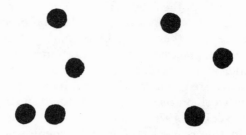

FIGURE 2. Initial dot pattern. From Spaulding, Rosenzweig, Huntzinger, Cromwell, Briggs, and Hayes (1980). Copyright 1980 by the American Psychological Association. Reprinted by permission of the publisher.

Lowest Central Nervous System Level

The search for the *lowest or simplest level of central nervous system activity* where a schizophrenic deficit may occur is still another strategy. A possible assumption behind this strategy is that the origins of schizophrenia may lie here and have secondary effects on higher levels. Granted, higher levels can also have secondary effects upon lower levels (Pribram, 1971). As I mentioned earlier, the examination of sensory acuity and simple reflexes has not yielded encouraging results. Shakow (1963) and his co-workers found that tapping speed, while deficient in some schizophrenics, was not deficient for all schizophrenic subgroups. The common denominator that did appear deficient was simple motor reaction time (Huston, Shakow, & Riggs, 1937; see also reviews by Nuechterlein, 1977a, 1977b). Schizophrenics were slower and more variable than normals in reaction time performance (see also Cancro, Sutton, Kerr, & Sugerman, 1971). Clinically, this result did not find its way into the defining criteria of schizophrenia; a broad range of other disorders are also characterized by slow reaction time. Among these are mental retardation, acute brain insult, chronic brain damage, and severe depression.

One derivative of the reaction time methodology has indeed tended to be relatively more characteristic of schizophrenia. This is reaction time crossover (or redundancy deficit). Its history is briefly summarized here. When Rodnick and Shakow (1940) launched their investigation of reaction time in schizophrenia, they systematically varied the preparatory intervals (PIs) in two ways (see Figure

Preemptive Thinking and Schizophrenia Research

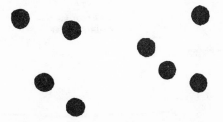

FIGURE 3. Second dot pattern. From Spaulding et al. (1980). Copyright 1980 by the American Psychological Association. Reprinted by permission of the publisher.

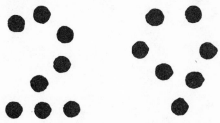

FIGURE 4. Potential integration of two dot patterns. From Spaulding et al. (1980). Copyright 1980 by the American Psychological Association. Reprinted by permission of the publisher.

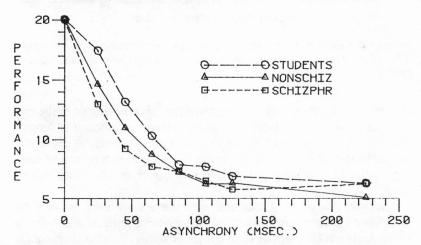

FIGURE 5. Report of integrated pattern as a function of interstimulus interval: a decay function. From Spaulding et al. (1980). Copyright 1980 by the American Psychological Association. Reprinted by permission of the publisher.

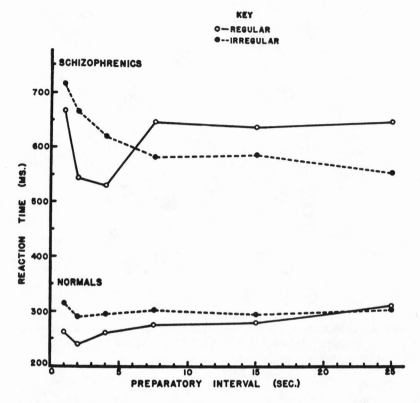

FIGURE 6. Reaction time in schizophrenic and normal subjects as a function of length and regularity of preparatory interval. From Rodnick and Shakow (1940).

6). Not only did they vary the length of the forewarning periods, but they also varied the schedule of presentation. A random PI length from trial to trial was referred to as an irregular series. A presentation of blocks of trials with the same PI was referred to as a regular series, the PI changing only when shifting from one block to the next.

A remarkable finding occurred with these variations. As may be seen from Figure 6, normal subjects are faster in general and, what's more, faster in the regular than irregular series. Presumably, this is because the regular series provides more information—that is, a basis for predicting PI length on each subsequent trial. The crossover among normals with a 25-second foreperiod is not statistically reliable and is sometimes referred to as the "weak form." However, when schizophrenics are given preparatory intervals beyond the 5-second level, this regularity of forewarning not only ceases to be advantageous but even becomes detrimental. This has been called the "crossover effect" (RTX).

The stability of the crossover phenomenon is reflected by the fact that, though discovered during the era before psychotropic drugs, it is still observed and seems impervious to drug effects (e.g., Bellissimo & Steffy, 1972).

The focus upon this crossover phenomenon may be divided historically into the "Shakow era" and the "Steffy era." During the Shakow era a major question was the significance of the point of crossover and its relevance to loss of psychological set. Also, several studies were done to determine if a shorter or longer preparatory interval on the trial immediately previous could explain crossover (e.g., Zahn, Rosenthal, & Shakow, 1963).

Steffy became interested in reaction time crossover because the poor performance of schizophrenics with regular forewarning periods appeared to contradict commonsense expectation. Why would relevant information be not only ineffective but indeed apparently harmful to performance? The series of studies by him and his co-workers have yielded many findings, only some of which can be noted here. For general reviews, see Steffy (1978) and Cromwell (1975).

The crossover effect appeared earlier to be characteristic only of process schizophrenics (Steffy, 1978). Reactive schizophrenics and the affectively disordered showed clearly lower levels of crossover. Subsequently, however, crossover has been identified in the elderly M. E. Strauss, Wagman, & Quaid, 1983) and in those with temporal-lobe epilepsy (Greiffenstein, Milberg, Lewis, & Rosenbaum, 1981). Therefore it is not entirely specific to process schizophrenics. Depending on whether subordinative or propositional thinking is used, this nonspecificity is a basis for viewing crossover as weaker in value for understanding schizophrenia or as more provocative to new ideas (which must incorporate these temporal-lobe and aging effects with process schizophrenia).

A question had lingered whether the crossover results from regular trials becoming slower, irregular trials becoming faster, or both. This was answered through the use of isotemporal sets by Bellissimo and Steffy (1975). In this technique an arbitrary series of four regular trials with 7-second PIs are interpolated within a longer series of irregular trials, and the trial-to-trial change in reaction time is plotted. This research yielded the conclusion that repeating the identical PI led primarily to slowing in regular trials, not quickening in irregular trials. For this reason the descriptive terms redundancy-associated deficit and redundancy deficit have been appropriately introduced as substitutes for the term crossover. Other studies identified conditions in which the effect could be either enhanced or eliminated (e.g., Schneider & Cauthen, 1982; Galbraith, & Steffy, 1980).

Ironically, with these new findings, reaction time crossover (RTX) has come to be viewed less often as a strategy for hunting the *lowest* level of central nervous system function on which schizophrenic deficit occurs. A broad range of cognitive factors appear to influence it and reveal its complexity.

Reaction time crossover in first-degree relatives of schizophrenics was studied by De Amicis and Cromwell (1979). Not trusting the clinical criteria alone, for reasons already stated, they required additional dimensions in index-subject selection. For relatives to be chosen for study the index patients not only had to meet the DSM-II clinical criteria for schizophrenia across time and the Elgin criteria for process schizophrenia, but they also had to show a minimum amount of RTX. Findings revealed that the first-degree relatives of these patients also showed crossover—to a lesser extent than their schizophrenic relative but significantly more than normal controls. Greater magnitude of crossover in the patients was found to be positively related to (*a*) the mean magnitude of crossover among each patient's relatives (De Amicis, Huntzinger, & Cromwell, 1981) and (*b*) the greater number of psychiatric hospitalizations among each patient's relatives.

This study illustrates not only a familial effect of crossover in schizophrenia but also again the different ways results can be conceptualized. Those with preemptive thinking would criticize the study as weak because the formal criteria for schizophrenia in index cases were not rigidly embraced; thus nothing can be concluded about DSM-III schizophrenia as such. Those with subordinative thinking would immediately raise a useful question about whether crossover exists in relatives of noncrossover schizophrenics and whether a useful subtyping would be possible on this basis. Those with propositional thinking would ask whether reformulating defining criteria of schizophrenia along the lines of crossover would lead to greater predictability of familial transmission, to better treatment decisions or outcome predictions, or to better prediction of risk within relative groups.

Earliest Evidence in Life Span

Another strategy is to identify variables or events at the *earliest point in the life span* where they are valid in predicting later onset of the disorder. An interim strategy is to identify differences between offspring with one schizophrenic parent and those with normal parents. This interim strategy is usually incorporated into longitudinal schizophrenia high-risk studies (oriented to predicting later psychotic breakdown from antecedent variables). Notable pioneers in high-risk research have been Fish (1957), Sobel (1961), Mednick and Schulsinger (1968), and Garmezy (1974a, 1974b). The most consistently replicated difference so far revealed between high- and normal-risk offspring has concerned vigilance/span of apprehension (Asarnow, Steffy, MacCrimmon, & Cleghorn, 1977; Erlenmeyer-Kimling & Cornblatt, 1978; Rutschman, Cornblatt, & Erlenmeyer-Kimling, 1977; Nuechterlein, 1981; Neuchterlein, Phipps-Yonas, Driscoll, & Garmezy, 1982). Other reported differences include ratings by peers and teachers of early school and social behavior (Fisher, 1980; Fisher, Harder, & Kokes, 1980; Harder, Kokes, Fisher, & Strauss, 1980; Fisher, Kokes, Harder, & Jones, 1980) and P300 amplitude of evoked response during a discriminative press-button response to two randomly presented stimuli (Friedman, Vaughn, & Erlenmeyer-Kimling, 1982). As I will note later, it is incorrect to assume that variables having these group differences also predict subsequent onset of illness.

The one-ill-parent strategy for risk research is popular for several reasons. The 12% to 15% risk makes this group more likely to yield immediately useful results than a study of the general population, who have about 1% risk. Yet one-ill-parent subjects are less difficult to find than subjects of even greater risk: offspring of two schizophrenic parents or persons who have identical twins who are schizophrenic.

Factors in Healthy Relatives

A related strategy has been to search for and study factors not only present in patients but also present in their *healthy relatives*. This strategy and the previous one are also attractive because they eliminate or reduce the innumerable "consequent effects" described earlier: effects of drugs, institutionalization, self-labeling, labeling by others, selective removal from drugs as based upon obscure criteria, and so on.

When deviant factors are identified uniquely in this group, they serve as candidate hypotheses for either environmental or genetic vulnerability to schizophrenia. The choice of interpretation—genetic or environmental—is usually based upon a rationale that is perhaps one of the weakest in psychiatric research: when the environmental transmission of a particular trait seems inconceivable, then the presumption of genetic transmission is invoked. Such was hypothesized in the case of eye tracking (Holzman, Proctor, Levy, Yasillo, Meltzer, & Hurt, 1974), RTX (De Amicis & Cromwell, 1979), and evoked response (Friedman et al., 1982).

ERRORS IN INTERPRETING
RISK AND TRANSMISSION FINDINGS

The two strategies just described—searching for deviations in healthy relatives and in patients before the onset of illness—have similarities and differences worthy of comment. Both strategies converge when using unaffected individuals as the target population. Yet their purposes are very different. The ultimate goal of the early-risk strategy is to predict longitudinally the onset of schizophrenic illness. The goal of the healthy-relatives strategy is to identify the mechanisms of transmission of disease propensity among family members.

Much confusion can occur, and has occurred, in interpreting what is a high-risk or vulnerability indicator, a familial factor, a biological factor, a genetic influence, or a socioenvironmental influence. Some of the errors of interpretation leading to this confusion are as follows:

The "Risk sans Environment" Error

High risk or vulnerability does not have to mean *biological* high risk or vulnerability, nor does it have to mean familial vulnerability. The study by Goldstein, Judd, Rodnick, and Alkire (1968) of outcome for disturbed adolescents represents a productive example of increased risk not identified through psychopathology in the parents that is biologically or even behaviorally transmitted to the child.

The Impatient Risk Researcher Error

A difference found between high-risk and non-high-risk offspring does not have to mean that a vulnerability or predictive factor of onset of later psychosis has been found. By analogy, the fact that patients with and without myocardial infarction differ in denial of hostility (and many other variables) does not mean these variables predict myocardial infarction (Cromwell, Butterfield, Brayfield, & Curry, 1977). Indeed, the factors predicting heart attack are relatively separate from those where group differences are found. Likewise, the factors predicting schizophrenia probably are relatively separate from those in which risk/nonrisk group differences are found.

The Vulnerocentrism Error

Even if a variable does prove itself successful in longitudinal prediction of onset in the offspring or other relatives of a schizophrenic, it does not mean this same variable predicts onset of schizophrenia in general. The vast majority of people who become schizophrenic do not have a parent or close relative who is schizophrenic. Thus they do not fall into this premorbid category of high risk. There is no basis yet for assuming that correct predictions of onset among one-ill-parent, high-risk subjects will also apply to predicting onset of schizophrenia in the population at large.

The Bad Seed Error

Familial transmission does not have to mean genetic (or even biological) transmission. "Familial" simply means that something "runs in the family," whether hair color, low socioeconomic status, or preference for the Republican party (e.g., Cavalli-Sforza, Feldman, Chen, & Dornbusch, 1982). Depending upon one's enthusiasm and persuasion, familial factors are still sometimes looked upon primarily as genetic. For example, Kety et al. (1968) demonstrated that process schizophrenics who had been adopted and reared apart from their families of origin had biological relatives who were schizophrenic. If these effects are environmental, they would have to be prebirth or perinatal environmental effects. Since this does not seem highly likely, the preferred interpretation is that the effects are genetic. However, it is erroneous to conclude absolutely that this is so. For converging support toward a genetic interpretation, increased interest focuses upon the concordance of schizophrenia in paternal half-siblings (rare cases indeed!), since they do not share the same pre- and perinatal environment.

Another example of nongenetic, nonbiological familial transmission is strongly suggested by the work of Wynne, Singer, and Toohey (1976), who demonstrated that adoptive parents of schizophrenics showed communication deviance.

The "Holy Grail" Error

If a familial influence in schizophrenia is indeed genetic, this does not have to mean that the genetic transmission of disorder, or any portion thereof, is contributed by alleles that are schizophrenia-specific. The clinical manifestations of schizophrenia could potentially be produced by genetic influence that simply impairs central nervous system functioning and ability to cope; following this, nongenetic factors may be the determinants that "specify" an outcome of schizophrenia rather than some other resolution. The most thoughtful position on these matters in recent years has been that of Spring and Zubin (1977), who have emphasized the interaction of underlying vulnerability and the environmental events that modify the threshold of susceptibility for overt schizophrenic episodes.

The Chauvinistic Clinician Error

Whatever genetic influence occurs in schizophrenia, whether specific or nonspecific, does not mean that manifest clinical schizophrenia can be usefully studied as a genetic phenotype itself (or as a one-to-one product of any other specific biological variable). The wide contemporary recognition that nongenetic factors contribute to overt schizophrenic episodes makes the direct genetic study of the clinical phenomenon as such patently absurd.

What is the alternative? Recalling the earlier part of this chapter, we are reminded that a finite number of variables have been identified that have been kept segregated from the defining criteria of schizophrenia but that are nonetheless associated with it. While it is clear that "clinical" schizophrenia is a "mixed bag" of genetic and environmental contributions, it is an open question whether these specific "associated variants" are under more clearly isolated genetic control. And if they are under isolated genetic control, it is an open question whether this control is specific to some families and not others or whether specific combinations of variants must be present to produce overt onset.

The Heterophobic Error

Another remarkable confusion exists between populational heritability of a genetic trait and whether it follows clearly identified transmission (Mendelian) laws within a given family pedigree. Those who hold to preemptive and subordinative thinking about schizophrenia, as described earlier, will typically cling to notions of specificity regarding the traditional construct of schizophrenia. For such thinkers it would be unattractive or intolerable to assume that genetic influences vary widely from family to family or that the rules of transmission might be clearer if the traditional defining criteria of the disorder were forsaken. It would also be unattractive or intolerable to assume that genetic transmission of specific traits should be studied within specific families (i.e., hypotheses of segregation and linkage) unless some formidable heritability coefficient were found for that trait in the general population. It is as if the trait must be not only schizophrenic related but also prominent and homogeneously distributed in the total schizophrenic population as well.

In other words, preemptive and subordinative thinking has produced the classic impasse. If one is to cling to the traditional thinking about schizophrenia, it is uprooting to consider variables outside the defining criteria of schizophrenia as serious candidates for study. Since clinically defined schizophrenia does not fit any clear pattern of genetic distribution, it is uprooting to think that a more specific variant—not part of the defining clinical criteria—might have such a fit. Since schizophrenia is preemptively viewed by some as a homogeneous entity affecting 1% of the population, it is uprooting to think that heritability might not be important when the role of a given genetic trait within a given family is investigated. In short, it is uprooting to think that research effort might be saved rather than lost by putting aside the traditional "plumbing" we call schizophrenia and examining new propositions.

THE SCHIZOPHRENIA-RELATED VARIANT:
A DIFFERENT STRATEGY

By implication I have argued that progress in schizophrenia research depends upon at least some propositional thinking—in other words, that the continued attempt to organize the data of schizophrenia investigations around central interview-based defining criteria is a bankrupt notion. While some would legitimately argue that an essence is still to be gleaned from clinical variables in the ABCD network of relation, it seems in perspective that the decades of study by outstanding and keenly perceptive clinicians should have revealed it by now. What is more, there seems to be little gain in a continued rearrangement of the furniture in the DSM fortress. Rearranging the same symptoms into more clever categories is not likely to make a DSM-IV or other edition more appointing in its effect.

Propositional thinking demands a search for better prediction within the ABCD framework. Each time better prediction is attained, a basis is set for new and different defining. Each such innovation demands a complete reassessment of correlates to the new construct, and the process begins again. How do we conduct this search? It may be necessary to shift our primary attention first to schizophrenia-related variants and then, as a later step, to do the research that bridges these variants to the clinical manifestations.

A *schizophrenia-related variant*, as proposed here, is a variable (a) significantly associated with clinically defined schizophrenia (but not highly so and not specific to it; otherwise we would get into the same problems we are trying to escape), (b) present in affected individuals before, during, and after episodes of illness, and (c) present also in healthy relatives (at least first-degree relatives) to an extent greater than in individuals with no known major mental disorder in self or family.

Once these variants are identified, they should be studied without regard to their specificity to clinically schizophrenic patients. The classification of individuals based upon a variant may include people not now considered clinically ill, or it may exclude some who would be considered clinically ill within the present criterion boundaries. We need only remember that at one time in history the deviation in blood sugar level was seen as an interesting variant of diabetes, not as part of the defining criteria. The laboratory identification of a syphilis spirochete was merely associated with the elaborately worked out syndrome of general paresis, not considered part of the defining criteria (see Lewis, 1974). Research in infectious disease did not progress through a careful path of factor analysis of coughs and sneezes.

In this section I will describe an ongoing study to illustrate how one can study schizophrenia yet break free from these shackles of current schizophrenia definition. The study is not offered as the crucial or only way to achieve progress; my major thesis is simply that it is time to look elsewhere.

This particular illustrative study applies schizophrenia-related variants to the study of genetics of schizophrenia. Other applications outside genetics are equally possible. First the method of the ongoing study, then the central questions to be answered by the research, then more peripheral nongenetic questions will be addressed. After this description of the study and its purpose, I shall comment on genetic concepts not currently familiar to all professionals in the mental health field. Finally, I shall comment on how preemptive thinking in schizophrenic genetics research has obstructed progress in the field.

The Pedigree Study of Schizophrenia-Related Variants

The target population of the study is three groups of extended families. Although the major goal is a within-family analysis of traits across generations, a selection of three kinds of families is important for descriptive purposes: those with (*a*) multiple cases, (*b*) single cases, and (*c*) no traceable evidence of schizophrenia in the family pedigree. As the first step in accepting eligible families into the study the formal schizophrenia criteria are used as "entry criteria." Once these entry criteria are met, it makes no difference whether a given family member is or has been overtly ill with schizophrenia; the attention thereafter is upon the independent variables, that is, the schizophrenia-related variants throughout the family pedigree.

The variants chosen have been demonstrated to different degrees as schizophrenia related and are under active study by various co-investigators.[1] They include reaction time crossover and related

1. The active co-investigators and collaborators in the study are Monte S. Buchsbaum, evoked response psychophysiology; Richard Doherty, DNA polymorphism genetics; William G. Iacono, eye tracking psychophysiology; Kenneth Kidd, programmed linkage analysis and DNA polymorphism genetics; Dennis Murphy, monoamine oxidase biochemistry; Lawrence G. Space, computer applications;

reaction time variables, vigilance/span of apprehension, visual evoked response augmenting/reducing, blood platelet monoamine oxidase, plasma dopamine beta hydroxylase, dichotic listening, and smooth-pursuit eye tracking. In addition to these schizophrenia-related variants, a number of other clinical and demographic measures are applied: the Schizophrenia and Affective Disorders Scale (SADS) clinical interview, Chapman, Chapman, and Raulin scales of anhedonia (1976) and perceptual aberration (1978), affective rating scale (Knight, Roff, Barnett, & Moss, 1979), Harris Test of Lateral Dominance, Golden and Meehl (1979) schizoidia items, a life events measure of stress (Sameroff & Rosenzweig, Note 3), and other demographic information. In addition to the plasma and platelet analyses, blood samples are also used to assay a range of genetic mapping markers.

The logistics of the study call for the various investigators to prescribe equipment, denote procedure, and train a central technical staff to collect data on all subjects. After this the members of respective families are brought to the University of Rochester in small groups or singly, admitted to the Clinical Research Center, and given the 1½ day battery of procedures.

Once the groups of relatives have been examined, the data on the schizophrenia-related (and clinical) variants will be submitted to segregation analysis and other types of genetic analysis. The purpose of segregation analysis is to determine whether the distribution of a given variant within a family conforms to a simple Mendelian distribution such as single dominant gene transmission. That it does conform does not prove the mode of transmission to be such, but it does provide a basis for another analytic step, namely, linkage analysis.

Genetic linkage analysis correlates the distribution of a variant of unknown chromosomal location in correspondence to each of a set of mapping markers. A mapping marker, referred to above, is a genetic trait whose chromosomal location is known. If the presence/absence of an investigated variant corresponds across generations with the presence/absence of a given marker, then one has a basis for concluding that the investigated variant is on the same chromosome as the genetic

Bonnie Spring, dichotic listening psychopathology; Jack Adams-Webber, general clinical assessment; and Lowell R. Weitkamp, genetic marker assays and linkage analysis. The project is supported primarily by National Institute of Mental Health grant MH-34114 and National Institutes of Health Division of Research Resources grant RR-00044.

marker—and, even more, on the same segment of chromosome that, by the process of meiosis, was inherited from one or the other parent. Thus, to the degree that the variant represents a risk that the individual will become schizophrenic, the location of the variant allows a refinement in defining genetic risk. Currently, genetic risk can be denoted through family membership—for example, with one schizophrenic parent. If the current type of research proves successful, different risk estimates could be made within families (e.g., from sibling to sibling) and at a more accurate level. Instead of a 15% risk for offspring with one ill parent, some offspring would be designated well above 15% risk and others well below that level.

Beyond the primary questions of genetic segregation and linkage, other questions remain—not all of which can be answered in a single study. For example, while some evidence has been found that each of the schizophrenia-related variants is familial, little or nothing is known about how they relate to each other. If variants are orthogonal, a basis is created for hypothesizing that separate and independent factors may be in operation. An intercorrelation among the variants may be the result of any number of reasons, genetic and nongenetic.

Other questions concern how the schizophrenia-related variants distribute themselves vis-à-vis the overt manifestation of schizophrenia. A preemptive polygenetic view would hold that families highly loaded with overt schizophrenia would also be highly loaded with schizophrenia-related variants, in number, magnitude, or both. An alternative view is that it is possible for one or more schizophrenia-related variants to be distributed among families (or affected families only) regardless of the number or severity of overt cases of schizophrenia. This view would be compatible with the notion that whatever familial (likely genetic) influences predispose schizophrenia, the precipitation of the overt case is primarily under environmental control. Thus it is possible for single-instance, or even no-instance, families to have as great or as similar a distribution of a schizophrenia-related variant as a multiple-instance family.

Still another related question is whether a single variant, the sum or magnitude of deviant variants present, or specific combinations or patterns of variants are necessary for schizophrenia to occur. A parellel question is whether environmental experience relevant to psychotic breakdown must be viewed as a simple-magnitude function of stress, a simple function of the resulting inconsistencies in conceptual structure, or a qualitatively and/or developmentally patterned phenomenon.

Important Genetic Distinctions

Genetic linkage should be sharply distinguished from genetic association. Genetic association refers to the correlation between genetic traits among unrelated individuals in the population. Such association may occur for many reasons, such as different phenotypic expressions originating from the same gene, genetic linkage, or, as with sickle-cell anemia and black skin, a genetic independence. As mentioned earlier, the intercorrelation (association) among variables has been one common basis for classification. The evolving of a more useful *diagnostic* classification, however, depends upon how tightly the assessment variables enter into the ABCD structure, thus allowing better treatment decision, prevention, and prognosis. How well the variables are associated with each other (genetically or otherwise) is only of secondary interest in terms of their possible common source of variance.

It has often been assumed that the genetic influences responsible for schizophrenia are rare and must conform to the populational base rate of 1% for schizophrenia in the general population. This is not necessarily the case. For example, consider the hypothetical possibility that two specific genetic factors are necessary to precipitate schizophrenia. Assume one of them is highly frequent in the population, say 50%, and the other is rarer, say 2%. If both variants are present, and if this represents the sufficient condition, then the population rate for schizophrenia would indeed be 1%. Or, choosing a more appropriate stress × vulnerability model (Spring & Zubin, 1977), assume that one variant is present in 50% of the population, the other necessary variant is present in 4% of the population, and the necessary environment to precipitate schizophrenia occurs 50% of the time. Again, this combination of circumstances would produce a 1% populational base rate for overt schizophrenia. The message in these examples is that much is yet to be known empirically about the number and interaction among schizophrenia-related variants and that some specific genetic determinants may indeed be highly frequent in the population. It is premature to begin positing specific models to show how genetic factors account for schizophrenia in the population. An unending number of models are possible, and only empirical knowledge can reject the inappropriate ones.

Another distinction to be made—already referred to—is between the genetic transmission analyses (segregation, linkage, etc.) and epidemiological descriptions (populational base rates, concordance among given relative pairs, heritability coefficients, etc.). The former concern nonparametric statistical inference that focuses on intrafamilial transmission. The inferences from specific families do not necessarily generalize to the total population. The later concern primarily parametric analyses concerning the existence and characteristics of a genetic trait in the population. The latter contribute little to the understanding of the mechanism of transmission or practical clinical questions that distinguish among members within specific families.

Preemptive Thinking among Genetic Researchers

The genetic studies of schizophrenia have focused almost solely upon the clinically manifest condition as the genetic variable — that is, the phenotype. And through twin, relative pairs, adoptee, and other research paradigms, we know that schizophrenia runs in some families. At least some genetic contribution can readily be hypothesized. We also know that the distribution of schizophrenia within any given family currently defies an understanding in terms of mechanism of transmission — type of gene constituency and Mendelian pattern. We also know that most schizophrenic patients have no known relatives diagnosed as schizophrenic. Since the clinically defined concept has preempted a search for a more appropriate phenotype (or phenotypes), one is forced into genetic interpretations of polygenic transmission, incomplete penetrance, or both.

Another approach, which also has assumed that clinical schizophrenia is the one and only variable to study, has been to move away from the search for a specific genetic mechanism to the study of populational base rates and heritability coefficients (i.e., genetic epidemiology). In a more and more exquisite fashion, such studies strengthen the hypothesis that a familial contribution indeed exists, and some research questions, trivial with respect to locus of transmission or practical clinical impact, are answered. However, these efforts move away from the goal of understanding how genetic variables contribute to schizophrenia in a given individual. Stated differently, the sole contribution of most past genetic studies in schizophrenia (e.g., as reviewed by Gottesman & Shields, 1982) is to confirm that something is transmitted; they do not answer what is transmitted or how. The extant assumption is that "symptoms" are transmitted.

Preemptive thinkers would not value a variant that was not specific to schizophrenia. Rather than change their central construct of what the problem area is, they would prefer to devalue the variant as unimportant. The subordinative view would require that the variant at least be either specific to a subtype of schizophrenia or clearly delineated as common to schizophrenia and some other disorder such as affective psychosis. The propositional thinking proposed here does not require these assumptions. To the contrary, relinquishing the assumption of specificity allows a variant to be valuable so long as it enhances the ABCD interrelations of *any* disorder. For example, reaction time crossover may turn out to contribute to the understanding of aging and temporal lobe epilepsy as well as process schizophrenia. Blood platelets monoamine oxidase may play a major role in a group of disorders now classified variously as schizophrenic and affective. Although schizophrenia is genetically influenced, there may be no such thing as a genetic influence specific to schizophrenia. With propositional thinking the historical lines of demarcation in diagnoses and their etiology become productively blurred.

A final step of illogic, already mentioned briefly, comes in how the preemptive thinker views the nature of schizophrenia-related variants. First, since the variants are not part of the defining criteria, they are by definition not highly relevant but instead are only loosely or remotely related to schizophrenia. Second, if they are nevertheless subordinated to and clearly associated with schizophrenia, then they are assumed to share characteristics similar to the central schizophrenia construct. In other words, if schizophrenia can be explained only by polygenic or incomplete penetrance models, then it is inconceivable that the specific variants can be explained in any other way.

A basic rationale in the study described above is that these lines of thinking must be challenged, that the global clinical definition of schizophrenia is not the appropriate phenotype for genetic study, and that the genetic mechanism for each respective schizophrenia-related variant, whether single dominant transmission or otherwise, is a worthy candidate for study.

Final Comment

Like all research strategies, the one just illustrated is not without its hazards. The ultimate goal would be to change the defining criteria for schizophrenia in such a way that the ABCD interrelations are tightened and that schizophrenia may thereby be more effectively prevented or cured. One hazard is that the genetic sources of influence, though hypothesized as present, may not be the most important ones. Variables primarily under environmental control may be more important. Second, the schizophrenia-related variants studied, though shown to be familial, have environmental sources of variance as well. Thus one must be mindful whether the genetic or environmental contribution (or both) mediates the schizophrenic behavior. Third, the probability of finding schizophrenia-related variants linked to genetic markers is low (but if found the payoff is high). Fourth, if and when a given variant has indeed been found to segregate and link, this does not mean it is a part of the causal pathway that produces clinical schizophrenia. Instead, the variant may be an unimportant by-product of some genetic influence that produces schizophrenia, or it may reflect an innocent gene that is closely linked on the same chromosome with another gene that is indeed implicated in schizophrenia. On the other hand, this strategy is nevertheless one of the appealing alternatives by which to study schizophrenia without the problems I described earlier.

Still another by-product is the possibility of identifying variants that decrease, rather than increase, the likelihood of clinical schizophrenia. If, as some suggest (Jaynes, 1977), schizophrenialike thinking and behavior were at one time in the evolution of man a normal part of his condition, then the notion of a specific "protecting" or "inhibitor" gene would be plausible.

Along with these hazards and by-products, we might expect that the genetic understanding of schizophrenia would progress with (*a*) the identification of schizophrenia-related variants through the investigation of numerous variables; (*b*) the determination of the segregation and linkage status of each, if any; (*c*) the determination of what characteristics, combinations, and patterns of variants, along with various types of stressing factors or other life experiences, produce or inhibit schizophrenia; (*d*) the identification of interventive variables that ward off, ameliorate, or prevent this debilitating process; and (*e*) the formalization of these antecedent/consequent relations into the formal language of diagnostic nomenclature.

REFERENCE NOTES

1. Nideffer, R. N., Space, L. G., Cromwell, R. L., & Dwyer, P. Speed vs. accuracy in choice reaction time of good and poor premorbid schizophrenics. Unpublished manuscript.
2. Kar, B. C. Muller-Lyer illusion in schizophrenics as a function of field distraction and exposure time. M.A. thesis, George Peabody College for Teachers, Nashville, Tennessee, 1967.
3. Sameroff, A., and Rosenzweig, L. H. Life events scale. Unpublished manuscript, 1981.

REFERENCES

American Psychiatric Association. *Diagnostic and statistical manual of mental disorders* (3rd ed.). Washington, D.C.: American Psychiatric Association, 1980.
Asarnow, R. F. The search for the psychobiological substrate of schizophrenia: A perspective from studies of children at risk for schizophrenia. In R. Tarten (Ed.), *The child at risk*. New York: Oxford University Press, 1983.
Asarnow, R. F., Cromwell, R. L., & Rennick, P. M. Cognitive and evoked response measures of information processing in schizophrenics with and without a family history of schizophrenia. *Journal of Nervous and Mental Disease*, 1978, **166**, 719–730.
Asarnow, R. F., & Mann, R. Size estimation in paranoid and nonparanoid schizophrenics: A test of the stimulus redundancy formulation interpretation. *Journal of Nervous and Mental Disease, 1978*, **166**, 96–103.
Asarnow, R. F., Steffy, R. A., MacCrimmon, D. J., & Cleghorn, J. M. An attentional assessment of foster children at risk for schizophrenia. *Journal of Abnormal Psychology, 1977*, **86**, 267–275. Reprinted in L. C. Wynne, R. L. Cromwell, and S. Matthysse (Eds.), *The nature of schizophrenia*. New York: John Wiley, 1978.
Bellissimo, A., & Steffy, R. A. Redundancy-associated deficit in schizophrenic reaction time performance. *Journal of Abnormal Psychology, 1972*, **80**, 299–307.
Bergman, G., & Spence, K. W. Operationism and theory in psychology. *Psychological Review*, 1941, **48**, 1–14.
Bleuler, E. *Dementia praecox oder die Gruppe der Schizophrenien*. Leipzig: Deuticke, 1911. Translated by J. Zinkin as *Dementia praecox, or The group of schizophrenias*. New York: International Universities Press, 1950.
Bridgman, P. W. *The logic of modern physics*. New York: Macmillan, 1927.
Buchsbaum, M. S. Average evoked response and stimulus intensity in

identical and fraternal twins. *Physiological Psychology, 1974,* **22,** 365–370.
Buchsbaum, M. S., Ingvar, D. H., Kessler, R., Waters, R. N., Capeletti, J.,
van Kammen, D. P., King, A. C., Johnson, J. J., Manning, R. G., Flynn, R.
M., Mann, L. S., Bunney, W. E., Jr., & Sokoloff, L. Cerebral glucography
with position tomography in normals and in patients with schizophrenia.
Archives of General Psychiatry, 1982, **39,** 251–260.
Buchsbaum, M. S., Murphy, D. L., Coursey, R. D., Lake, C. R., & Zeigler,
M. G. Platelet monoamine oxidase, plasma dopamine-beta-hydroxylase
and attention in a "biochemical high risk" sample. In L. C. Wynne, R. L.
Cromwell, & S. Matthysee (Eds.), *The nature of schizophrenia.* New York:
John Wiley, 1978.
Cancro, R., Sutton, S., Kerr, J., & Sugerman, A. A. Reaction time and
prognosis in schizophrenia. *Journal of Nervous and Mental Disease,* 1971,
153, 351–359.
Cavalli-Sforza, L. L., Feldman, M. W., Chen, K. H., & Dornbusch, S. M.
Theory and observation in cultural transmission. *Science,* 1982, **218,**
19–27.
Chapman, L. J., Chapman, J. P., & Raulin, M. L. Scales for physical and
social anhedonia. *Journal of Abnormal Psychology,* 1976, **85,** 374–382.
Chapman, L. J., Chapman, J. P., & Raulin, M. L. Body-image observation in
schizophrenia. *Journal of Abnormal Psychology,* 1978, **87,** 399–407.
Cornblatt, B., & Erlenmeyer-Kimling, L. Early attentional predictors of
adolescent behavioral disturbances in children at risk for schizophrenia.
In N. Watt, J. Anthony, L. C. Wynne, & J. Rolff (Eds.), *Children at risk for
schizophrenia: A longitudinal perspective.* New York: Cambridge University
Press, 1983.
Cromwell, R. L. Stimulus redundancy and schizophrenia. *Journal of Nervous
and Mental Disease,* 1968, **146,** 360–375.
Cromwell, R. L. Assessment of schizophrenia. *Annual Review of Psychology,*
1975, **26,** 593–619.
Cromwell, R. L. Ethics, umbrage, and the ABCDs. *Minnesota Education,*
1976, **2,** 42–47.
Cromwell, R. L. Eight decades focus on symptom classification is enough: A
discussion. In M. J. Goldstein (Ed.), *Preventive intervention in psychopathology: Are we ready?* Washington, D.C.: U.S. Government Printing Office,
1982.
Cromwell, R. L., Butterfield, E. C., Brayfield, F. M., & Curry, J. J. *Acute
myocardial infarction: Reaction and recovery.* Saint Louis, Mo.: C. V. Mosby,
1977.
Cromwell, R. L., & Dokecki, P. R. Schizophrenic language: A disattention
interpretation. In S. Rosenberg & J. H. Koplin (Eds.), *Developments in
applied psycholinguistic research.* New York: Macmillan, 1968.
Cromwell, R. L., Strauss, J. S., & Blashfield, R. K. Criteria for classification
systems. In N. Hobbs (Ed.), *Issues in the classification of children: A handbook*

of categories, labels, and their consequences. San Francisco: Jossey-Bass, 1975.

Davis, D. W., Cromwell, R. L., & Held, J. M. Size estimation in emotionally disturbed children and schizophrenic adults. *Journal of Abnormal Psychology,* 1967, **72,** 395–401.

De Amicis, L. A., & Cromwell, R. L. Reaction time crossover in process schizophrenic patients, their relatives, and control subjects. *Journal of Nervous and Mental Disease,* 1979, **167,** 593–600.

De Amicis, L. A., Huntzinger, R. S., & Cromwell, R. L. Brief communication: Magnitude of reaction time crossover in process schizophrenic patients in relation to their first degree relatives. *Journal of Nervous and Mental Disease,* 1981, **169,** 64–65.

Dingemans, P., Space, L. G., & Cromwell, R. L. Repertory grid, consistency, and schizophrenia. In J. Adams-Webber (Ed.), *Personal constructs: Theory and application.* Toronto: Academic Press, 1983.

Doane, J. A., West, K. L., Goldstein, M. J., Rodnick, E. H., & Jones, J. E. Parental communication deviance and affective style: Predictors of subsequent schizophrenia spectrum disorders in vulnerable adolescents. *Archives of General Psychiatry,* 1981, **38,** 679–685.

Erlenmeyer-Kimling, L., & Cornblatt, B. Attentional measures in a study of children at high-risk for schizophrenia. *Journal of Psychiatric Research,* 1978, **14,** 93–98.

Fish, B. The detection of schizophrenia in infancy. *Journal of Nervous and Mental Disease,* 1957, **125,** 1–24.

Fisher, L. Child competence and psychiatric risk. I. Model and method. *Journal of Nervous and Mental Disease,* 1980, **168,** 323–331.

Fisher, L., Harder, D. W., & Kokes, R. F. Child competence and psychiatric risk. III. Comparisons based on diagnosis of hospitalized patients. *Journal of Nervous and Mental Disease,* 1980, **168,** 338–342.

Fisher, L., Kokes, R. F., Harder, D. W., & Jones, J. E. Child competence and psychiatric risk. VI. Summary and integration of findings. *Journal of Nervous and Mental Disease,* 1980, **168,** 353–355.

Friedman, D., Vaughn, H. G., Jr., & Erlenmeyer-Kimling, L. Cognitive brain potentials in children at risk for schizophrenia: Preliminary findings and methodological considerations. *Schizophrenia Bulletin,* 1982, **8,** 514–531.

Galbraith, K. J., & Steffy, R. A. Intensity of imperative signed influences on redundancy deficit and latency in process schizophrenics. *Journal of Nervous and Mental Disease,* 1980, **168,** 542–549.

Garmezy, N. Children at risk: The search for the antecedents of schizophrenia. Part 1. Conceptual models and research methods. *Schizophrenia Bulletin,* 1974, no. 8, 14–90. (a)

Garmezy, N. Children at risk: The search for the antecedents of schizophrenia. Part 2. Ongoing research programs, issues, and interventions. *Schizophrenia Bulletin,* 1974, no. 9, 55–126. (b)

Golden, R. R., & Meehl, P. E. Detection of the schizoid taxon with MMPI indicators. *Journal of Abnormal Psychology*, 1979, **88**, 217–233.

Goldstein, M. J., Judd, L. L., Rodnick, E. H., & Alkire, A. A. A method for studying social influence and coping patterns within families of disturbed adolescents. *Journal of Nervous and Mental Disease*, 1968, **147**, 233–251.

Gottsman, I. I., & Shields, J. *Schizophrenia: The epigenetic puzzle*. Cambridge: Cambridge University Press, 1982.

Greiffenstein, M., Milberg, W., Lewis, R., & Rosenbaum, G. Temporal lobe epilepsy and schizophrenia: Comparison of reaction time deficits. *Journal of Abnormal Psychology*, 1981, **90**, 105–112.

Haracz, J. L. The dopamine hypothesis: An overview of studies with schizophrenic patients. *Schizophrenia Bulletin*, 1982, **8**, 438–469.

Harder, D. W., Kokes, R. F., Fisher, L., & Strauss, J. S. Child competence and psychiatric risk. IV. Relationship of patient diagnostic classifications and parent psychopathology severity to child functioning. *Journal of Nervous and Mental Disease*, 1980, **168**, 343–347.

Holzman, P. S., Proctor, L. R., Levy, D. L., Yasillo, N. J., Meltzer, H. Y., & Hurt, S. W. Eyetracking dysfunctions in schizophrenic patients and their relatives. *Archives of General Psychiatry*, 1974, **31**, 143–151.

Huston, P. E., Shakow, D., & Riggs, L. A. Studies of motor function in schizophrenia. 2. Reaction time. *Journal of Genetic Psychology*, 1937, **16**, 39–82.

Jaynes, J. *The state of consciousness and the breakdown of the bicameral mind*. New York: Houghton Mifflin, 1977.

Jensen, D. D. Operationism and the question "Is this behavior learned or innate?" *Behaviour*, 1960, **17**, 1–8.

Jensen, D. D. Polythetic biopsychology: An alternative to behaviorism. In J. H. Reynierse (Ed.), *Current issues in animal learning: A colloquium*. Lincoln, Neb.: University of Nebraska Press, 1970.

Kantor, J. R. The operational principle in the physical and psychological sciences. *Psychological Record*, 1938, **2**, 3–32.

Kelly, G. A. *The psychology of personal constructs* (Vols. 1 and 2). New York: Norton, 1955.

Kety, S. S. Neurochemical and genetic bases of psychopathology: Current status. *Behavior genetics*, 1982, **12**, 93–100.

Kety, S. S., Rosenthal D., Wender, P. H., & Schulsinger, F. The types and prevalence of mental illness in the biological and adoptive families of adopted schizophrenics. In D. Rosenthal & S. S. Kety (Eds.), *The transmission of schizophrenia*. New York: Pergamon Press, 1968.

Klein, D. N. Relation between current diagnostic criteria for schizophrenia and the dimension of premorbid adjustment, paranoid symptomatology, and chronicity. *Journal of Abnormal Psychology*, 1982, **91**, 319–325.

Knight, R. A., Roff, J. D., Barnett, J., & Moss, J. L. Concurrent and predictive validity of thought disorder and affectivity: A 22-year follow-up of acute schizophrenics. *Journal of Abnormal Psychology*, 1979, **88**, 1–12.

Knight, R., Sherer, M., & Shapiro, J. Iconic imagery in overinclusive and nonoverinclusive schizophrenics. *Journal of Abnormal Psychology*, 1977, **86**, 245–255.

Lewis, N. D. C. American psychiatry from its beginnings to World War II. In S. Arieti (Ed.), *American handbook of psychiatry*. New York: Basic Books, 1974.

Lykken, D. T. Statistical significance in psychological research. *Psychological Bulletin*, 1968, **70**, 151–159.

Magaro, P. Size estimation in schizophrenia as a function of censure, diagnosis, premorbid adjustment, and chronicity. *Journal of Abnormal Psychology*, 1969, **74**, 306–313.

McCormick, P., & Broekema, V. Size estimation, perceptual recognition, and cardiac rate response in acute paranoid and nonparanoid schizophrenics. *Journal of Abnormal Psychology*, 1978, **87**, 385–398.

Mednick, S. A., & Schulsinger, F. Some premorbid characteristics related to breakdown in children with schizophrenic mothers. In D. Rosenthal & S. S. Kety (Eds.), *The transmission of schizophrenia*. New York: Pergamon Press, 1968.

Meehl, P. E. Theory testing in psychology and physics: A methodological paradox. *Philosophy of Science*, 1967, **34**, 104–115.

Neale, J. M., & Cromwell, R. L. Size estimation of schizophrenics as a function of stimulus presentation time. *Journal of Abnormal Psychology*, 1968, **73**, 44–48.

Nuechterlein, K. H. Reaction time and attention in schizophrenia: A critical evaluation of the data and theories. *Schizophrenia Bulletin*, 1977, **3**, 373–428. (a)

Nuechterlein, K. H. Refocusing on attentional dysfunctions in schizophrenia. *Schizophrenia Bulletin*, 1977, **3**, 457–469. (b)

Nuechterlein, K. H. Signal detection in vigilance tasks and behavioral attributes among offspring of schizophrenic mothers and among hyperactive children. *Journal of Abnormal Psychology*, 1981, **92**, 4–28.

Nuechterlein, K. H., Phipps-Yonas, S., Driscoll, R. M., & Garmezy, N. The role of different components of attention in children vulnerable to schizophrenia. In M. J. Goldstein (Ed.), *Preventive intervention in schizophrenia: Are we ready?* Washington, D.C.: U.S. Government Printing Office, 1982.

Nuechterlein, K. H. Sustained attention among children vulnerable to adult schizophrenia and among hyperactive children. In N. F. Watt, J. E. Anthony, L. C. Wynne, & J. Rolff (Eds.), *Children at risk for schizophrenia: A longitudinal perspective*. New York: Cambridge University Press, 1983.

Orlov, Y. F. The wave logic of consciousness: A hypothesis. *International Journal of Theoretical Physics*, 1982, **21**, 37–53.

Osgood, C. E. *The measurement of meaning*. Urbana: University of Illinois Press, 1957.

Oshins, E., & McGoveran, D. . . . Thoughts about logic about thoughts . . . : The question "schizophrenia?" In B. H. Banathy (Ed.),

Systems science and science. Proceedings of the Society for General Systems Research, San Francisco, January 7–10, 1980. Louisville, Ky.: Society of General Systems Research, 1980. Reprinted in W. Gray, J. W. Fidler, & J. R. Battista (Eds.), *General systems theory and the psychological sciences.* Seaside, Calif.: Intersystem Publications, 1983.

Pribram, K. H. *Languages of the brain: Experimental paradoxes and principles in neuropsychology.* Monterey, Calif.: Brooks/Cole, 1971.

Rodnick, E. H., & Shakow, D. Set in the schizophrenic as measured by a composite reaction time index. *American Journal of Psychiatry,* 1940, **97,** 214–225.

Romano, J. On the nature of schizophrenia: Changes in the observer as well as the observed (1932–1977). *Schizophrenia Bulletin,* 1977, **3,** 532–559. (a)

Romano, J. Requiem or reveille: Psychiatry's choice. *Bulletin of the New York Academy of Medicine.* 1977, **53,** 787–805. (b)

Rutschman, J., Cornblatt, B., & Erlenmeyer-Kimling, L. Sustained attention in children at risk for schizophrenia: Report on a continuous performance test. *Archives of General Psychiatry,* 1977, **34,** 571–575.

Schneider, R. D., and Cauthen, N. R. Locus of reaction time change in schizophrenic and normal subjects. *Journal of Nervous and Mental Disease,* 1982, **170,** 231–240.

Shakow, D. Psychological deficit in schizophrenia. *Behavior Science,* 1963, **8,** 275–305.

Shakow, D. Some thoughts about schizophrenic research in the context of high risk studies. *Psychiatry,* 1973, **36,** 353–365.

Silverman, J. The problem of attention in research and theory in schizophrenia. *Psychological Review,* 1964, **71,** 352–379.

Sneath, P. H. A., & Sokal, R. R. *Numerical taxonomy: The principles and practice of numerical classification.* San Francisco: W. H. Freeman, 1973.

Snyder, S. H. Dopamine and schizophrenia. In L. C. Wynne, R. L. Cromwell, & S. Matthysse (Eds.), *The nature of schizophrenia.* New York: John Wiley, 1978.

Sobel, D. E. Children of schizophrenic patients: Preliminary observations on early development. *American Journal of Psychiatry,* 1961, **118,** 512–517.

Space, L. G., & Cromwell, R. L. Personal constructs among schizophrenic patients. In S. Schwartz (Ed.), *Language and cognition in schizophrenia.* Hillsdale, N.J.: Lawrence Erlbaum Associates, 1978.

Spaulding, W. D., Rosenzweig, L. H., Huntzinger, R. D., Cromwell, R. L., Briggs, D., & Hayes, T. Visual pattern integration in psychiatric patients. *Journal of Abnormal Psychology,* 1980, **89,** 635–643.

Spohn, H. E., Lacoursiere, R. B., Thompson, K., & Coyne, L. Phenothiazine effects on psychological and psychophysiological dysfunction in chronic schizophrenia. *Archives of General Psychiatry,* 1977, **34,** 633–644.

Spring, B., & Zubin, J. Vulnerability: A new view of schizophrenia. *Journal of Abnormal Psychology,* 1977, **86,** 103–126.

Steffy, R. A. An early cue sometimes impairs process schizophrenic performance. In L. C. Wynne, R. L. Cromwell, & S. Matthysse (Eds.), *The nature of schizophrenia*. New York: John Wiley, 1978.

Stevens, S. S. The operational basis of psychology. *American Journal of Psychology*, 1935, **47**, 323–330. (a)

Stevens, S. S. The operational definitions of psychological concepts. *Psychological Review*, 1935, **42**, 512–527. (b)

Strauss, J. S., & Carpenter, W. T. Prediction of outcome in schizophrenia. *Archives of General Psychiatry*, 1972, **27**, 739–746.

Strauss, J. S., Carpenter, W. T., & Bartko, J. J. The diagnosis and understanding of schizophrenia. Part 3. Speculations on the processes that underlie schizophrenic symptoms and signs. *Schizophrenia Bulletin*, 1974, No. 11, 61–75.

Strauss, M. E., Foureman, W. C., & Parwatikur, S. D. Schizophrenics' size estimation of thematic stimuli. *Journal of Abnormal Psychology*, 1974, **83**, 117–123.

Strauss, M. E., Wagman, A. M. I., & Quaid, K. A. Preparatory interval influences in reaction time of elderly adults. *Journal of Gerontology*, 1983, **38**, 55–57.

Tolman, E. C. An operational analysis of "demands." *Erkenntnis*, 1936, **6**, 383–390.

Vaughn, C. E., & Leff, J. P. The influence of family and social factors on the course of psychiatric illness. *British Journal of Psychiatry*, 1976, **129**, 125–137.

Venables, P. H. Input dysfunction in schizophrenia. In B. A. Maher (Ed.), *Progress in experimental personality research* (Vol. 1). New York: Academic Press, 1964.

Wynne, L. C., Singer, M., & Toohey, M. Communication of the adoptive parents of schizophrenics. In J. Jerstad & E. Ugelsad (Eds.), *Schizophrenia 75: Psychotherapy, family studies, research*. Oslo: Universitetsforlaget, 1976.

Zahn, T. P., Rosenthal, D., & Shakow, D. Effects of irregular preparatory intervals in reaction time in schizophrenia. *Journal of Abnormal and Social Psychology*, 1963, **67**, 44–52.

Cerebral Mechanisms, Autonomic Responsiveness, and Attention in Schizophrenia[1]

P. H. Venables

University of York

INTRODUCTION

Some sections of this chapter review and summarize well-established findings, while other sections are frankly speculative and attempt to draw together areas of work in ways with which the reader may disagree. I have purposely presented more than a passive compilation of material, and if the provocative nature of the presentation does stimulate the reader into refutation of the position taken it will have served its purpose.

I shall follow several lines of argument to intermediate positions that permit temporary conclusions, then attempt to draw together these possible approaches into reasonable cohesion.

Since this subject matter centers on schizophrenia, the first step is to define this disorder from a somewhat limited point of view, though the restricted scope introduced here is not used by some of the authors cited.

After a period in which the florid symptoms of schizophrenia have been taken as defining characteristics (e.g., Schneider 1959), now the pendulum seems to be moving back toward the definition Kraepelin (1913) made at the beginning of the century. Kety (1980), in his Maudsley lecture to the Royal College of Psychiatrists in London, made this point clearly: "We would define syndromes more homogeneous in symptomatology . . . were we to restrict the

1. This paper was prepared with the help of grants from the Leverhulme Trust and the Wellcome Trust for research on children at risk for schizophrenia.

term schizophrenia to its original concept of a chronic disorder of thought and feeling in which insidious onset, the premorbid personality qualities and the fundamental features described by Kraepelin and Bleuler were the defining characteristics" (p. 426). He emphasizes that this chronic or, better, *continuous* form of the disorder should be distinguished from acute psychoses, which "do not have the type of onset or course, the family history, the fundamental symptoms, the prognosis or response to treatment that are associated with schizophrenia."

In like manner Crow (1980), albeit based largely on a contrast between forms of the disorder having a presumed biochemical and structural etiology, defines type I and type II forms. The defining characteristics of the former are the positive symptoms of hallucinations and delusions, not leading to chronic disability and with no intellectual impairment. Type II shows the negative symptoms of affective flattening, poverty of speech, and loss of drive, characteristic of a defect state, with possible intellectual impairment. The outcome in this form is generally thought to be unfavorable. Type II is essentially what Kraepelin was defining in 1913: "The weakening of judgement, of mental activity and of creative ability, the dulling of emotional interest and the loss of energy, the loss of the inner unity of psychic life would have to be reckoned among the fundamental disorders of dementia praecox" (p. 6). He then goes on to say: "while all the remaining morbid symptoms especially hallucinations and delusions would be regarded as more secondary accompanying phenomena" (p. 6).

Since the approach taken in this chapter is developmental, inevitably I lean toward a definition of the disorder that emphasizes the existence of premorbid characteristics that portend an unfavorable development—a Kraepelinian point of view. However, developments since the turn of the century demand that his stand not be adopted too rigidly, and I shall consider deviations from his position.

PREMORBID INTELLECTUAL IMPAIRMENT

Kraepelin's (1913) definition cites weakening of judgment, mental activity, and creative ability, and Crow (1980) also considers the possibility of intellectual impairment.

In their classic paper "Psychological Deficit," Hunt and Cofer (1944) noted that "no investigator, to our knowledge, has been able to obtain predisorder test results (of intelligence) for patients in his sample." The studies up to that time, therefore, though making ingenious attempts to estimate premorbid intellectual level, could not establish definitely whether schizophrenic patients' deficit in intelligence was a continuation of that shown premorbidly or was as a result of their current clinical status.

Many studies since then have helped to determine whether such patients show intellectual impairment before the disorder, a question important in light of statements such as that by Claridge (1972, p. 7): "Thus it may be that the very creative person, though highly disposed to schizophrenia does not become clinically psychotic because high general intelligence confers some immunity in the form of adequate intellectual and personality reserves." Similarly, Lehmann (1966, p. 186) makes the point that "non-paranoid schizophrenic patients have a primary, possibly constitutional susceptibility . . . to be subject to the impact of a higher number of discrete sensory stimuli per time unit" than other individuals. If a person can cope with this supernormal influx of stimuli, then he might become creative. (As Dellas and Gaier 1970 say, creative individuals deploy their attention more widely and tend not to screen out the irrelevant.) On the other hand, Lehmann says, if the patient's "central processing apparatus" does not match in performance the extraordinary sensitivity of his input apparatus, "then his integration breaks down and he may become psychotic."

Two points arise from Lehmann's statement. First, the attention of the schizophrenic—or possibly the preschizophrenic—is wider or less selective than normal. Second, Lehmann is talking about central processing efficiency, which while conceptually comparable to the notion of general intelligence is not necessarily the same thing.

In relation to the first point Venables (1964, p. 41) wrote, "The acute . . . patient is characterized by an inability to restrict the range of his attention so that he is flooded by sensory impressions from all quarters." More recent empirical studies show little need to modify that early statement except perhaps to emphasize that "acute" in this instance means "early in the disease process" rather than acute psychosis as a diagnostic entity.

Later in this chapter I shall discuss the attentional mechanisms involved in the "wide deployment of attention," but first let us assess what data support the notion that low intellectual performance is a predisposing factor for schizophrenia.

The most recent review of earlier studies is in a paper by Worland, Weeks, Weiner, and Schechtman (1982). The authors state that "despite some evidence to the contrary, there is reason to conclude that intellectual deficit is an early concomitant of schizophrenia and is evident long before the emergence of adult illness."

A striking study is that by Offord and Cross (1971), who obtained information from school records for patients diagnosed as schizophrenic and with no additional complications such as alcoholism or epilepsy. They found that those with childhood IQs under 80 had a mean first hospitalization age of 21, whereas those with IQs of 100 or over had a mean age of 30. The intermediate IQ group were first hospitalized at a mean age of 25.4 years. By age 40 the low IQ group had been hospitalized for a mean of 206.5 months, the intermediate group for 112.3 months, and the high IQ group for only 12 months.

A later study by Offord (1974) looked at the IQs of male and female schizophrenics, their like and unlike siblings, and unrelated controls, based on measurements taken during their school careers. It was found that the mean IQ of male schizophrenics was 88.2; their male siblings averaged 95.9, their female siblings 93.8, and their matched controls 100.6. The IQs of female schizophrenics averaged 97.1, not significantly different from any of their three control groups, which averaged 96.3, 97.0, and 101.8, respectively. The finding thus exemplifies the point that lower premorbid IQ in schizophrenics is found among males but not among females. The sex difference is also seen in a study by Rieder, Broman, and Rosenthal (1977). They showed that IQ measured at the age of 7 was lower in the children of schizophrenic parents than in the children of matched controls and that male offspring were almost entirely responsible for this difference.

The stage at which the low IQ of children at risk for schizophrenia is manifest is addressed by Worland et al. (1982). The children in their study were tested first at a mean age of 7.9 years and again at 15.6 years, with Wechsler scales providing data on verbal, performance, and full-scale IQ. The study showed no effect of parental diagnosis on performance or full-scale IQ. However, an interaction between time of testing and parental diagnosis showed that there was a decline in verbal IQ between first and second testing for the children of schizophrenics but not those of normal parents. The data were not divided by sex of offspring.

Gruzelier, Mednick, and Schulsinger (1979), using data from the second major study on high risk for schizophrenia in Copenhagen, found that children of schizophrenic parents showed lower verbal but not performance IQ at ages 10 to 13 than children of normal parents.

A different approach to that of familial selection for risk was used in Mauritius (Venables, 1978; Venables, Mednick, Schulsinger, Raman, Bell, Dalais, & Fletcher, 1978). These investigators started with psychophysiological screening of a population of 1,800 3-year-old children, selecting risk groups by electrodermal orienting response characteristics. Two groups were thought to be at risk for schizophrenia. Children in the first group had a hyperactive pattern of electrodermal responses, with short latency, high amplitude, and short recovery characteristics similar to those shown premorbidly by children in the original Copenhagen high-risk study who later succumbed to schizophrenia (Mednick, Schulsinger, Teasdale, Schulsinger, Venables, & Rock, 1978) and also shown by some adult schizophrenics (e.g., Gruzelier & Venables, 1972; Frith, Stevens, Johnstone, & Crow, 1979). The second group of children showed no electrodermal responsivity whatever, a characteristic exhibited by some 40–50% of adult schizophrenic patients (Bernstein, Firth, Gruzelier, Patterson, Straube, Venables, & Zahn, 1982). Data on the differential characteristics of schizophrenic "responders" and "nonresponders" suggest that the latter are most often described as showing "emotional withdrawal", "conceptual disorganization," "affective flatness," and "motor retardation." In comparison "responders" are characterized by ratings of "manic state" anxiety, psychotic belligerence, and attention-demanding behavior (Gruzelier, 1976; Straube, 1979). It seems likely, on this basis, that it is the nonresponders who are close to the classic pattern of schizophrenia outlined by Kraepelin.

The Kraepelinian definition of schizophrenia, which gives weight to negative symptoms, inadequate premorbid status, and probable unfavorable outcome, suggests that "true" Kraepelinian schizophrenia is the form characterized as "process" or "poor premorbid" (Klorman, Strauss, & Kokes, 1977). A particular feature of this class of patients is inadequate premorbid sexual adjustment; they tend to be single rather than married. There is thus a paradox in the "traditional" high-risk design that uses children of schizophrenic parents as the sample. If schizophrenic patients have children, then they have a lower probability of being "process" or "poor premorbid" in classification. If this characteristic is heritable, which seems not unlikely, then their children may be less apt to show the premorbid impairment on which high-risk design is predicated. The present success of familial high-risk studies suggests that this analysis is not wholly correct. Nevertheless, the lack of report of hyporesponsivity shown by children of schizophrenic parents in the classic Mednick and Schulsinger (1968) high-risk study suggests a bias in the direction of selection of a nonprocess sample. It should also be borne in mind that only some 10% of schizophrenic patients have schizophrenic parents (Rosenthal, 1970), again suggesting a bias in familial high risk work.

The technique used in Mauritius—taking a whole age group of the population in one area as a sample, then selecting groups for further study on the basis of their electrodermal characteristics—is a step toward overcoming the familial bias. It does, however, demand some faith in the effectiveness of psychophysiological screening procedures.

Garmezy (1974), in his review of high-risk studies, lacked this faith. Considering the Mauritius research, he said:

> The critical question that remains, however, is the appropriateness of using deviant psychophysiological functioning in children as a criterion of risk. Issues related to the legitimacy of using such a criterion on the basis of existent data, the stability of such measures over time, when obtained from pre-schoolers and the markedly different social and psychological environment of Mauritius are only several factors that raise questions about the direction of the proposed study. (p. 76)

Whether the selection procedures have been successful can be confirmed only when some of the total sample become schizophrenic. But we can obtain some confirmation if it can be shown that the psychophysiologically selected groups behave differently from one another in ways that are in accord with data from other developmental studies of schizophrenia. Such an analysis is presented by Venables, Dalais, Mitchell, Mednick, and Schulsinger (1983). The experimental sample comprises two risk groups of children who at age 3 either showed hyperresponsive patterns of electrodermal activity or were electrodermal nonresponders. A control group matched to these groups for race and sex was selected on the basis of median electrodermal responsivity. At age 6 the children's intellectual status was tested with performance subtests of the Wechsler Pre-School and Primary Scale of Intelligence and for verbal intelligence by the Reynell Developmental Language Scales (Reynell &

Huntley, 1971). At age 9 the children were rated by their teachers on a scale developed by Rutter (1967), which produced clear factors of "aggression-hyperactivity" and "worried-fearfulness" (Venables, Fletcher, Dalais, Mitchell, Schulsinger, & Mednick, 1983). Both risk groups scored significantly lower on the aggression-hyperactivity factor than the control groups, and in addition the males among the nonresponder group were significantly lower than all other groups on verbal intelligence. The intelligence data thus fit with the data reviewed above. The combination of aggression and intelligence data is also in close accord with work reported by Roff and Knight (1980) indicating that low intelligence and low levels of aggressiveness measured at age 11 predict markedly unfavorable schizophrenic outcome at age 40.

In summary, therefore, there is growing evidence that the weakening of mental activity (Kraepelin, 1913), if thought of as synonymous with impairment of intelligence, is found in the premorbid state among those who later develop schizophrenia or appear vulnerable to developing it in the future. There is also some suggestion that this association may be confined to males and may be particularly apparent when *verbal* intelligence is considered.

At this point I will suggest a speculative hypothesis to account for the low level of intelligence, to be taken up later in relation to other aspects of behavior.

Kroll and Madden (1978) carried out a study in which a "memory stimulus" was presented to the center of a subject's visual field and a subsequent "test stimulus" was presented within the right or left visual field. Subjects had to decide as rapidly as possible whether the test stimulus matched the memory stimulus. Stimulus material consisted of upper- and lower-case letters. Decision times with different fields of presentation were related to subjects' "verbal scholastic aptitude" test scores. Results indicated that "high verbals tend to show the strongest hemisphere differences in that they show different patterns for the left and right visual field presentations on same and different case presentations. . . . The data suggest that Low Verbals carry out the same type of processing in both hemispheres."

Based on this result, therefore, I suggest that low verbal intelligence is shown in (male, process) schizophrenics because they tend to process both spatial and verbal material within the same hemisphere.

The idea that carrying out verbal and spatiotemporal functions in the same hemisphere is disadvantageous is in accord with the theory of Kinsbourne and Hicks (1978) known as the "functional cerebral space model." This model states that "limitations on dual task performance are due to intertask interference within a highly linked 'cerebral space.'" The degree of interference is a function of the "functional distance" between the cerebral control centers. This functional distance is of course markedly reduced if the operations are carried out within the same cerebral hemisphere. That such an explanation may be valid for the finding of low verbal IQ in preschizophrenic *males* is supported by the data reviewed by Buffery and Gray (1972), which suggest that female children tend to develop hemispheric specialization earlier than males, who may process both verbal and spatial material in either hemisphere up to a later age. It is quite clear, however, that this explanation of low intelligence in schizophrenics and preschizophrenics is speculative and gains strength only when other material supports it. This material will be reviewed later.

EMOTIONAL IMPAIRMENT AS A FEATURE OF SCHIZOPHRENIA

In his definition of schizophrenia Kraepelin also emphasizes "dulling of emotional interest" as characteristic of the disorder. The feature is also seen as one of the cardinal characteristics of schizophrenia by Meehl (1962), who calls it "anhedonia", defined as "a marked widespread and refractory defect in pleasure capacity— which is one of the most consistent and dramatic behavioural signs of the disease" (p. 829). Meehl also includes "cognitive slippage" as one of the critical signs of schizophrenia, and this too emphasizes the area reviewed in the previous section.

The important thing to note about Meehl's (1962) approach is that it is both developmental and dimensional. He speaks of an initial condition of "schizotoxia," an "integrated neural defect" that he sees as "all that can be spoken of as inherited." Schizotaxia, then, is seen as a predisposition to develop schizophrenia. "The imposition of social learning history upon schizotaxic individuals results in a personality organization . . . the schizotype." The schizotype is within the range of normal persons, but if the social environment the schizotaxic individual experiences is sufficiently adverse this will lead to a breakdown, with identifiable schizophrenia.

One of the difficulties in studying a schizophrenic patient in hospital is that his condition is the result not only of the primary disease process (the schizotaxia) but also of the way others react to him as his behavior becomes unusual and of his own reaction to his increasing disorder. Thus features of emotional behavior that are part of the primary disease process are inextricably overlaid with reactions to the developing disorder.

Because of this it is important to study primary characteristics in children before the disorder has developed or in normal persons with schizotypic traits. One can argue, somewhat indirectly, that if normal persons exhibiting anhedonic traits show the same characteristics on other measures as do schizophrenic patients, then anhedonia may be thought of as a primary characteristic of schizophrenia. Work in this area has been stimulated by the development of scales for measuring physical and social anhedonia by Chapman, Chapman, and Raulin (1976). Physical anhedonia is measured by such items as "The beauty of sunsets is greatly overrated," and social anhedonia is typified by the item "Having close friends is not as important as many people say."

About half the population of adult schizophrenic patients appear to be electrodermal nonresponders (Bernstein et al., 1982). Furthermore, the material reviewed in the previous section suggests that nonresponders tend to be characterized more by negative than positive of symptoms. We might therefore expect that subjects classed as anhedonic would show hyporesponsive electrodermal patterns. Simons (1981) examined electrodermal and heart-rate responses to a series of orienting tones. His subjects were undergraduates selected on the basis of their high scores (anhedonics) or mean scores (controls) on the physical anhedonic scale of Chapman et al. (1976). Results showed a significantly greater incidence of nonresponders and fast habituators (subjects showing only one or two orienting responses; Patterson & Venables, 1978) among the anhedonics than among the controls. This pattern in the electrodermal modality was supported by heart-rate orienting data, which showed smaller primary and secondary deceleration in anhedonic subjects than in controls.

Anhedonic subjects also show patterns of cortical evoked responsivity similar to those shown by schizophrenics; but before describing these findings let me review the material from research on schizophrenic patients.

In 1972 Roth and Cannon conducted a study in which they measured averaged evoked responses to series of frequent and infrequent auditory stimuli, based on the first report of a late positive wave with a peak latency of about 300 msecs (P300) by Sutton, Braren, John, and Zubin (1965), which occurred as a response to uncertain but not to certain stimuli. In accordance with earlier work, Roth and Cannon found that in normal subjects a large P300 was elicited by infrequent stimuli, whereas this component was absent in response to frequent stimuli. In contrast, schizophrenic patients showed minimal P300 response components to the infrequent stimuli, which were not different from those to frequent stimuli. This result was replicated in further studies by Roth, Horvath, Pfefferbaum, and Kopell (1980), Roth, Pfefferbaum, Horvath, Berger, and Kopell (1980), and Roth, Pfefferbaum, Kelly, Berger, and Kopell (1981). A test frequently used in studies of attention in schizophrenics, the Continuous Performance Test (CPT), provides a similar paradigm in the visual modality to that used by Roth and his colleagues in the auditory modality. In the CPT the subject has to respond to rare target visual stimuli presented in the context of frequent nontarget stimuli. Pass, Klorman, Salzman, Klein, and Kaskey (1980) report on a study that used the CPT to elicit averaged evoked responses. Schizophrenics had a smaller P300 response component and a smaller amplitude difference between critical and noncritical stimuli than nonpsychotics.

The occurrence of smaller P300 response components to rare stimuli in schizophrenic patients thus appears to be reasonably well established. Simons (1982) reports a study in which event-related potentials collected in nonsignal (orienting) and signal (constant foreperiod RT task) conditions were examined, using anhedonic and control subjects. The nonsignal conditions are considered analogous to the "frequent" or "nontarget" conditions, and the signal conditions correspond to the "infrequent" or target conditions in the studies reviewed above. No differences in evoked potential between anhedonics and controls are shown in the nonsignal conditions. However, whereas in the signal conditions the control subjects showed a large (15μV) P300 ERP component, the anhedonics showed only a small (6μV) P300 component. The result obtained for the anhedonic group is thus comparable to that obtained with schizophrenic patients, supporting the notion that anhedonia may be a fundamental aspect of schizophrenia.

In this context, however, let us return to the original analyses of the anhedonia scale by Chapman et al. (1976), who presented data on the distribution of responses of schizophrenic and control groups on the physical and social anhedonia scales. In the normal group the distribution of physical anhedonia scores is clearly unimodal, but in the schizophrenic group the distribution shows bimodality. One mode is at the same point as for the normals while the other mode gives the clear impression of a second subgroup among the schizophrenic patients. The suggestion is that a high degree of anhedonia is characteristic of some but not all schizophrenic patients. Associating this anhedonia scale with measures of premorbid adjustment suggests that poor-premorbid patients tend to be anhedonic, supporting my general position that it is the "continuous" type of schizophrenic as defined by Kraepelin who may be characterized by "dulling of emotional interest."

FUNCTIONAL CEREBRAL ASYMMETRY
IN SCHIZOPHRENIA

The findings in the literature generally suggest an impairment of left-hemisphere activity in adult schizophrenics (see, for instance, the considerable data presented in Gruzelier & Flor-Henry, 1979). It is not my purpose to contradict this position; rather, let us examine the nature and origin of left-hemispheric impairment. I have presented these points elsewhere (Venables 1980), but to integrate them with the ideas already offered in this chapter I will repeat them here. The essential point is that the left-hemispheric defect seen in adult schizophrenics might arise from overloading of that hemisphere because of a prior right-hemispheric dysfunction. Two sources stimulated this suggestion. In 1978 Mesulam and Geschwind proposed that dysfunction of the right parietal lobe might result in disturbances of selective attention similar to those apparent in schizophrenia. Their proposal stemmed from the examination of data from stroke patients: "as a consequence of the cerebral lesion these patients develop a dramatic impairment in selective attention, the ability to maintain and direct vigilance is impaired; distractibility by irrelevant stimuli is augmented and the ability to maintain a coherent stream of thought or to perform a sequence of goal directed behaviour is severely compromised" (p. 162).

The parallel with the attentional disturbance reported in schizophrenia is seductive, but the words used to describe the impairment do not help us decide at which points in the information-processing sequence impairment is found. The second difficulty is that unilateral neglect is thought to be characteristic of patients with parietal-lobe lesions (e.g., Critchley 1953), and no report of unilateral neglect in schizophrenic patients has been made. Nevertheless, since it is not suggested that there is structural damage to the parietal lobe in schizophrenia, this may not be a major stumbling block to using Mesulam and Geschwind's idea as a tentative starting point.

The other impetus to this line of thought was a report by Itil, Hsu, Saletu, and Mednick (1974), which analyzed EEG data collected as part of a study initiated in Copenhagen by Mednick and Schulsinger (Mednick, Mura, Schulsinger, & Mednick, 1971; Orvaschel, Mednick, Schulsinger, & Rock, 1979.) The subjects were children tested in 1972, when their mean age was about 11 years, and data are presented on the first 100 children studied from a total sample of some 250. The data relevant to this paper are from children of schizophrenic parents and children of normal parents and consist of 10 minutes of EEG recorded for left and right frontal, central, temporal, parietal, and occipital leads. Period analyses showed that children at risk had less alpha, more fast beta, and more delta activity than normals. The most significant differences between high- and low-risk children were in the *right* temporal to parietal lead. These data are in contrast to other material in the literature on adult schizophrenics, where there is a fairly consistent report of abnormalities of EEG spectra from the left hemisphere (e.g., Flor-Henry, Koles, Bo-Lassen, & Yeudall, 1975).

Against the findings of Itil et al. (1974), we might cite the results of Gruzelier, Mednick, and Schulsinger (1979), who used the same source of subjects but reported that children of schizophrenic parents showed lower verbal but not lower performance IQs than children of normal parents. They interpret this as showing a left-hemispheric deficit in their subjects. But, as suggested earlier, low verbal intelligence may occur when both verbal material and spatial material are processed in the same hemisphere. If the EEG findings in this instance can be interpreted as showing a right-hemispheric disturbance in these children, then it is possible that the impairment in their verbal behavior is due to the narrowing of functional cerebral space, as suggested by Kinsbourne and Hicks (1978) and as proposed above.

Neuropsychological data gathered with standard test batteries are sometimes cited in support of left-hemispheric dysfunction in schizophrenia. One such study is that of Abrams and Taylor (1979), who used the Reitan modification of the Halstead-Lepman aphasia screening test with groups of carefully diagnosed schizophrenic and affective-disorder patients and controls. Compared with control subjects, significantly more schizophrenics made errors associated with dominant temporal/temporoparietal dysfunction. However, they also made more nondominant parietal errors than controls, thus suggesting a right- as well as left-sided dysfunction in adult schizophrenic patients.

It is, however, experimental data that particularly raise the question of the nature of left-hemispheric dysfunction and its possible precursors. Gur (1979) presented pairs of pictures to subjects either successively or simultaneously. The subjects' task was to detect the subtle difference between the members of each pair and to point as rapidly as possible to the region of the picture where the difference lay. To relate performance to hemispheric specialization, the task was given to groups of subjects who were left-brain damaged and right-brain damaged. This preliminary investigation showed that left-hemisphere-damaged patients were equally fast with successive and simultaneous presentation, whereas right-hemisphere-damaged patients were significantly slower during simultaneous presentation. Following this preliminary study, the main experiment was conducted on groups of paranoid and nonparanoid schizophrenics and controls. All subjects had had hospital admissions before the current one and were right handed. No significant differences were found between paranoid and nonparanoid schizophrenics, so their results were combined. Whereas controls performed equally fast with both presentation modes, the schizophrenics were slower in the simultaneous-presentation condition. The same result was obtained when the schizophrenic sample was divided into chronic and acute groups based on number of hospitalizations, onset of syndrome, and clinical evaluation. A subsidiary study on depressed patients showed that they responded euqally fast in both presentation modes, so the hemispheric asymmetry shown in this study appears to be confined to schizophrenic patients.

Gur's interpretation of the results is that: "This finding supported the hypothesis of left hemisphere overactivation in schizophrenics since it parallelled the pattern found for right hemisphere damaged patients who presumably used left hemisphere strategies." She also suggests that "schizophrenics are triply disabled by having a dysfunctional left hemisphere, by failing to shift processing to the right and by an overactivation of the dysfunctional hemisphere." A simpler explanation is that schizophrenics may have (or have had) a dysfunctional right hemisphere and that the left hemisphere is overactivated because it now carries out both its own normal processing and that transferred to it because of right-hemisphere dysfunction.

Gur (1978) and Schweitzer, Becker, and Welsh (1978) measured lateral eye movements to assess asymmetry in hemispheric activation. The studies used the findings initially presented by Kinsbourne (1972) to support the notion that eye movements to the left indicate activation of the contralateral (i.e., right) hemisphere and vice-versa. Studies subsequent to Kinsbourne's (e.g., Gur, Gur, & Harris, 1975) have shown that additional factors, such as experimenter location, modify the position suggested by the original findings; nevertheless, both Gur and Schweitzer suggest that eye movements do provide a substantial index of lateral cerebral activation.

Gur (1978, p. 234) found that "schizophrenics, paranoid and non-paranoid, manifest a higher proportion of rightward eye-movements than do controls." From this she concluded that "if eye directionality is taken as a measure of hemispheric activation, we may conclude that schizophrenics activate their left hemisphere to a larger extent than do controls."

Similarly, Schweitzer et al. (1978) reported that schizophrenics, diagnosed as exhibiting two out of four of Bleuler's fundamental symptoms, produced more rightward lateral eye movements than controls. They thus suggested that "schizophrenic patients initiated the processing of spatial-emotional, verbal-emotional and verbal non-emotional questions in their left frontal hemisphere more often than controls." After discussing their results Schweitzer et al. suggest that "the appearance of greater left hemisphere activity in the patient group may thus actually reflect a lack of right hemisphere reciprocal inhibition and/or modulation of incoming information" (p. 984). Gur (1978) makes a similar statement in discussing the eye-movement results. She says, "Schizophrenia can be considered an expression of a shift from right to left hemisphericity, a result of a failure of right hemisphere strategies to cope with reality stresses" (p. 235).

The eye-movement data, however, are only part of the material Gur (1978) provides. The other study she conducted used dot location or syllable identification, with the material presented tachisto-scopically to the right or left visual field. On the dot-location (spatial) task both controls and schizophrenics performed better when the material was presented to the right hemisphere. However, while normal controls processed syllables better in the left hemisphere, the reverse seemed true in schizophrenics. Gur interprets these findings as showing that "schizophrenics showed a right hemisphere superiority both on the verbal and on the spatial tests, indicating left hemisphere dysfunction in the initial processing of verbal information" (p. 231). Thus her interpretation is in direct contrast to the position taken here, that left-hemisphere overactivity appears to result from the right hemisphere's inability to undertake its normal functions.

Schweitzer (1982) has questioned the interpretation of Gur's (1978) "verbal" results. He points out that "the material which Gur used for 'verbal' presentation was meaningless consonant-vowel-consonant stimuli presented in a vertical format" (p. 657). Schweitzer suggests that, since this material lacks semantic content and is presented as a spatial construct, it may be inadequately processed by the overactive left hemisphere, and that "subsequent processing in a visuo-spatial mode may then account for error in phonemic analysis and observed relative right hemisphere superiority" (p. 657). Whether or not Schweitzer's interpretation is correct, it appears in the introduction to a study that provides strong evidence that spatial material is processed in the left hemisphere in schizophrenic patients. The method uses a stimulus (S1) consisting of a word and a shape arranged in random vertical order. This stimulus, which has a duration of 64 msec, is presented either to the right or to the left of a central fixation point. At the end of the 64 msec presentation of S1, either the word or the shape is erased and the remaining stimulus element (S2) is displayed for a further 32, 64, or 96 msec. The subject is then asked to state whether the part of S1 that was erased first had, to his perception, disappeared before or at the same time as S2. Under the "shape" condition subjects were led to believe that the word and shape would appear simultaneously, but that the word would always disappear first or at the same time as the shape.

Since the word always disappeared first, a judgment of "same" indicated that the subject had failed to observe the shape stimulus following the word offset. "Thus the shape condition measured a subject's ability to detect a rapidly appearing shape while the reverse held for the word condition" (p. 658).

Results showed that both normal and schizophrenic groups processed verbal stimuli better in the left than in the right hemisphere. In contrast, while normals processed the spatial stimuli more effectively in the right than in the left hemisphere, the reverse was true of the patients. Thus the schizophrenics appear to show advantage in processing both verbal and spatial stimuli in the left hemisphere.

Schweitzer interprets these results in accord with the thesis of this chapter:

> Thus while these data are consistent with previous reports of left hemisphere overactivity in schizophrenics . . . they do not add strong support to the conclusion of a *primary* deficit in the schizophrenic's left hemisphere or a primary focus of *dysfunction* there. Rather these data suggest that schizophrenics' left hemisphere advantage for spatial detection may be a *compensatory* reaction to a fundamental deficit in the processing of spatial material by the right hemisphere. (pp. 670–671)

These data, which support the idea that both verbal and spatial stimuli are processed in the left hemisphere in schizophrenic patients, receive confirmation from a source quite dissimilar to the performance material of Schweitzer and Gur. Stevens and her colleagues (Stevens, Bigelow, Denney, Lipkin, Livermore, Rauscher, & Wyatt, 1979; Stevens and Livermore, 1982) conducted studies in which EEG activity was telemetered from schizophrenic patients during observation of their behavior. The studies are particularly important in that most of the patients taking part were not receiving medication, in contrast to the Schweitzer and Gur studies, where the patients were on drug regimens. The first study (Stevens et al.) reported that: "Although patients resembled control subjects in desynchronizing the left temporal EEG during the performance of verbal tasks, in contrast to controls they also desynchronized activity over the left temporal region during performance of spatial tasks" (p. 259).

In the second study (Stevens & Livermore, 1982) the results are not quite so clear-cut, indicating appropriate lateral shifts in alpha power between hemispheres during verbal and spatial tasks in control subjects. However, although patients desynchronized left temporal activity during verbal tasks, during spatial tasks they "exhibited a scatter of power without significant lateralized predominance over either temporal lobe during the spatial task" (p. 393).

In summary, the data reviewed here are in general consistent with the idea that left-hemispheric overactivity, sometimes resulting in performance deficits interpreted as left-hemispheric dysfunction, may be due to the overemployment of that hemisphere as it takes on functions normally carried out by the right hemisphere. The intellectual impairment of schizophrenic patients, particularly in verbal tasks, thus might be due to verbal and spatiotemporal tasks' being carried out in the same hemisphere.

If left-hemisphere overactivity is due to (primary) right-hemisphere dysfunction, it is important to seek data that are consistent with the idea that some of the features shown by patients with right-hemisphere dysfunction are akin to those shown by schizophrenics.

It should perhaps be reiterated at this point that the type of patient being discussed here is the Kraepelinian "continuous" or "process" schizophrenic, and the thesis of right-hemispheric primary dysfunction refers particularly to such patients. Mesulam and Geschwind (1978) suggested that the attentional disturbances shown by patients with right parietal lesions were similar to those shown by schizophrenics, and there are data suggesting that emotional impairment is a feature of schizophrenia, including anhedonia, or the inability to experience pleasure. The inability to recognize emotional expression in others may be considered another facet of the same impairment and might be allied to the lack of social competence schizophrenic patients exhibit.

A recent study by Walker, Marwit, and Emory (1980) showed that schizophrenic patients were impaired, compared with controls, in their ability to recognize eight different expressions of emotion in photographs. In general it replicated earlier studies, but it was more extensive in that it included childhood schizophrenics whom the authors considered to show features that were precursors of adult characteristics of process schizophrenia. Furthermore, the adult sample was restricted to process patients. The results indicated no diagnosis by age interaction or diagnosis by type of emotion interaction in scores on recognition accuracy. Recognition of all emotions was impaired over the whole age range examined.

Kolb and Taylor (1981) asked patients with right- and left-hemisphere lesions to match photographs displaying emotions and also sentences describing the same emotions. Patients with lesions of the right hemisphere were significantly impaired on the photograph-matching task, whereas patients with lesions of the left hemisphere were significantly impaired on the verbal test.

The latter finding at first seems in contrast to studies by Wechsler (1973) and by Heilman, Scholes, and Watson (1975), which showed that patients with right-hemisphere lesions had difficulty comprehending or remembering the affective content of speech passages. However, in the Kolb and Taylor study it was clearly the verbal content of the material that was being processed, whereas in the other two studies, though the material was verbal, the emotional content was conveyed by tone of voice and thus might be considered akin to the photographic expression of emotion in the earlier studies.

A relevant study employing normal subjects is that of Safer and Leventhal (1977), who presented material in three varieties of tone of voice and three levels of content or meaning to right and left ears. Most subjects receiving material through the left ear (right hemisphere) used tone-of-voice cues to rate the material, while those receiving stimulation of the right ear (left hemisphere) used content cues. The authors suggest that this indicates right-hemisphere specialization for processing emotional information.

Taken together, and in light of the impairment of emotional behavior seen in schizophrenics, these studies suggest that an impairment of affective performance is consonant with a postulated right-hemisphere dysfunction in these patients.

Processing of stimuli with spatial content, has already been discussed as being a function optimally dealt with by the right hemisphere. Sound localization might legitimately be considered a spatial processing function. Altman, Balonov, and Deglin (1979) examined the ability of depressed patients to localize sounds in a free field or as a result of temporally displaced dichotic stimulation after left- or right-hemisphere electroshock seizures. Left-side ECT caused no impairment of sound localization. By contrast, right-side ECT caused gross disorder of both sound localization and lateralization. Studies by Balogh, Schuck, and Leventhal (1979) and Balogh and Leventhal (1982) examined schizophrenics' ability to localize sound in space. In the first study free-space conditions were used, and the schizophrenic patients were designated process, nonparanoid. The schizophrenics were significantly impaired compared with normal and nonschizophrenic patient controls. In the second study, which used dichotic stimulation, apparent localization was produced either by conditions of temporal asynchrony or by amplitude difference of the signal between ears. No differences were shown between patients and controls under the amplitude condition. Under the temporal condition, however, there were differences between the two groups.

Although the second experiment by Balogh and Leventhal (1982) makes simple interpretations of sound localization dysfunction difficult, in general the studies reviewed can reasonably be interpreted to support right-hemispheric dysfunction in process schizophrenia.

It has been stated earlier that electrodermal hyporesponsivity appears to be characteristic of a high proportion of adult schizophrenics and may be particularly evident in the process or continuous type of patient. Heilman, Schwartz, and Watson (1978) studied patients with right- and left-hemisphere lesions, and also controls, presenting mild shock stimuli and recording electrodermal responses from the hand ipsilateral to the lesion. They showed that patients with right-hemisphere lesions had higher levels of skin resistance than those with left-hemisphere lesions and than the controls, which did not differ from each other. The patients with left-hemisphere lesions had the highest amplitude of response, with the right-hemisphere patients lower and controls intermediate; five of the seven right-hemisphere patients had no recordable responses. These data suggest a close similarity between patients with right-hemisphere lesions and process schizophrenics, while the electrodermal hyperresponsivity shown in left-lesion patients suggests that left-hemisphere dysfunction produces behavior similar to that of those "schizophrenic" patients with more florid symptoms.

Similar results were obtained by Morrow, Vrtunski, Kim, and Boller (1981) using slides with and without emotional content as stimuli. Again, right-hemisphere-damaged patients showed virtually no response to either emotional or nonemotional stimuli, though the results differed from those of Heilman et al. (1978), with the left-hemisphere patients showing slightly impaired responsivity compared with the controls, particularly with the emotional stimuli.

In both sets of studies electrodermal responsivity was recorded from the hand ipsilateral to the lesion, making interpretation more equivocal than if bilateral recordings had been made. But with this reservation these studies appear to provide further convergent evidence that process or continuous schizophrenia is consistent with right-hemisphere dysfunction.

A fairly consistent finding over the years has been the slowness of response of nonparanoid schizophrenic patients on the typical simple reaction time (RT) task. An early example is provided by Venables and O'Connor (1959), who divided chronic unmedicated schizophrenic patients into four groups according to two rating scales measuring "activity-withdrawal" and paranoid tendencies. Items scored in the direction of withdrawal were consonant with descriptions of Kraepelinian "process" schizophrenia. Patients classed as withdrawan, either paranoid or nonparanoid, and as active nonparanoid showed mean reaction times to auditory stimuli between 600 and 700 msec. They were distinguished from the other "schizophrenic" group, the "active paranoids," and from a normal control group, who had simple auditory RT values on the order of 400 and 300 msec respectively. Howes and Boller (1975) conducted an auditory RT study using patients with right- and left-hemisphere lesions and controls. Patients with right-hemisphere lesions had mean RTs of 635 msec, those with left-hemisphere lesions 334 msec, and normal controls 228 msec. The findings for the neuropsychiatric patients thus closely parallel those from schizophrenics, with the right-lesion and process schizophrenic patients having closely comparable values and the left-lesion patients having RTs that matched those of functional disorder patients, who might be thought of as intact or monosymptomatic paranoid.

Heilman and Van den Abell (1979a, 1979b) sought to explain the findings of Howes and Boller (1975). Using normal subjects, they showed that in a forewarned reaction time paradigm "warning stimuli projected to the right hemisphere reduced reaction time of the right hand more than warning stimuli projected to the left hemisphere reduced left hand reaction times" (1979a, p. 315). They also report (1979b) that, when EEG alpha power is measured from right and left parietal lobe sites, "while the left parietal lobe desynchronizes more to right sided (visual warning) stimuli, the right parietal lobe desynchronizes equally to right and left stimuli" (p. 586). They thus state that "the left hemisphere attends to contralateral stimuli while the right hemisphere attends to both ipsilateral and contralateral stimuli." These results suggest that functional disturbance of the right hemisphere might bring about general changes in attention and performance like those reported in the studies reviewed above, compatible with some of the disturbances of function exhibited by process schizophrenics.

ATTENTIONAL DISORDERS IN SCHIZOPHRENIA

The notion that nonparanoid schizophrenic patients are constitutionally susceptible to being "flooded by sensory impressions" was introduced earlier, but the nature of this "wide deployment of attention" was deferred for later discussion. Let me now return to this topic and present arguments even more speculative than those given earlier. A degree of consistency with some of the points made before is possible, and I will attempt to provide a skeletal model of the nature of the schizophrenic attentional defect.

Early discussions of schizophrenic attentional dysfunction often used the concepts of current models. Thus Broadbent's (1958) seminal book *Perception and Communication* provided the basis for some contemporary experimental studies on schizophrenics. Broadbent, however, largely concentrated on one facet of the topic that might be labeled "selective attention."

Bleuler, in his *Textbook of Psychiatry* (1924), already had things to say about this selective aspect of attention, which he termed "vigility." He wrote, "if we are performing an important experiment we observe what is relevant to it, everything else is entirely lost to our sense" (p. 40), which sums up Broadbent's position. Moray (1959) and Treisman (1960) later introduced modifications to this position by quesioning Bleuler's use of "entirely" and showing that unwanted material was attenuated rather than "entirely lost."

Bleuler, however, distinguishes "vigility" from "tenacity," the latter defined as "the ability to keep one's attention fixed on a certain subject continuously." This aspect, which we might now define as sustained attention, Kraepelin (1913) saw to be disordered in schizophrenic patients. He suggested that "it is quite common for them to lose both inclination and ability on their own initiative to keep their attention fixed for any length of time."

The two aspects of "sustained" and "selective" attention continue to be treated separately in studies on attention in schizophrenia, but most of the work to be discussed here is concerned with the latter aspect.

Nevertheless, active research on sustained attention is currently being pursued, and it has its origins in Kraepelin's time. Diefendorf and Dodge (1908) studied smooth-pursuit eye tracking in schizophrenic patients, showing that they were deficient in this process and made steplike motions of the eyes as they attempted to maintain target fixation. Kraepelin (1913) cited this study, saying, "In psychological experiments the patients cannot stick to the appointed exercise . . . perhaps the experience related by Diefendorf and Dodge that patients do not usually follow a moving pendulum continuously as normal persons do, but intermittently and hesitatingly may be explained by a similar disorder of attention." This technique was resurrected by Holzman, Proctor, and Hughes (1973) and has given rise to a wealth of subsequent work.

Neurons in the parietal lobe (area 7) are specialized for smooth visual tracking (Mountcastle, Lynch, Georgeopoulos, Sakata, & Acuna, 1975). In discussing neurons in areas 5 and 7 with special functions, these authors also report that "eighteen of these neurons were functionally related to the co-ordination of the visual fixation of an arm projection towards desired objects in immediate extra personal space. They were all located in the posterior bank of the intra parietal sulcus in the most anterior portion of area 7; 17 of the 18 were located in the right hemispheres of five different animals." While extrapolation from single neuron studies to functional disorders in schizophrenia is clearly hazardous, this sort of finding clearly deserves further exploration and gives some support to the idea of parietal lobe dysfunction in schizophrenia.

Here, however, the focus is on selective attention. In support of a disturbance of selective attention in schizophrenia the work McGhie and Chapman (1961) is often cited, where they report statements by "early" schizophrenics. One of the difficulties of using this report as evidence is that so little is said about the diagnostic principles used in classifying the patients. We are told only that "the subsequent course of the illness confirmed the original diagnosis" (of schizophrenia). Nevertheless, if we do accept the material as reporting experiences of schizophrenics in the early stages of their illness, it does provide an important description of attentional disturbance.

Patients report (p. 104): "The sounds are coming through to me but I feel my mind cannot cope with everything, it's difficult to concentrate on any one sound. It's like trying to do different things at the same time." "I am attending to everything at once and as a result I do not really attend to anything." "Everything seems to go through me, I just can't shut things out." Numerous reports of the same kind are provided.

An even more dramatic and even more often quoted report is that of MacDonald (1960, p. 218), but again there are diagnostic problems. MacDonald says, "I still don't know whether I had schizophrenia, what kind of schizophrenia I had, and I don't think I want to know." Nevertheless her report, subtitled "Living with Schizophrenia," is of interest. She states: "What I want to explain if I can, is the exaggerated state of awareness in which I lived, before during and after my acute illness." She then goes on to say: "the mind must have a filter which functions without our conscious thought, sorting stimuli and allowing only those which are relevant to the situation in hand to disturb consciousness . . . what had happened to me . . . was a breakdown in the filter and a hodge-podge of unrelated stimuli were distracting me from things which should have had my undivided attention."

These reports were produced in the context of Broadbent's (1958) model of a selective filter protecting a limited-capacity single channel in man's information flow system. A breakdown in this filter was thus used as an image for the defect found in the acute phase of this schizophrenic disorder. (MacDonald writes about the "exaggerated state of awareness *before, during and after*" the acute stage of the illness, thus emphasizing the continuous nature of her disability.) Models of attentive processes have, however, advanced since 1958, and it is appropriate to examine schizophrenic attentional disorders in the light of more recent proposals.

The problem is, however, that there is as yet no real consensus within experimental psychology about the mechanisms involved in attentive processes. In the 1960s the main alternative to a selective filter early in the chain of information processing was the concept of "late" selection initially proposed by Deutsch and Deutsch (1963), with the selection emphasizing less what stimulus to attend than what response to make. Thus all stimuli were thought to be processed up to a late stage with their characteristics intact until the final selection for response.

It is unlikely at present that anyone would maintain a pure "early selection" or "late selection" theory. Far more acceptable is a model like that of Broadbent (1971), which combines the features of both earlier positions. In this the "filtering" early selection (or stimulus set) is based on a few sample characteristics of the stimulus array (e.g., male or female voice; data presented to the left or right ear). On the other hand, the late selection "pigeon holing" (or response set) is based on categorization using more complex cognitive processing. A similar view is that of Treisman and Gelade (1980), denoted as the "feature integration theory of attention," in which "features are registered early automatically and in parallel across the visual field, while objects are identified separately and only at a later stage which requires focussed attention." In much the same way Broadbent (1977), defining pigeonholing, says, "in the case of pigeon-holing, however, the relevant and irrelevant stimuli do not differ by any single feature. Rather, there is a set of responses or pigeon holes which are distinguished from each other by various combinations of sensory features. . . . Pigeon holing therefore requires more processing than filtering does."

So far, the information-processing system has been viewed as unidirectional, but the ideas outlined suggest a more interactive approach. Kahneman (1973), for instance, suggests that the early stage of processing may yield a partial analysis of the input, and that resources are then made available to take in additional material. Broadbent (1977) outlines this as follows; "there is an early and relatively passive stage in which evidence arrives from the senses and suggests possible interpretation of the situation. The most promising of these interpretations is then verified by active interrogation of the sensory field to check whether certain stimulus features are present which have not previously been detected." Furthermore, he suggests that this verification stage need not wait for the early stage of information intake if it is primed by the semantic context. The same sorts of ideas are present in theories arising from work with animals. Wagner (1976), for instance, talks of "self-generated priming" through recent presentation of a stimulus and "retrieval generated priming" through exposure to stimuli previously associated with that stimulus.

Thus, more recent theories make use of two processes: an early or global stage, and a later local, detailed, focal attention stage. Broadbent (1977) suggests that what he has designated the filtering process may involve what Neisser (1967) called "pre-attentive processes." These, preattentive processes make use of natural groupings of the environment—arrangements in space, groupings by color, rhythmical groupings of sounds, and so on—and as such provide the basis for the filtering process.

If we admit the possibility of interaction between global and focal stages of attention, however, even though the "natural" groupings of the environment provide the basis for early passive sectioning, there is still a need for a speedy verification stage by which the range of interesting possibilities to be selected is modified. This means that very detailed experiments must be conducted to critically eluci- date processes that may be operating—or that, in the case of schizo- phrenia, may be operating inefficiently. Thus descriptions such as those of McGhie and Chapman (1961) and MacDonald (1960) do not provide enough evidence to base theories on.

A further seductive and popular line of thought has some paral- lels to those just outlined. Schneider and Shiffrin (1977) and Shiffrin and Schneider (1977) have presented a detailed theory of controlled and automatic information processing. They state that:

> Automatic processing is learned in long term store, is triggered by appropriate inputs and then operates independently of the subject's control. An automatic sequence can contain compo- nents that control information flow, attract attention and gov- ern overt responses. Automatic sequences do not require atten- tion. . . . Controlled processing is a temporary activation of nodes in sequence. . . . It requires attention, uses up short term capacity and is often serial in nature. (p. 51)

Controlled processing appears to have many of the characteristics of the focal-attention, pigeonholing processes of the models outlined earlier in that it is sequential and takes up central capacity. Automa- tic processing is not a necessary equivalent of preattentive process- ing or filtering, and Broadbent (1982) outlines some of the difficul- ties raised by this concept.

Although Schneider and Shiffrin's ideas have not yet had exten- sive influence on work with schizophrenics, there is some sugges- tion that there is a failure of automatic processing in schizophrenia so that activity must proceed at a level of consciously controlled sequential processing. One patient of McGhie and Chapman's (1961), for instance, reported, "I have to do everything step by step, nothing is automatic now. Everything has to be considered." Another said, "People just do things but I have to watch first to see how you do things. I have to think out most things first and know how to do them before I do them" (p. 105).

Frith (1979) presents a theory which is a slightly modified of the idea of a failure of automatic processing in schizophrenia, suggest- ing that in schizophrenics automatic processes, though still avail- able, attract attention. "In essence it is suggested that the basic cognitive defect associated with schizophrenia is an awareness of automatic processes which are normally carried out below the level of consciousness." Now, however, those who theorize about failures of attention in schizophrenics are more concerned with the use of ideas of preattentive processing, filtering, and pigeonholing. Before I address that topic, however, I shall review another relevant area.

Hillyard and his colleagues (e.g., Hillyard, Picton, & Regan, 1978) have conducted studies on event-related potentials using paradigms that can be interpreted in terms of the theories of pigeonholing and filtering. A representative example is that by Hink, Hillyard, and Benson (1978). In this study four consonant-vowel (CV) stimuli were spoken to each subject's left ear in a male voice and to the right ear in a female voice. Subjects were told to attend to one channel at a time, left or right, and to detect and respond to one of the four CV stimuli. Thus channel selection was a filtering task, whereas target detection, being based on complex phonemic cues, was a pigeonholing task. Attention to channels, the filtering task, was reflected in the size of the N1 component of the evoked potential, while attention to the CV target was reflected in the size of the P3 component. Thus the idea that different attentional functions are independent factors is supported by their reflection in different event-related components. Such event-related potentials, when measured using appropriate paradigms, also enable us to investigate schizophrenic dysfunctions.

The work of Roth and his colleagues, referred to earlier, showed that P300 (P3) was reduced or absent in paradigms where a rare, uncertain target had to be detected in a context of frequent targets. In these studies the amplitude of N1 to the infrequent signals did not differ between schizophrenics and normals. This finding of a reduced P300 in schizophrenics was also shown in a study by Pass, Klorman, Salzman, Klein, and Klaskey (1980), which used the Continuous Performance Test and measured event-related potential to rare (target) and frequent stimuli. Again a smaller P300 was shown by schizophrenic patients. A similar experiment by Cohen, Sommer, and Hermanutz (1982) used rare and frequent clicks as the stimuli. Schizophrenics again showed a smaller P300 component than normals. An interesting additional factor in this study, however, was that the patients were divided into electrodermal responders and nonresponders. The latter, who may be thought of as exemplifying the negative diagnostic features that characterize process schizophrenics, showed both a diminished P300 component and a small N220 (N2) component.

Naataanen and Michie (1979), in a review of "endogenous negative potentials," say, "there is solid evidence for the existence of an endogenous negative component with a peak latency of approximately 200 msec in response to a deviating stimulus in a repetitive stimulus background. . . . The component, called N2 or N200 or mismatch negativity . . . was elicited by a stimulus deviation *whether attention was directed to this stimulus or not*" (p. 258; italics added). The finding of Cohen et al. is important because it appears to show that N2, as the precursor of P3, is deficient in process schizophrenics and that impaired pigeonholing indexed by a small P3 may be due to the patients' inability to detect the mismatch involved in the perception of rare stimuli rather than being a function of their unwillingness to undertake the task. This finding apparently has not been replicated. However, figure 3 in Roth, Horvath, Pfefferbaum, and Kopell (1980) shows an absence of N2 in schizophrenics where the lack of significant differences in this component between schizophrenics and normals may be accounted for because the schizophrenics included both electrodermal responders and nonresponders.

These studies suggest that schizophrenics show deficits in a component of the ERP that has been associated with pigeonholing or response set but not with filtering. This conclusion is in line with that of Hemsley and Richardson (1980), who studied shadowing of binaurally presented material. Their findings could be interpreted in terms of a defect in pigeonholing but not in filtering.

In the study by Pass et al. (1980) referred to earlier, event-related potentials elicited by target and nontarget stimuli on the Continuous Performance Test (CPT) provided evidence for a pigeonholing defect, and the actual performance on versions of the test gives evidence in the same direction. The test has been used with additional distractor stimuli; Pass et al. (1980) presented clicks and flashes to the subject and used a version of the CPT in which a critical target letter had to be picked out from other nontarget letters. This is evidence that distraction stimuli can be separated from task stimuli by simple characteristics of modality and space. Thus, if an early filtering process is intact in schizophrenics, there should be no effect of distraction in either schizophrenics or normals. This was found to be true. On the other hand, Asarnow and MacCrimmon

(1978) used a task involving target and nontarget digits with the distraction of a voice reading digits. In this instance, although there was a difference in modality between task and distraction stimuli, the need to process at a focal attention level may have been far greater, and one would expect distraction to have an effect with schizophrenic patients, who would be expected to have a pigeonholing defect. The subjects in this instance were acute and remitted schizophrenics and controls. The acute patients showed such impaired performances under both distraction and nondistraction conditions that the additional effect of distraction could not be seen. But in the remitted patients the distraction produced impaired performance not shown in the nondistraction condition, thus suggesting that a pigeonholing defect may be a relatively permanent indicator of schizotaxis.

This emphasis on dysfunction in the later aspects of information processing in schizophrenia at first appears out of line with a recent report by Schwartz-Place and Gilmore (1980). In this study, a numerosity task was used in which process schizophrenics and normal subjects were to report the number of lines presented in a tachistoscope display. The lines could appear either alone or in the context of circles (as performance of schizophrenics and controls was comparable, but when lines had to be counted in the presence of circles the performance of the schizophrenics deteriorated while that of the normal controls was not affected. In a second experiment subjects were to report the number of all the lines displayed as the experimenter manipulated their orientation and grouping. In this task the schizophrenics' performance was better than that of the normals, whose reports were influenced by the direction or spatial grouping of the lines. The authors interpret the results as indicating that schizophrenics fail to engage a preattentive process and thus fail to group stimuli in an initial global analysis of the stimulus array.

It appears that these results may be interpreted in two ways. The studies already reviewed, while suggesting that schizophrenics have a major deficit in later information processing at the level of pigeonholing or focal attention, do not rule out an earlier attentional defect. Furthermore it is not clear from evoked-potential work that N1, which appears to be related to filtering, necessarily also reflects processing at a preattentive level.

The second form of interpretation builds on the interactive view of processing presented earlier, by which later stages of processing may "prime" the earlier global attentive stage, and perhaps this priming may take place by the use of the semantic context.

A failure in later processing could thus make it appear that there was failure in earlier processing, particularly where priming was by instruction, as in the Schwartz-Place and Gilmore (1980) study, rather than by "natural grouping." Choosing between these two views is not possible at this point, and may indeed not be necessary. In the next section I shall attempt to reach a tentative conclusion by again examining hemisphere function in the context of attention and attentional disturbance.

ATTENTION AND THE CEREBRAL HEMISPHERES

Views on the role of the hemispheres in information processing are as difficult to summarize as views on the processes involved in information processing in general. Cohen (1982) probably states the most reasonable view when she draws a distinction between fixed-structure and dynamic-process models. The former depend on findings such as those that place the function of expressive language in the left hemisphere, while the latter are more in line with studies that show apparent changes in hemisphere function over time and with varying instructions. Unfortunately, this reasonably flexible view enables practically anything to be explained; some degree of bias therefore needs to be introduced into ideas about hemisphere function, and this probably reflects some of the bias that actually exists because there is some reality in the fixed-structure model.

Thus one can agree with Hellige, Cox, and Litvac (1979) that "the greatest danger is to overlook the complexities that we might wish did not exist" (p. 277) yet note that their results on information-processing tasks "suggest that the left hemisphere functions as a typical limited-capacity information processing system" (p. 251). The role of the right hemisphere as a "global" processor is outlined, for instance, by Kinsbourne (1974) when he writes, "Input is grouped according to Gestalt laws so that the perceptual field is segmented or structured . . . patients with right posterior cerebral lesions who suffer from visuo-spatial agnosia behave as though this pre-attentive structuring had not occurred" (p. 278). He thus expresses the idea that the right hemisphere is constantly processing general gestalts from the perceptual field in an automatic and generally unconscious fashion and that the right hemisphere adjusts the direction of attention so that left-hemisphere focus may be appropriately brought to bear. The degree of automaticity considered here is that of the preattentive perceptual process, not that of the total chain of control spoken about by Schneider and Shiffrin (1977).

A similar idea is expressed by workers in the very different field of electrodermal conditioning. Maltzman, Langdon, Pendery, and Wolff (1977), discussing their results in this area, suggest that both the conditioned response and the unconditioned response may in their terms be considered different forms of orienting responses (OR). They go on to suggest that "the physiological basis for the two kinds of OR's may be the hemispheric asymmetry of the cerebral control mechanism for the GSR. The involuntary OR is largely determined by the right hemisphere, whereas the voluntary OR is primarily under left hemisphere control" (p. 168).

The (automatic) monitoring of the environment by preattentive processes (located in the right hemisphere) is very much in line with ideas about the nature of the orienting response as a mechanism elicited when the external environment does not match the cortical representation of the subject's world built up in an internal memory model (Sokolov, 1963).

Tomlinson-Keasey, Kelly, and Burton (1978) presented pictorial or symbolic stimuli singly to either right or left visual hemifield and asked subjects to decide whether the first stimulus of a pair matched the second stimulus. The results showed that the right hemisphere processed unmatched stimuli more effectively than the left. The authors in discussion suggest that "the cortex is constantly monitoring the environment for unique stimuli or stimuli that do not match. . . . That the right hemisphere might be functionally specialized to assist in such monitoring fits with the descriptions of the right hemisphere that highlights the processing of more global information" (p. 221).

Here again is the suggestion that the right hemisphere serves as a preattentive processor segregating the perceptual world, in this instance into novel and familiar stimuli. Perhaps one of the most important papers in this context, however, is that of Dawson and Schell (1982), successors to Corteen and Wood (1972), which has been widely cited as supporting the notion (Treisman 1960) that stimuli presented to the unattended ear in a dichotic listening task are monitored to a partial level of analysis but without conscious awareness.

The Corteen and Wood (1972) study involved a two-phase procedure. In the first phase a semantic category was made significant by associating words within that category (city names) with an electric shock. During the second phase the words were presented (without a shock) as part of the message to the nonattended ear in a dichotic-listening and verbal-shadowing task. During this second phase semantically related words as well as the originally shocked words elicited more skin conductance responses than nonshocked control words.

The difficulty with this study was whether the subjects really failed to attend to the previously shocked words in the instructed, nonattended ear or whether they temporarily switched attention on presentation of the critical words.

A number of subsequent studies have been concerned with this issue, and the Dawson and Schell (1982) study is the culmination of this series. It incorporated the use of unrelated words presented to the attended ear, a recognition questionnaire with a known false-positive rate to measure memory of specific words in the nonattended ear, and the counterbalancing of ears receiving the nonattended message across subjects. The results showed that electrodermal responses (EDRs) were elicited by significant (i.e., preshocked) words presented on the nonattended channel. For the subgroup of subjects that had significant words presented to the right ear (left hemisphere), EDRs were elicited by those words only when there were independent indications of shift of attention. In contrast, for that subgroup of subjects that had the significant words presented to the left ear (right hemisphere), EDRs were elicited by these words even on trials on which there were no shifts in attention.

Thus the evidence suggests that the right hemisphere can automatically monitor the environment to the extent of partial analysis of a semantic category without conscious awareness. Although Dawson and Schell (1980) present this result and their interpretation with caution, they are in line with the position described earlier, and the possibility of semantic analysis in the right hemisphere accords with the material reviewed by Searleman (1977).

These studies show that the right hemisphere appears capable of automatic, unaware analysis of the structure of the environment even when that structure is determined by semantic categories. This capability does not necessarily determine that material will always be processed in this way, and the dynamic distribution of resources discussed by Cohen (1982) should always be kept in mind. A somewhat similar view is held by Kinsbourne (1982), who emphasizes that normal interaction between the hemispheres is not based so much on categorical functions of the hemispheres, "but rather refers in the most general and basic terms to the manner in which understanding grows" (p. 419). Kinsbourne suggests that "the right hemisphere fits successive acts of information extraction or insights with a framework that is based on the initial overview of the scope of the problem and makes it possible by preserving the unbalancing effect of the shifting focus of attention, by holding it in context" (p. 418). Of the role of the left hemisphere, he suggests: "Finally the whole pattern is represented, not in its original undifferentiated state but in analytic detail and preserving a proper balance between attributes. These analytic processes are left hemisphere" (p. 418).

SUMMARY: WHERE HAVE WE GOT TO?

I have tried to concentrate on examining possible dysfunction in "continuous," "process" schizophrenics rather than those patients in whom florid symptoms flare up and then subside. This emphasis derives from my return to the original ideas of Kraepelin and Bleuler on the nature of schizophrenia. I am proposing essentially a developmental view of schizophrenia—that there is, in the adult schizophrenic, evidence for a dysfunction of left-hemispheric processes that takes the form of overactivity in that hemisphere, resulting in an inadequacy of focal attention and of categorizing or pigeonholing. I suggest that the overactivity of the left hemisphere is in part due to activities' being transferred to it because of inadequacies of the right hemisphere at some stage of the developmental process.

There is evidence that spatial processes normally carried out in the right hemisphere appear to be undertaken by the left hemisphere in schizophrenic patients. In line with this is the suggestion that low IQ, particularly low verbal IQ, of schizophrenics results from this intrusion of normally right-hemisphere processes into the left hemisphere, with a consequent effective reduction of "functional cerebral space."

Low IQ as a precursor of schizophrenia appears to be found particularly in males rather than females. Seeman (1981) discusses gender differences in the onset of schizophrenia. Following the general agreement that the onset of schizophrenia is later in women than in men (e.g., Kramer, 1978), Seeman suggests that this may be a function of the more complete lateralization in males than in females, and the faster and more quickly terminated development of lateralization of function in girls than in boys. Of particular importance is her idea that sex hormones may "act at critical developmental periods to protect against dopaminergic activity," and that "this protective function may be particularly important for left hemisphere functions" (p. 137). The lateral asymmetry of the distribution of neurotransmitters is well established in nonhuman animals (e.g., Glick, Jerussi, & Zimmerberg, 1977), but other data (Oke, Keller, Mefford, & Adams, 1978) show evidence for lateral asymmetry of distribution in man.

Clearly none of this material is other than speculative, but it does suggest a way future research might attempt to link sex differences in schizophrenia with the development of lateral functions. The hypothesis of this chapter that left-hemisphere overactivity in adult schizophrenics is a result of prior right-hemisphere disturbance carries with it the possibility of two kinds of mechanisms. The first, that in some way the right-hemisphere dysfunction is relatively permanent, is suggested by the evidence reviewed earlier that some of the dysfunctions of process schizophrenics are seen in patients with right-hemisphere lesions. A second possibility is that the right-hemisphere disturbance was "functional" and relatively transient but occurred at a critical stage, so that it brought about the "permanent" transfer of right-hemisphere functions to the left hemisphere, resulting in the disabilities outlined. This is more in accord with a view that takes into account different rates of lateral development in the two sexes. A third possibility is that there is a *relative* imbalance of lateral function. An earlier version of this idea put forward by Venables (1977) suggested that even in normal subjects the left hemisphere might be a "weaker" nervous system than the right, using the terminology of Pavlovian and neo-Pavlovian workers (e.g., Nebylitsyn & Gray, 1972). If schizophrenics have a general tendency toward a "weak" nervous system (Pavlov 1941), then the left hemisphere may be even more prone than in normals to develop "transmarginal inhibition" or, in more Western terms, performance inefficiencies owing to increased arousal. This rather tentative point of view does provide the elements of another alternative model.

Analyzing the nature of the attentive defect in schizophrenia as one of categorizing or pigeonholing or of focal attention is in line with the suggestion that these are essentially left-hemisphere functions. These dysfunctions are readily seen as occurring as a disorder of left-hemisphere function caused by overloading rather than by a lesion in that hemisphere.

The overloading might occur because functions are transferred from right to left hemisphere, since spatial functions appear to be located in the left hemisphere in schizophrenics; but it might also occur because an earlier part of the information-processing chain, thought of as the total attentive process, is defective and thus overloads the later focal-attention (left hemisphere) system. In this instance that may be a disturbance in early preattentive processes that causes too much material to be dealt with in a conscious focal fashion. Myslobodsky, Mintz, and Tomer (1979) suggest that "the primary involvement of the left hemisphere in schizophrenics may simply favour the solution of analytic material and even offer a sequential analytic solution as a substitute where a typical parallel holistic analysis is required" (p. 133). I suggest that a sequential analytic solution is used *because* of the failure of parallel holistic analyses. This parallel system, on the basis of material reviewed, is normally seen as biased toward the right hemisphere.

The failure of preattentive holistic processes, however, may occur not because of a direct dysfunction of the right hemisphere but because of a lack of retroactive "priming" of these processes by the more analytic later functions. Such a failure is in the "verification" process.

In this hypothesis of a "primary" right-hemisphere dysfunction leading to left-hemisphere overloading, I have not explicitly considered the specific location of that dysfunction. The review by Mesulam and Geschwind (1978) that provided the starting point for my proposals invoked disturbances of the right parietal lobe as underlying attentional disturbances in schizophrenia. Abrams and Taylor (1979) showed that disorder of the nondominant parietal lobe was involved in schizophrenia, Kinsbourne (1974) suggested the involvement of the right posterior region of the brain as a holistic processor, and, more tentatively, Mountcastle et al. (1975) suggested that the parietal areas are involved in smooth-pursuit eye tracking. Cox and Ludwig (1979) also provide data showing an increase in soft neurological signs related to parietal (and frontal) dysfunction. Although their data did not relate soft neurological signs to particular brain areas, Quitkin, Rifkin, and Klein (1976) also showed an increase in such soft signs in schizophrenics of a subtype characterized by premorbid social incompetence but not in schizophrenics with mixed characteristics. Furthermore, the asocial schizophrenics also exhibited low IQ. Thus this study is congruent with those previously reviewed.

The material discussed here, though drawn together in a speculative fashion, points to areas where future research might be undertaken with profit. In conclusion, let us look briefly at two recent theoretical presentations that take up the same general points raised here.

Callaway and Naghdi (1982) examine the distinction between automatic parallel processes and controlled serial processes in the human information-processing system. They suggest that "In schizophrenia only the controlled serial system seems disordered, the automatic parallel system remains normal or may even appear supernormal" (p. 339). Clearly the first part of this statement is in agreement with my position; a possible disagreement arises from the second, probably because of their broad application of the term "automatic." For instance, they include preattentive processing, along with Schneider and Shiffrin's (1977) ideas on automatic processing, a conjunction to which Broadbent (1982) would probably object. Here I have tried to confine the (right hemisphere) preattentive type of processing to early aspects of the attentional system, and apart from a brief discussion I have not considered automatic processing as a whole system in the way Callaway and Naghdi have done. Thus the conflict is more apparent than real. Insofar as both attempts aim to "link research on schizophrenia to a growing body of work on human information processing" (Callaway & Naghdi, 1982, p. 346) they are in accord. While Callaway and Naghdi's model does not involve lateralization of processing, the work of Gruzelier and his colleagues—the other theoretical viewpoint to be examined—is centered on ideas of lateral dysfunction.

In studies involving orienting responses to low-intensity stimuli, Gruzelier (1973), Gruzelier and Venables (1974) and Gruzelier and Hammond (1978) showed that schizophrenics tended to give larger right-hand than left-hand electrodermal responses. The opposite asymmetry was found in patients with depressive psychoses. About half the schizophrenic patients tested, however, were not responsive to these low-intensity tones. In a study that used higher-intensity (90db) tones, Gruzelier, Eves, Connolly, and Hirsch (1981) showed that all patients were responsive to some extent. Gruzelier, Eves, Connolly, and Hirsch (1981) and Gruzelier and Manchanda

(1982) showed that schizophrenics differed in their lateral response pattern to these 90db tones. Those giving greater right-hand than left-hand responses showed mainly negative symptoms characteristic of the continuous, process patients described by Kraepelin and Bleuler and emphasized here. In contrast, those with larger left-hand than right-hand responses "had many positive, florid features associated with psychosis of good prognosis" (Gruzelier & Manchanda 1982, p. 493).

This very important finding is difficult to interpret because of the lack of definite evidence to connect lateral asymmetries in the hands with asymmetry of brain function.

Gruzelier and Manchanda (1982) interpret their findings to suggest that patients with larger left-hand electrodermal responses and with pressured speech and flight of ideas have an overactivation of left-hemisphere function, "whereas sluggish thinking and speech impoverisation sometimes to the point of muteness which characterized the group with larger right hand responses implies a reduction in left hemisphere activation" (p. 493).

The difficulty lies in the word "activation." If Gruzelier and colleagues were talking about hemispheric *activity*, or performance, following an inverted U-shaped function in which increased arousal implies diminished activity, then my suggestion that the overloading of the left hemisphere and its consequent increased arousal imply less effective performance agrees with Gruzelier's ideas.

Gruzelier, Eves, and Connolly (1981) presented normal subjects with 70db and 90db tones. Their results showed that slow habituation and more frequent responding were associated with higher response amplitudes on the right hand, whereas fast habituation and less frequent responses were associated with higher left response amplitudes. If the association is made between nonresponding to 70db tones and negative symptoms, as suggested earlier, then the association of greater right-hand than left-hand responding with features of process schizophrenia in Gruzelier and Manchanda (1982) and greater right-hand than left-hand responding with more frequent responding and lower habituation in Gruzelier, Eves, and Connolly (1981) would seem anomalous. The latter authors show a strong association between a laterality index and numbers of nonspecific responses such that a higher right than left pattern of response is shown by subjects with large numbers of nonspecific responses. If nonspecific responses may be considered an index of general arousal (a somewhat controversial assumption), then we may suggest that higher right than left electrodermal responsivity is associated with high arousal. Bearing in mind the findings of Venables and Wing (1962), which suggested an association of "withdrawal"—or in current terminology negative symptoms—with measures of high arousal, then the association of greater right than left responsivity with negative symptoms receives some support.

Venables's (1957) "activity-withdrawal" scale was successful in distinguishing schizophrenic from manic patients with an accuracy of 83% (Klein, 1982), and it was this scale that Venables and Wing (1962) used to determine the relation described above.

To show alignment between Gruzelier's theory and mine we can also invoke an inverted U-shaped curve, which in conjunction with ideas of lateral balance can explain almost anything.

I have presented a set of mutually supportive suggestions concerning the development of schizophrenia. If they do no more than generate discussion they will have been successful; if they generate attempts at experimental verification or disproof, they will have been very successful.

REFERENCES

Abrams, R., & Taylor, M. A. Laboratory studies in the validation of psychiatric diagnoses. In J. Gruzelier & P. Flor-Henry (Eds.), *Hemisphere asymmetries of function in psychopathology.* Amsterdam: Elsevier/North-Holland, 1979.

Altman, J. A., Balonov, L. J., & Deglin, V. L. Effects of unilateral disorder of the brain hemisphere function in man on dimensional learning. *Neuropsychologia*, 1979, **17**, 295–301.

Asarnow, R. F., & MacCrimmon, D. J. Residual performance deficit in clinically remitted schizophrenics: A marker of schizophrenia? *Journal of Abnormal Psychology*, 1978, **87**, 597–608.

Balogh, D. W., & Leventhal, D. B. The use of temporal and amplitude cues by schizophrenics, psychiatric controls and aged normals in auditory lateralization. *Journal of Nervous and Mental Disease*, 1982, **170**, 553–560.

Balogh, D. W., Schuck, J. R., & Leventhal, D. B. A study of schizophrenics' ability to localize the source of sound. *Journal of Nervous and Mental Disease*, 1979, **167**, 484–487.

Bernstein, A. S., Frith, C. D., Gruzelier, J. H., Patterson, T., Straube, E., Venables, P. H., & Zahn, T. P. An analysis of the skin conductance orienting response in samples of American, British and German schizophrenics. *Biological Psychology*, 1982, **14**, 155–211.

Bleuler, E. *Textbook of psychiatry.* New York: Macmillan, 1924.

Broadbent, D. E. *Perception and communication.* New York: Pergamon Press, 1958.

Broadbent, D. E. *Decision and stress.* London and New York: Academic Press, 1971.

Broadbent, D. E. The hidden pre-attentive process. *American Psychologist,* 1977, **32,** 109–118.

Broadbent, D. E. Task combination and selective intake of information. *Acta Psychologica,* 1982, **50,** 253–290.

Buffery, A. W. H., & Gray, J. A. Sex differences in the development of spatial and linguistic skills. In C. Ounsted and D. C. Taylor (Eds.), *Gender differences: Their ontogeny and significance.* Edinburgh: Churchill Livingstone, 1972.

Callaway, E., & Naghdi, S. An information processing model for schizophrenia. *Archives of General Psychiatry,* 1982, **39,** 339–347.

Chapman, L. J., Chapman, J. P., & Raulin, M. L. Scales for physical and social anhedonia. *Journal of Abnormal Psychology,* 1976, **85,** 374–382.

Claridge, G. The schizophrenias as nervous types. *British Journal of Psychiatry,* 1972, **121,** 1–17.

Cohen, G. Theoretical interpretation of lateral asymmetries. In J. G. Beaumont (Ed.), *Divided visual field studies of cerebral organization.* London: Academic Press, 1982.

Cohen, R., Sommer, W., & Hermanutz, M. Auditory event related potentials in chronic schizophrenics: Effect of electrodermal response type and demands on selective attention. In D. Kemali (Ed.), *Clinical neurophysiological aspects of psychopathological conditions.* Basel: Karger, 1982 (forthcoming).

Corteen, R. S., & Wood, B. Autonomic responses to shock associated words in an unattended channel. *Journal of Experimental Psychology,* 1972, **94,** 308–313.

Cox, S. M., & Ludwig, A. M. Neurological soft signs and psychopathology, I. Findings in schizophrenia. *Journal of Nervous and Mental Disease,* 1979, **167,** 161–164.

Critchley, M. *The parietal lobes.* London: Arnold, 1953.

Crow, T. J. Molecular pathology of schizophrenia: More than one disease process? *British Medical Journal,* 1980, **280,** 66–68.

Dawson, M. E., & Schell, A. M. Electrodermal responses to attended and non-attended significant stimuli during dichotic listening. *Journal of Experimental Psychology: Human Perception and Performance,* 1982, **8,** 315–324.

Dellas, M., & Gaier, E. L. Identification of creativity: The individual. *Psychological Bulletin,* 1970, **73,** 55–73.

Deutsch, J. A., & Deutsch, D. Attention: Some theoretical considerations. *Psychological Review,* 1963, **70,** 80–90.

Diefendorff, A. R., & Dodge, R. An experimental study of the ocular reactions of the insane from photographic records. *Brain*, 1908, **31**, 451–489.

Flor-Henry, P., Koles, Z. J., Bo-Lassen, P., & Yeudall, L. T. Studies of the functional psychoses: Power spectral EEG analysis. *IRCS Medical Science, Psychiatry and Clinical Psychology*, 1975, **3**, 87.

Frith, C. D. Consciousness, information processing and schizophrenia. *British Journal of Psychiatry*, 1979, **134**, 225–235.

Frith, C. D., Stevens, M., Johnstone, E. C. & Crow, T. J. Skin conductance responsivity during acute episodes of schizophrenia as a predictor of symptomatic improvement. *Psychological Medicine*, 1979, **9**, 101–106.

Garmezy, N. (with Streitman, G.). Children at risk: The search for the antecedents of schizophrenia. I. Conceptual models and research methods. II. Ongoing research programs, issues and intervention. *Schizophrenia Bulletin*, 1974, **8**, 14–90, and **9**, 55–125.

Glick, S. D., Jerussi, T. P., & Zimmerberg, B. Behavioural and neuropharmacological correlates of nigrostriatal asymmetry in rats. In S. Harnad, R. W. Doty, L. Goldstein, J. Janes, & G. Krauthamer (Eds.), *Lateralization in the nervous system*. New York: Academic Press, 1977.

Gruzelier, J. H. Bilateral asymmetry of skin conductance activity and levels in schizophrenics. *Biological Psychology*, 1973, **1**, 21–42.

Gruzelier, J. H. Clinical attributes of schizophrenic skin conductance responders and non-responders. *Psychological Medicine*, 1976, **6**, 245–249.

Gruzelier, J. H., Connolly, J. F., & Hirsch, S. R. Altered brain functional organisation in psychosis: Brain-behaviour relationships. In J. Mendlewicz & H. M. van Praag (Eds.), *Advances in biological psychiatry*, vol. 6, pp. 54–59. Basel: Karger, 1979.

Gruzelier, J. H., Eves, F., & Connolly, J. Reciprocal hemispheric influences on response habituation in the electrodermal system. *Physiological Psychology*, 1981, **9**, 313–317.

Gruzelier, J. H., Eves, F., Connolly, J., & Hirsch, S. Orienting habituation, sensitization and dishabituation in the electrodermal system of consecutive drug free admissions for schizophrenia. *Biological Psychology*, 1981, **12**, 187–210.

Gruzelier, J. H., & Flor-Henry, P. (Eds.). *Hemisphere asymmetries of function in psychopathology*. Amsterdam: Elsevier/North-Holland, 1979.

Gruzelier, J. H., & Hammond, N. The effects of chlorpromazine on psychophysiological, endocrinal and information processing measures in schizophrenia. *Journal of Psychiatric Research*, 1978, **14**, 167–182.

Gruzelier, J. H., & Manchanda, R. The syndrome of schizophrenia: Relations between electrodermal response, lateral asymmetries and clinical ratings. *British Journal of Psychiatry*, 1982, **141**, 488–495.

Gruzelier, J. H., Mednick, S., & Schulsinger, F. Lateralised impairments in the WISC profiles of children at genetic risk for psychopathology. In J. Gruzelier & P. Flor-Henry (Eds.), *Hemisphere asymmetries of function in psychopathology*. Amsterdam: Elsevier/North-Holland, 1979.

Gruzelier, J. H., & Venables, P. H. Skin conductance orienting activity in a heterogeneous sample of schizophrenics. *Journal of Nervous and Mental Disease*, 1972, **155**, 277–287.

Gruzelier, J. H., & Venables, P. H. Bimodality and lateral asymmetry of skin conductance orienting activity in schizophrenics: Replication and evidence of lateral asymmetry in patients with depression and disorder of personality. *Biological Psychiatry*, 1974, **8**, 55–73.

Gur, R. E. Left hemisphere dysfunction and left hemisphere overactivation in schizophrenia. *Journal of Abnormal Psychology*, 1978, **87**, 226–238.

Gur, R. E. Cognitive concomitants of hemispheric dysfunction in schizophrenia. *Archives of General Psychiatry*, 1979, **36**, 209–274.

Gur, R. E., Gur, R. C., & Harris, L. J. Cerebral activation as measured by subjects' lateral eye movements is influenced by experimenter location. *Neuropsychologia*, 1975, **13**, 35–44.

Heilman, K. M., Scholes, R., & Watson, R. T. Auditory affective agnosia. *Journal of Neurology, Neurosurgery and Psychiatry*, 1975, **38**, 69–72.

Heilman, K. M., Schwartz, H. D., & Watson, R. T. Hypoarousal in patients with neglect syndrome and emotional indifference. *Neurology*, 1978, **28**, 229–232.

Heilman, K. M., & Van den Abell, T. Right hemispheric dominance for mediating cerebral activation. *Neuropsychologia*, 1979, **17**, 315–321. (a)

Heilman, K. M., & Van den Abell, T. Right hemispheric dominance for attention. *Neurology*, 1979, **29**, 586. (b)

Hellige, J. B., Cox, P. J., & Litvac, L. Information processing in the cerebral hemispheres: Selective hemispheric activation and capacity limitations. *Journal of Experimental Psychology: General*, 1979, **108**, 251–279.

Hemsley, D. R., & Richardson, P. H. Shadowing by context in schizophrenia. *Journal of Nervous and Mental Disease*, 1980, **168**, 141–145.

Hillyard, S. A., Picton, T. W., & Regan, D. Sensation, perception and attention: Analysis using ERPs. In E. Callaway, P. Tueting, & S. H. Koslow (Eds.), *Event related brain potentials in man*. New York: Academic Press, 1978.

Hink, R. F., Hillyard, S. A., & Benson, P. J. Event related brain potentials and selective attention to acoustic and phonetic cues. *Biological Psychology*, 1978, **6**, 1–16.

Holzman, P. S., Proctor, L. R., & Hughes, D. W. Eye-tracking patterns in schizophrenia. *Science*, 1973, **181**, 179–181.

Howes, D., & Boller, F. Simple reaction time: Evidence for focal impairment for lesions of the right hemisphere. *Brain*, 1975, **98**, 317–332.

Hunt, J. McV., & Cofer, C. Psychological deficit in schizophrenia. In J. McV. Hunt (Ed.), *Personality and the behaviour disorders*. New York: Ronald Press, 1944.

Itil, T. M., Hsu, W., Saletu, B., & Mednick, S. A. Computer EEG and auditory evoked potential investigations in children at high risk for schizophrenia. *American Journal of Psychiatry*, 1974, **131**, 892–900.

Kahneman, D. *Attention and effort*. New York: Academic Press, 1973.

Kety, S. S. The syndrome of schizophrenia: Unresolved questions and opportunities for research. *British Journal of Psychiatry*, 1980, **136**, 421–426.

Kinsbourne, M. Eye and head turning indicates cerebral lateralization. *Science*, 1972, **176**, 539–541.

Kinsbourne, M. Mechanisms of hemispheric interactions in man. In M. Kinsbourne & W. L. Smith (Eds.), *Hemispheric disconnection and cerebral function*. Springfield, Ill.: Thomas, 1974.

Kinsbourne, M. Hemispheric specialization and the growth of human understanding. *American Psychologist*, 1982, **37**, 411–420.

Kinsbourne, M., & Hicks, R. E. Functional cerebral space: A model for overflow, transfer and interference effects in human performance. In J. Requin (Ed.), *Attention and performance*, vol. 7. Hillsdale, N.J.: Lawrence Erlbaum, 1978.

Klein, D. N. Activity-withdrawal in the differential diagnosis of schizophrenia and mania. *Journal of Abnormal Psychology*, 1982, **91**, 157–164.

Klorman, R., Strauss, J. S., & Kokes, R. F. Pre-morbid adjustment in schizophrenia. III. The relationship of demographic and diagnostic factors to measures of adjustment in schizophrenia. *Schizophrenia Bulletin*, 1977, **3**, 214–225.

Kolb, B., & Taylor, L. Affective behaviour in patients with localized cortical excisions: Role of lesion site and side. *Science*, 1981, **214**, 89–91.

Kraepelin, E. *Dementia praecox and paraphrenia*. Translated by R. M. Barclay. Edinburgh: Livingstone, 1913.

Kramer, M. Population changes and schizophrenia, 1970–1985. In L. C. Wynne, R. L. Cromwell, & S. Matthyse (Eds.), *The nature of schizophrenia*. New York: Wiley, 1978.

Kroll, N. E. A., & Madden, D. J. Verbal and pictorial processing by hemisphere as a function of the subject's verbal scholastic aptitude test score. In J. Requin (Ed.), *Attention and performance*, vol. 7. Hillsdale, N.J.: Lawrence Erlbaum, 1978.

Lehmann, H. Pharmacotherapy of schizophrenia. In P. Hoch & J. Zubin (Eds.), *Psychopathology of schizophrenia*. New York: Grune and Stratton, 1966.

MacDonald, N. Living with schizophrenia. *Canadian Medical Association Journal*, 1960, **82**, 218–221.

Maltzman, I., Langdon, B., Pendery, M., & Wolff, C. Galvanic skin response–orienting reflex and semantic conditioning and generalization with different unconditioned stimuli. *Journal of Experimental Psychology: General*, 1977, **106**, 141–171.

McGhie, A., & Chapman, J. Disorders of attention and perception in early schizophrenia. *British Journal of Medical Psychology*, 1961, 34, 103–116.

Mednick, S. A., Mura, E., Schulsinger, F., & Mednick, B. Perinatal conditions and infant development in children with schizophrenic parents. *Social Biology*, 1971, **18**, 103–113.

Mednick, S. A., & Schulsinger, F. Some pre-morbid characteristics related to breakdown in children with schizophrenic mothers. In D. Rosenthal & S. S. Kety (Ed.), *The transmission of schizophrenia*. New York: Pergamon Press, 1968.

Mednick, S. A., Schulsinger, F., Teasdale, T. W., Schulsinger, H., Venables, P. H., & Rock, D. R. Schizophrenia in high-risk children: Sex differences in pre-disposing factors. In G. Serban (Ed.), *Cognitive defects in the development of mental illness*. New York: Brunner/Mazel, 1978.

Meehl, P. E. Schizotaxia, schizotypy and schizophrenia. *American Psychologist*, 1962, **17**, 827–838.

Mesulam, M.-M., & Geschwind, N. On the possible role of the neo-cortex and its limbic connections in attention and schizophrenia. In L. C. Wynne, R. C. Cromwell, & S. Matthyse (Eds.), *The nature of schizophrenia*. New York: Wiley, 1978.

Moray, N. Attention in dichotic listening: Affective cues and the influence of instructions. *Quarterly Journal of Experimental Psychology*, 1959, **9**, 56–60.

Morrow, L., Vrtunski, P. B., Kim, Y., & Boller, F. Arousal responses to emotional stimuli and laterality of lesion. *Neuropsychologia*, 1981, **19**, 65–71.

Mountcastle, V. B., Lynch, J. C., Georgeopoulos, A., Sakata, H., & Acuna, C. Posterior parietal association cortex of the monkey: Command functions for operations within extra personal space. *Journal of Neurophysiology*, 1975, **38**, 871–908.

Myslobodsky, M., Mintz, M., & Tomer, R. Asymmetric reactivity of the brain and components of hemispheric imbalance. In J. Gruzelier & P. Flor-Henry (Eds.), *Hemisphere asymmetries of function in psychopathology*. Amsterdam: Elsevier/North-Holland, 1979.

Naataanen, R., & Michie, P. T. Different variants of endogenous negative brain potentials in performance situations: A review and classification. In D. Lehmann & E. Callaway (Eds.), *Human evoked potentials: Applications and problems*. New York: Plenum, 1979.

Nebylitsyn, V. D., & Gray, J. A. *Biological bases of individual behaviour*. New York: Academic Press, 1972.

Neisser, U. *Cognitive psychology*, New York: Appleton-Century-Crofts, 1967.

Offord, D. R. School performance of adult schizophrenics, their siblings and age mates. *British Journal of Psychiatry*, 1974, **125**, 12–19.

Offord, D. R., & Cross, L. A. Adult schizophrenia with scholastic failure or low IQ in childhood. *Archives of General Psychiatry*, 1971, **24**, 431–436.

Oke, A., Keller, R., Mefford, I., & Adams, R. N. Lateralization of norepinephrine in the human thalamus. *Science*, 1978, **200**, 1411–1413.

Orvaschel, H., Mednick, S. A., Schulsinger, F., & Rock, D. The children of psychiatrically disturbed parents. *Archives of General Psychiatry*, 1979, **36**, 691–695.

Pass, H. L., Klorman, R., Salzman, L. F., Klein, R. H., & Kaskey, G. B. The late positive component of the evoked response in acute schizophrenics during a test of sustained attention. *Biological Psychiatry*, 1980, **15**, 9–20.

Patterson, T., & Venables, P. H. Bilateral skin conductance and skin potential in schizophrenic and normal subjects: The identification of the Fast Habituator group of schizophrenics. *Psychophysiology*, 1978, **15**, 556–560.

Pavlov, I. P. *Conditioned reflexes and psychiatry*. Translated by W. H. Gantt. New York: International Universities Press, 1941.

Quitkin, F., Rifkin, A., & Klein, D. F. Neurologic soft signs in schizophrenia and character disorders. *Archives of General Psychiatry*, 1976, **33**, 845–853.

Reynell, J., & Huntley, R. M. C. New scales for the assessment of language development in young children. *Journal of Learning Disabilities*, 1971, **4**, 549–557.

Rieder, R. O., Broman, S. H., and Rosenthal, D. The offspring of schizophrenics. II. Perinatal factors and IQ. *Archives of General Psychiatry*, 1977, **34**, 789–799.

Roff, J. D., & Knight, R. Preschizophrenics: Low IQ and aggressive symptoms as predictors of adult outcome and marital status. *Journal of Nervous and Mental Disease*, 1980, **168**, 129–132.

Rosenthal, D. *Genetic theory and abnormal behavior*. New York: McGraw-Hill, 1970.

Roth, W. T., & Cannon, E. H. Some features of the auditory evoked response in schizophrenics. *Archives of General Psychiatry*, 1972, **27**, 466–471.

Roth, W. T., Horvath, T. B., Pfefferbaum, A., & Kopell, B. S. Event related potentials in schizophrenics. *Electroencephalography and Clinical Neurophysiology*, 1980, **48**, 127–139.

Roth, W. T., Pfefferbaum, A., Horvath, T. B., Bergen, P. A., & Kopell, B. S. P3 reduction in auditory evoked potentials of schizophrenics. *Electroencephalography and Clinical Neurophysiology*, 1980, **49**, 497–505.

Roth, W. T., Pfefferbaum, A., Kelly, A. F., Bergen, P. A., & Kopell, B. S. Auditory event related potentials in schizophrenia and depression. *Psychiatry Research*, 1981, **4**, 199–212.

Rutter, M. A children's behaviour questionnaire for completion by teachers. *Journal of Child Psychology-Psychiatry*, 1967, **8**, 1–11.

Safer, M. A., & Leventhal, H. Ear differences in evaluating emotional tones of voice and verbal content. *Journal of Experimental Psychology: Human Perception and Performance*, 1977, **3**, 75–82.

Schneider, K. *Clinical psychopathology.* Translated by M. W. Hamilton. New York: Grune and Stratton, 1959.

Schneider, W., & Shiffrin, R. M. Controlled and automatic human information processing. I. Detection, search, and attention. *Psychological Review,* 1977, **84,** 1–66.

Schwartz-Place, E. J., & Gilmore, G. C. Perceptual organization in schizophrenia. *Journal of Abnormal Psychology,* 1980, **89,** 409–418.

Schweitzer, L. Evidence of right cerebral hemisphere dysfunction in schizophrenic patients with left hemisphere overactivation. *Biological Psychiatry,* 1982, **17,** 655–673.

Schweitzer, L., Becker, E., & Welsh, H. Abnormalities of cerebral lateralization in schizophrenia patients. *Archives of General Psychiatry,* 1978, **35,** 982–985.

Searleman, A. A review of right hemisphere linguistic capabilities. *Psychological Bulletin,* 1977, **84,** 503–528.

Seeman, M. V. Gender and onset of schizophrenia: Neurohumoral influences. *Psychiatric Journal of the University of Ottawa,* 1981, **6,** 136–138.

Shiffrin, R. M., & Schneider, W. Controlled and automatic human information processing. II. Perceptual learning, automatic attending and a general theory. *Psychological Review,* 1977, **84,** 127–188.

Simons, R. F. Electrodermal and cardiac orienting in psychometically defined high-risk subjects. *Psychiatry Research,* 1981, **4,** 347–356.

Simons, R. F. Physical anhedonia and future psychopathology: An electrocortical continuity. *Psychophysiology,* 1982, **19,** 433–441.

Sokolov, E. N. *Perception and the conditioned reflex.* New York: Macmillan, 1963.

Stevens, J. R., Bigelow, L., Denney, D., Lipkin, J., Livermore, A. H., Rauscher, F., & Wyatt, R. J. Telemetered EEG and EOG during psychotic behaviour in schizophrenia. *Archives of General Psychiatry,* 1979, **36,** 251–262.

Stevens, J. R., & Livermore, A. Telemetered EEG in schizophrenia: Spectral analysis during abnormal behaviour episodes. *Journal of Neurology, Neurosurgery, and Psychiatry,* 1982, **45,** 385–395.

Straube, E. R. On the meaning of electrodermal non-responding in schizophrenia. *Journal of Nervous and Mental Disease,* 1979, **167,** 601–611.

Sutton, S., Braren, M., John, E. R., & Zubin, J. Evoked potential correlates of stimulus uncertainty. *Science,* 1965, **150,** 1187–1188.

Tomlinson-Keasey, C., Kelly, R., & Burton, J. K. Hemispheric changes in information processing during development. *Developmental Psychology,* 1978, **14,** 214–223.

Treisman, A. M. Contextual cues in selective listening. *Quarterly Journal of Experimental Psychology,* 1960, **12,** 242–248.

Treisman, A. M., & Gelade, G. A feature integration theory of attention. *Cognitive Psychology,* 1980, **12,** 97–136.

Venables, P. H. A short scale for rating "activity-withdrawal" in schizophrenics. *Journal of Mental Science*, 1957, **103**, 197–199.

Venables, P. H. Input dysfunction in schizophrenia. In B. Maher (Ed.), *Advances in experimental personality research*, vol. 1. New York: Academic Press, 1964.

Venables, P. H. The electrodermal psychology of schizophrenics and children at risk for schizophrenia: Current controversies and developments. *Schizophrenia Bulletin*, 1977, **3**, 28–48.

Venables, P. H. Psychophysiology and psychometrics. *Psychophysiology*, 1978, **15**, 302–315.

Venables, P. H. Primary dysfunction and cortical lateralization in schizophrenia. In M. Koukkou, D. Lehmann, & J. Angst (Eds.), *Functional states of the brain: Their determinants*. Amsterdam: Elsevier/North-Holland, 1980.

Venables, P. H., Dalais, J. C., Mitchell, D. A., Mednick, S. A., & Schulsinger, F. Outcome at age 9 of psychophysiological selection at age 3 for risk of schizophrenia. *Bristol Journal of Developmental Psychology*, 1983, **1** (in press).

Venables, P. H., Fletcher, R. P., Dalais, J. C., Mitchell, D. A., Schulsinger, F., & Mednick, S. A. Factor structure of the Rutter "Children's Behaviour Questionnaire" in a primary school population in a developing country. *Journal of Child Psychology and Psychiatry*, 1983, **24**, 213–222.

Venables, P. H., Mednick, S. A., Schulsinger, F., Raman, A. C., Bell, B., Dalais, J. C., & Fletcher, R. P. Screening for risk of mental illness. In G. Serban (Ed.), *Cognitive defects in the development of mental illness*. New York: Brunner/Mazel, 1978.

Venables, P. H., & O'Connor, N. Reaction times to auditory and visual stimulation in schizophrenic and normal subjects. *Quarterly Journal of Experimental Psychology*, 1959, **11**, 175–179.

Venables, P. H., and Wing, J. K. Level of aurousal and subclassification of schizophrenia. *Archives of General Psychiatry*, 1962, **7**, 114–119.

Wagner, A. R. Priming in S.T.M.: An information processing mechanism for self-generated or retrieval generated depression in performance. In T. J. Tighe & R. N. Leaton (Eds.), *Habituation: Perspectives from child development, animal behaviour and neurophysiology*. Hillsdale, N.J.: Lawrence Erlbaum, 1976.

Walker, E., Marwit, S. J., & Emory, E. A cross-sectional study of emotion recognition in schizophrenics. *Journal of Abnormal Psychology*, 1980, **89**, 428–436.

Wechsler, A. F. The effect of organic brain disease on recall of emotionally charged versus neutral narrative texts. *Neurology*, 1973, **23**, 130–135.

Worland, J., Weeks, D. G., Weiner, S. M., & Schechtman, J. Longitudinal, prospective evaluations of intelligence in children at risk. *Schizophrenia Bulletin*, 1982, **8**, 135–141.

Converging Models of Cognitive Deficit in Schizophrenia[1]

Raymond A. Knight

Brandeis University

*P*rogress in the study of the cognitive deficiencies of schizophrenics has been slow, and the methodological dilemmas facing those who investigate this area have been manifold (Blaney, 1978; Chapman & Chapman, 1973; Cromwell, 1972; Neale & Oltmanns, 1980; Salzinger, 1973). One of the major stumbling blocks until recently has been the paucity of adequate cognitive models to guide the search for deficient processes. Because of this gap early hypotheses were forced to be too vague and global (e.g., Lang & Buss, 1965; McGhie & Chapman, 1961; Silverman, 1964). Such lack of specificity made it difficult to test and discomfirm such notions, and a mass of contradictory, inconclusive studies resulted. When some specificity was introduced (e.g., Mednick, 1958; Salzinger, 1971; Storms & Broen, 1969), it was done within a behavioral framework that ultimately was shown to be an inadequate vehicle for studying both perception and cognition (Neisser, 1967, 1976, 1982).

The combination of numerous methodological pitfalls and little guidance from a fruitful theoretical perspective led to a stagnation marked by an absence of the cumulative knowledge so characteristic of an adequately functioning science. Two solutions to this dilemma

1. Recent research from my laboratory reported in this chapter was supported in part by a grant from the Scottish Rite Schizophrenia Research Program, Northern Masonic Jurisdiction, United States. I would especially like to thank Judith Sims-Knight for her numerous substantive contributions at many stages of this chapter. Without her help as a sounding board for many of the ideas presented here, they would not have reached their current stage of development. I am also greatly indebted to Michael Berbaum, Paul Blaney, David Elliott, Maurice Hershenson, and Daniel Klein for their helpful comments on earlier versions of this chapter. Finally, thanks are due to Edith Rosenberg for her help in tracking down all the references.

have emerged. One (Chapman & Chapman, 1973) has aimed at carefully isolating descriptive principles for schizophrenics' behavior rather than attempting to postulate underlying hypothetical mechanisms and has proposed a task-oriented approach to one of the major methodological difficulties in this research—the general deficit problem. This solution finds its roots in the individual difference, psychometric tradition and proposes stringent psychometric control procedures to counteract artifactual results. It attempts to specify schizophrenics' differential deficits by finding tasks on which their poor performance cannot be accounted for by their general performance inefficiencies. Those who have embraced this approach have provided important insights into the task characteristics that have distorted experimental results.

The other approach has embraced the new theoretical models and paradigms of cognitive psychology and has focused on attempting to uncover and isolate the specific processes that are deficient in schizophrenics' encoding, storage, and retrieval of information. This approach is part of a larger movement in psychology away from less theoretical, more behavioral, descriptive approaches to scientific inquiry. Advocates of this more explicitly theoretical approach feel that less-theoretical investigation strategies have reached the limits of their usefulness. They have not been successful in perception and cognition (Haber, 1974; Neisser, 1967), and their generativity has been questioned in personality research (Loevinger, 1972) and in psychological assessment (Millon, 1977). Paul Meehl, who earlier (1945, 1957) believed that a "dustbowl empiricism" that keeps its sights on criterion validity was sufficient to create an adequate data base for scientific growth, now thinks that psychological theory must guide every level of test development from item construction to clinical interpretation (Meehl, 1972). Indeed, Meehl (1978) attributes much of the slow progress in "soft" psychology to the weakness of psychological theory and to psychologists' failure to subject what theories they do have to sufficient risk of discomfirmation.

The process-oriented, theoretical approach has recently been applied to a number of areas of schizophrenics' cognitive process (e.g., Knight, Sherer, & Shapiro, 1977; Koh, 1978; Rochester, 1978; Hemsley, 1975) and has resulted in a small but growing body of cumulative knowledge that has eliminated certain explanations for schizophrenics' deficiencies and provided some clear paths for future research. In this chapter I will focus on one portion of this research, that on schizophrenics' early visual processing deficiencies. By placing recent findings within the context of new theoretical developments in cognitive psychology and putting the strategies used to generate these data within a larger philosophical context, I hope to give us a clearer perspective on where we are and where we are going. Moreover, an examination of the methods and paradigms that have already been used and those that are available to us suggests some alternative solutions to important methodological difficulties in this area such as the "general deficit" problem. The process approach is, of course, not without its problems. I will conclude my consideration of this strategy with a summary of some of the major theoretical and practical difficulties we face.

SCHIZOPHRENICS' EARLY
VISUAL PROCESSING DEFICIENCIES

The hypothesis that some attentional/information processing dysfunction is an important distinguishing characteristic of schizophrenics has existed for a considerable time (Bleuler, 1950; Kraepelin, 1919). It has been invoked as an explanatory construct to account for schizophrenics' descriptions of their experiences (Freedman & Chapman, 1973; McGhie & Chapman, 1961) and has been used to integrate a large number of research studies that have found schizophrenics deficient on a wide variety of laboratory tasks (Lang & Buss, 1965; Silverman, 1964; Venables, 1964, 1977). A number of theorists (e.g., Ornitz, 1969; Maher, 1972; Meehl, 1962; Rochester, 1978) have hypothesized that an attentional/information processing disturbance might constitute the primary vulnerability to schizophrenia. Such speculations have been bolstered by data suggesting that some attentional dysfunction is found in nonpsychotic schizotypic individuals (Steronko & Woods, 1978), in schizotypal patients (Braff, 1981), and in a significant subsample of children at increased risk for adult schizophrenia (Asarnow, Steffy, MacCrimmon, & Cleghorn, 1978; Erlenmeyer-Kimling & Cornblatt, 1978; Grunebaum, Weiss, Gallant, & Cohler, 1974; Rutschmann, Cornblatt, & Erlenmeyer-Kimling, 1977). Also, other data suggest that this deficit is a consistent trait of schizophrenics, evidenced in the remitted as well as acute stages of the disorder (Asarnow & MacCrimmon, 1978; Miller, Saccuzzo, & Braff, 1979).

Such a global summary of the attention literature sounds shiny and bright, but in reality it is tarnished. Although this literature seems to present tantalizing convergences and to hold the promise of leading to important deficient processes in schizophrenics, a close examination reveals critical flaws. As I mentioned in my introduction, the early formulations of models of schizophrenics' attentional deficit were for the most part vague and unspecified, and there is no agreement in this literature on the underlying processes that might account for the deficiencies in task performance. Although the information processing "revolution" (Haber, 1974) has provided precise, well-specified constructs, it is difficult to relate these processes to performance on most of the measures used in the earlier studies (e.g., object sorting, size estimation, size constancy, competing information). Thus any attempts to translate most early studies into information processing structures seem futile (Haber, 1969). Indeed, subsequent research has even suggested that some of the early tasks were not measuring attention at all (Price & Eriksen, 1966; Strauss, Foureman, & Parwatikar, 1974; Walker & Green, 1982). It is not surprising that the various tasks in this early research have been shown to bear little empirical relation to each other (Kopfstein & Neale, 1972). In my review of early visual processing in schizophrenia, therefore, I will focus only on those studies that have used tasks that can be directly related to processing models.

Before considering the early visual information processing studies on schizophrenics, it is important to sketch in broad strokes a general processing model. A hallmark of information processing models has been the compartmentalization of perception and memory into registers through which new information flows in its passage from the senses to final storage. These registers and their associated transfer operations constitute the various hypothesized stages of processing. One of the earliest models (Atkinson & Shiffrin, 1968, 1971) hypothesized three gross stages: the icon, short-term memory (STM), and long-term memory (LTM). Although this model is by no means universally accepted (Craik & Lockhart, 1972; Holding, 1971; Haber, 1983), and though in the course of this chapter I will reject the classical formulation of the icon, it is a convenient backdrop for beginning my discussion, and it and related models have provided a conceptual context for many experimental psychopathologists. In this model iconic memory, the most elementary visual stage, called "the first visual cognitive process" (Neisser, 1967), is a short-lived, high-capacity, fairly complete store. STM is working memory and contains the processes necessary to maintain ongoing task performance. It has a limited capacity and decays within about 15 seconds unless prevented by some rehearsal strategy. LTM, the final component, is the archive or long-term repository of information, which also supports STM functioning.

The first studies on schizophrenics' early visual information processing focused, as had some of the earlier studies on normals, on span of apprehension and iconic imagery. The span of apprehension studies have all used a similar procedure. The subject is required to identify which of two target letters (usually T or F) is present in a tachistoscopically flashed stimulus array. Complexity is manipulated by varying the number of irrelevant stimuli in the array. These studies have demonstrated rather consistently that both acute and remitted schizophrenics (Asarnow & MacCrimmon, 1978; Neale, 1971; Neale, McIntyre, Fox, & Cromwell, 1969) and a subgroup of children vulnerable to schizophrenia (Asarnow et al., 1978) showed a significantly greater decrement than normal controls in the accuracy of detection of a target stimulus as the number of nonrelevant elements in the array increased. Davidson and Neale (1974) varied the similarity of nonrelevant letters to the target letter in a span of apprehension paradigm and found that schizophrenics, like normals, were adversely affected by increasing target-noise similarity. These authors suggested that at this level schizophrenics have stimulus processing operations similar to those of normals but perform them more slowly. Their results have to be interpreted with some caution, however, because their diagnostic criteria were not specified.

Very different results were obtained when, instead of testing detection of a rapidly flashed array, a sequential visual search paradigm was employed. In these studies subjects searched for a particular target in a visual display. Russell and R. G. Knight (1977) found that schizophrenics' rate of increase in response time as the number of letters in a display increased was equivalent to normals in three separate tasks measuring visual search. They also found that schizophrenics' response times averaged about one second longer than those of controls. They attributed this to slow search setup time or to longer time required to organize a response, not to slowness of processing. In a subsequent study Russell, Consedine, and R. G. Knight (1980) had their subjects search displays of varying sizes for targets drawn from a memorized set of one, three, or six letters. Process schizophrenics were found to be equal to controls in the rate at which response time rose as a function of the product of memory set and display size. Controls did, however, show faster response times. Such results were consistent with their earlier study and confirmed a similar study by other investigators (Koh, Szoc, & Peterson, 1977). Russell and R. G. Knight concluded from their studies that there was no perceptual deficit in schizophrenia and that investigators should look at higher-level processes. This conclusion not only ignored the span of apprehension data I have just reviewed, it also failed to account for the results of several studies examining schizophrenics' iconic memory.

Since iconic memory was first isolated and measured by Sperling (1960), it has generated an extensive and at times controversial literature. At first it was widely agreed that this large-capacity, uncoded memory with its short duration and rapid decay was an important component of early processing. Early controversies centered on whether Neisser's (1967) term *cognitive* was appropriate to describe the store, whether information was read off this store in parallel or in series (Dick, 1974), and what its true duration was (e.g., Haber, 1971; Haber & Hershenson, 1980). Numerous techniques were developed to measure the icon. Indeed, the explosion of such techniques contributed substantially to the discrepancies in estimating the icon's duration, and some techniques were seen as methodologically more sound than others (Long, 1980). Recently there has been more serious questioning of the role of the icon in perceptual processing (Haber, 1983; Turvey, 1977), and some good evidence has been found to suggest that the classical icon really encompasses two stages (e.g., Phillips, 1974; Potter, 1976). In presenting the early iconic memory studies of schizophrenics, I will describe them within the classical icon model in which they were conceived and executed and will follow the developments of the model as they evolved from the data.

Sperling (1960) developed a paradigm that maximized the possibility of tapping a perceptual trace. He presented supraspan matrices of letters for very short exposure durations, and after the offset of the stimulus he indicated with a cue which particular row to report (partial report). Subjects were able to report with great accuracy items in the designated row even though they were unable to report all the letters when asked (full report). Sperling concluded from such data that the subject retains a visual or iconic image of the stimulus that decays within one second unless it is verbally encoded in STM. In this paradigm the earmarks of an adequately functioning icon are the superiority in performance when only partial report is required and the cue immediately follows the target, and the rapid decay in this superiority as the interval between the offset of the target array and the onset of the cue is increased. Using an adaptation of Sperling's paradigm, Knight, Sherer, and Shapiro (1977) found that good-prognosis overinclusive schizophrenics and nonpsychotic, psychiatric controls showed both characteristics of an adequately functioning icon—partial-report superiority and rapid iconic memory decay. Poor-prognosis, nonoverinclusive schizophrenics, however, demonstrated no partial-report superiority, and their decay slopes were flat, suggesting some deficiency in functioning at this stage.

Delay-of-masking-effect procedures have been conceptualized as affecting the icon (Haber & Standing, 1969; Neisser, 1967; Spencer, 1969) and have thus been used to assess its functioning and duration (Long, 1980). In the backward-masking paradigm at various durations after the offset of a target stimulus (TS), a masking stimulus (MS—usually a patterned, but meaningless configuration) is presented. When MS is presented at short intervals after TS, performance is at chance levels. As the interstimulus interval (ISI) increases, performance improves until it finally equals the no-mask level. Several backward-masking studies have found deficiencies in schizophrenics' iconic memory. Saccuzzo, Hirt, and Spencer (1974) tested delusional and chronic, nondelusional schizophrenics as well as nonschizophrenic, psychiatric controls and college student controls. In their procedure to establish functional equivalence of all subjects' icons in the no-mask condition, they found that compared with all other groups the nondelusional, chronic schizophrenics required the longest critical stimulus duration (CSD—the shortest stimulus duration at which the target can be accurately recognized 80% of the time). Moreover, distinctly different patterns of performance in backward-masking performance emerged for the schizophrenics and the controls. The controls' performances in this task replicated those of normals in other studies (Kahneman, 1968); the patterned mask interfered with the processing of the TS only when it was presented within 100 msec of the TS offset. For both delusional and chronic, nondelusional schizophrenics the processing of the TS was adversely affected even when the patterned MS was presented up to 250–300 msec after its offset. These results have subsequently been replicated in several studies that have demonstrated further that: (*a*) the longer CSD effect and the vulnerability to masking at longer ISIs is characteristic only of poor premorbid nonparanoid, not good premorbid paranoid schizophrenics (Saccuzzo & Braff, 1981); (b) good premorbid paranoids do show an impaired critical ISI, but this is reversible with small amounts of practice (Saccuzzo & Braff, 1981); (c) both remitted process schizophrenics (Miller, Saccuzzo, & Braff, 1979) and nonmedicated schizotypal patients (Braff, 1981) are hypervulnerable to pattern backward masking; (d) all schizophrenics perform adequately in a forward-masking task (i.e., when MS precedes TS) (Saccuzzo & Braff, 1981); (e) subjects with other psychopathologies, mania and depression, do not show these same masking deficiencies (Braff, 1981; Brody, Saccuzzo, & Braff, 1980; Saccuzzo & Braff, 1981); (f) elderly subjects (mean age 67.8) (Brody et al., 1980) and subjects intoxicated with marijuana (Braff, Silverton, Saccuzzo, & Janowsky, 1981) do not show the same pattern of deficiencies as poor-prognosis schizophrenics; (g) medication levels cannot explain the patterns of results obtained (Braff & Saccuzzo, 1981; Brody et al., 1980; Saccuzzo et al., 1974); and (h) both schizophrenics with normal intelligence and mentally retarded schizophrenics show equal vulnerability to backward masking, suggesting that intellectual factors do not play a significant role in the deficit (Saccuzzo, Braff, & Sprock, 1982).

Although the results of both the partial-report and backward-masking techniques strongly suggested some deficiencies specific to poor-prognosis schizophrenics at the earliest stage of processing and promised to provide an explanation for schizophrenics' inferior span of apprehension performance, neither procedure could pinpoint the specific nature of schizophrenics' processing difficulties. Thus new procedures were required to define the deficit more precisely. The prevalent model of the icon (Dick, 1974) suggested multiple explanations for the partial-report and masking results that could be divided into two categories—deficiencies in the icon itself and in the transfer of information from the icon to subsequent stages.

A deficient iconic storage—that is, an icon that is inadequately formed, abnormal in duration, or smaller than normal in capacity— would account for the inferior performance of the poor-prognosis nonoverinclusives in Knight, Sherer, and Shapiro's (1977) study. Also, Saccuzzo et al. (1974) argued that their chronic, nondelusional schizophrenics may have had an initially weaker icon, and that all schizophrenics' icons may have taken abnormally long to decay. As they noted, too slow an iconic decay would be as maladaptive as too quick a decay, since the incompletely disposed images might interfere with the formation of subsequent icons. The flat decay functions of the poor-prognosis schizophrenics in Knight, Sherer, and Shapiro's (1977) study were consistent with this explanation.

Various deficiencies in the transfer of information from its spatial array on the icon to subsequent sequential verbal encoding could have accounted equally well for these data. For instance, the partial-report technique we used required not only that the subject process the letter array, but that he or she also process, analyze, and respond to a cue. If the poor-prognosis schizophrenics were the high-redundancy, slow processors described by Cromwell (1975), who thus complied with Yates's (1966) slow processing hypothesis, the time required to process the cue might have been long enough to offset any advantage they may have gained from partial report's reduction in output interference. Such slowness of processing could also account for Saccuzzo et al.'s (1974) data, and indeed has currently become the favored hypothesis of that research group (Saccuzzo & Braff, 1981). The cue in the partial-report technique also directs the subject to attend selectively to a specific subset of letters in the array and to transfer these into STM first. Any difficulty in "disattending" (Cromwell & Dokecki, 1968) from an accustomed stimulus "reading" and switching to the appropriate subset would clearly be disadvantageous. Finally, although the nature of processing from the icon was controversial (Dick, 1974), deficits in either parallel or sequential transfer could account for the data.

Since none of the studies described could differentiate between specifically iconic or transfer dysfunctions, we (Knight, Sherer, Putchat, & Carter, 1978) sought a task to measure the icon, independent of transfer. To test the capacity and decay of the icon, unconfounded by possible transfer difficulties or deficits at subsequent stages, one needed a task that (*a*) did not, as the partial-report technique does, use a cue that consumes time that would otherwise be employed in processing the display; (*b*) required a minimum of set breaking; (*c*) involved the transfer of only a relatively small amount of information, so as not to overload any subsequent stages of processing and thereby tax these capacities; (*d*) seemed to need less practice than Sperling's technique; and yet (*e*) convincingly tested the functioning of the icon. To meet these specifications, we developed a variation of a technique first used by Eriksen and Collins (1967, 1968). Their stimuli were patterns of white dots on a black background.

Although the dots appeared random, when two complementary patterns were superimposed, an embedded syllable was evident. They were able to measure the duration of the iconic image by varying the delay between the presentation of two complementary dot patterns. As expected, recognition of the syllable decreased with increased interstimulus interval. Instead of dot patterns, we employed pictures of common objects as stimuli. The pictures were constructed so that when each single slide was tachistoscopically flashed for 100 msec, it appeared as random lines, but when the complementary slides were flashed simultaneously, the object depicted was readily apparent. By varying the interstimulus interval between complementary picture pairs, we were able to test the capacity and duration of the icon in schizophrenics. We found that all the subtypes of schizophrenics tested had intact icons. Surprisingly, however, our adaptation of the stimulus integration technique produced substantially longer estimates of the duration of the icon for both normals and schizophrenics than had occurred in Eriksen and Collins's original study.

Subsequently, Spaulding, Rosenzweig, Huntzinger, Cromwell, Briggs, and Hayes (1980), using a dot integration procedure similar to that employed by Eriksen and Collins, perfectly replicated Eriksen and Collins's 100 msec decay functions and found, like Knight et al. (1978), that schizophrenics' icons were intact and decayed as normals' icons did. If one ignores the duration discrepancy between the Spaulding et al. (1980) and Knight et al. (1978) studies, one could argue that both strongly support the adequacy of schizophrenics' icons. One could then conclude by elimination that transfer functions might be the source of schizophrenics' difficulties on the partial-report and masking tasks. As I have indicated, "transfer deficit" is a generalization for a number of possibly deficient encoding variables, including the speed of encoding, the location of the stimulus on the icon, the selective direction of attention to that stimulus, and the strategies of parallel or sequential processing from the icon.

The initially puzzling discrepancy in decay functions between our picture integration task and the dot integration task of Eriksen and Collins (1967, 1968) sent me scurrying to the normal cognitive literature for an explanation and ultimately provided the spark for our next study. Converging evidence suggested that the classical icon model was inadequate and that many of the tasks measuring iconic memory had confounded two processing stages—the first a large-capacity sensory store that lasts 100 msec (Phillips, 1974) and

that some have equated with visual persistence in the photorecep-
tors (Long, 1980), and the second a limited-capacity, schematic store
(short-term visual or conceptual memory, which I will refer to as
STVM) that is maximally efficient over the first 600 msec (Phillips,
1974; Potter, 1975, 1976).

Following evidence that suggested the existence of a schematic
representation of visual structure (Kroll, Parks, Parkinson, Bieber,
& Johnson, 1970; Meudell, 1972; Posner, 1969), Phillips (1974)
extended the Eriksen and Collins (1967, 1968) paradigm to relatively
uncoded matrix block patterns in an attempt to specify the characteristics of this hypothesized schematic store. Studying the same/
different comparisons of two successively presented block matrices
with half of the cells randomly blackened, he varied pattern
complexity, pattern movement, and masking. He found strong
evidence to support two separate memory stages. The first he called
the sensory storage. It had a high capacity and could handle large
block patterns efficiently. It was tied to a particular spatial position,
was easily masked, and was short in duration (about 100 msec).
Finally, since matrix size had little effect on reaction time, elements
in this store seemed to be processed concurrently and independently. The second stage, called STVM, was limited in capacity, not tied
to spatial position, not affected by a pattern mask, and maximally
efficient over the first 600 msec. Since reaction time increased with
matrix size during this stage, it seemed to require some sequential
processing of elements.

Potter (1975, 1976; Potter & Levy, 1969) came to a two-process
hypothesis from very different data. She was interested in whether
pictures presented in rapid sequence and subsequently not recognized were processed and momentarily understood or simply not
identified. Presenting sequences of 16 pictures for exposure durations ranging from 113 to 333 msec with zero ISI, she found that at
the most rapid exposure subjects could identify a particular picture
when cued with a picture (72% correct) or a descriptive title (64%
correct), but at that exposure they could not subsequently recognize
the picture (11% correct). Identification was measured by the subject's pressing a telegraph key as soon as the target was detected.
The subject's reaction time determined correctness of identification.
The subsequent memory task was an old/new recognition test cor-
rected for guessing. Identity asymptoted at 250 msec (Potter, 1976),
but picture recognition (which was only 30% correct at 250 msec)
continued to improve until 2 seconds (Potter & Levy, 1969). When,

however, a patterned mask (which blocked only *visual* processing) was used instead of, as in the previous sequential search presentation, another picture, over 80% of the pictures were remembered after an exposure of only 120 msec. Potter concluded from such data that a subsequent picture in the sequential search paradigm acted as a conceptual mask and interfered with a higher-level, postidentification processing. She hypothesized, therefore, that there are two processes in visual encoding. The first is the process of identification, whose median duration is 100 msec or less and which is susceptible to pattern masking. The second is the process of short-term conceptual memory, which reaches median duration at 400 msec and is not susceptible to pattern masking but can be affected only by a cognitive mask (i.e., a mask that requires the processing of new information). This second stage seems to provide a brief working span in which the consolidation necessary for subsequent retention can be initiated. Its similarity to Phillips's (1974) STVM is striking.

This new model not only resolved some of the discrepant findings about normal cognition (e.g., Long, 1980), it also permitted an explanation and integration of the seemingly contradictory findings about schizophrenics' early visual processing dysfunction. The reason for the difference in decay functions between Eriksen and Collins's dot stimuli and our picture stimuli was clearly a difference in the complexity of the stimuli. Their stimuli were sufficiently complex that they could be maintained only in sensory store. Our easily encodable line drawings could, like the less complex matrices in the Phillips (1974) study, be partially encoded in the more schematic STVM. By this interpretation Spaulding et al.'s (1980) dot integration results support the adequacy of schizophrenics' sensory store and indicate that it decays within 100 msec. Our picture results suggest that schizophrenics had sufficient form integration ability to identify very simple forms in STVM. That schizophrenics' sensory store decays within 100 msec has important implications for the backward-masking studies. The performance decrements caused by a pattern mask at ISIs greater than 100 msec must be due to interference with schizophrenics' processing in STVM. Normals' processing in this stage can only be affected by a cognitive (meaningful) mask. Potter (1976) has argued that the cognitive mask is disruptive because it interferes with the consolidation of meaningful information by requiring the processing of new meaningful information. This leads to two possible explanations that could account for the backward-masking deficit—either poor-prognosis schizophrenics process the information in the pattern mask as meaningful (or at least they are not as efficient as normals at quickly determining the lack of meaning and terminating further processing) or they have an unstable STVM that is more easily disrupted than that of normals.

To test these hypotheses, we (Knight, Elliott, & Freedman, Note 1) adapted a backward-masking recognition paradigm that Hulme and Merikle (1976) had developed to test the postexposure processing of pictures of complex, colored, naturalistic scenes. To their pattern-mask condition (a random array of colored shapes) we added random-noise-mask (a dense matrix randomly filled with dark or light dots) and cognitive-mask (a photograph of a real-world scene—Potter, 1976) conditions, thereby enabling an assessment of the hypothesis that poor-prognosis schizophrenics tend to process the pattern mask as if it were a cognitive mask, while good-prognosis schizophrenics process the pattern mask the same way as normals. More specifically, if either of the mask-processing hypotheses is correct, there should be an interaction between subgroup, mask type, and stimulus onset asynchrony (SOA, the total processing time from TS onset to MS onset). For good-prognosis schizophrenics, as for nonschizophrenics, the pattern mask should be relatively ineffective at longer SOAs (200–300 msec), but the cognitive mask should disrupt their picture processing at this interval. For poor-prognosis schizophrenics, the pattern mask should function more like the cognitive mask. The random-noise mask should do little to block processing and thus should provide a control condition. It should be noted parenthetically that neither a slowness of processing nor a general deficit hypothesis could generate the prediction of this complex pattern.

In this study colored pictures of real-world scenes and objects were followed at varying SOAs with one of the three masks described above. After each block of 12 trials (i.e., 12 picture-mask pairs, with each block having one mask type), each subject's memory for the pictures was tested using a four-picture multiple-choice recognition task. The results of this experiment are shown in Figures 1 and 2. Figure 1 presents the critical interaction. To control for general deficiencies in responding, the results are presented as difference scores from no-mask performance. As can be seen in this figure, we obtained the significant three-way interaction we predicted. Normals, nonschizophrenics (primarily affective disorders), and good premorbid schizophrenics all differentiated pattern-mask

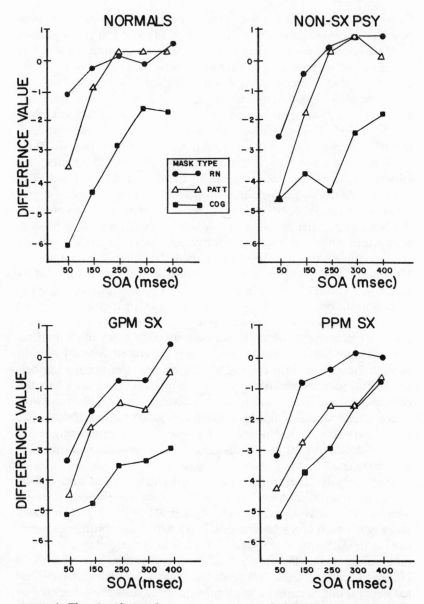

FIGURE 1. The significant three-way interaction between groups (normals, nonschizophrenic psychotics, good premorbid schizophrenics, and poor premorbid schizophrenics), mask type (random noise, pattern, and cognitive), and SOA, F (24, 336) = 1.80, p = .013, for the difference scores between the average no-mask conditions and each mask x SOA condition.

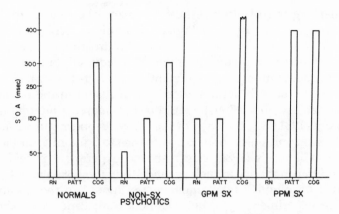

FIGURE 2. Depiction of the SOA level at which each mask type (random noise, pattern, cognitive) for each group (normals, nonschizophrenic psychotics, good premorbid schizophrenics, poor premorbid schizophrenics) first reached equivalence to no-mask performance ($p > .025$).

and cognitive-mask conditions. Only the poor premorbid schizophrenics performed equivalently in the two conditions. Figure 2, which presents graphically the SOAs at which each group in each condition first performed equivalently to their no-mask performance, also shows this same result. Only the poor premorbid schizophrenics performed equivalently on the pattern-mask and cognitive-mask conditions.

The picture-masking study corroborated our hypothesis that poor-prognosis schizophrenics respond to a pattern mask the same way they respond to a cognitive mask. It was still not clear from this study alone which of two possible explanations might account for their performance. One hypothesis was that they have a perceptual organization dysfunction that does not allow them to determine as efficiently as normals the meaninglessness of the mask, so they process this material enough that it acts like a meaningful cognitive mask. The second hypothesis was that poor-prognosis schizophrenics have some instabilities in their STVM that make this stage vulnerable to distractors that do not affect normals' STVM. Fortunately, two investigations from two other laboratories clearly support the first alternative. In two numerosity experiments Place and Gilmore (1980) asked poor premorbid schizophrenics and drug-abusing controls to judge the number of lines appearing in a display flashed tachistoscopically for less than 20 msec. In their first experiment a group of either vertical or horizontal lines appeared by themselves or with circles (a "noise" condition). Schizophrenics were able to count the lines as well as controls in the no-noise condition when no selective attention was required, but they had difficulty judging numerosity when the circles were present. Since a single feature, straightness, sufficed for inclusion in the relevant stimulus set, the "noise" task would be considered a filtering task (Broadbent, 1981). On the basis of these results one might wrongly attribute schizophrenics' poor performance to a filtering problem. Place and Gilmore's (1980) clever second experiment provides a different interpretation. In their second study they presented three categories of stimuli—(a) homogeneous lines, like the no-noise stimuli in experiment 1; (b) heterogeneous/adjacent lines —both vertical and horizontal lines presented in the same set with same-orientation lines grouped; and (c) heterogeneous/non-adjacent—with both orientation lines presented without adjacent grouping of similar lines. The task was to count all lines. Controls' performance declined from (a) to (c). Schizophrenics found all three types equally easy, and in fact their overall performance on all three conditions was significantly *better* than that of controls. These results suggest that, before counting, controls automatically organized the lines in conditions (b) and (c), and this organization interfered with their counting. Since poor premorbid schizophrenics presumably did no such automatic chunking, their perception of numerosity proceeded unabated.

A second investigation also supports the perceptual organization deficit hypothesis. Cox and Leventhal (1978) tested process, non-paranoid schizophrenics, reactive, paranoid schizophrenics, and nonschizophrenic psychiatric controls on three tasks measuring "preattentive" processes (Neisser's [1967] term for initial perceptual organization). In a disparate figure task adapted from Beck (1972), subjects were required to count tilted and inverted figures embedded in an array of upright figures. Their second task, a variant of a visual suffix task developed by Kahneman (1973), briefly displayed a series of relevant digits followed by irrelevant trailing zeros. The subject's task was to recall the last three digits, but only memory for the last digit was scored. The final task was a figure recognition test, again adapted from Beck (1972). Here they tested a subject's ability to detect quickly the presence of inverted figures, shown in the corners of a square matrix. When the tasks were administered in standard format, the process schizophrenics' performance was significantly worse than that of both reactives and controls on all three tasks. When enrichment conditions were introduced that provided subjects with the perceptual organization by explicitly visually discriminating the perceptual target (e.g., in the disparate figure task the tilted and inverted figures were highlighted by doubling their thickness), the performance of the process schizophrenics differentially improved so that group differences were eliminated on two of the three tasks. On the third task, the visual suffix task, process schizophrenics showed differential improvement on the enriched condition relative to the controls, but not relative to the reactive schizophrenics. Overall, these results strongly suggest that process schizophrenics do not automatically organize their perceptual world in the same way reactive schizophrenics and controls do.

Thus three disparate paradigms converge in the same deficit explanation. Place and Gilmore (1980) demonstrated in their numerosity task that because poor-prognosis schizophrenics did not perceptually organize stimuli they were immune to an interference that disrupted controls' performance. Cox and Leventhal (1978) tested process schizophrenics on tasks that required perceptual organization, found them deficient, and differentially improved their performance by providing them with the perceptual organization they had had difficulty generating themselves. Finally, in our picture-masking study poor premorbid schizophrenics were excessively vulnerable to a pattern mask at longer ISIs than controls because their deficient perceptual organization did not allow sufficiently rapid differentiation between meaningless and meaningful information.

A perceptual organization deficit is also consistent with a number of the other early visual processing results I have reviewed. Obviously, the explanation for the backward-masking results of Saccuzzo and his colleagues is the same as that for the picture-masking study. Because of poor-prognosis schizophrenics' perceptual organization deficit, the pattern mask acts for them as a cognitive mask acts for normals and thus affects performance at longer ISIs. It is interesting that Braff and Saccuzzo (1981) have had to posit a separate dysfunction to account for poor premorbids' CSD results. They have hypothesized that schizophrenics' need for a longer stimulus duration to achieve adequate target recognition is due to "impaired sensory registration," while the masking deficit is due to "slow processing of stimuli." The perceptual organization hypothesis more parsimoniously explains both with the same deficit. The CSD results simply reflect the greater amount of time it takes poor premorbids to schematize even very familiar stimuli like letters.

The span of apprehension and partial report results are also amenable to a perceptual organization explanation. As I indicated earlier, the most consistent span of apprehension finding has been that schizophrenics' accuracy of target detection declines relative to controls' as the number of irrelevant elements in the array increases. It seems that when single letters are presented for reasonably long durations without interference, schizophrenics' perceptual organizational abilities are not strained. As the field becomes more cluttered, requiring more rapid organization of the elements and the field, schizophrenics' performance declines. The partial-report data can be similarly explained. Because of their limited perceptual organization ability it seems that poor-prognosis schizophrenics process single elements sequentially from the matrix rather than chunking larger units for processing in parallel. Cuing a portion of the matrix to reduce output inference does not benefit such element-by-element processing. In tasks that require sequential search and comparison, like the visual search paradigms reviewed earlier (Koh et al., 1977; Russell & R. G. Knight, 1977; Russell, Consedine, & R. G. Knight, 1980), schizophrenics seem to function more adequately.

The studies thus far reviewed do not allow further specification of the nature of poor-prognosis schizophrenics' perceptual organization deficit. It is clearly not an absolute deficit. Indeed, schizophrenics must be able to do some minimal amount of perceptual organization, or they could perform no cognitive task. We have seen that schizophrenics can fuse stimuli within their sensory store (Spaulding et al., 1980) and can schematize simple visual line representations sufficiently for integration with a complementary representation (Knight et al., 1978). Moreover, their visual search of a stimulus that is present until processing ceases seems intact (Russell & R. G. Knight, 1977). Their perceptual organization seems to break down when the stimuli are less familiar (the numerosity data: Place & Gilmore, 1980) or when their schematization abilities are taxed by increasing the number of units to be processed (the partial-report and span data: Knight, Sherer, & Shapiro, 1977; Neale, 1971; Neale et al., 1969), by decreasing the amount of time available to process a single unit (the CSD results: Saccuzzo & Braff, 1981), or by creating a situation in which rapid organization is necessary for the completion of the task (the backward-masking results: Saccuzzo & Braff, 1981; Knight et al., Note 1). A brief consideration of this hypothesized deficit in light of some current cognitive models suggests paradigms that can be used to specify this deficit's parameters further and provides a theoretical framework for speculation about how a perceptual organization deficit interfaces with other hypotheses about schizophrenics' cognitive deficiencies.

Before proceeding it is important to emphasize a crucial point that has remained in the background of my discussion until now. This involves the major issue of typology. The perceptual organization deficit has been found consistently in only one subgroup of schizophrenics, the poor premorbids. Good premorbids in most paradigms do not evidence this processing deficiency. The premorbidity dimension has long been associated with prognostic utility (e.g., Zigler & Phillips, 1961). Both poor social competence, which is definitional of poor premorbidity, and flat affect and inappropriate affect, which have been major characteristics of the poor premorbids in our samples (Levin, Hall, Knight, & Alpert, Note 2), predict poor outcome (Astrup & Noreik, 1966; Jansson, 1968; Knight, Roff, Barrnett, & Moss, 1979; Langfeldt, 1969; Prentky, Lewine, Watt, & Fryer, 1980; Strauss & Carpenter, 1972). It has remained, however, very controversial whether dichotomizing this premorbidity dimension really isolates different types of patients. Some have argued (Gottesman & Shields, 1982) that the present state of our knowledge does not permit us to determine whether poor premorbids constitute an essential core of a genetically homogeneous spectrum disorder or a separate type with a specific etiology. Recently, new data have been injected into this controversy. A number of studies have suggested two distinct types of schizophrenics, related to the old good premorbid/poor premorbid dichotomy, but revolving around a new cluster of symptoms. The poor premorbid type is characterized by negative symptoms, cognitive deficits, neuropsychological impairment, poor response to treatment, perhaps structural abnormalities like cerebral ventricular enlargement, and no association with a change in dopaminergic transmission (Andreasen & Olsen, 1982; Andreasen, Olsen, Dennert, & Smith, 1982; Crow, 1980; Golden, Moses, Zelazowski, Graber, Zatz, Horvath, & Berger, 1980; Johnstone, Crow, Frith, Husband, & Kreel, 1976; Rieder, Donnelly, Herdt, & Waldman, 1979; Weinberger, Bigelow, Kleinman, Klein, Rosenblatt, & Wyatt, 1980; Weinberger,

Cannon-Spoor, Potkin, & Wyatt, 1980). The complementary good premorbid type manifests the opposite cluster of symptoms. An empirical cluster analytic investigation of rigorously diagnosed schizophrenics (Farmer, McGuffin, & Spitznagel, 1983) has also generated two distinct groups similar to the two I have just described—an early onset, poor premorbid group with "hebephrenic" symptoms like blunted affect, incoherent speech, and bizarre behavior, and a later onset, good premorbid group with well-organized delusions. Although the results have not always been consistent (Jernigan, Zatz, Moses, & Berger, 1982; Nasrallah, Jacoby, McCalley-Whitters, & Kuperman, 1982), the basic trend of these recent investigations has been consistent with the differences found in the cognitive research. The specific performances and symptom clusters that have evolved are sufficiently compelling to mandate the continued examination of these subtypes in future research. Indeed, if more comprehensive criteria become available that specify the typology better and provide more accurate type assignment, it will be important for cognitive psychopathologists to include such criteria in their assessment batteries. Premorbidity is clearly only a gross correlate of the typology. Whether this typology ultimately leads to the isolation of specific etiologies or simply permits the identification of core schizophrenics, it should continue to play a central role in our research on schizophrenics' cognitive deficiencies.

COGNITIVE MODELS OF EARLY VISUAL PROCESSING

Modern theories of attention can be categorized along a number of dimensions. One dichotomization, especially relevant to the results discussed in the previous section, distinguishes between theories that emphasize the passive or receptive characteristics of processing and those that focus on the active and constructive aspects of perception. Proponents of the former (Broadbent, 1958, 1971; Deutsch & Deutsch, 1963; Treisman, 1969) stress the complexity of the stimulus information that is presented to the senses at any time and that can potentially overload the system. They have been more concerned with tasks of divided attention (Kahneman & Treisman, in press) and have postulated various filtering mechanisms that select specific information at particular stages in a limited-capacity processing system. A major issue addressed by these investigators has been the site of attentional restriction, whether it is at an early or a late stage (Norman, 1976). Since these researchers' models have been relatively unconcerned with perceptual organization, they have contributed little to research on the topic. Much of the research and theorizing about schizophrenics' attentional deficiencies has been conducted within this framework and has hypothesized that abnormal filtering mechanisms of one sort or another are central to schizophrenics' cognitive deficits (e.g., McGhie, 1970; Nuechterlein, 1977; Payne, Mattussek, & George, 1959; Wishner & Wahl, 1974; Schwartz, 1978, 1982).

The theorists with a more active bent have emphasized the variety of responses a subject can initiate in any instance. They have seen perceptual overload as more a problem of adopting the appropriate set so as to avoid incoherence (Neisser, 1976; Posner, 1978) than of protecting the system from stimulus overload. Their research has been concerned more with focused or selective than with divided attention (Kahneman & Treisman, in press), and they have sought to explore issues of automaticity and perceptual organization in information processing (Posner, 1978; Shiffrin & Schneider, 1977).

As Kahneman and Treisman (in press) have indicated, there was something of a paradigm shift in attention research in the 1970s. The research pendulum swung away from filter models toward automatic processing. Since the converging lines of evidence I have reviewed point to a perceptual organization rather than a filtering deficit in poor-prognosis schizophrenics, and since the aim of this section is to explore the nature and consequences of such a deficit, I will focus on selected automaticity theories and limit my consideration of filter theories to Kahneman and Treisman's (in press) compromise, which deals with some of the problems of an exclusively automatic theory of perception.

Neisser's (1967) systematic treatise of perception brought the constructivist orientation into the mainstream of theorizing about information processing. He distinguished between *focal attention* and *preattentive* processes. The former he described as having both analytic and synthetic characteristics in that it both extracts and constructs details from the limited aspect of the visual or auditory world that has been preestablished by preattentive processes. Neisser described the preattentive processes as "wholistic" or "global" processors that segregate objects from each other and help direct further processing. They chunk the raw materials of perception and thereby lay the groundwork for the subsequent, more detailed analyses of focal attention.

Neisser (1976) subsequently narrowed his definition of preattentive processes and seems now to exclude acquired automatic skills from this category. In his new model he emphasizes the active, cyclic nature of perception. He views schemata as structures that are internal to the perceiver and central to the perceptual cycle. They are an "active array of physiological structures and processes" (Neisser, 1976, p. 54). They anticipate information and prepare and direct the perceiver. They accept sensory information, are modified by that information, and direct the exploration of subsequent information. In his model there is no need for filters. Selection is an active, positive process. Perceivers pick up what they have schemata for and simply do not process the rest. There is no need to inhibit anything. For Neisser (1976, p. 87), "Attention is nothing but perception."

Many other models subsequently included processes very similar to Neisser's focal attention and preattentive processes. Perhaps the most detailed, best-developed, and most extensively integrated with other models is that presented by Shiffrin and Schneider (1977). Their model represents to some degree a compromise between the two extreme camps into which I have divided perceptual theorizing. While they see perception as an active process and reject the passive, filter-oriented view of attentional selectivity, they also reject constructivist, "top-down" conceptions.

In their theory of information processing they hypothesize two fundamental processing modes: *controlled* and *automatic*. The former, so called because they manipulate or control the flow of information in and out of STM and into LTM, are analogous to, but somewhat broader than, Neisser's focal-attention processes. They include rehearsal, memory searching, coding, and decisions of all sorts. According to Shiffrin and Schneider (1977) they are flexible, easily initiated and altered. They require little training, their performance level stabilizes very quickly, and they are readily adapted to novel situations. Their major drawback is that their capacity is limited to that of STM, and their functioning requires attention. In contrast, automatic processes, which are most like Neisser's original conception of preattentional processes, are virtually unaffected by load, demand little capacity, and need attention only when the target is presented. Shiffrin and Schneider's (1977; Schneider &

Shiffrin, 1977) data indicate that these processes require considerable training to develop, but once established they become permanently and rather inflexibly entrenched and difficult to suppress. Even more extensive training is needed to alter or reverse such processes than to learn them initially. These processes are hypothesized to operate in parallel. Once a particular input configuration occurs, the process runs automatically to completion. These two processing modes complement each other and are hypothesized to have numerous advantages for the system. As automatic processing develops, it reduces attentional demands, freeing capacity for controlled operations. Thus performance improves, and the efficient use of the limited capacity available is optimized. At the same time the duality of the system continues to maintain both flexibility for novel situations (controlled processes) and immediate accessibility for important stimulation (automatic detection).

One final model, closely related on several dimensions to Shiffrin and Schneider's model, deserves consideration—the two-stage discriminability model of visual matching proposed by Kroll and Hershenson (1980). This model and its supporting data provide a bridge between the general processing models I have just discussed and the STVM models that guided our research. Moreover, its demonstration that a two-stage model very similar to Shiffrin and Schneider's can explain what had been perplexing findings in another paradigm attests to the generativity and validity of the model and increases our confidence in using such a model to help explain and investigate schizophrenics' processing deficiencies.

Kroll and Hershenson (1980) originally generated their model to explain the paradox that *same* judgments tend to be made faster than *different* judgments in matching tasks (Nickerson, 1972, 1973, 1978). A logical analysis of matching-task demands suggested that the reverse should have occurred. To determine that two patterns are different seems to involve simply the identification of a single discrepancy, and hypothetically processing could terminate with such a discovery. In contrast, a judgment of pattern identity seems to require a detailed, exhaustive comparison to rule out any discrepancies. Thus by this analysis one would hypothesize, contrary to the empirical data, that *different* judgments should be faster than *same* judgments.

To explain this paradox Kroll and Hershenson posited a model with a wholistic and an analytic processor arranged in tandem to form two processing stages. They hypothesized that fast *same* and some fast *different* judgments represent the output of the first-stage wholistic comparator. Slow *different* responses are the result of additional processing through an analytic, element-by-element sequential processor. The degree of discriminability of the stimulus pair determines whether a response is made after wholistic comparison or whether further sequential analysis is necessary before a response can be made.

The pattern of results of a series of studies has provided substantial support for this model. In a matching paradigm Kroll and Hershenson (1980) presented six-letter strings for durations of 100 or 1,000 msec. The *different* arrays were either easy to discriminate (all of the six letters were different in the two pairs) or hard to discriminate (the arrays differed by only one letter). In two separate experiments the results were consistent. The differences in discriminability determined the speed of both *same* and *different* responses. When hard discriminations were included in the stimulus set, wholistic processing became inefficient and serial processing predominated. The presence of only easy stimuli facilitated wholistic, rapid, first-stage decisions. Moreover, the limitation of stimulus exposure affected *same* responses at both levels of discriminability, but *different* responses only for the hard-to-discriminate arrays. That *different* responses to the easy-to-discriminate stimuli were unaffected by stimulus duration suggested that the decision was based on information available from the first 100 msecs—that is, that the first decision stage used a rough estimate (wholistic comparison) of the difference between the letter strings. Furthermore, the faster stimulus duration had more effect on the matching latencies of both the *same* and *different* responses when the discrimination was difficult than when it was easy, suggesting that the brief exposure forced the termination of processing the hard-to-discriminate stimuli before completion of the task. This produced fast response latencies but larger error rates. In contrast, the easy-to-discriminate arrays were rapidly and accurately matched on the basis of an initial, wholistic stage of comparison for which the 100 msec exposure provided sufficient information.

The serial position data also supported the two-stage model. For the short-duration stimuli, when the second stage cannot be involved and thus the serial comparison should not be performed, the reaction times for all serial positions should be approximately equal. For these stimuli the response latencies were similar for all positions except the leftmost. For long-duration stimuli the hard-to-discriminate arrays should be passed on to a second-stage sequential processing, producing an increasing left-right serial position function. As expected, reaction time and errors increased from left to right for these stimuli.

Rosen and Hershenson (1983) tested the model in a different manner. They constructed stimuli that were designed to facilitate processing in one of the two stages. They combined four (of eight possible) geometric shapes in either a square or a linear arrangement. According to the two-stage model, the square arrangement of elements should facilitate wholistic, stage-one comparison and inhibit serial processing in the second stage, while the linear arrangement of elements should facilitate only second-stage processing. Degree of discriminability and stimulus duration were varied to provide differential predictions for each configuration-duration combination at each stage of processing. All of the predicted patterns were obtained for both response latency and accuracy scores.

Finally, in another test of the model, Ryder (1979) used stimuli in which both shape and orientation were varied. One set contained pairs of letters, and two sets contained pairs of "random" polygons. Subjects were instructed to base their comparisons either on shape alone, on orientation alone, on both shape and orientation, or on either shape or orientation. Ryder's complex predictions from the two-stage model were supported in almost every detail.

There are important parallels between Kroll and Hershenson's (1980) two-stage discriminability model and Shiffrin and Schneider's (1977) model. The wholistic, stage-one comparator is directly analogous to the automatic processing mode. Both process stimuli rapidly (within 100 msec) and deal in parallel with whole units rather than with separate elements. Kroll and Hershenson's analytic processor would qualify as a controlled processor—a sequential, more flexible, and possibly more easily initiated process. The experimental paradigms these investigators have chosen to study their first-stage, automatic processor reflect their theoretical biases and to some degree color their descriptions of this stage. Shiffrin and Schneider have chosen stimuli and paradigms that require extensive practice before automatic processing becomes evident. They therefore focus on the learning and associative aspects of this processing. Hershenson and his students have manipulated stimulus characteristics that affect discrimination and thus have emphasized the structural or Gestalt characteristics to which their stage responds. These different approaches are, of course, complementary. Structures found to facilitate automatic or wholistic processing in adults without extensive practice might simply be the result of previous learning. It is interesting to speculate on whether certain perceptual configurations inherently lend themselves to automatic processing (see, e.g., some of the early-appearing Gestalt principles [Bower, 1982] and Neisser's [1976] related discussion).

The two-stage discriminability model can also be integrated with the iconic memory studies (Eriksen & Collins, 1967, 1968) and the work of Potter (1975, 1976) and Phillips (1974) that guided our research. The wholistic comparison stage of the discriminability model, like Potter's identification stage, processes wholistic, easily discriminable "major" themes. The large variety of themes easily identified in Potter's paradigm might be partially a function of the experimental paradigm employed, in which automaticity was facilitated by the use of the name or picture "cue." Like Phillips's (1974) sensory store, elements in the wholistic stage, as in Shiffrin and Schneider's (1977) automatic mode, seem to be processed in parallel. All three models (Phillips, Potter, and Kroll & Hershenson) propose that processing in the first stage is virtually complete within the first 100 msec. The serial analysis stage of the discriminability model, like both Phillips's and Potter's STVM memory, requires more processing time, and like Phillips's STVM, seems to require the sequential analysis of elements.

There are, however, some important distinctions among these models. Phillips's sensory store is susceptible to visual masking and, like the storage assessed by Eriksen and Collins (1967, 1968), decays rapidly (within 100 msec). It seems to be a literal, veridical image reverberation that is a high-capacity, and possibly peripheral, store, which Long (1980) would identify with the icon proper but Haber (1983) would equate with visual perseveration. Both Potter's and Kroll and Hershenson's initial stages (identification and wholistic analysis) are, like Shiffrin and Schneider's automatic processing, processes on that storage and should not be confused with the storage itself. These initial processes seem to be able to garner their required information within the time limitations of the sensory store but do not seem isomorphic with that store. This is important for our interpretation of the schizophrenic processing studies, since it means that evidence for equal decay of schizophrenics' sensory store (Knight et al., 1978; Spaulding et al., 1980) cannot constitute proof of the adequacy of the wholistic processing stage.

The several models I have thus far reviewed and their accompanying validation data indicate that, despite some fundamental differences in theoretical perspectives, there is increasing agreement among investigators on some of the basic parameters of early visual processing. Converging evidence from experiments in backward masking, stimulus integration, physical and name matching, picture identification and recognition, and visual and memory search all suggest two underlying early processes arranged in tandem—an automatic, wholistic initial perceptual organizer and a sequential, analytic, more narrowly focused controlled processor.

Even some earlier proponents of filter theories have moved to compromise with these automaticity models. Kahneman and Treisman (in press) argue that the construct of automaticity, especially the "display board model" proposed by Shiffrin and Schneider (1977), cannot explain by itself all the phenomena in early visual processing. It still has difficulty accounting for many of those results from the more complex divided-attention paradigms for which the "filter" mechanism was proposed. Most important, a model that hypothesizes that perception works by activating semipermanent structures in long-term memory has no way of representing the perceptual unity of objects and events. To fill this gap and to replace the defunct "filter," they propose a new mechanism, a perceptual analogue of *episodic* memory, which they call an *object file*. These temporary files are opened on any object in the perceptual field and maintain the continuity and identity of these objects in a specific episode. They are defined by physical characteristics, especially spatiotemporal, and provide a mechanism for attention to be applied to particular objects or specific spatial locations rather than to nodes in long-term memory. Interestingly, these files seem to be opened automatically. Kahneman and Treisman suggest that attention may not affect the accumulation of information in an object file, only the dissemination from it, and that attention is directed toward such an object file by specific physical characteristics. Thus, in addition to accounting for the complex stimulus location findings that Kahneman and Treisman (in press) report in their chapter, it also could be used to explain how early selection on elementary features occurs, since these files store (and therefore select) only elementary features.

Kahneman and Treisman's (in press) alternative view clearly allays any unfounded suspicions that early perception is now tied up in a neat bundle, waiting for the experimental psychopathologist simply to apply it to schizophrenia. Yet, though this compromise model introduces a new mechanism and to some degree restricts the "automaticity model," it still recognizes the viability of a modified form of the construct. Moreover, it does allow an initial specification of early kinds of perceptual organization that might be helpful in schizophrenia research. It has been convincingly argued that schizophrenics' stimulus-set "filtering" seems to be intact (Schwartz, 1982). This suggests, therefore, that their "episodic object file" perceptual memory should function adequately and that the perceptual organization deficit might be limited specifically to configural and semantic schemata.

The experimental research I have presented suggests that the poor premorbid schizophrenics' initial configural and semantic organization of a stimulus into a unified perceptual whole was deficient. In the context of the cognitive models I have described this would constitute some deficiency in perceptual schema formation, in automaticity, or in the wholistic stage of processing. These models suggest that such a deficiency could have wide-ranging consequences for performance on other cognitive tasks and for specific aspects of schizophrenics' behavior and phenomenology. Since automatic processes serve functionally to expand capacity by reducing the load on controlled processes, any impairment or inefficiency in their operation would essentially limit capacity. The degree of deficit would relate directly to vulnerability to stimulus or task overload. Thus an automatic processing dysfunction would be consistent with the greater decrements in performance schizophrenics experience with any conditions that increase load (R. G. Knight & Russell, 1978). In the Shiffrin and Schneider (1977) model, overload would mean not only that some stimuli would remain unprocessed, but also that controlled processing would be limited. Thus, for example, findings that when distractors are introduced, schizophrenics reduce rehearsal (i.e., lose their primacy effect; Oltmanns, 1978) or show decreased recall for shadowed speech (Pogue-Geile & Oltmanns, 1980) would be consistent with an automatic processing deficit. It is important to point out that it might be quite difficult to predict a priori exactly which controlled process would be affected in an overload condition. This might vary radically with changes in instruction or task structure. Thus, in their attempt to replicate with some modifications the Pogue-Geile and Oltmanns (1980) study, Frame and Oltmanns (Note 3) found that *shadowing* and not *recall* was affected in distractor conditions. Both the Pogue-Geile and the Frame studies, despite their seemingly contradictory findings, are consistent with the proposed automatic processing deficit. More generally, the proposed deficit would be consistent with all those theories that implicate impairments in schizophrenics' controlled processing (Koh, 1978; Neale & Oltmanns, 1980; Rochester, 1978), since such a deficit would make controlled processes excessively vulnerable to overload. In this regard it is noteworthy that when care is taken to ensure successful organization of mnemonic material at encoding (Koh, Kayton, & Streicker, 1976; Koh & Peterson, 1978) or when a self-paced organization of stimuli is permitted (Larsen & Fromholt, 1976), schizophrenics' recall deficit is ameliorated. This suggests that they can employ appropriate controlled strategies but do not do so in more typical recall paradigms. A depletion in the necessary attentional capacity for controlled processing because of deficient automatic processing might possibly explain such results.

Neissler's (1976) characterization of perceptual organization as cyclic and directive in nature suggests other possible implications of a deficit in such schema formation. In his formulation, as these perceptual skills develop, a person moves from being "stimulus bound" to being more "inner directed." An impairment in schema-organization skills, resulting in schemata that are either inappropriately or poorly formed for the task demands, would leave the individual less in control and more susceptible to being driven by whatever stimuli are either immediately present or most salient. Thus the proposed deficit could provide the mechanism responsible for the behaviors and laboratory performances of schizophrenics described by Salzinger's immediacy hypothesis (Salzinger, this volume; Salzinger, Portnoy, & Feldman, 1978).

It has been argued (Chapman & Chapman, 1973) that any theory of schizophrenics' cognitive deficiencies should be able to give some account for the experiences of patients. Accounts of stimulus overload and of difficulties in concentrating and "focusing attention" are common in schizophrenics' self-reports (Freedman, 1974; McGhie & Chapman, 1961). Since the perceptual organization of schemata works to reduce stimulus load and the cyclic anticipation and reformulation of such schemata help set the direction for subsequent processing, a deficiency in such organization could create a fragmented perceptual field, where individual elements are processed separately rather than as parts of cohesive wholes and the direction of attention is not focused. In this situation schizophrenics would experience the stimulus overload and problems in concentration and focusing that they report.

In these first two sections I have presented some of the converging evidence that has accumulated both in research on normal early visual processing and in the study of schizophrenics' early processing deficit, and I have attempted to demonstrate some of the many consistencies across these areas. In both of these areas the research approach method that has sparked these advances has been process oriented. It is to the nature and methodological advantages of this approach that I will turn my attention in the next section.

THE METHODOLOGICAL BENEFITS OF A PROCESS-ORIENTED APPROACH

The review above indicates that recent developments in the research on perception and cognition of both normals and schizophrenics are converging on models that allow a more precise, and therefore more disconfirmable, set of concepts about the nature of schizophrenics' processing deficiencies. Moreover, a number of studies point to specific perceptual organization deficiencies in poor-prognosis schizophrenics that might have substantial power for explaining many aspects of their cognitive performance.

Before the advent of well-defined, process-relevant models, the investigators of schizophrenics' cognitive deficiencies were forced to proceed either by trial and error or under the guidance of vague models (Neale & Cromwell, 1970, 1977), that often seemed to bear little resemblance to the tasks employed. Two rational strategies emerged to systematize and guide the search for consistency. Both understandably shied away from underlying processes and focused on the isolation and investigation of a single, differentiating task. One sought tasks that differentiated schizophrenics from other pathological groups and attempted to determine the conditions and subject variables that affected performance on the task—whether it improves with medication, is worse in schizophrenics with a family history of schizophrenia, is found in children vulnerable to schizophrenia, and so on (cf. Kornetsky & Orzack, 1978, for a review of an excellent example of this approach). A second, related strategy again found a task that differentiated schizophrenics from other groups and sought to isolate what particular aspects of the task were most correlated with schizophrenia. The attempted isolation of the crossover phenomenon (Bellissimo & Steffy, 1972; Cromwell, 1975; Nideffer, Neale, Kopfstein, & Cromwell, 1971; Zubin, 1975) is a good example of this approach. This strategy should not be confused with more process-oriented task decomposition, which requires a priori models and quantification of theoretical constructs in specific terms (Embretson, 1983; Posner, 1978; Siegler & Vago, 1978; Sternberg, 1979). Lacking such theoretical constructs to guide their search, task-oriented investigators, when they did narrow differential performance parameters, had to limit their speculations about the nature of schizophrenics' deficiencies to task-descriptive rather than mechanism-specific explanations. Although both of these strategies have contributed to our general understanding of the importance of some input deficit in schizophrenia, they have not substantially advanced our knowledge of the specific processes involved in this dysfunction, because they have not been able to generalize from their particular task to different tasks supposedly measuring the same phenomenon.

In addition, these task-oriented approaches were found vulnerable to several methodological difficulties that made problematic even their point of departure, the isolation of a differentiating task. It became obvious to many that finding schizophrenics deficient on any *single* task provided little insight into their cognitive capabilities, since their performance was deficient on numerous seemingly unrelated tasks (Maher, 1974). A *differential*-deficit strategy emerged to address this difficulty. It was argued that if two dependent measures were employed and schizophrenics were compared with controls on both tasks, a relatively greater deficiency on one task could be taken as evidence for a *differential* deficit. This strategy had the added advantage of reducing somewhat the interpretative problem posed by "nuisance variables" such as the sociomedical consequences of the disorder (medication, institutionalization, etc.). It could often be argued that such third-variable alternatives could not provide a viable explanation for any group-by-task interaction that was found (Neale & Oltmanns, 1980).

The differential-deficit strategy was, however, shown to have a serious flaw, one that required substantial methodological rehabilitation. Chapman and Chapman (1973) argued convincingly that an artifactual differential deficit may be produced in any single experiment by an inappropriate selection of dependent measures. They reasoned that if one accepts the notion of a general cognitive deficit in schizophrenia (i.e., that schizophrenics in general tend to perform more poorly than normal controls on many cognitive tasks), differential performance on two tasks might occur simply as a function of the unequal discriminating power of the tasks chosen. That is, more reliable, and therefore more discriminating, tasks might produce group differences that are absent when less discriminating tasks are employed. To remedy this situation, the Chapmans (1973, 1978) proposed that experimental and control tasks must be made equivalent in both difficulty and reliability.

As Blaney (1978) has pointed out, the Chapmans' solution to the discrimination problem still left serious unresolved dilemmas in the task-oriented approach. Their exclusive focus on reliability and discrimination totally neglected problems of construct validity. Ensuring that tasks were reliable and equally discriminating did not guarantee that such tasks were measuring homogeneous constructs. In the likely event that a task tapped multiple processes, it was impossible to determine which process was responsible for any differences that were obtained.

More important, however, the Chapmans' solution of balancing psychometric characteristics, particularly level of difficulty, does not in most instances afford an appropriate solution for process-oriented researchers, since it can often be achieved only at the expense of confounding the hypothetical processes being compared. In many information processing and cognitive paradigms, stimulus and task-difficulty level provide an essential manipulation for assessing underlying hypothetical processes. The Kroll and Hershenson (1980) model I discussed earlier is an excellent example. Their model hypothesizes that it is the difficulty of stimulus discriminability that determines whether a particular response can be made by the wholistic processor or whether the decision must be passed on to the sequential, analytic processor. Various manipulations of stimulus discriminability constitute an essential component for testing their model. Here, to match on discrimination difficulty is to unmatch on process. This reliance on difficulty manipulation is so prevalent in cognitive paradigms that to require matched tasks would eliminate many powerful analytic tools from the process-oriented researcher's arsenal. Fortunately, such a requirement is not necessary, since the process approach yields its own strategies for addressing the artifact problem.

To understand how a process-oriented research approach is able to finesse these methodological dilemmas, it is necessary to consider the available strategies within the larger context of the philosophy of science. Although I share Reichenbach's (1958) concern that scientists should get on with the business of science and leave philosophical inquiry to more qualified specialists, lest such concerns paralyze the scientist's "pioneering spirit," I believe that in this instance some philosophical reflection can be helpful in advancing the scientific enterprise.

Basically, the major methodological distinction between the task and process orientations lies in the degree to which each relies on theoretical, a priori models to guide the search for truth. Those who use a task orientation lean more heavily toward an inductivist, Baconian strategy, hoping that the presuppositionless observation of performance differences will yield a consistent description of schizophrenics' cognitive behavior that can in some way provide a "marker" for this disorder. This "marker" can serve as a feature to distinguish schizophrenics from those with other psychopathologies, as a prodromal indicator of those vulnerable to the disorder, as a sign predictive of the recurrence of a psychotic episode, and so forth. The emphasis here is on the sign or symptom value of the task and its potential as a discriminating factor.

The task-oriented approach is, of course, never completely atheoretical. As Popper (1972) has convincingly demonstrated, the very selection of what to observe, or in this case what tasks to administer, necessarily implies the application of some theory, however vague or ineffable. It was also the case that before the influx of the new perceptual and cognitive theories, researchers attempted to generate descriptive theories of schizophrenics' cognitive deficiencies that integrated performance differences on various tasks. Lacking precise models and paradigms, such theories had to remain inexact, and thus they were difficult to test. Consequently, researchers had little choice but to continue gathering valid individual bits of discriminating, descriptive task data, hoping that such an accumulation would form the basis for a more theoretical formulation of the disorder. They were thereby forced because of their inadequate models to rely more on induction, a method that has been described as the "despair of philosophy" (Whitehead, 1925). With the advances in information processing and cognitive psychology models, dependence on induction is no longer mandatory. Coupled with Popper's (1959, 1972) solution to the induction dilemma, which restored logic to science and gave a firm philosophical base to a theoretical orientation, these new models

provided important techniques to advance research on schizophrenics' cognitive deficiencies.

Popper (1959, 1972) has defended the basic premise that mere
repeatability of observation can never justify a universal. In fact,
more generally, he has argued that in the logic of science it is
impossible to prove or justify any hypothesis. Any such attempt
necessarily results in a fallacious affirmation of the consequent.
Rather, one must employ a valid logical argument, *modus tollens*
$(A \rightarrow B, \sim B, \therefore \sim A)$. Since it is valid only to disconfirm a theory, one
enhances the credibility of a particular theory by eliminating
competing hypotheses. Valid hypotheses are statements that are
determined to have low probability of future disconfirmation—
provided, of course, that they are highly falsifiable, so that they can
be eliminated when wrong. Objective criteria for such theories can
be specified (Popper, 1959). Such theories, in contrast to vague or
tautological statements, must have high empirical content (i.e., be
precise) and high explanatory power (universality) so that from
them a large range of specific testable states can be deduced. Popper
(1959) has argued that such precision and universality will result in
theories that have a lower prior probability of being true and
therefore are more falsifiable.

Several obvious conclusions for the process-oriented researcher
of schizophrenics' cognitive deficit immediately follow from this
philosophical position. First, theory construction is essential for
scientific progress. Second, advancement of our knowledge hinges
on our ability to create falsifable theories that can be tested in
situations that put them at grave risk of disconfirmation. A particular theory is corroborated by surviving severe tests of its validity,
and the greater the diversity and difficulty of such tests, the greater
a theory's validity. Indeed, both inductivists and noninductivists
alike would agree that such refutatory or negative evidence contributes more to our knowledge than confirmatory evidence. Third,
the only way to achieve falsifiability is to create theories that make
precise predictions about particular performance patterns, and from
which we can derive many diverse predictions.

Cognitive psychology has matured sufficiently, especially in the
area of early visual processing, that not only does it provide paradigms that yield precise, predictable results, but also, as exemplified
in the cognitive research I reviewed, many of its structures and
processes can be measured by several paradigms. Thus, the process-oriented researcher can assess a particular process from several

perspectives. Although the outcomes of these different measures are not such that they provide exactly equivalent estimates of the same theoretical quantity, they are sufficiently precise to permit specific predictions in advance of testing of the *function patterns* that would occur under conditions of adequate and inadequate performance. Thus, an analogy of Feigl's "triangulation of logical space" (Meehl, 1978) can be achieved by assessing the consistency of performance of schizophrenics across these multiple processing paradigms. Armed with such theories, we can take advantage of several research strategies for addressing the Chapmans' psychometric artifact problem that elude the task-oriented researcher. All four of the process-oriented solutions I will discuss center on the use of clear a priori theoretical models and their quantification in specific terms to guide the designing of experiments and the interpretation of their results. Consistent with their Popperian roots, each solution demands that such theories be highly falsifiable and that experiments be designed to put them at high risk for disconfirmation.

The first strategy is eminently consistent with Popperian principles, since it works to *disconfirm* alternative specific deficit theories—or, more positively put, it seeks to demonstrate the *adequacy* of schizophrenics' abilities in particular stages or processes. This strategy works against schizophrenics' general cognitive deficiencies and can avoid the pitfalls of the psychometric artifact by *convincingly* demonstrating competence. The simple lack of *between-group differences* would not constitute convincing evidence, since this same result could be obtained simply by an inappropriate choice of task level (a ceiling or floor effect) or by using an unreliable task. Convincing evidence means that both schizophrenics and controls must achieve a predicted *pattern* of performance either across the levels of a well-validated task or across a number of theoretically integrated tasks that have been shown to tap various components of a process. If both groups perform in accord with the specific predictions of a cognitive model (no group-by-levels interaction and significant *within*-group-levels performance differences in the appropriate directions), this would be convincing prima facie evidence of the adequacy of the assessed process. Many examples of such findings were reviewed in the first section of this chapter. For instance, the data supporting the intactness of schizophrenics' iconic decay (Knight et al., 1978; Spaulding et al., 1980) and the adequacy of schizophrenics' visual and memory search (Russell & R. G. Knight, 1977; Russell et al., 1980) are good examples of this strategy. It would be difficult to argue that schizophrenics' parallel decay slopes or search functions are the product of anything but adequate processing capacities. A general deficit explanation, even buffered with a psychometric artifact, could not explain such competence. This general strategy has been used widely in studying a number of cognitive as well as perceptual skills in schizophrenics (Knight & Sims-Knight, 1980; Koh, 1978; Rochester, 1978; Rochester, Harris & Seeman, 1973).

The second, third, and fourth strategies take advantage of the diversity of converging paradigms that have been developed in cognitive psychology. The numerous paradigms not only give us readily available, well-validated experimental models that can be used to put a particular deficit theory at severe risk for disconfirmation, but also provide enough variety and flexibility of design so we can create experiments that help circumvent the psychometric artifact dilemma. The key to these solutions lies in having a sufficient grasp of the operation of the hypothesized deficient process so that the pattern of results predicted for the malfunctioning of this process cannot be predicted by a general cognitive deficit. In such an approach the general deficit hypothesis, which is the alternative explanation requiring the Chapmans' psychometric controls, becomes a competing model. It is the task of the process-oriented researcher to demonstrate the inferior explanatory power of this model and thereby discount the artifactual interpretation.

The second strategy, which is the rarest but the most powerful, uses this variety and flexibility of design to create experiments in which the hypothesized deficiency in schizophrenics' processing predicts their *superiority* of performance in a particular condition. An excellent example of this strategy is Place and Gilmore's (1980) numerosity task, in which the perceptual organization deficit actually made poor-prognosis schizophrenics perform better than controls in those conditions in which normals' intact automatic organizational ability intefered with completing the task. Clearly, such a finding cannot be explained by a general cognitive deficit, and thus the psychometric artifact interpretation cannot apply to this study. Moreover, since both tasks (distraction and orientation) were found to discriminate in opposite directions, matching could not change the direction of differences.

The third and fourth strategies cannot eliminate the psychometric artifact interpretation in a single experiment as do the first two. Rather, they seek to establish a pattern of results over a series of studies that is both consistent with the hypothesized specific deficit model and either inconsistent with predictions from the general deficit model (the relative superiority strategy) or problematic for that model (the multiparadigm strategies). They thereby support the superior explanatory and predictive power of the specific over the general deficit model and reduce the probability that the results are artifactual.

The third strategy is closely related to the superior performance strategy described above but requires only relative rather than absolute performance superiority by the schizophrenics. Since relative superiority still results in inferior performance by schizophrenics, a single such finding, even if compared with an established baseline performance, could be explained by a general deficit. For instance, an experimental condition that introduced a manipulation that negatively affected controls' performance but did not affect schizophrenics' performance could easily be interpreted as having *less* discriminating power than the baseline control condition. The key to this strategy lies in a knowledge both of ways the operation of a particular process can facilitate and interfere with performance and of those task and stimulus characteristics that increase and decrease the demands placed on a particular process. By manipulating the effects of a process and the demands placed on the operation of that process, one can create across a number of studies a *pattern* of relatively superior and inferior performances compared with an established baseline that would be inconsistent with a general cognitive deficit.

An example of a paradigm that can be structured so that an adequately functioning perceptual organization will facilitate or interfere with performance is the Flanker Test (Eriksen & Eriksen, 1974; LaBerge, 1981).[2] In this method one directs a subject's attention to one item or attribute and measures the processing of another item. In its original form (Eriksen & Eriksen, 1974), subjects were asked to identify target letters when noise letters flanked the target on either side—thus the name Flanker Test. Since normals process the "flanker" stimuli automatically, and since the nature of the

2. Although this hypothetical example serves to illustrate the relative-superiority strategy, it must be emphasized that the Flanker paradigm cannot be used in the manner described until several crucial preliminary studies have been completed. Specifically, for this paradigm to assess poor premorbids' perceptual organization, it must first be demonstrated that their facilitation and inhibition (Proctor, 1981; Krueger & Shapiro, 1981) are functioning adequately in their wholistic processing stage.

relation of the target to the flanker affects speed of processing of the target (i.e., facilitates or inhibits the processing of the target), the task can be used effectively to assess the influence of the units that are automatically chunked and processed from the flanker. Thus it can be set up so that the automaticity is reflected in either a decrement or an increment in performance. Consequently, if poor-prognosis schizophrenics are deficient in their unitization (perceptual organization), they will exhibit no decrement in processing the target where normals will be handicapped, and they will be less able to benefit from conditions where normals are facilitated. Since the typical dependent measure in this task is the latency of target identification, superiority of the schizophrenics' performance would not be expected in any condition (Nuechterlein, 1977). Still, poor-prognosis schizophrenics' relative performance superiority, produced by their immunity to factors that are detrimental to normals' performance, would be difficult to explain by a general deficit model.

This design still requires some buttressing. It could be argued that the immunity of the schizophrenics to manipulation of the flankers simply reflects a general inability to cope with the task and their lack of sensitivity to any manipulations. Manipulation of *target* stimulus characteristics that increase and decrease the demands on perceptual organization capacities could counter this interpretation while yielding additional corroboration of the perceptual organization deficit model. Increasing such target demands should tax poor-prognosis schizophrenics' capabilities more than normals'; decreasing demands on perceptual organization should be more helpful to schizophrenics than to normals (Cox & Leventhal, 1978). The greater responsivity of schizophrenics to target manipulations would counter the criticism that their baseline and flanker performances are simply due to a basement effect that renders them insensitive to manipulations.

In this hypothetical example, the validity of the model would be corroborated by its ability to avoid disconfirmation in a variety of specific, jeopardizing tests. Moreover, the full series of studies, if consistent with the model, would create a pattern incompatible with the general deficit explanation. Why would poor-prognosis schizophrenics be immune to some factors that make normals worse and get much worse under conditions that have little effect on normals if their problem is simply general cognitive inefficiency? The inapplicability of the general deficit model would obviate the psychometric artifact interpretation. Indeed, the crucial issue here is not so much the differential discriminability between normals and schizophrenics on each condition as it is the pattern of responding of each group across conditions. Only the specific deficit model could predict the pattern. Therefore only this model survives disconfirmation.

The importance of an integrated series of studies is further exemplified by the Cox and Leventhal (1978) study discussed earlier. This study sought to establish the validity of a "preattentive" processing deficiency in poor-prognosis schizophrenics by demonstrating their differential improvement (i.e., relative superiority) compared with normals and good-prognosis schizophrenics under conditions that reduced demands on this process. Unfortunately, in all three tasks employed, the "enriched" conditions that placed fewer demands on perceptual organization were easier than the standard experimental tasks, leaving their results vulnerable to the psychometric artifact interpretation, since it might be argued that the "enriched" conditions were less discriminating because they were less reliable. Thus, while the study corroborated the perceptual organization model, it was confounded with a general deficit explanation. The multistudy approach I have described is designed to avoid this confounding.

The relative superiority strategy aims at finding tasks in which the pattern of results across tasks predicted by the specific deficit model will be inconsistent with and therefore disconfirm a general deficit explanation. Since the predictions of a general deficit model tend to remain vague because of their dependence on the fickle comparative psychometric characteristics of tasks and conditions, such an a priori specification of an inconsistent pattern is unrealistic for many information processing and cognitive tasks. Yet such tasks may be potentially important tools for further specifying the nature of schizophrenics' processing deficiencies. Within a process orientation we can find a basic rationale for guiding our use of such tasks and several strategies that will minimize the risks of being duped by artifactual results. I call this fourth group of strategies multiparadigmatic because their rationale focuses on the ability of the proposed deficit model to make specific a priori predictions of the pattern of results expected across several paradigms for both the adequate and the inadequate functioning of a process. As was true of the relative superiority strategy, this group of strategies requires a series of studies that address a single issue. The rationale hinges on the assumption that there is a small likelihood that the particular pattern of results predicted by the specific deficit model across multiple paradigms will coincide exactly with differential task or condition discriminability. The various strategies employed are all aimed at reducing the probability of such a confounding. To the degree that these strategies are successful, it can be argued that the consistent attainment of predicted patterns across a diversity of paradigms not only corroborates the specific model, but also gives reasonable assurance of the low risk that a general deficit might produce such results through a complex pattern of differential reliabilities.

The first of these multiparadigmatic strategies aims at reducing the variance of reliability among tasks by choosing those tasks whose consistency has been well established and demonstrating with controls that the particular versions of the task adapted for use with a psychopathological population closely replicate the predicted performance pattern. Although this does not assess reliability in the traditional way, it should achieve a similar end, since it is unlikely that the consistent replication of complex patterns of responding could be attained by tasks that did not have good reliability. One could also assess coefficient alphas within each condition as an additional check, but one should not choose tasks solely on the basis of high internal consistency values. Indeed, for our purposes we are more concerned with the consistency of the *pattern*, for which internal consistency within conditions is not a sufficient criterion. The strategy of choosing tasks with well-established patterns does not, of course, in any way guarantee the equality of reliability of tasks and conditions and is not suggested as a shortcut to the matching on discrimination. It is not appropriate for that purpose (Chapman & Chapman, 1978). To the degree, however, that careful selection and pretesting of paradigms can reduce the variance of reliability among various tasks and can ensure that only tasks of reasonable reliability are employed, the effects of differential discriminability can be attenuated.

The goal of the second multiparadigmatic strategy is to attempt whenever possible to choose or construct paradigms in which the predictions of the specific deficit model are not confounded with the obvious predictions of a general deficit coupled with differential task or condition discriminability. The Cox and Leventhal (1978) study I discussed above is an example of a paradigm in which the two predictions are completely confounded. Our backward-masking picture paradigm (Knight et al., Note 1) is an example of a task in which the two models are not confounded. First, our predictions were all relative to each group's no-mask baseline, removing some degree of general performance differences. Second, the critical prediction for the specific model was the level and slope of the decay function of the pattern mask relative to a random noise and cognitive mask. One could postulate several obvious patterns that might be expected if a general deficit were determining performance. The relative level of the pattern mask is not one of these. It is important to note that the difference between this strategy and the relative superiority strategy described earlier is that the pattern predicted by the model is not theoretically inconsistent with a general deficit and does not disconfirm it. It simply is not confounded with the obvious a priori predictions of a general deficit model. When a general performance deficit is a viable assumption, the artifactual effects of differential discriminability are so pervasive that any discrimination found could always post hoc be attributed to it. Since this artifact provides such a wide interpretive flexibility, any study that either lacks evidence directly disconfirming the general deficit interpretation or does not match tasks for discriminability could be challenged. Thus, although the pattern of results of our masking study suggests the low probability of an artifactual interpretation, it cannot completely escape this criticism. While in this single instance the low-probability artifactual explanation might have some plausibility, an increase in the number of additional corroborating studies, similarly designed but from diverse paradigms, decreases the credibility of the artifactual explanation.

In constructing studies for the multiparadigmatic strategy, other factors can also contribute to reducing the probability of artifactual results. One should of course make certain, in line with the logic of the differential deficit strategy, that one assesses tasks or conditions measuring processes that are hypothesized to be intact in schizophrenics. As I discussed earlier in my consideration of the first general strategy, disconfirming deficits, the simple lack of significant differences from controls on a single task provides weak support at best for the adequacy of schizophrenics' ability in a process, since low task-discriminatory power might produce the same result. Convincing support can be established only by the production of a predicted pattern across tasks or conditions. For instance, several performance characteristics of the poor premorbid schizophrenics on the random noise and cognitive mask conditions of our picture masking study indicate the adequacy of their performance in these conditions—in particular that they reached equivalent performance with the no-mask baseline at the same SOAs as normals and that both groups had similar decay slopes for both masking conditions. The demonstration of competency in nondeficient conditions, especially in conditions that bracket the predicted deficiency, indicates that the level of the task is sufficiently sensitive to the subjects' abilities, that lack of motivation or failure to engage the task cannot explain the results, and that if a "general" deficit is operating, the extent of this deficiency is limited and thus the name seems inappropriate.

Often, adapting cognitive paradigms for administration to psychotics is a difficult undertaking requiring extensive piloting. It is necessary to ensure not only that the tasks are accessible to patients, but also that they engage them and neither frustrate them with numerous discriminations beyond their capabilities nor require so many trials that they become bored and withdraw. If these basic characteristics are not achieved, the probability of eliciting a general deficit pattern of responding will be high. Moreover, within these confines it is essential that in the new adapted paradigm the predicted response patterns of the original paradigm are closely replicated with controls. Without this basic requirement the study is uninterpretable.

Finally, when possible, tasks should be chosen that provide, within the limits of the model being tested, the widest possible range of difficulty levels. This may in certain instances permit comparisons of the differential predictions of a specific model and the general deficit model. The general model will always predict greater discriminability at moderate difficulty levels. As conditions become more or less difficult, the variance of responding is restricted and the upper limit of reliability is reduced. A finding that a range of difficulty levels within a particular condition does not affect group discrimination (e.g., Knight, Sims-Knight, & Petchers-Cassell, 1977) lowers the probability that the result is produced by the psychometric artifact.

As we have seen, this final group of strategies aims at minimizing the potential effects of a general deficit while at the same time severely testing a specific model. Its weakness, compared with the absolute and relative superiority strategies, is that it does not clearly disconfirm the general deficit explanation. It only reduces its plausibility. It makes available to the researcher, however, those powerful, potentially informative paradigms that cannot be structured to disconfirm the general deficit. It has the advantage over the Chapmans' solution that it does not run the risk of confounding underlying processes by imposing matching on difficulty level. The cost of this advantage is that one study is inadequate to eliminate the general deficit explanation. If one pursues this solution with an awareness of the reliability problem and builds into one's designs as many as possible of the strategies I have discussed, the probability of hunting a snark for too long can be minimized and additional important data about the nature of the process being investigated can be gathered in each study.

It must be stressed that the efficacy of this strategy is anchored in the specificity of the a priori predictions generated by a model. Without this criterion outside of the task, one is vulnerable to being duped by artifacts and is forced to fall back to a psychometric solution for the general deficit problem. Carbotte's (1978) argument for a "converging operations" solution to the psychometric artifact missed this crucial point and thus did not provide a convincing alternative to matching. She seems to believe that simply choosing an information processing or cognitive paradigm ipso facto frees one from the concerns of differential discriminatory power. It does not. Too often studies choose a paradigm simply because it is "an interesting way to measure attention" and "might provide some insight into the hypothesized attention deficit in schizophrenia." All such studies are vulnerable to the Chapmans' criticisms and should be required to defend their results against the artifact interpretation.

Both for corroboration of the specific deficit model and for reduction of the probability of the general deficit explanation, the multiparadigmatic strategies I have outlined require consistency of prediction across a series of diverse but theoretically related paradigms. The mere replication of the same paradigm does not convincingly test a theory (Meehl, 1978) or dispel the psychometric artifact explanation. Thus the work of Saccuzzo, Braff, and their colleagues reviewed earlier, though important in specifying the subpopulation of schizophrenics vulnerable to backward-masking deficits and discounting various nuisance variables, does not by itself reduce general deficit criticisms. Their work is a good example of a task-oriented rather than a process-oriented approach. Although they have employed a well-established information processing paradigm, their studies have focused on the "marker" characteristics of their particular version of backward-masking paradigm rather than on identifying the mechanisms responsible for poor-prognosis schizophrenics' deficit on this task.

As I have been describing the strategies for countering the effects of a general deficit model, I have chosen examples from the early visual processing literature. It should be evident from these examples that there is thus far a strong case that the general deficit model has grave difficulties accounting for the body of results supporting a perceptual organization model. Other closely related deficits have been disconfirmed (Knight et al., 1978; Russell et al., 1980; Russell & R. G. Knight, 1977; Spaulding et al., 1980). One important study has demonstrated the superiority of schizophrenics' performance because of their deficient perceptual organization (Place & Gilmore, 1980). Finally, the results of a number of studies using multiple paradigms (e.g., Cox & Leventhal, 1978; Knight, Sherer, & Shapiro, 1977; Saccuzzo & Braff, 1981; Knight et al., Note 1) converge on this specific deficit. It must be admitted, of course, that not all of the studies in the multiparadigmatic example have employed the entire group of strategies I have suggested, and only two of these studies actually had a priori models that tested aspects of perceptual organization. To the degree that they have not included these important strategies, these studies are vulnerable to the general deficit explanation and require additional studies to bolster their position. On balance, however, the three strategies thus far employed corroborate that a specific deficit has been isolated. The poorer explanatory power of a general deficit for the pattern of results obtained in these studies does not relieve us of the need to continue striving to control for its possible consequences. Failure to do so will decrease the sensitivity of our investigations and make our results vulnerable to artifacts. Since we can address this alternative explanation without compromising the basic tenets of the process orientation, there is no reason to avoid this challenge.

Although most of my comments on the methodological advantages of a process-oriented approach have been directed at the important general deficit/psychometric artifact problem, the strategies described are more generally applicable to dealing with numerous nuisance variables that plague schizophrenia research (e.g., medication, patient motivation and cooperation, hospitalization; see Salzinger's chapter in this volume for a more detailed description of these variables). To the degree that our models are able to predict specific patterns of performance, despite the noise these nuisance variables contribute, we can be confident that we are not reading meaning into error variance. Once again, the greater the number of experiments in which our model can predict, the more certain of its validity we can be, especially if we can demonstrate that these nuisance variables vary across studies. Although it is possible that nuisance variables could coalesce to generate the complex patterns predicted by the model, the probability is sufficiently low to make it implausible. The major difficulty with the process solution to this problem, as I will discuss in more detail in the next section, occurs when our models do not predict the pattern of results.

One last point must be made on the benefits of the process orientation before I briefly examine the problems of this approach. As I have repeatedly emphasized, the key element in the process approach is the requirement of theory building—of creating specific, clear, falsifiable models. The inherent abstraction of such models benefits generativity. Creating a model can and should lead to new ways of thinking that reveal hitherto unknown relations (Whitehead, 1925, 1948). It can also provide connective links among processes whose relatedness is suspected, but where not even crude structures are available to bridge the gaps between them. One criterion for a viable model is the degree to which it sparks such connective jumps. Several examples of this kind of integration generated from the perceptual organization model were given in the second section of this chapter. More speculative links to other, more physiologically based areas are also possible. For instance, since such perceptual organization seems to be a right-hemisphere function (Moscovitch, 1979), a dysfunction in such organization could lead to the left-hemisphere overcompensation proposed by Walker and McGuire (1982). If a model of schizophrenics' cognitive deficit is to be truly generative, it must ultimately interface with the biological aspects of the disorder.

SOURCES OF DIFFICULTY IN THE PROCESS ORIENTATION

Although the process approach provides a general philosophical framework and specific methodological strategies for attacking some of the major problems facing researchers of schizophrenics' cognitive deficiencies, it is by no means a panacea. Many difficulties remain, some of which are intrinsic to the approach itself. In this section I will briefly discuss five of the more important ones: the difficulty of the multiplicity and flux of cognitive models, the need to develop and employ more appropriate and specific model-testing statistics, the problem of auxiliary theories, the compensatory skills dilemma, and the ever present taxonomic concerns. Each could be the focus of an entire paper. My purpose here is simply to highlight the general parameters of each problem.

The first difficulty for the process-oriented psychopathologist involves the constant change in existing cognitive models and the frequent presence of opposing models to explain the same phenomena. Since our ability to specify schizophrenics' deficit is limited both by the validity and resolution of existing models and by the sensitivity of the measures that have been developed to test these models, choosing the best model is a constant concern. In reviewing the literature, I noted that many early information processing studies on schizophrenics were guided by the classical iconic imagery model. This model is now being challenged for many reasons (Haber, 1983; Long, 1980; Turvey, 1977). Indeed, it was a newer formulation of early processing (Phillips, 1974; Potter, 1976) that ultimately led me to the integration I have presented. The conflicting findings of the schizophrenia research could not be reconciled within the classical model. Thus, specific advances in cognitive psychology helped to resolve conflicts I encountered in my research on schizophrenics. In fairness, it is important to point out that these very conflicts in the schizophrenia research motivated my search for better models in the normal cognitive literature, suggesting that, just as the investigation of brain-damaged patients can inform cognitive theories (Posner, 1981, 1982; Posner, Cohen, & Rafal, 1982), so too research on schizophrenics has the potential of advancing the cognitive field.

There currently exist numerous paradigms that can advance our knowledge about schizophrenics' processing deficiencies. I have touched on only a smattering in my review. From the progress that has already been made, it should be obvious that we can continue to make headway even with models that will eventually be replaced. The data from the Sperling and backward-masking paradigms are still useful, even though they were generated within a questionable model. It is also clear, however, that a more complete specification of the hypothesized perceptual organization dysfunction must await advances in our understanding of the nature of this early automatic unitization (LaBerge, 1981). Are there structures that lend themselves more easily to automatic processing? We know that infants respond to some elementary patterns at birth (e.g., Fantz, Fagan, & Miranda, 1975; Salapatek, 1975), and it has been demonstrated that three-month-old infants can detect perceptual invariance in some circumstances (Milewski, 1979; Gibson, Owsley, Walker, & Megaw-Nyce, 1979). Little is known, however, about the differential development of various perceptual structures. Do some kinds of perceptual organizations develop earlier than others? Are some learned more easily than others? Which structures are more likely to go awry in the development of schizophrenics? All of these are unanswered questions that are important for advancing our understanding of schizophrenics' cognitive deficit.

The first difficulty reflects, of course, the more general issue in science that all models are temporary structures and will eventually be replaced by superior versions (Popper, 1972, 1974). Although because of their abstract nature models are inherently artificial surrogates for the real world, they are not simply convenient summaries of empirical laws (Feigl, 1962) and cannot be dismissed, as Chapman and Chapman (1978) suggest, as existing only "in the eye of the beholder." As I discussed earlier, objective criteria for a model's viability can be established (Popper, 1959). Ironically, although the continuing change in models in a particular area and the presence of a multiplicity of models indicate that a convincing theoretical explanation of a process has not yet been found, they also reflect the vitality of the research in that area. So, while the instabilities of models of normal cognition make our task as experimental psychopathologists more difficult, that same process of theoretical development presages new understanding that will help to advance our knowledge of schizophrenics' processing deficiencies.

The second major difficulty for the process-oriented researcher involves the development and use of appropriate quantitative methods and statistical techniques to assist in testing the validity of our hypothesized models. Meehl (1978), in his scathing critique of the misapplication of significance testing in much of "soft" psychology, has condemned the frequent practice of refuting a straw-man null hypothesis and thinking that such a manipulation of the statistical power function amounts to anything but a "feeble corroboration of a theory." To remedy this situation Meehl has called for new quantitative techniques to assess the validity of theories and has offered his taxometric *consistency tests* as an example of a solution. Although I agree with the major thrust of Meehl's critique—that unless social scientists pay closer attention to their theoretical assumptions and conceptual frameworks no system of statistics will suffice—it strikes me that the real culprit is the weak null hypotheses and not significance testing per se. For instance, the process-oriented strategies that I have offered to solve the methodological dilemmas in research in schizophrenics' cognitive deficit do not suffer from Meehl's straw-man syndrome. Indeed, it could be argued (as I will argue below) that it is more likely that the substantial "noise" of error variance in this area might drown out the two- or three-way interaction "signals" that are required for corroboration of a specific deficit theory. More generally, it seems that it is how we use our significance tests, not the tests themselves, that is the problem. For example, we could avoid playing power function games if our models would simply specify what constitutes meaningful effect sizes (Cohen, 1969) and if a reasonable number of subjects were established a priori to test the model's predictions. More important, I agree with Meehl that it is time we move beyond the simple manipulation of our accustomed significance tests and develop theories that drive our statistical inquiries and proper statistics to test our models. The statistical tools for adequate model testing are available (Kerlinger & Pedhazur, 1973), and indeed there are some good examples of specific model-testing techniques (Bamber, 1979). One quantitative development that had been lacking until recently was the statistical integration of the experimental approach of the cognitive psychologists with the classical *nomological network* of Cronbach and Meehl (1955), which was developed and described in the context of individual difference research and is thus more amenable to correlational analysis. Embretson's (1983) beginning work along these lines is a welcome advance. Ultimately such an integration will be crucial to our ability to relate research on cognitive deficits to the complexly interrelated symptoms, behaviors, and physiological deficiencies of schizophrenics.

The third problem focuses on determining when disconfirmatory evidence is sufficiently convincing that it requires the rejection of a theory. This has been a long-standing problem in psychology (Cronbach & Meehl, 1955; Meehl, 1978) and has been particularly troublesome in experimental psychopathology (Maher, 1966). Central to this difficulty is the role played by "saving" or auxiliary theories that can be postulated as explanations for the failure of any particular experiment to corroborate the theory being tested (Lakatos, 1970). If an observation derived from a theory is disconfirmed, it is often difficult to determine whether the target theory itself, the auxiliary theories that link it to the measured observables, or some experimental particular was responsible for the negative result (Meehl, 1978). Thus the power of modus tollens is weakened to the degree that the theory is protected from disconfirmation by a buffer of auxiliary theories. As Meehl (1978) has pointed out, this situation is even more acutely problematic in certain areas of "soft" psychology where the independent testing of auxiliary theories is difficult and such theories face numerous methodological and "intrinsic subject matter" hazards (Meehl describes 20 such subject-matter difficulties). In addition, in some areas of psychology the connective link between the substantive theory and its auxiliaries may be so loose and inconsequential that the complete discrediting of an auxiliary theory leaves the substantive theory unscathed.

The dilemma the buffering effects of such auxiliaries pose to the process-oriented researcher of schizophrenics' cognitive deficiencies is substantial. I have argued that the major deterrent to the problems of general performance deficits and their accompanying threat of artifactual results owing to the psychometric characteristics of specific tasks lies in the ability of a model to predict complex performance patterns. Failure to predict such patterns should in strict Popperian logic lead us to conclude that we have not successfully isolated a specific cognitive deficit in schizophrenics. If a model has, however, been successful in predicting performance patterns in previous paradigms, it is not likely that we would so easily discard it. Rather, we would search for paradigm-specific or possibly typology-related auxiliary theory explanations, or we would look for experimental particulars like peculiar sampling or unusual medication schedules to bear the blame for the failure. Only after exhausting these alternative explanations would we take the negative results as a serious threat to the model. It is not difficult to see that such hedging, even though it can be defended as a research strategy (Meehl, 1978; O'Hear, 1980), greatly complicates the task of testing models of schizophrenics' cognitive processes, especially if one is using a multistudy, multiparadigm approach to solve the general deficit problem. It is most likely that models with a track record of some predictive success would be abandoned only when a study found results inconsistent with that model and these same results were also predicted a priori by a competing model. In such a case it might be demanded not only that the victorious model or theory get the right result, but also that it suggest reasons why the rival theory did not (Feyerabend, 1965). This of course puts the heavy burden on experimental psychopathologists to know cognitive models and paradigms well enough to create such discriminating experiments and to be motivated to put their pet theories to severe experimental tests.

In the general area of attention research there has historically been a relatively close link between substantive and auxiliary theories. Posner (1982), in a historical review, has argued that past processing theories have been incorporated into the basic methodology of studying attention so that both modern substantive theories and their measurement (auxiliary) base derive from the same source and are intimately connected. A rejection of the measurement base would indeed put the theories in jeopardy. For example, recent questioning of certain information processing measurement strategies has challenged some basic theoretical structures as artifacts of these measurement techniques (Haber, 1983). This close tie between substantive theory and measurement technique cannot, however, be unquestioningly assumed to operate in the assessment of schizophrenics' cognition. Reaction time is a good example of a dependent measure that has been both theoretically and methodologically important in information processing theories (Posner, 1982) and is the major dependent variable in many paradigms that might clarify schizophrenics' processing deficiencies. Unfortunately, it might prove problematic as an auxiliary measurement theory to assess schizophrenics' processing. The domain of variables that contributes to schizophrenics' reaction times is not yet completely clear. Recently, motor components (Rosofsky, Levin, & Holzman, 1982; Walker & Green, 1982) have been implicated, substantially complicating the more traditional cognitive processing explanations of schizophrenics' reaction time deficiencies. It seems that, in addition to the methodological problems of poor deficit sensitivity created by schizophrenics' long latencies and large response variances, we are now faced with the possibility that at least some of the variance of schizophrenics' reaction times is being contributed by a deficiency other than the one being assessed. Thus, to disconfirm a substantive theory of schizophrenics' processing using response latency requires demonstration that in the particular paradigm being employed this dependent measure is actually sensitive to the process being tested and not to some related deficit. This can, of course, be achieved only if one can specify a priori a pattern that implicates a specific deficit as opposed to psychomotor retardation or, better still, if one can predict a pattern that corroborates a competing deficit model. Not finding a predicted pattern could simply be a failure of the appropriateness of the auxiliary response latency theory for assessing schizophrenics' processing.

The fourth major difficulty is another that relates to the need to ensure that our measures accurately reflect performance on the target process. As Jenkins (1973, p. 159) has indicated, the "human being is a very flexible psychological machine: he is capable of being either a very simple machine or a very complex one." He is capable in some instances of substituting alternative strategies or processes to accomplish a particular goal. This point is well supported in the expert/novice literature, where it has been demonstrated that the expert has developed processing strategies that are lacking in the novice (see, e.g., review by Larkin, McDermott, Simon, & Simon, 1980). If the task is simple enough, both groups can achieve adequate performance, even though they might use different strategies. It is inappropriate to conclude from such data either that the expert does not have the more advanced strategy or that the novice possesses the expert's skill. So too, it is quite possible for us to structure a "perceptual organization" task that is simple enough that schizophrenics could perform it with a compensatory "controlled" or "sequential, analytic" processing strategy. Such data cannot be used to support the functional adequacy of schizophrenics' perceptual organization. It is therefore the difficult task of experimental psychopathologists to make certain they are adequately assessing the target process, while at the same time making the task sufficiently accessible to schizophrenics that they do not preclude adequate performance by eliciting either a general or an alternative deficit.

A fifth and final difficulty that plagues the process-oriented researcher is exclusive neither to the theoretically oriented nor to the investigator of schizophrenia. This is the pervasive problem of individual and subgroup differences. Even in research on normal populations it has been recognized that it is important to consider taxonomies of attention (Posner & Rothbart, 1981) and to be concerned with what skills and abilities different groups of subjects bring to cognitive tasks (Jenkins, 1981). This "difficulty" has been elevated to a major taxonomic and diagnostic concern in the area of schizophrenia, where investigators hold a wide range of opinions even on the existence (Spitzer, Williams, & Skodol, 1980) or nonexistence (Sarbin & Mancuso, 1980) of the disorder. Although I am obviously in agreement with those who think that ultimately some specifiable disorder or disorders will be identified by the label "schizophrenic," I am also troubled by the diagnostic flux in this area. It has been shown empirically that different research criteria for schizophrenia categorize the same populations in diverse ways (Overall & Hollister, 1979) and that each system relies heavily on different subject characteristics in the selection process (Marvinney, Rosenberg, & Knight, Note 4). Such variance in selection criteria could have substantial impact on the outcome of cognitive studies of schizophrenics. For example, in our backward-masking study, most of the nonschizophrenic psychotics had been diagnosed as schizophrenic by ward psychiatrists. The majority of these patients in this particular study happened to have poor premorbid histories. Had it not been our practice to rediagnose all patients, blind to their cognitive performance, according to Research Diagnostic Criteria (Spitzer, Endicott, & Robins, Note 5), these subjects would have been included in the poor premorbid schizophrenic group, and the adequacy of their performance would have masked the important interaction we predicted and found.

Not only is the careful diagnosis of the target population important, the research I reviewed earlier also indicates a marked heterogeneity even within samples of carefully diagnosed schizophrenics. Moreover, it is only the poor-prognosis subsample of schizophrenics that has consistently manifested a perceptual organization dysfunction. Good-prognosis schizophrenics' cognitive performances have often been indistinguishable from those of controls. Ignoring subdivisions within samples of schizophrenics can as easily lead to false conclusions as does the failure to exclude affectively disordered patients from schizophrenic samples.

As I indicated earlier in my brief, selective review of some of the typological research in schizophrenia, there is converging evidence suggesting that there are distinct subgroups within this class of patients. There is, however, no general consensus on which typology most adequately accounts for the heterogeneity of schizophrenics. Even the "premorbidity" typology I have used in my research requires greater specification. The premorbidity index that cognitive researchers have used might be at best a correlate of a complex of symptoms that need to be identified and measured. Moreover, our own follow-up research (Knight & Roff, 1983) suggests there are two developmental paths that lead to the final poor premorbid state. It might be that even this poor-prognosis group could be subdivided. Once again the process-oriented researcher of schizophrenics' cognitive deficiencies relies on advances in other areas. Construction of an adequate typology is an essential propaedeutic to advancement in the specification of cognitive deficiencies. Diagnostic confusion diminishes the sensitivity of our models and makes it more difficult to predict particular patterns of performance.

Thus my cursory review of the sources of difficulty encountered by process-oriented researchers indicates that, while the approach both supplies numerous strategies for addressing difficult methodological problems and has yielded sufficient cumulative knowledge about schizophrenics' cognitive deficiencies to attest to its viability as a research strategy, it is not a panacea, nor does it provide an easy road to success. While offering solutions to some problems, it raises others. Since, however, no other approach either equals its cumulative record or provides equivalent strategies both for dealing with the perplexing methodological problems that face us and for guiding future research, it seems for now to be the best game in town.

REFERENCE NOTES

1. Knight, R. A., Elliott, D. S., & Freedman, E. G. *Short-term visual memory in schizophrenics*. Manuscript in preparation for publication.

2. Levin, S., Hall, J. A., Knight, R. A., & Alpert, M. *Verbal and nonverbal expression of affect in speech of schizophrenic and affective disorder patients*. Manuscript in preparation for publication.

3. Frame, C. L., & Oltmanns, T. F. *Distraction and verbal information processing in schizophrenia: Specific effects or global capacity reduction?* Paper presented at the annual meeting of the American Psychological Association, Los Angeles, 1981.

4. Marvinney, D. A., Rosenberg, E., & Knight, R. A. *The identification of schizophrenics: Differential selection by five research diagnostic systems*. Paper presented at the annual meeting of the Eastern Psychological Association, Baltimore, April 1982.

5. Spitzer, R., Endicott, J., & Robins, J. *Research diagnostic criteria*. Unpublished manuscript, 1978. (Available from Biometrics Research, New York State Psychiatric Institute, 722 West 168th Street, New York, New York 10032.)

REFERENCES

Andreasen, N. C., & Olsen, S. Negative v. positive schizophrenia: Definition and validation. *Archives of General Psychiatry*, 1982, **39**, 789–794.

Andreasen, N. C., Olsen, S. A., Dennert, J. W., & Smith, M. R. Ventricular enlargement in schizophrenia: Relationship to positive and negative symptoms. *American Journal of Psychiatry*, 1982, **139**, 297–302.

Asarnow, R. F., & MacCrimmon, D. J. Residual performance deficit in clinically remitted schizophrenics: A marker of schizophrenia? *Journal of Abnormal Psychology*, 1978, **87**, 597–608.

Asarnow, R. F., Steffy, R. A., MacCrimmon, D. J., & Cleghorn, J. M. An attentional assessment of foster children at risk for schizophrenia. In L. C. Wynne, R. L. Cromwell, & S. Matthysse (Eds.), *The nature of schizophrenia: New approaches to research and treatment*. New York: Wiley, 1978.

Astrup, C., & Noreik, K. *Functional psychoses: Diagnostic and prognostic models*. Springfield, Ill.: Charles C. Thomas, 1966.

Atkinson, R. C., & Shiffrin, R. M. Human memory: A proposed system and its control processes. In K. W. Spence & J. T. Spence (Eds.), *The psychology of learning and motivation: Advances in research and theory* (Vol. 2). New York: Academic Press, 1968.

Atkinson, R. C., & Shiffrin, R. M. The control processes of short-term memory. *Scientific American*, 1971, **224**, 82–90.

Bamber, D. State-trace analysis: A method of testing simple theories of causation. *Journal of Mathematical Psychology*, 1979, **19**, 137–181.

Beck, J. Similarity grouping and peripheral discriminability under uncertainty. *American Journal of Psychology*, 1972, **85**, 1–19.

Bellissimo, A., & Steffy, R. A. Redundancy-associated deficit in schizophrenic reaction time performance. *Journal of Abnormal Psychology*, 1972, **80**, 299–307.

Blaney, P. H. Schizophrenic thought disorder: Why the lack of answers? In S. Schwartz (Ed.), *Language and cognition in schizophrenia*. Hillsdale, N.J.: Lawrence Erlbaum Associates, 1978.

Bleuler, E. *Dementia praecox or the group of schizophrenias*. New York: International Universities Press, 1950.

Bower, T. G. R. *Development in infancy* (2nd ed.). San Francisco: Freeman, 1982.

Braff, D. L. Impaired speed of information processing in nonmedicated schizotypal patients. *Schizophrenia Bulletin*, 1981, **7**, 499–508.

Braff, D. L., & Saccuzzo, D. P. Information processing dysfunction in paranoid schizophrenia: A two-factor deficit. *American Journal of Psychiatry*, 1981, **138**, 1051–1056.

Braff, D. L., Silverton, L., Saccuzzo, D. P., & Janowsky, D. S. Impaired speed of visual information processing in marijuana intoxication. *American Journal of Psychiatry*, 1981, **138**, 613–617.

Broadbent, D. E. *Perception and communication.* Oxford: Pergamon Press, 1958.

Broadbent, D. E. *Decision and stress.* New York: Academic Press, 1971.

Broadbent, D. E. Selective and control processes. *Cognition,* 1981, **10,** 53–58.

Brody, D., Saccuzzo, D. P., & Braff, D. L. Information processing for masked and unmasked stimuli in schizophrenia and old age. *Journal of Abnormal Psychology,* 1980, **89,** 617–622.

Carbotte, R. M. Converging operations or matched control tasks? *Journal of Psychiatric Research,* 1978, **14,** 313–316.

Chapman, L. J., & Chapman, J. P. *Disordered thought in schizophrenia.* New York: Appleton-Century-Crofts, 1973.

Chapman, L. J., & Chapman, J. P. The measurement of differential deficit. *Journal of Psychiatric Research,* 1978, **14,** 303–311.

Cohen, J. *Statistical power analysis for the behavioral sciences.* New York: Academic Press, 1969.

Cox, M. D., & Leventhal, D. B. A multivariate analysis and modification of a preattentive, perceptual dysfunction in schizophrenia. *Journal of Nervous and Mental Disease,* 1978, **166,** 709–718.

Craik, R. I. M., & Lockhart, R. S. Levels of processing: A framework for memory research. *Journal of Verbal Learning and Verbal Behavior,* 1972, **11,** 671–684.

Cromwell, R. L. Strategies for studying schizophrenic behavior. *Psychopharmacologia,* 1972, **24,** 121–146.

Cromwell, R. L. Assessment of schizophrenia. In M. R. Rosenzweig & L. W. Porter (Eds.), *Annual Review of Psychology* (Vol. 26). Palo Alto, Calif.: Annual Reviews, 1975.

Cromwell, R. L., & Dokecki, P. R. Schizophrenic language: A disattention interpretation. In S. Rosenberg & J. H. Koplin (Eds.), *Developments in applied psycholinguistics research.* New York: Macmillan, 1968.

Cronbach, L. J., & Meehl, P. E. Construct validity in psychological tests. *Psychological Bulletin,* 1955, **52,** 281–302.

Crow, T. J. Molecular pathology of schizophrenia: More than one disease process? *British Medical Journal,* 1980, **280,** 66–68.

Davidson, G. S., & Neale, J. M. The effects of signal-noise similarity on visual information processing of schizophrenics. *Journal of Abnormal Psychology,* 1974, **83,** 683–686.

Deutsch, J. A., & Deutsch, D. Attention: Some theoretical considerations. *Psychological Review,* 1963, **70,** 80–90.

Dick, A. O. Iconic memory and its relation to perceptual processing and other memory mechanisms. *Perception and Psychophysics,* 1974, **16,** 575–596.

Embretson (Whitely), S. Construct validity: Construct representation versus nomothetic span. *Psychological Bulletin,* 1983, **93,** 179–197.

Eriksen, B. A., & Eriksen, C. W. Effects of noise letters upon the identification of a target letter in a nonsearch task. *Perception and Psychophysics*, 1974, **16**, 143–149.

Eriksen, C. W., & Collins, J. F. Some temporal characteristics of visual pattern perception. *Journal of Experimental Psychology*, 1967, **74**, 476–484.

Eriksen, C. W., & Collins, J. F. Sensory traces versus the psychological moment in the temporal organization of form. *Journal of Experimental Psychology*, 1968, **77**, 376–382.

Erlenmeyer-Kimling, L., & Cornblatt, B. Attentional measures in a study of children at high-risk for schizophrenia. In L. C. Wynne, R. L. Cromwell, & S. Matthysse (Eds.), *The nature of schizophrenia: New approaches to research and treatment*. New York: Wiley, 1978.

Fantz, R. L., Fagan, J. F., III, & Miranda, S. B. Early visual selectivity as a function of pattern variables, previous exposure, age from birth and conception, and expected cognitive deficit. In L. B. Cohen & P. Salapatek (Eds.), *Infant perception: From sensation to cognition*. Vol. 1. *Basic visual processes*. New York: Academic Press, 1975.

Farmer, A. E., McGuffin, P., & Spitznagel, E. L. Heterogeneity in schizophrenia: A cluster-analytic approach. *Psychiatry Research*, 1983, **8**, 1–9.

Feigl, H. Philosophical embarrassments of psychology. *Psychologische Beiträge*, 1962, **6**, 340–364.

Feyerabend, P. K. Problems of empiricism. In R. G. Colodny (Ed.), *Beyond the edge of certainty*. Englewood Cliffs, N.J.: Prentice-Hall, 1965.

Freedman, B. J. The subjective experience of perceptual and cognitive disturbances in schizophrenia: A review of autobiographical accounts. *Archives of General Psychiatry*, 1974, **30**, 333–340.

Freedman, B. J., & Chapman, L. J. Early subjective experience in schizophrenic episodes. *Journal of Abnormal Psychology*, 1973, **82**, 46–54.

Gibson, E. J., Owsley, C. J., Walker, A., & Megaw-Nyce, J. Development of the perception of invariants: Substance and shape. *Perception*, 1979, **8**, 609–619.

Golden, C. J., Moses, J. A., Jr., Zelazowski, R., Graber, B., Zatz, L. M., Horvath, T. B., & Berger, P. A. Cerebral ventricular size and neuropsychological impairment in young chronic schizophrenics. *Archives of General Psychiatry*, 1980, **37**, 619–623.

Gottesman, I. I., & Shields, J. *Schizophrenia: The epigenetic puzzle*. Cambridge: Cambridge University Press, 1982.

Grunebaum, H., Weiss, J. L., Gallant, D., & Cohler, B. J. Attention in young children of psychotic mothers. *American Journal of Psychiatry*, 1974, **131**, 887–891.

Haber, R. N. Information-processing approaches to visual perception: An introduction. In R. N. Haber (Ed.), *Information-processing approaches to visual perception*. New York: Holt, Rinehart and Winston, 1969.

Haber, R. N. Where are the visions in visual perception? In S. Segel (Ed.), *Imagery*. New York: Academic Press, 1971.

Haber, R. N. Information processing. In E. C. Carterette & M. P. Friedman (Eds.), *Handbook of perception*. Vol. 1. *History and philosophical roots of perception*. New York: Academic Press, 1974.

Haber, R. N. The impending demise of the icon: A critique of the concept of iconic storage in visual information processing. *Behavioral and Brain Sciences*, 1983, **6**, in press.

Haber, R. N., & Hershenson, M. *The psychology of visual perception* (2nd ed.). New York: Holt, Rinehart and Winston, 1980.

Haber, R. N., & Standing, L. G. Direct measures of short-term visual storage. *Quarterly Journal of Experimental Psychology*, 1969, **21**, 43–54.

Hemsley, D. R. A two-stage model of attention in schizophrenia research. *British Journal of Social and Clinical Psychology*, 1975, **14**, 81–89.

Holding, D. H. The amount seen in brief exposures. *Quarterly Journal of Experimental Psychology*, 1971, **23**, 72–81.

Hulme, M. R., & Merikle, P. M. Processing time and memory for pictures. *Canadian Journal of Psychology*, 1976, **30**, 31–38.

Jansson, B. The prognostic significance of various types of hallucinations in young people. *Acta Psychiatrica Scandinavica*, 1968, **44**, 401–409.

Jenkins, J. J. Language and memory. In G. A. Miller (Ed.), *Communication, language, and meaning: Psychological perspectives*. New York: Basic Books, 1973.

Jenkins, J. J. Can we have a fruitful cognitive psychology? In H. E. Howe, Jr., & J. H. Flowers (Eds.), *Nebraska Symposium on Motivation* (Vol. 28). Lincoln: University of Nebraska Press, 1981.

Jernigan, T. L., Zatz, L. M., Moses, J. A., & Berger, P. A. Computed tomography in schizophrenics and normal volunteers. I. Fluid volume. *Archives of General Psychiatry*, 1982, **39**, 765–770.

Johnstone, E. C., Crow, T. J., Frith, C. D., Husband, J., & Kreel, L. Cerebral ventricular size and cognitive impairment in chronic schizophrenia. *Lancet*, 1976, **2**, 924–926.

Kahneman, D. Methods, findings, and theory in studies of visual masking. *Psychological Bulletin*, 1968, **70**, 404–425.

Kahneman, D. *Attention and effort*. Englewood Cliffs, N.J.: Prentice-Hall, 1973.

Kahneman, D., & Treisman, A. Changing views of attention and automaticity. In R. Parasuraman, D. R. Davies, & J. Beatty (Eds.), *Variants of attention*. New York: Academic Press, in press.

Kerlinger, F. N., & Pedhazur, E. J. *Multiple regression in behavioral research*. New York: Holt, Rinehart and Winston, 1973.

Knight, R. A., & Roff, J. D. Childhood and young adult predictors of schizophrenic outcome. In D. Ricks & B. Dohrenwend (Eds.), *Origins of psychopathology: Research and public policy*. Cambridge: Cambridge University Press, 1983.

Knight, R. A., Roff, J. D., Barrnett, J., & Moss, J. L. Concurrent and predictive validity of thought disorder and affectivity: A 22-year follow-up of acute schizophrenics. *Journal of Abnormal Psychology*, 1979, **88**, 1–12.

Knight, R. A., Sherer, M., Putchat, C., & Carter, G. A picture integration task for measuring iconic memory in schizophrenics. *Journal of Abnormal Psychology*, 1978, **87**, 314–321.

Knight, R. A., Sherer, M., & Shapiro, J. Iconic imagery in overinclusive and nonoverinclusive schizophrenics. *Journal of Abnormal Psychology*, 1977, **86**, 242–255.

Knight, R. A., & Sims-Knight, J. E. Integration of visual patterns in schizophrenics. *Journal of Abnormal Psychology*, 1980, **89**, 623–634.

Knight, R. A., Sims-Knight, J. E., & Petchers-Cassell, M. Overinclusion, broad scanning, and picture recognition in schizophrenics. *Journal of Clinical Psychology*, 1977, **33**, 635–642.

Knight, R. G., & Russell, P. N. Global capacity reduction and schizophrenia. *British Journal of Social and Clinical Psychology*, 1978, **17**, 275–280.

Koh, S. D. Remembering of verbal materials by schizophrenic young adults. In S. Schwartz (Ed.), *Language and cognition in schizophrenia*. Hillsdale, N.J.: Lawrence Erlbaum Associates, 1978.

Koh, S. D., Kayton, L., & Streicker, S. K. Short term memory for numerousness in schizophrenic young adults. *Journal of Nervous and Mental Disease*, 1976, **163**, 88–101.

Koh, S. D., & Peterson, R. A. Encoding orientation and the remembering of schizophrenic young adults. *Journal of Abnormal Psychology*, 1978, **87**, 303–313.

Koh, S. D., Szoc, R., & Peterson, R. A. Short-term memory scanning in schizophrenic young adults. *Journal of Abnormal Psychology*, 1977, **86**, 451–460.

Kopfstein, J. H., & Neale, J. M. A multivariate study of attention dysfunction in schizophrenia. *Journal of Abnormal Psychology*, 1972, **80**, 294–298.

Kornetsky, C., & Orzack, M. H. Physiological and behavioral correlates of attention dysfunction in schizophrenic patients. *Journal of Psychiatric Research*, 1978, **14**, 69–79.

Kraepelin, E. *Dementia praecox and paraphrenia* (R. M. Barclay, trans.). Edinburgh, Scotland: Livingstone, 1919.

Kroll, J. F., & Hershenson, M. Two stages in visual matching. *Canadian Journal of Psychology*, 1980, **34**, 49–61.

Kroll, N. E. A., Parks, T., Parkinson, S. R., Bieber, S. L., & Johnson, A. L. Short-term memory while shadowing: Recall of visually and of aurally presented letters. *Journal of Experimental Psychology*, 1970, **85**, 220–224.

Krueger, L. E., & Shapiro, R. G. A reformulation of Proctor's unified theory for matching-task phenomena. *Psychological Review*, 1981, **88**, 573–581.

LaBerge, D. Unitization and automaticity in perception. In H. E. Howe, Jr., & J. H. Flowers (Eds.), *Nebraska Symposium on Motivation* (Vol. 28). Lincoln: University of Nebraska Press, 1981.

Lakatos, I. Falsification and the methodology of scientific research programs. In I. Lakatos & A. Musgrave (Eds.), *Criticism and the growth of knowledge.* Cambridge: Cambridge University Press, 1970.

Lang, P. J., & Buss, A. H. Psychological deficit in schizophrenia. II. Interference and activation. *Journal of Abnormal Psychology,* 1965, **70,** 77–106.

Langfeldt, G. Schizophrenia, diagnosis, and prognosis. *Behavioral Science,* 1969, **14,** 173–182.

Larkin, J., McDermott, J., Simon, D. P., & Simon, H. A. Expert and novice performance in solving physics problems. *Science,* 1980, **208,** 1335–1342.

Larsen, S. F., & Fromholt, P. Mnemonic organization and free recall in schizophrenia. *Journal of Abnormal Psychology,* 1976, **85,** 61–65.

Loevinger, J. Some limitations of objective personality tests. In J. N. Butcher (Ed.), *Objective personality assessment: Changing perspectives.* New York: Academic Press, 1972.

Long, G. M. Iconic memory: A review and critique of the study of short-term visual storage. *Psychological Bulletin,* 1980, **88,** 785–820.

Maher, B. A. *Principles of psychopathology: An experimental approach.* New York: McGraw-Hill, 1966.

Maher, B. A. The language of schizophrenia: A review and interpretation. *British Journal of Psychiatry,* 1972, **120,** 3–17.

Maher, B. A. Editorial. *Journal of Consulting and Clinical Psychology,* 1974, **42,** 1–3.

McGhie, A. Attention and perception in schizophrenia. In B. A. Maher (Ed.), *Progress in experimental personality research* (Vol. 5). New York: Academic Press, 1970.

McGhie, A., & Chapman, J. Disorders of attention and perception in early schizophrenia. *British Journal of Medical Psychology,* 1961, **34,** 103–116.

Mednick, S. A. A learning theory approach to research in schizophrenia. *Psychological Bulletin,* 1958, **55,** 316–327.

Meehl, P. E. The dynamics of "structured" personality tests. *Journal of Clinical Psychology,* 1945, **1,** 296–303.

Meehl, P. E. When shall we use our heads instead of the formula? *Journal of Counseling Psychology,* 1957, **4,** 268–273.

Meehl, P. E. Schizotaxia, schizotypy, schizophrenia. *American Psychologist,* 1962, **17,** 827–838.

Meehl, P. E. Prefatory comment. In L. D. Goodstein & R. I. Lanyon (Eds.), *Readings in personality assessment.* New York: Wiley, 1972.

Meehl, P. E. Theoretical risks and tabular asterisks: Sir Karl, Sir Ronald, and the slow progress of soft psychology. *Journal of Consulting and Clinical Psychology,* 1978, **46,** 806–834.

Meudell, P. R. Short-term visual memory: Comparative effects of two types of distraction on the recall of visually presented verbal and nonverbal material. *Journal of Experimental Psychology,* 1972, **94,** 244–247.

Milewski, A. E. Visual discrimination and detection of configural invariance in 3-month infants. *Developmental Psychology*, 1979, **15**, 357–363.

Miller, S., Saccuzzo, D., & Braff, D. Information processing deficits in remitted schizophrenics. *Journal of Abnormal Psychology*, 1979, **88**, 446–449.

Millon, T. *Millon clinical multiaxial inventory manual*. Minneapolis: National Computer Systems, 1977.

Moscovitch, M. Information processing and the cerebral hemispheres. In M. S. Gazzaniga (Ed.), *Handbook of behavioral neurobiology*. Vol. 2. *Neuropsychology*. New York: Plenum, 1979.

Nasrallah, H. A., Jacoby, C. G., McCalley-Whitters, M., & Kuperman, S. Cerebral ventricular enlargement in subtypes of chronic schizophrenia. *Archives of General Psychiatry*, 1982, **39**, 774–777.

Neale, J. M. Perceptual span in schizophrenia. *Journal of Abnormal Psychology*, 1971, **77**, 196–204.

Neale, J. M., & Cromwell, R. L. Attention and schizophrenia. In B. A. Maher (Ed.), *Progress in experimental personality research* (Vol. 5). New York: Academic Press, 1970.

Neale, J. M., & Cromwell, R. L. Attention and schizophrenia: Postscript. In B. A. Maher (Ed.), *Contributions to the psychopathology of schizophrenia*. New York: Academic Press, 1977.

Neale, J. M., McIntyre, C. W., Fox, R., & Cromwell, R. L. Span of apprehension in acute schizophrenics. *Journal of Abnormal Psychology*, 1969, **74**, 593–596.

Neale, J. M., & Oltmanns, T. F. *Schizophrenia*. New York: Wiley, 1980.

Neisser, U. *Cognitive psychology*. New York: Appleton-Century-Crofts, 1967.

Neisser, U. *Cognition and reality: Principles and implications of cognitive psychology*. San Francisco: Freeman, 1976.

Neisser, U. Memory: What are the important questions? In U. Neisser (Ed.), *Memory observed: Remembering in natural contexts*. San Francisco: Freeman, 1982.

Nickerson, R. S. Binary-classification reaction time: A review of some studies of human information-processing capabilities. *Psychonomic Monograph Supplement*, 1972, **4** (17, Whole No. 65).

Nickerson, R. S. The use of binary-classification tasks in the study of human information processing: A tutorial survey. In S. Kornblum (Ed.), *Attention and performance IV*. New York: Academic Press, 1973.

Nickerson, R. S. On the time it takes to tell things apart. In J. Requin (Ed.), *Attention and performance VII*. Hillsdale, N.J.: Lawrence Erlbaum Associates, 1978.

Nideffer, R. M., Neale, J. M., Kopfstein, J. H., & Cromwell, R. L. The effect of previous preparatory intervals upon anticipatory responses in the reaction time of schizophrenic and nonschizophrenic patients. *Journal of Nervous and Mental Disease*, 1971, **153**, 360–365.

Norman, D. A. *Memory and attention: An introduction to human information processing* (2nd ed.). New York: Wiley, 1976.

Nuechterlein, K. H. Reaction time and attention in schizophrenia: A critical evaluation of the data and theories. *Schizophrenia Bulletin,* 1977, **3,** 373–428.

O'Hear, A. *Karl Popper.* London: Routledge and Kegan Paul, 1980.

Oltmanns, T. F. Selective attention in schizophrenic and manic psychoses: The effect of distraction on information processing. *Journal of Abnormal Psychology,* 1978, **87,** 212–225.

Ornitz, E. M. Disorders of perception common to early infantile autism and schizophrenia. *Comprehensive Psychiatry,* 1969, **10,** 259–274.

Overall, J. E., & Hollister, L. E. Comparative evaluation of research diagnostic criteria for schizophrenia. *Archives of General Psychiatry,* 1979, **36,** 1198–1205.

Payne, R. W., Mattussek, P., & George, E. I. An experimental study of schizophrenic thought disorder. *Journal of Mental Science,* 1959, **105,** 627–652.

Phillips, W. A. On the distinction between sensory storage and short-term visual memory. *Perception and Psychophysics,* 1974, **16,** 283–290.

Place, E. J. S., & Gilmore, G. C. Perceptual organization in schizophrenia. *Journal of Abnormal Psychology,* 1980, **89,** 409–418.

Pogue-Geile, M. F., & Oltmanns, T. F. Sentence perception and distractibility in schizophrenic, manic, and depressed patients. *Journal of Abnormal Psychology,* 1980, **89,** 115–124.

Popper, K. R. *The logic of scientific discovery.* New York: Basic Books, 1959.

Popper, K. R. *Objective knowledge: An evolutionary approach.* Oxford: Clarendon Press, 1972.

Popper, K. R. Replies to my critics. In P. Schilpp (Ed.), *The philosophy of Karl Popper.* La Salle, Ill.: Open Court, 1974.

Posner, M. I. Abstraction and the process of recognition. In J. T. Spence & G. H. Bower (Eds.), *Psychology of learning and motivation: Advances in research and theory* (Vol. 3). New York: Academic Press, 1969.

Posner, M. I. *Chronometric explorations of mind.* Hillsdale, N.J.: Lawrence Erlbaum Associates, 1978.

Posner, M. I. Cognition and neural systems. *Cognition,* 1981, **10,** 261–266.

Posner, M. I. Cumulative development of attentional theory. *American Psychologist,* 1982, **37,** 168–179.

Posner, M. I., Cohen, Y., & Rafal, R. D. Neural systems control of spatial orienting. *Philosophical Transactions of the Royal Society of London,* 1982, **298,** 187–198.

Posner, M. I., & Rothbart, M. K. The development of attentional mechanisms. In H. E. Howe, Jr., & J. H. Flowers (Eds.), *Nebraska Symposium on Motivation* (Vol. 28). Lincoln: University of Nebraska Press, 1981.

Potter, M. C. Meaning in visual search. *Science,* 1975, **187,** 965–966.

Potter, M. C. Short-term conceptual memory for pictures. *Journal of Experimental Psychology: Human Learning and Memory*, 1976, **2**, 509–522.

Potter, M. C., & Levy, E. I. Recognition memory for a rapid sequence of pictures. *Journal of Experimental Psychology*, 1969, **81**, 10–15.

Prentky, R. A., Lewine, R. R. J., Watt, N. F., & Fryer, J. H. A longitudinal study of psychiatric outcome: Developmental variables vs. psychiatric symptoms. *Schizophrenia Bulletin*, 1980, **6**, 139–148.

Price, R. H., & Eriksen, C. W. Size constancy in schizophrenia: A reanalysis. *Journal of Abnormal Psychology*, 1966, **71**, 155–160.

Proctor, R. W. A unified theory for matching-task phenomena. *Psychological Review*, 1981, **88**, 291–326.

Reichenbach, H. *The philosophy of space and time* (M. Reichenbach & J. Freund, trans.). New York: Dover Publications, 1958.

Rieder, R. O., Donnelly, E. F., Herdt, J. R., & Waldman, I. N. Sulcal prominence in young chronic schizophrenic patients: CT scan findings associated with impairment on neuropsychological tests. *Psychiatry Research*, 1979, **1**, 1–8.

Rochester, S. R. Are language disorders in acute schizophrenia actually information-processing problems? In L. C. Wynne, R. L. Cromwell, & S. Matthysse (Eds.), *The nature of schizophrenia: New approaches to research and treatment*. New York: Wiley, 1978.

Rochester, S. R., Harris, J., & Seeman, M. V. Sentence processing in schizophrenic listeners. *Journal of Abnormal Psychology*, 1973, **82**, 350–356.

Rosen, K. S., & Hershenson, M. Tests of a two-stage model of visual matching. *Perceptual and Motor Skills*, 1983, **56**, 343–354.

Rosofsky, I., Levin, S., & Holzman, P. S. Psychomotility in the functional psychoses. *Journal of Abnormal Psychology*, 1982, **91**, 71–74.

Russell, P. N., Consedine, C. E., & Knight, R. G. Visual and memory search by process schizophrenics. *Journal of Abnormal Psychology*, 1980, **89**, 109–114.

Russell, P. N., & Knight, R. G. Performance of process schizophrenics on tasks involving visual search. *Journal of Abnormal Psychology*, 1977, **86**, 16–26.

Rutschmann, J., Cornblatt, B., & Erlenmeyer-Kimling, L. Sustained attention in children at risk for schizophrenia: Report on a continuous performance test. *Archives of General Psychiatry*, 1977, **34**, 571–575.

Ryder, J. M. *Symmetry relations in visual matching*. Unpublished doctoral dissertation, Brandeis University, 1979.

Saccuzzo, D. P., & Braff, D. L. Early information processing deficit in schizophrenia: New findings using schizophrenic sub-groups and manic control subjects. *Archives of General Psychiatry*, 1981, **38**, 175–179.

Saccuzzo, D. P., Braff, D. L., & Sprock, J. The effect of mental retardation and schizophrenia on information processing. *Journal of Nervous and Mental Disease*, 1982, **170**, 102–106.

Saccuzzo, D. P., Hirt, M., & Spencer, T. J. Backward masking as a measure of attention in schizophrenia. *Journal of Abnormal Psychology*, 1974, **83**, 512–522.

Salapatek, P. Pattern perception in early infancy. In L. B. Cohen & P. Salapatek (Eds.), *Infant perception: From sensation to cognition*. Vol. 1. *Basic visual processes*. New York: Academic Press, 1975.

Salzinger, K. The immediacy hypothesis of schizophrenia. In H. M. Yaker, H. Osmond, & F. Cheek (Eds.), *The future of time: Man's temporal environment*. Garden City, N.Y.: Doubleday, 1971.

Salzinger, K. *Schizophrenia: Behavioral aspects*. New York: Wiley, 1973.

Salzinger, K., Portnoy, S., & Feldman, R. S. Communicability deficit in schizophrenics resulting from a more general deficit. In S. Schwartz (Ed.), *Language and cognition in schizophrenia*. Hillsdale, N.J.: Lawrence Erlbaum Associates, 1978.

Sarbin, T. R., & Mancuso, J. C. *Schizophrenia: Medical diagnosis or moral verdict?* Elmsford, N.Y.: Pergamon Press, 1980.

Schneider, W., & Shiffrin, R. M. Controlled and automatic human information processing. I. Detection, search, and attention. *Psychological Review*, 1977, **84**, 1–66.

Schwartz, S. Language and cognition in schizophrenia: A review and synthesis. In S. Schwartz (Ed.), *Language and cognition in schizophrenia*. Hillsdale, N.J.: Lawrence Erlbaum Associates, 1978.

Schwartz, S. Is there a schizophrenic language? *Behavioral and Brain Sciences*, 1982, **5**, 579–626.

Shiffrin, R. M., & Schneider, W. Controlled and automatic human information processing. II. Perceptual learning, automatic attending, and a general theory. *Psychological Review*, 1977, **84**, 127–190.

Siegler, R. S., & Vago, S. The development of a proportionality concept: Judging relative fullness. *Journal of Experimental Child Psychology*, 1978, **25**, 371–395.

Silverman, J. The problem of attention in research and theory in schizophrenia. *Psychological Review*, 1964, **71**, 352–379.

Spaulding, W., Rosenzweig, L., Huntzinger, R., Cromwell, R. L., Briggs, D., & Hayes, T. Visual pattern integration in psychiatric patients. *Journal of Abnormal Psychology*, 1980, **89**, 635–643.

Spencer, T. J. Some effects of different masking stimuli on iconic storage. *Journal of Experimental Psychology*, 1969, **81**, 132–140.

Sperling, G. The information available in brief visual presentations. *Psychological Monographs*, 1960, **74** (11, Whole No. 498).

Spitzer, R. L., Williams, J. B. W., & Skodol, A. E. DSM-III: The major achievements and an overview. *American Journal of Psychiatry*, 1980, **137**, 151–164.

Sternberg, R. J. The nature of mental abilities. *American Psychologist*, 1979, **34**, 214–230.

Steronko, R. J., & Woods, D. J. Impairment in early stages of visual information processing in nonpsychotic schizotypic individuals. *Journal of Abnormal Psychology*, 1978, **87**, 481–490.

Storms, L. H., & Broen, W. E., Jr. A theory of schizophrenic behavioral disorganization. *Archives of General Psychiatry*, 1969, **20**, 129–144.

Strauss, J. S., & Carpenter, W. T. The prediction of outcome in schizophrenia. I. Characteristics of outcome. *Archives of General Psychiatry*, 1972, **27**, 739–746.

Strauss, M. E., Foureman, W. C., & Parwatikar, S. D. Schizophrenics' size estimations of thematic stimuli. *Journal of Abnormal Psychology*, 1974, **83**, 117–123.

Treisman, A. M. Strategies and models of selective attention. *Psychological Review*, 1969, **76**, 282–299.

Turvey, M. T. Contrasting orientations to the theory of visual information processing. *Psychological Review*, 1977, **84**, 67–88.

Venables, P. H. Input dysfunction in schizophrenia. In B. A. Maher (Ed.), *Progress in experimental personality research* (Vol. 1). New York: Academic Press, 1964.

Venables, P. H. Input dysfunction in schizophrenia: Postscript. In B. A. Maher (Ed.), *Contributions to the psychopathology of schizophrenia*. New York: Academic Press, 1977.

Walker, E., & Green, M. Motor proficiency and attentional-task performance by psychotic patients. *Journal of Abnormal Psychology*, 1982, **91**, 261–268.

Walker, E., & McGuire, M. Intra- and interhemispheric information processing in schizophrenia. *Psychological Bulletin*, 1982, **92**, 701–725.

Weinberger, D. R., Bigelow, L. B., Kleinman, J. E., Klein, S. T., Rosenblatt, J. E., & Wyatt, R. J. Cerebral ventricular enlargement in chronic schizophrenia: An association with poor response to treatment. *Archives of General Psychiatry*, 1980, **37**, 11–13.

Weinberger, D. R., Cannon-Spoor, E., Potkin, S. G., & Wyatt, R. J. Poor premorbid adjustment and CT scan abnormalities in chronic schizophrenia. *American Journal of Psychiatry*, 1980, **137**, 1410–1413.

Whitehead, A. N. *Science and the modern world*. New York: Macmillan, 1925.

Whitehead, A. N. *An introduction to mathematics*. Oxford: Oxford University Press, 1948.

Wishner, J., & Wahl, O. Dichotic listening in schizophrenia. *Journal of Consulting and Clinical Psychology*, 1974, **42**, 538–546.

Yates, A. J. Data-processing levels and thought disorder in schizophrenia. *Australian Journal of Psychology*, 1966, **18**, 103–117.

Zigler, E., & Phillips, L. Social competence and outcome in psychiatric disorder. *Journal of Abnormal and Social Psychology*, 1961, **63**, 264–271.

Zubin, J. Problem of attention in schizophrenia. In M. L. Kietzman, S. Sutton, & J. Zubin (Eds.), *Experimental approaches to psychopathology*. New York: Academic Press, 1975.

Psychosis and Schizophrenia[1]

Peter A. Magaro
Ohio State University

*T*his year's symposium, entitled Theories of Schizophrenia and Psychosis, is timely because it allows a presentation of the distinctions between the psychotic process and the basic nature of schizophrenia. In experimental design terms, this symposium marks another step in the evolution of a more precise specification of the schizophrenic disorder. By separating the elements inherent in the psychosis from those processes inherent in schizophrenia, we remove one more distortion in the experimental lens focused upon the causes of pathological behavior. I believe this symposium clearly marks a new direction because I think it will no longer be acceptable to confound one process with the other in our research designs. This says only that investigators have recognized a distinction between the effects of the disorder and the disorder itself and are searching for the means to operationalize these processes as they affect our dependent variables.

I shall address this important development in the field before presenting a conception of the basic cognitive and neurological processes I believe are unique to schizophrenia. This discussion therefore will be in three parts: the first will present a view of psychosis as it relates to schizophrenia; the second will present a theory of cognition in schizophrenia that will serve as a revision of my initial theory (Magaro, 1980); and the third will attempt to derive hypotheses about the effect of psychosis on the schizophrenic process.

1. Portions of this work were supported by the Scottish Rite Schizophrenia Research Program, NMJ, USA.

SCHIZOPHRENIA AND PSYCHOSIS

From the time schizophrenia became a separate category, and even before, there has been an intense interest in separating the underlying process unique to schizophrenia from the symptoms manifest in the psychosis. For instance, Bleuler (1911; translation, 1950) struggled to unravel the characteristics fundamental to the disorder from what he considered accessory symptoms.

As far as we know, the fundamental symptoms are characteristic of schizophrenia, while the accessory symptoms may also appear in other types of illness. Nevertheless, even in such cases close scrutiny often reveals peculiarities of genesis or manifestation of a symptom, which are only found in schizophrenia. We can expect that gradually we will come to recognize the characteristic features in a great number of these accessory symptoms.

A description of the symptoms can be based only on clear-cut cases. But it is extremely important to recognize that they exist in varying degrees and shadings on the entire scale from pathological to normal; also the milder cases, latent schizophrenics with far less manifest symptoms, are many times more common than the overt, manifest cases. Furthermore, in view of the fluctuating character which distinguishes the clinical picture of schizophrenia, it is not to be expected that we shall be able to demonstrate each and every symptom at each and every moment of the disease. (p. 13)

Within such a disease perspective of symptoms and process, psychosis is intimately intertwined with schizophrenia, since psychotic behavior is only the manifestation of a disease as it erupts in a set of bizarre symptoms or subsides into a residual or dormant state. The fundamental symptoms are basic characteristics such as the thought disorder, while secondary symptoms are observable signs such as hallucinations. The secondary signs, however, are manifestations of fundamental signs; hence the diagnostic necessity to identify those unique schizophrenic signs, even though Bleuler (1950) recognized that such secondary symptoms fluctuated over time and were present in other psychiatric conditions and in individuals exhibiting little or no pathology. Unfortunately, the unique secondary signs have never been established. The research literature on diagnosis tells us the same story today as Bleuler (1950) described at the beginning of the century. There are few accessory symptoms that exist solely for schizophrenia.

The attempt to define schizophrenia in terms of symptom markers constantly encounters severe and possibly insurmountable problems. One example that is receiving attention these days is the presence in schizophrenia of signs commonly associated with depression. Moller and Zerssen (1982), using the Inpatient Psychiatric Scale, examined 81 schizophrenics after admission to a psychiatric hospital. Of these 81, 50% showed some sign of anxious depression and 63% exhibited a marked depressive-apathetic syndrome. However, only 15% of those hospitalized developed depression during their stay. Moller and Zerssen (1982) also found depression in patients who eight years previously had been diagnosed as schizophrenic. Finally, Johnson (1981) found depression to be frequent in schizophrenics hospitalized for the first time, during acute relapse both with and without drugs, and on medication and free from acute symptoms. Also, in following 30 schizophrenics over a two-year period, he found that 70% experienced a depressive incident during that time. Going the other way, Pope and Lipinsky (1978) found classic schizophrenic symptoms in 20–50% of validated manic-depressive cases they reviewed. Given that they could discern no set of symptoms unique to schizophrenia, they concluded that schizophrenia and manic-depression are very difficult to distinguish as separate entities. Similarly, symptoms thought to be hallmarks of schizophrenia, such as anhedonia and thought disorder, have been found not to be specific to schizophrenia (Abrams & Taylor, 1977; Harrow, Grinkle, Holzman, & Kayton, 1977; Harrow & Quinlan, 1977).

What seems most germane to our interest is that diagnostic symptoms are elusive because psychosis is not a sole property of any one diagnostic group. It is not surprising that schizophrenics, like everyone else, exhibit depressive mood states. Such symptoms come and go depending upon the environmental stresses encountered. Bleuler (1978), summarizing data on almost 2,000 schizophrenics over a twenty-two-year period of observation, has concluded that the accessory signs are neither progressive nor constant in all cases. He supports this contention by pointing out that at least 25% of schizophrenics have recovered and remained recovered, while only 10% remain either severe or hospitalized—that is symptomatic. Strauss, Kokes, Carpenter, and Ritzler (1978), find the same result. On interviewing 40 schizophrenics again two years after hospitalization, they found that 15% had no impairment, while an additional 40% were functioning at levels that, though indicative of some dysfunction, were not seriously impaired. In other words, the signs of the psychosis come and go, but schizophrenia may remain.

This discussion is not about problems in the reliability or validity of diagnostic signs. I am interested in such issues solely as they retard our search for underlying psychological and neurological processes in the schizophrenic individual. What has been recognized is that psychosis has a life of its own—or, in experimental terms, determinants that could predict behavior distinct from those that predict schizophrenic behavior. When we think of psychosis as being constituted by the disease process alone, psychotic behavior becomes only the beacon that leads the investigator to the schizophrenic. Unfortunately, when schizophrenics are detected through their psychosis and studied as specimens, their situational context is often ignored. For instance, we have become aware of how environmental conditions—such as a state hospital with its peculiar nutritional, social, and stimulus conditions—or temporary state conditions produce actions that could be mistaken for schizophrenic behavior. The recognition and control of such confounding subject variables are not new in the study of schizophrenia, and they have been reviewed extensively in many places (Buss, 1965; Chapman & Chapman, 1973; Neale & Oltmanns, 1980). In the same vein, the psychosis itself, including the cognitive disorganization and the perception by the individual and others that he is disturbed, can determine behavior mistakenly thought to be a reflection of the schizophrenic process. Much past research has utilized signs of a psychosis such as thought disorder, hallucinations, or delusions to mark the presence of schizophrenia. The schizophrenic is then examined, and conclusions are drawn about the schizophrenic condition. At this point such a procedure is not sufficient. Current investigations now require the investigator to disentangle the effects of schizophrenia from the effects of psychosis on the dependent variable. As we will see, the two effects are not easy to separate, especially in some research designs, but specific questions concerning one process or the other demand more process-specific answers. From the viewpoint of experimental pathology, the question is how to study schizophrenia without being misled by the confounding effects of the secondary aspects inherent in the pathology.

If we study schizophrenia by assessing behavior, such as on a laboratory task, we are intent on examining an underlying process, be it cognitive or neurological. It is now mandatory to consider whether the behavior measured reflects this underlying process, unique to the disorder, or reflects secondary conditions such as the psychosis. For example, schizophrenics usually perform worse than normal controls. This may be because the psychosis retards the motor system and, if so, it should occur in most psychotic groups, as found by Rosofsky, Levin, and Holzman (1982). In effect, we are seeking not correlates of the disorder—behavior as symptoms and behavior on laboratory tasks—but cause-and-effect relationships between the process and the behavior, be it symptoms or laboratory task performance. I initially will focus upon this distinction between psychosis and schizophrenia, especially as they relate to the development of research strategies, not only because of the spirit of this symposium but because eventually I intend to relate ideas about psychosis to ideas about schizophrenia. Although this has not often been done in the investigation of cognitive processes, it has been an active concern in the study of hemispheric specificity and has led to some interesting data that I will discuss.

I will use the term pathology in a general way to include many secondary aspects of the schizophrenic condition. Psychosis will refer to the extent of symptoms during the schizophrenic episode, which may vary in duration. There have been many efforts to categorize symptom dimensions in terms of extent and duration, such as rapidity of onset or length of the disorder. In some cases it is clear that the extent or duration of symptoms is being considered, whereas in others it seems that the degree of the schizophrenic process is being assessed. For example, the distinction between acute and chronic may indicate an extent dimension by which the acute condition contains extensive florid symptoms as opposed to a chronic state with an enduring moderate to low degree of symptomatology. On the other hand, this usage may indicate a duration dimension, with acute representing a more sudden reactive condition while chronic reflects a more long-term process condition.

I will use the term psychosis as a general label for the extent of symptomatology as it reflects the activity of a psychotic process. Later I will consider the measures of duration as they partially reflect the same dimension. To help me chart the domain of psychosis, I will rely on terms used by Cromwell and Spaulding (1978) as well as by Zubin and Spring (1977). They speak of "markers of vulnerability" that are basic schizophrenic traits or core indicators of schizophrenia comparable to the fundamental symptoms of Bleuler. These are distinguished from "symptom markers," or accessory symptoms, which indicate psychotic episodes and thus are modified as the degree of pathology changes. As we will see, many investigators have already employed such distinctions in their research designs. Cromwell and Pithers (1981), for instance, have expanded upon the trait markers to develop a diagnostic approach to schizophrenia and a research strategy that attempts to examine the correlates of core processes in other aspects of schizophrenia. This thinking is expanded upon in Cromwell's chapter in this volume.

Research Designs and the Separation of Psychosis from Schizophrenia

To begin with, I shall sample some research designs that have attempted to struggle with the issue of core or symptom markers. Holzman (1974) has directly confronted the question of core versus symptom markers in the investigation of smooth-pursuit eye movements. What is remarkable about this line of investigation is that he has employed research strategies to clearly distinguish the specific type of eye movement in schizophrenics from the effects of psychosis in terms of situational conditions and individual differences. A set of studies (reviewed in Holzman, 1982) examined treatment states such as attention or motivation that are not intrinsic to the disorder but are secondary aspects and may be related to situational conditions or the psychosis. They found that the particular eye movement in schizophrenia was not diminished when other temporary states such as distraction were manipulated. An interesting research strategy was to administer to normals a distraction task simulating the inattention or distraction supposedly inherent in the psychosis. Even under distraction conditions, normals did not exhibit the smooth-pursuit eye movement deficit of schizophrenics (Lipton, Levin, and Holzman, 1980). These authors also examined the effect of another transient confounding factor—medication—and found the smooth-pursuit eye movement deficit independent of medication and unique to schizophrenia. Patients on medication who are not schizophrenic do not show the core process, and when schizophrenics are removed from medication the core process is still evident (Holzman, 1982). The most often cited work was the finding of the same pursuit movement in the relatives of schizophrenics who were not on medication (Holzman, 1974; Holzman, Meltzer, Kringlen, Levy, Haberman, & Davis, 1979). Thus, from this data one would have to discount the effects of the psychosis itself, in terms of either phase or severity or treatments on the dependent variable, smooth-pursuit eye movement.

However, other studies (Shagass, Amadeo, & Overton, 1974; Holzman, 1982) find that psychosis as manifested in other diagnostic types produces the same smooth-pursuit eye movement found in schizophrenics. Manic-depressives exhibit the same core markers. Among young middle-class schizophrenics who have not been ill more than two years, the impairment rate is 50%, the same as the prevalence rate among manic-depressives. Chronic schizophrenics undergoing long-term hospitalization demonstrate an 85% rate of impairment. The suggestion here is that the smooth-pursuit eye movement may be not a vulnerability marker of schizophrenia but a symptom marker reflecting the duration of pathology, or the measure may be a core marker for schizophrenia and a symptom marker for another condition, mania. Iacono, Peloquin, Lumry, Valentine, and Tuason (1982) found that unipolar and bipolar affectives in remission do differ from schizophrenics. Schizophrenics produce more tracking errors, especially compared with unipolar affectives. The conclusion from these studies comparing schizophrenics with affectives could be that manics will produce the smooth-pursuit movement deficit when they are psychotic and appear like schizophrenics, who produce the behavior even in the nonpsychotic state. Manics when nonpsychotic do not exhibit the behavior that is prevalent in schizophrenics, supporting the idea that the deficit is a vulnerability marker for schizophrenia.

Holzman (1982) tends to consider the smooth-pursuit eye movement dysfunction more closely related to the psychotic process than to schizophrenia. More specifically, he has related the impaired smooth-pursuit eye movement to the degree of thought disorder, which may be considered a transient state created by the psychosis. Evidence for this position is derived from studies by Shagass, Roemer, and Amadeo (1976) and by Holzman, Levy, and Proctor (1976), who found that as the conceptual demands of the eye-movement task increase, such as by reading arabic numerals on the swinging pendulum, the eye-movement disorder decreases. The question then becomes whether this experimental manipulation is managing the psychosis or a core process, conceptual order, which could produce the same result. I will present some evidence that such experimental manipulation actually aids a conceptual structuring, which improves the performance of nonparanoid schizophrenics because it is a core-process problem.

At this point the careful work of Holzman on the issue of core and symptom markers nicely places the question in experimental terms, allowing a resolution. On one hand, we find temporary states such as inattention and motivation or treatment effects such as medication affecting the core process, but on the other hand we find manics displaying the effect and change occurring with another treatment, conceptual order. A possible interpretation of this contribution is that the dependent measure is a core marker for schizophrenia and a symptom marker for mania. The answer is not final concerning symptoms or vulnerability, but it is important that the question is being pursued experimentally.

Some work, focusing upon recidivism, has produced fascinating results that could be clearly interpreted in terms of symptom markers. The work of Leff (1976; Vaughn & Leff, 1976) attempted to find the specific family determinants that produce the psychotic behavior leading to rehospitalization. There is greater relapse if there is high emotional content in the home environment, especially if it is critical and even more so if it is directed against the personality of the person rather than his maladjusted behavior. On the other hand, such family conditions also could be considered a vulnerability factor (Garmezy, 1982). Basically the idea is that schizophrenics are over sensitive to censure, so that family condition acts as a "trigger" to elicit a basic schizophrenic process such as withdrawal. According to this view, sensitivity to censure is a precursor to the present condition. However, there is little evidence that such family conditions are unique to schizophrenia and do not produce pathological behavior in other groups. Of course one could argue either way, and there is some evidence that such family conditions elicit a core process, since they can be observed during adolescence and are related to schizophrenic episodes in later life (Goldstein, Held, & Cromwell, 1978). However, the research designs supporting this view were not constructed to deal with the question of core and symptom markers. As the authors explain, there are other family conditions that are required to enter into a predictor of schizophrenia, such as affective style, but even with such combined predictors there is only limited evidence that such results are related to schizophrenia and not to pathology in general (Rodnick, Goldstein, Doane, & Lewis, 1982).

Although this very interesting and careful work has extended our understanding of how we might modify communication-deviance problems in pathological families as well as elucidate the intrafamilial interactions, they were undertaken at a time when dimensions of core and symptom markers were not a prime concern, and the traditional diagnostic system was deemed adequate for identifying schizophrenia. It may be that without appropriate control groups they are only finding the precursors to pathology in general and have focused upon a set of stressors that should produce pathology but not necessarily schizophrenia.

Neale (1982) makes this point most clearly when he notes that, as long as high-risk studies do not use other pathological groups as controls, the children of schizophrenics will always differ from other children, just as adult schizophrenics always differ from normal controls. Few high-risk studies, initially developed to find core markers, can tell if the results would also be found with children of patients in other diagnostic groups, such as unipolar or bipolar depressives. Neale (1982) goes further into the issue of deficit specificity, reviewing a number of information processing markers found in high-risk children. In comparisons with children of those with depressive disorders, the uniqueness of the deficits disappeared. In effect, such results are not pathognomonic of schizophrenia. Again, psychosis may be important to study, but it should not be confused with schizophrenia.

Zubin (1975) delineated the core versus symptom marker issue most precisely by asking what type of attention—sustained, shifting, or selective—is a core marker and which are symptom markers. Spring and Zubin (1978) reported results that defined vulnerability markers as performance anomalies not present in nonschizophrenic patients or healthy controls but occurring in nonaffected siblings and in a schizophrenic proband; the disorder persisted in recovered schizophrenics. Symptom markers should occur only in symptomatic schizophrenic patients, not in remitted patients. They then described the research methodology following from such distinctions, specifically the procedures needed to control for irrelevant performance factors. Their results are extremely instructive because they compare the performance of various psychotic groups and find points of divergence and convergence.

Neuchterlein, Phipps-Yonas, Driscoll, and Garmezy (1982) studied attention in children at risk for schizophrenia because of having a schizophrenic mother, comparing them with hyperactive children. One might expect these groups to be at similar levels of pathology or even expect the hyperactive children to be more pathological, since they were identified by present behavior rather than by the behavior of their parents. They found some attentional measures related to schizophrenic children but not to hyperactive children, though there is no way of telling whether these constituted a precursor to psychosis or a core marker for schizophrenia, since the children of schizophrenics also developed other pathological conditions. In effect, the study does show that some attentional measures are not related to hyperactivity, but the design does not allow the question whether they are related to risk of schizophrenia independent of other forms of pathology.

Using EEG measures, Itil et al. (1977) found that schizophrenics produce faster beta, higher average frequency, decreased alpha, and lower amplitude. After treatment, however, beta is reduced and alpha is increased. Does this suggest an investigation into the core process or a symptom correlate? Going further, Saletu, Itil, Arat, and Akpinar (1973) found that the average evoked potential measures of shorter latency, smaller amplitude, and greater intra-individual variability are found in schizophrenia. Moreover, the greater the pathology as defined by a measure of thought disorder, the greater these deficits—especially amplitude, which is related to clinical manifestation of the disorder (Saletu, 1980). This suggests that EEG results reflect the degree of psychosis, not schizophrenia, in that when symptom markers such as clinical manifestations or thought disorder change, the dependent variable changes. Core markers are expected to be stable.

Up to this point I have sampled some research designs that have asked about core processes and considered the effects of psychosis. We can see that the means of controlling for the secondary aspects of the disorder can vary depending on the questions being asked. For instance, in asking about the present behavior of schizophrenic children, a control group of equal pathology is required. If the study is designed to find early expression of vulnerability markers in at-risk children of schizophrenic mothers, then the children of parents in other pathological groups must be incorporated into the design lest we be left with some high-risk children producing such behavior and others producing other behavior. There is no class of behavior unique to children at risk for schizophrenia and not shared by other high-risk children. Just as in work with adult schizophrenics, we are looking for processes unique to schizophrenia, not to psychosis.

Dimensions of Psychosis

At this point, I shall try to flesh out the psychosis construct, first differentiating it from other dimensions of pathology. Let us reserve psychosis for the extent of the pathology at any one point in time — the intensity or degree of symptomatology that interferes with normal functioning. I will narrow this conception by discussing operational definitions that have been employed to control for the effects of confounding subject dimensions related to the secondary effects of the disorder. Pathology is a multidimensional construct including such elements as the duration of the disorder, its severity, the rapidity of onset, the degree of disorganization, the extent of symptomatology, the level of social adjustment, the extent of treatment (such as hospitalization), and the diagnosis. Figure 1 illustrates the relation between various subject dimensions. The list presented there could go on, especially if one is attempting to predict outcome by symptom markers. However, here we are mainly interested in aspects of the condition that influence current behavior, specifically in experimental measures. Hence the subject dimensions of greatest concern are those that can reliably distinguish between levels of the disorder. I do not intend to be inclusive, but I hope to instigate a discussion about the dimensions that usually have been considered in the experimental investigation of schizophrenia.

Much of this discussion may be old hat to some investigators, since most work today has already heeded such advice. Ritzler (1981), however, did not find such clear adherence to controls for psychosis when he reviewed journal articles on schizophrenia published between 1970 and 1978. He found that 73% of the control groups used as comparisons for the schizophrenic sample were nonpsychiatric. Of this group, 68% were normals. Nonpsychotic psychiatric controls were used 27% of the time, and psychotic controls were used only 11% of the time. By 1977 that percentage was 22%, and in 1978, 23%. Ritzler (1981) also makes the point that we

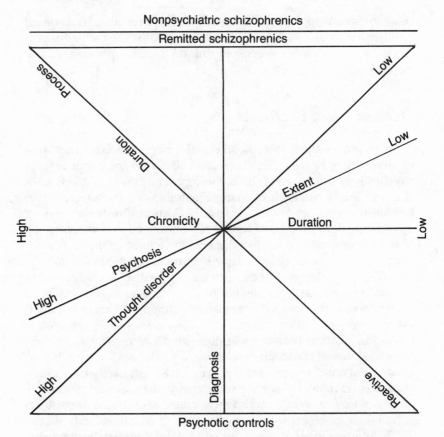

FIGURE 1. Dimensions of pathology and research strategies to control for the effect of psychosis. (Relation of dimensions to one another does not imply degree of correlation.)

know little about the characteristics of schizophrenics as compared with psychotics in general.

Let me begin by describing the means that have been used to cope with this problem. A study done in our laboratory more than ten years ago (Magaro & Vojtisek, 1971) illustrates the attention being given to one confounding subject dimension. We administered the Embedded Figures Test (EFT) to acute and chronic nonparanoid schizophrenics, paranoid schizophrenics, and other psychiatric patients, mainly alcoholics, divided by level of premorbid adjustment. The major result was that chronicity, defined in terms of years of hospitalization, was the main factor related to EFT performance.

Overall, the chronic patient of any diagnosis was more field-dependent than the acute patient, who was similar to normal controls. In effect, chronicity was more closely related to performance level than to diagnosis such as schizophrenia or alcoholism. We analyzed galvanic skin response amplitude and basal level in the same manner. Chronicity was the main determiner of differences between schizophrenics and other groups (Magaro, 1980). Others have found the same effect. Kopfstein and Neale (1971) report that schizophrenics and nonschizophrenic patients who were also considered psychotic did not differ in level of performance on size estimation tasks when length of hospitalization was considered. Silverman, Berg, and Kantor (1965) found that long-term prisoners did not differ from chronic schizophrenics on a number of perceptual tasks.

These studies did not control for psychosis in terms of extent of symptoms but used length of hospitalization and thus indirectly the duration of symptomatology. A chronicity measure may also indirectly measure level of psychosis, but chronicity is not equivalent to psychosis in terms of extent or duration because it also taps another dimension, the effects of long-term hospitalization. When degree of pathology is controlled for by this means, group differences on many dependent variables disappear. It is not clear just what dimension within the length-of-hospitalization measure—extent, or duration of symptomatology, or hospitalization—accounts for the variance on the dependent variable independent of the experimental manipulation.

The effects of pathology have been controlled for through other measurement techniques that may be closer to the extent of the pathology. Ritzler and Rosenbaum (1974) examined the degree of proprioception in long-term schizophrenic patients and found the customary deficit for schizophrenics compared with normal controls. Later, however, Ritzler (1977) separated his schizophrenic patients into levels of premorbid adjustment (for convenience I will label the dimension process-reactive) and compared them with neurotics, normals, and another psychotic group (manic-depressive, depressive psychosis, and amphetamine psychosis) who were also divided along the process-reactive dimension. The dependent variables were the same proprioception measures used in the prior study (Ritzler & Rosenbaum, 1974). The major result was that the process patients, schizophrenic and nonschizophrenic, performed worse than the reactive patients, both schizophrenic and nonschizophrenic. To be more accurate, only the poor-process non-paranoid schizophrenics exhibited the deficit, along with the other process nonschizophrenic psychotic group. A process paranoid schizophrenic group did not differ from the other control groups or the reactive groups on at least one proprioception measure.

This study introduces an old friend in research in schizophrenia, the process-reactive dimension. This dimension reflects the duration of symptomatology, as does chronicity, but it also reflects the extent of psychosis. The Ritzler studies illustrate that when we control for psychosis by assessing the process-reactive dimension in other psychotic patients, we lose another deficit unique to schizophrenia. Such results suggest that when we assess psychosis by the process-reactive dimension, the dependent variable may reflect this dimension and not the effect of a core marker.

Otteson and Holzman (1976) continued this line of investigation by direct examination of the issue of psychosis and schizophrenia. They note that the work on cognitive controls, which are relatively stable within a person over time, yields ambiguous results for schizophrenics. They believe this is because the usual examination of schizophrenics actually reflects schizophrenic disorganization rather than the schizophrenic process. In their terms, the cognitive control variables are trait variables and must be distinguished from psychotic disorganization, which is a state variable. We see conflicting results on cognitive variables, they contend, because they reflect different aspects of the state condition rather than the trait. In a rather extensive examination of cognitive measures, they found that schizophrenic deficits were a function of degree of disorganization—they called it patienthood or general organismic disequilibrium—that is not specific to any particular diagnostic group. They examined degree of pathology by comparing all psychiatric patients with normal controls, psychiatric patients with nonpsychotic patients, and psychotics diagnosed as schizophrenic with psychotics diagnosed as nonschizophrenic. They also assessed the degree of thought disorder of schizophrenics and nonschizophrenics and found that schizophrenics exhibited greater thought disorder. Unfortunately, however, they did not directly relate this variable to cognitive performance, which would have lent further credence to their main finding that cognitive disorganization was the major factor related to test performance. On a complex factor analysis of a large number of cognitive tasks such as the Stroop, Size Estimation, and Rod-and-Frame tests, the aspects of test performance that were related to inefficiency rather than to a difference in cognitive styles produced between-group differences. In effect, the same cognitive styles found in normals are characteristic of clinical populations, with no distinction between schizophrenic and nonschizophrenic patients, and the differences found between groups were based on level of disorganization. On some measures psychotic patients of any label did more poorly than nonpsychotics. The researchers did find subgroup differences within schizophrenia, in that process schizophrenics did worse than reactives on some measures. Unfortunately, they did not assess process-reactive status of nonschizophrenics, or they may not have found this subgroup difference to be unique to schizophrenia; as in the Ritzler (1977) study, they might have found that the process patient of any category did worse than the corresponding reactive patient. However, their conclusion is of the most interest. They conclude that there is no evidence for specific cognitive controls of any group, and that level of disorganization is mainly responsible for lowered performance on measures of cognitive style. Of interest to this discussion is their research strategy of separating laboratory task performance into the efficiency component, reflecting disorganization, and a cognitive component reflecting a core process. They also initiate the idea of assessing the degree of thought disorder in all patients, since it could be directly related to performance independent of diagnostic grouping. In Figure 1, I present thought disorder as a separate dimension relative to psychosis, but in fact it may be the best measure of the extent of psychosis.

The studies above controlled for the effects of psychosis by comparing schizophrenics with other psychotics or by assessing the degree of pathology as reflected in the process-reactive dimension or level of chronicity. When such controls are used, we find that effects on the dependent variable are related mainly to secondary aspects of the disorder, not to schizophrenia. The Otteson and Holzman (1976) concept of a level of disorganization or disequilibrium that can be measured in each diagnostic group is a way to disentangle the confounding effects of a dimension of psychosis. Such work indicates that schizophrenics at least should be compared with other psychotics and that both groups should be assessed on a direct measure of psychosis.

Means of controlling for other forms of pathology with high-risk children are exemplified in a study by Harvey, Winters, Weintraub, and Neale (1981). Children of schizophrenics, unipolar and bipolar depressives, and normals were tested on a digit-span measure of distractibility. Although schizophrenics were not alone in exhibiting distractibility, they were distinct in the type of deficit they showed. The researchers concluded that the schizophrenics had problems with controlled information processing. Such a vulnerability marker was indicated because only the children of schizophrenics made errors at the beginning of the digit-span list when distractors were present. Employing children of depressives in the research design controls for pathology in the home, or possibly in the children themselves, and allows the assertion that the specific problem is unique to the children of schizophrenics.

Oltmanns (1978) obtained the same result on the same task with adult schizophrenics, who differed from normals on the early segment of a digit-span list; when schizophrenics were compared with a control group of manics, however, their uniqueness disappeared, and they did not differ from manics on a number of measures. Thus, although children of schizophrenics differ from children of depressives, adult schizophrenics do not differ from manic patients. The Oltmanns (1978) study controlled for level of present pathology and suggested that the distractibility results might be related to a particular condition, the thought disorder: "It may be that distractibility is more directly related to this particular symptom than to any diagnostic category" (Oltmanns, 1978, p. 224).

Another way to deal with this issue is to study individuals who can be identified as schizophrenic but have never experienced a psychotic episode. This method has been used by the Chapmans (Chapman & Chapman, 1980), who have examined the core process in schizophrenia by testing nonpsychotic schizophrenics identified by scale measures such as anhedonia and social withdrawal (Numbers & Chapman, 1982), mainly in terms of predicting psychosis in normal individuals who may have particular traits but not exhibit any psychosis. One such trait is anhedonia. Chapman and Chapman (1976) describe anhedonia as a lowered ability to experience pleasure, and some authors have considered this a basic characteristic of schizophrenia (Bleuler, 1950; Rado, 1956, 1962). Further, this loss of pleasure is considered to lead to inappropriate behavior and social isolation (Meehl, 1973). Chapman and Chapman (1976) postulate that differences in level of premorbid functioning may be a function of differences in anhedonia. On measures of physical and social anhedonia, schizophrenics appeared more anhedonic than normal males, but not all schizophrenic subjects scored as anhedonic. Within the schizophrenic sample, hedonics and anhedonics differed in premorbid functioning, hedonics being more reactive than anhedonics. Further, these authors note that the relation between process-reactive and anhedonia scales suggests that anhedonia may be an enduring trait in those who possess it.[2]

Another way to control for psychosis is offered by Asarnow and MacCrimmon (1978). In their review of the literature on attention and information processing, they found only two studies that used clinically remitted schizophrenics, although remitted patients experience minimal pathology and thus could exhibit core schizophrenic processes without the effects of psychosis. Asarnow and Asarnow (1982) also reported that a span-of-apprehension task differentiated remitted schizophrenics from "partially recovered" manic-depressives. However, they identified only a small group of remitted schizophrenics who performed differently from manic-depressives on this task. Such a result suggests that it may be the more psychotic and less remitted, though discharged, patient who still exhibits this deficit because the measure is psychosis-dependent. Certainly the use of remitted schizophrenics or partially recovered manics does not indicate that the secondary aspects of the disorder are absent. One could certainly assume that patients show less psychosis in the remitted stage than on admission, but discharge does not necessarily guarantee absence or decrease of symptoms. Comparing two remitted groups may amount to comparing groups with similar levels of pathology, so that the dependent variable is similarly affected by psychosis in each group. However, group differences in psychosis may also be present in judgments of remission for different diagnostic groups; thus, level of psychosis between groups should be independently assessed.

To summarize, I have discussed some ways to control for level of psychosis that are presented in Figure 1. There are two main research strategies. One is to examine specific subject dimensions that could be correlated with the dependent variable, the other is to compare the schizophrenics with other groups that share the same level of psychosis or exhibit no psychosis. Subject dimensions that control for level of pathology are chronicity, degree of thought disorder, and a process-reactive continuum. A thought-disorder measure would be the most direct measure of the extent of the

2. I am indebted to Mark Johnson for relating work on depression to the issue of psychosis.

disorder, and the chronicity measure would best reflect duration. The process reactive continuum may reflect both dimensions. Certainly other measures are available for assessing degree of psychosis or extent of pathology. The Lorr (1953) scales for inpatient and outpatient populations, devised for this purpose, measure dimensions of psychosis in terms of symptom content. Three other inventories that measure degree of pathology are the Structural Clinical Interview (Burdock & Hardesty, 1969), the Psychotic Symptoms Inventory (PSI) (Harrow & Silverstein, 1977), and the Schedule for Affective Disorders and Schizophrenia (SADS) (Endicott & Spitzer, 1978). The PSI is based upon the Present State Examination (Wing, Cooper, & Sartorius, 1974) and includes all eleven of Schneider's first-rank symptoms (Schneider, 1959) as well as other signs such as delusions, hallucinations, and sensory aberrations. This scale yields an "overall psychotic symptoms" value indicative of the severity of psychotic symptoms. The Structural Clinical Interview yields an overall level of psychopathology score, as well as yielding ten subscores of dimensions of pathology (Sollod & Lapidus, 1977). Finally, the SADS-C provides a measure of pathology focusing upon the one-week period before the interview. This interview provides an overall level of function (global assessment scale) as well as yielding severity ratings along eight dimensions. The SADS-C is designed to be used repeatedly, thus monitoring severity from one period to the next. Since the 1978 publication of the Research Diagnostic Criteria, a host of research endeavors have utilized this instrument, propelling it toward being the standard research instrument to measure level of pathology.

The control group approach has used equivalent psychotics, remitted schizophrenics, and nonsymptomatic schizophrenics. The expectation is that the latter two groups have no psychosis, so that this value is near zero, and thus that dependent variable effects are due to schizophrenia. Both approach strategies have their merits, but the best strategy may be a combination of the two where control groups are used and the degree of psychosis is assessed within each group. Let me add one other dimension that may reflect level of psychosis—diagnosis itself as presented in the current diagnostic system.

Diagnosis as a Dimension of Pathology

The present diagnostic system attempts to characterize a disease as reflected by presented symptoms. We use this system to isolate individuals exhibiting the core process that underlies the pathological state. Thus it is accepted that the diagnostic label contains the signs manifested by a core disorder. Although I do not disagree with this approach, it must be accepted that the diagnostic system contains by its nature a degree or level of pathology.

Stone (1968) had psychiatrists estimate the magnitude and category of impairment of fifteen psychotic diagnoses. The resulting judgmental continuum was related to the external validity criteria of IQ, scores on a psychoticism scale, and length of hospital stay through a psychophysical power-law function. In effect, diagnostic judgments of the severity of a disorder agree with other measures of severity. Hence a diagnostic judgment about which diagnostic category best fits the behavior of the individual is made on the basis of severity within the individual rather than particular signs of a diagnostic category. The diagnostic categories thus are applied on the basis of the extent of the psychosis exhibited rather than the type of psychosis, the class of signs summarized in the syndrome.

Figure 2 presents the relation between level of pathology and a diagnosis of some type of schizophrenia that could be adapted from the DSM-III. I suspect the extent of the psychosis would be the major element in the diagnosis, ordered in terms of degree of pathology. I will also include the paranoid dimension, since I will be discussing the core traits of that group along with those of schizophrenics. I have previously discussed in detail the necessity of separating paranoids from nonparanoid schizophrenics (Magaro, 1980, 1981; *Schizophrenia Bulletin*, 1981, 7, no. 4, presents a thorough discussion of this distinction in regard to process, symptom, and treatment).

Beginning at the low-pathology end of the diagnostic dimension in Figure 2, there are schizophrenic personalities who may be well adjusted but share particular traits. This may be the group studied by Chapman and others who examine people in the normal population as defined by a particular MMPI profile or particular schizophrenic trait measures. The schizoid personality disorder may also fall into this grouping. The schizotypical and schizophreniform disorders seem to be middle points in terms of level of psychosis. The reactive schizophrenic may also be included in this middle

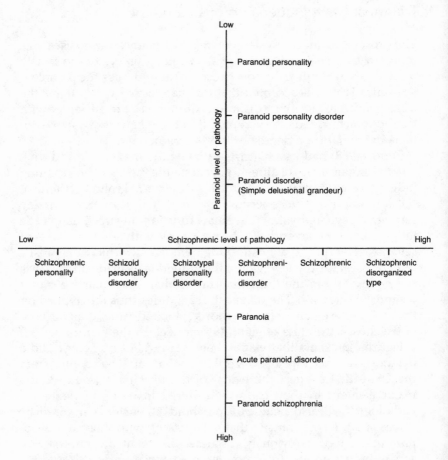

FIGURE 2. Levels of pathology for schizophrenics and paranoids as adapted from DSM-III.

range, while the process schizophrenic may be more obviously psychotic. At the end point is the disorganized schizophrenic that in the older terminology would be the hebephrenic subtype. Other schizophrenic categories used in DSM-III—such as acute, latent, and residual—may all relate to this dimension. It would be difficult to separate such a symptom continuum into discrete categories, since symptom behavior can easily change from day to day.

In summary, there are a number of dimensions of the secondary aspects of schizophrenia. Some may be situationally based, and others may be individual differences. All, however, have the potential for confounding experimental results in terms of the effects of core schizophrenic processes. Some measures of pathology, especially of duration, have been employed in most research designs for the past ten years. Other direct measures of psychosis such as thought-disorder indexes are relatively recent. The more such measures are employed, the more difficult it is to find results unique to schizophrenia. However, some agreement is arising concerning the cognitive processes that may be unique to this disorder. The following section describes such core processes in terms of information-processing strategies and hemispheric laterality.

SCHIZOPHRENIC COGNITION

I shall now present a revision of integration theory (Magaro 1980, 1981) in terms of current data on the core processes in schizophrenia and the effect of the psychosis. Let me begin with an analogy. If you examine a tapestry from a distance you see a pattern, but if you look closely you see only individual threads. A piano can produce a set of notes, the scale, that can be combined in certain ways to create music. The threads or the notes are the structure, the elements, of a complex process—the tapestry or the composition. Psychology has always wondered about the relation between man as a process and his structure—between the psychological and the physical, the mind and the body. Which notes in a structural sense create the psychological state that is man in thought and action?

Here we are concerned with schizophrenics and with their cognition relative to their neurological structure. A set of studies performed in our laboratory demonstrate what I believe to be the cognitive traits specific to schizophrenia—the fugue, so to speak, that the schizophrenic creates from the notes available—and that will be the theme carried contrapuntally throughout the orchestra. I then will review our work on hemispheric preferences—the notes, so to speak, that are the elements of the fugue. I will discuss two sets of core markers, one involved with information processing and one involved with hemisphere specialization. In our work we control for psychosis by usually using psychotic controls, by using only acute patients who are generally only reactives, and by measuring the degree of thought disorder in all groups. We thus focus upon the schizo-

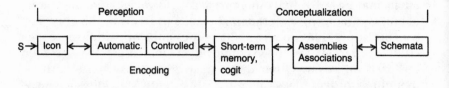

FIGURE 3. An information-processing model illustrating terms and processes.

phrenic compared with appropriate control groups with assessed level of psychosis, not the schizophrenic devoid of psychosis.

Results from information-processing stages such as encoding cannot be clearly understood independent of the effect of other stages. Similarly, the data generated by various research paradigms aimed at different information-processing stages can best be understood in a complete context. Looking at only one area of investigation such as recall memory or an evoked potential would be like listening just to the horns in a concert and ignoring the reeds. Obviously the score could not be appreciated.

Figure 3 presents a model (Magaro, 1980) that attempts to organize the major research on information processing in schizophrenia. First let me draw attention to the bidirectional nature of information flow. Neisser (1976) used the term figural synthesis to capture the idea that knowledge is a constant dialectic between conceptual elements and the perceptual elements more closely tied to stimulus events. Hence at the encoding stage there is not merely a simple designation of iconic features but also an imposition of form generated by expectancies of content or associations in memory. However, it is not just the content of memory that can influence what is encoded, but the degree of conceptual organization. Although it is clear that stimulus attributes influence the way we process a stimulus field, the degree of association of elements in memory—the assemblies in Figure 3—also can affect encoding. Both concepts and percepts interact in deriving information. It is my thesis that schizophrenic subtypes differ in the way information flows so that preference is given to information generated either by the concept or by the percept. Whereas my previous theory focused upon the integration of perceptual and conceptual knowledge, my present orientation looks at these processes as separate channels that the person switches between depending upon situational demand and upon individual predispositions considered information-processing strategies.

This conception of directional information flow is not much different from some theories of information processing. Rabbitt (1979) is explicit in his concepts of data-driven and memory-driven information processing. His interesting series of studies showed that older individuals could be characterized by deficits in memory-driven processes, although data-driven processes were intact. Such directional processing is related to structural conditions in terms of central nervous system conditions that parallel my conception that the information processing of schizophrenics and paranoids is embedded in hemispheric preferences.

Within the information-processing model presented in Figure 3 there are a number of stages, for lack of a better term, that must be considered in a total context. The first is the short-term memory trace, the icon. It seems fairly clear that schizophrenics of any type have no problem with the strength of the icon (Magaro & Page, 1982). However, most work investigating the degree of processing off the icon indicates deficits in schizophrenics (Magaro, 1980, 1981).

Encoding

The encoding process is not a single phenomenon but can be performed in different ways. I have concentrated upon two types of encoding, serial and parallel, or controlled and automatic, following the usage of Shiffren and Schneider (1977). Schneider and Shiffrin (1977) empirically and quantitatively demonstrated the operation of what they labeled automatic and controlled processing. In their admirably thorough review, they demonstrated the action of an automatic processing strategy. Through repeated practice, a sequence of memory nodes are formed that become active in response to a particular stimulus input without the necessity of active control by the individual. In this stage, the processing of material is automatic, because an element in the stimulus activates the cognit—the basic unit of further conceptualization. Once activated and practiced, automatic processing is difficult to modify or ignore. It is not limited by memory load or number of distractors and requires only an initial discrimination of stimulus elements into sets that are practiced.

Controlled processing, on the other hand, is a sequential search operation that processes each element in the set and is a function of set size and memory load. Controlled processing can be seen in a task that requires serial comparison of a list of words to find a match. The process is under the control and attention of the subject and makes extensive use of short-term memory storage to consider all matching possibilities, which also provides greater accuracy in novel situations. The two processes operate in different types of situations, depending upon experience and upon the degree of categorization of the items in search. Automatic processing is much faster than controlled processing because the latter is serial in nature and dependent upon memory load.

Either process can be used for gathering information. I believe that nonparanoid schizophrenics, (I will label this group schizophrenics) engage the automatic process in most situations, although certainly not where a serial processing is required to determine the nature of the stimulus. Such persons will prefer to use the automatic process and report global percepts or elementary concepts. They will, however, employ the nonpreferred controlled processing, although poorly, to produce a more detailed and accurate (at least in terms of consensually validated concepts or categories) picture of the world if so required. However, schizophrenics will be less adept at controlled processing and more adept at automatic processing. Hence, on most laboratory tasks they will appear slow or inaccurate, because such tasks usually require serial processes performed in a limited time period. Specifically, I predict that schizophrenics will perform as well as normals in experiments that demand automatic processing and be deficient in experiments that require controlled processing. While schizophrenics may sometimes use controlled processing, they will do so more slowly because it is not a preferred strategy.

Controlled processing is most characteristic of paranoid schizophrenics (I will label this group paranoids). The paranoid dimension is shown in Figure 2, with the paranoid schizophrenic representing the end point in degree of pathology. Here information is processed in an active serial search, with reliance upon the category. This does not mean the paranoid never uses automatic processing. In fact, I propose that, in well-practiced situations, the lack of novelty creates the discriminative set where automatic processing can operate. I predict that the paranoid will prefer controlled processing when confronted with most situations and will maintain that process for a longer period. The information-processing strategy used will depend upon the novelty of the task. The greatest deficit will occur when automatic processing is required, and a concept should have the least influence on the percept.

Type of encoding, therefore, is partially related to the strength of association in memory. Controlled processing relies upon the establishment of a particular recognizable category in the memory set that is searched for in the stimulus pattern. This is not to say that automatic processing does not require specific objects in memory, but since it does not require an item-by-item search, the target in the stimulus field must be clearly distinguishable in order to be detected. Let me illustrate how the increase in discriminability can improve the accuracy of automatic processing.

A recent study that measured each process found that nonparanoid schizophrenics exhibited a deficit in the preattentive process while paranoid schizophrenics did not (Cox & Leventhal, 1978). On different measures of preattention such as counting the tilted figures in a matrix of upright figures or detecting inverted figures in a set of upright figures, nonparanoid schizophrenics took longer or made more errors. Of most interest was a procedure called enrichment, an attempt to enhance the stimulus elements that directly affected preattentive discriminability. Here the schizophrenics improved their performance to the levels of the paranoids and psychiatric controls. This suggests that, although the paranoids had no difficulty discriminating and reporting stimulus elements, the nonparanoids did not focus upon the relevant stimulus elements and required a greater discriminability to separate elements or engage in serial processing. Once stimulus elements were made more discriminable, the nonparanoids improved their performance level. Other groups did not demonstrate this effect. We might say that the increased discriminability allowed those who were employing an automatic type of processing to improve their performance because the stimulus field became discriminated enough to allow an automatic process to work efficiently. When the stimulus field was less discriminable, a controlled processing was more effective. Paranoids used controlled processing in the first place, so increased target discriminability did not produce much of an advantage. Nonparanoids, however, used an automatic processing, which is favorably affected by an increase in stimulus discriminability.

A series of studies in our laboratory investigated the hypothesis that schizophrenics prefer automatic processing and paranoids prefer controlled processing. Pic'l, Magaro, and Wade (1979) presented dots or letters to the right or left hemisphere. The task was to recognize as many letters as possible from a four-letter array or to count the dots in eight arrays ranging from three to ten dots each. The schizophrenic group was subdivided into paranoid and non-paranoid schizophrenics by the Maine Scale (Magaro, Abrams, & Cantrell, 1981), and the control groups were normals and other psychiatric patients, mainly with major affective disorders. I should note, especially in reference to the prior discussion on psychosis, that the Maine Scale attempts to assess paranoid or schizophrenic status without relying solely on present symptom status. It attempts to measure symptoms at any time period, such as at admission, to assess diagnostic class. In letter naming the left hemisphere produced more letter identification than the right for all groups. Non-paranoid schizophrenics also showed the hemisphere effect and recognized fewer letters than the controls. They were especially deficient in the left hemisphere. However, an examination of the effects of other subject dimensions negated this finding.

Our measure of pathology was a thought-disorder measure, the Expanded Similarities Test, which Hamlin and Lorr (1971) have found to differentiate between normals, neurotics, and psychotics and to be the key variable in a factor related to psychosis. This measure, as well as educational level, differentiated among groups. Psychiatric controls and nonparanoid schizophrenics had less education than paranoid schizophrenics and normals, which in itself may reflect duration of pathology. On the thought-disorder dimension, psychiatric controls and normals were equal, while paranoid and nonparanoid schizophrenics were high. Most important, both of these measures significantly correlated with performance on the letter task in both hemispheres. To make a long story short, once educational level was partialed out of the analysis of variance, nonparanoid schizophrenics no longer differed from controls. Taylor, Redfield, and Abrams (1981) also found that education was related to differences in both right- and left-hemisphere performance on a neuropsychological test battery.

Interestingly, the covariance analysis of level of pathology only equated groups in the left hemisphere. When pathology was equated for right-hemisphere performance, the nonparanoid schizophrenics were still different from controls. The hint was that

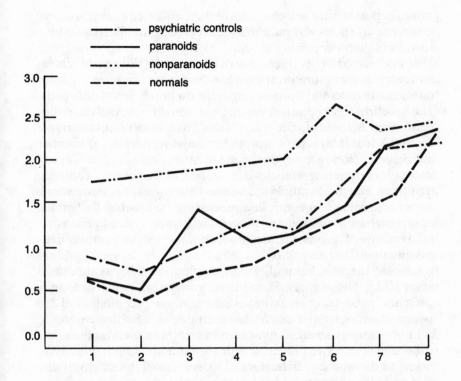

FIGURE 4. Dot enumeration, combining hemispheres. From Pic'l, Magaro, & Wade, 1979.

level of disorganization or psychosis may be directed to performance in one hemisphere more than in the other. However, since the task was a left-hemisphere task and the right hemisphere would not have been so much involved, and also since educational level accounted for the nonparanoid schizophrenic deficit, we ignored this finding and went on. I will, however, bring it up again when I discuss other results that indicate a specific effect of the psychosis on hemispheres.

The dot task produced no hemisphere effect, but nonparanoid schizophrenics made more errors across both hemispheres. The next analysis pointed to a possible reason. As Figure 4 shows, when we examined errors over dot numbers, we found that nonparanoid schizophrenics stayed relatively constant from small to large arrays while others made more errors as the array size increased. This pattern of performance suggested a particular strategy employed by nonparanoids and not by paranoids that could be interpreted within our information-processing model.

We interpreted the performance of paranoids in dot enumeration as indicating that more errors occur when there are more dots to count. In the controlled-processing function presented by Schneider and Shiffrin (1977), the number of figures in the field produces the same effect. Accuracy is dependent upon the number one can count before the icon fades. Schizophrenics, however, exhibit the same number of errors across five display sizes, possibly indicating automatic processing. Normals and nonschizophrenic controls performed like the paranoids. The conclusion was that paranoids, like others, engage in controlled processing on this task, whereas schizophrenics use automatic processing. However, this particular task is not most commonly used to distinguish between controlled and automatic processing.

A recent thesis (Chamrad, 1982) adopted the letter-search task reported by Neisser (1963) to directly examine controlled and automatic processing in schizophrenics. Chamrad attempted to specify the characteristic processing strategies used by paranoid and nonparanoid schizophrenics when searching for a target letter embedded within two particular types of stimulus fields, contexts of dissimilar or similar distractors. Neisser (1967) noted that the relation of the target's configuration to that of the context (distractors) plays an important role. While automatic processes will suffice in distinguishing a target letter from very dissimilar letters, controlled processing is necessary in locating a target letter within similar distractor items where it is necessary to distinguish particular angles, open spaces, parallel lines, and such.

We hypothesized that paranoid schizophrenics would conduct a serial, controlled analysis of the letter arrays even when this detailed analysis was unnecessary—that is, in the arrays where the target item was in sharp contrast to distractors. Nonparanoids would rely upon an automatic strategy, quickly scanning the lists and searching for distinguishing features. This strategy suffices in processing the arrays where the target is in contrast to the distractor set, but when the target is not easily distinguishable from the distractors nonparanoids are forced into controlled processing, a mode of processing at which they are not especially adept. Thus processing time should be slower, although the controlled processing function or slope should be equivalent to that of other groups.

Figure 5 presents the X̄ reaction time-slope values of each group in the dissimilar and similar distractor lists. The higher the value on the graph, the steeper is the slope, representing a more serial type of processing. As can be seen, the first three blocks, which contained the dissimilar distractors, show paranoids to be distinguishable from all other groups. They serially processed while all other groups processed in a more automatic fashion, as expected from task characteristics. In looking at the next three trial blocks, 4–6, where the distractor was similar to the target, all groups increased their slope, with paranoids tending to be even more exact but not differing significantly from all control groups. There also was a tendency for a higher overall reaction time or higher intercepts for nonparanoid schizophrenics, but this did not reach significance. These results indicate that paranoids employ a controlled processing strategy even when a faster, more automatic strategy will suffice. The nature of the first three trial blocks allowed for automatic processing, which all groups except the paranoids took advantage of. In tasks requiring controlled processing, they are comparable to other groups.

Regarding the hypothesis that paranoids and nonparanoids employ distinct processing strategies and that these strategies vary according to characteristics of the stimulus field, it is important that nonparanoids were able to adapt their processing strategies to task demands. The first time they were presented with the similar distractors, trial block 4, their slope was the flattest and their intercept the highest; but by the next trial block they had begun to process serially. The dissimilar context allowed more of a choice of strategic processing; accordingly, paranoids employed controlled processing while both nonparanoids and controls employed automatic processing. However, the similar context did not allow as much choice. The task demanded controlled processing, and all subjects responded accordingly, though nonparanoids had the greatest difficulty making this adjustment. The two variations of this visual search task, therefore, were able to elicit two distinct processing strategies in nonparanoids but only one strategy in paranoids. This same rigidity of response by paranoids appeared in the dichotic listening tasks I will discuss later when I present laterality results.

At this point let me note only that the task imposed structural limitations on the strategies employed. While nonparanoids may be

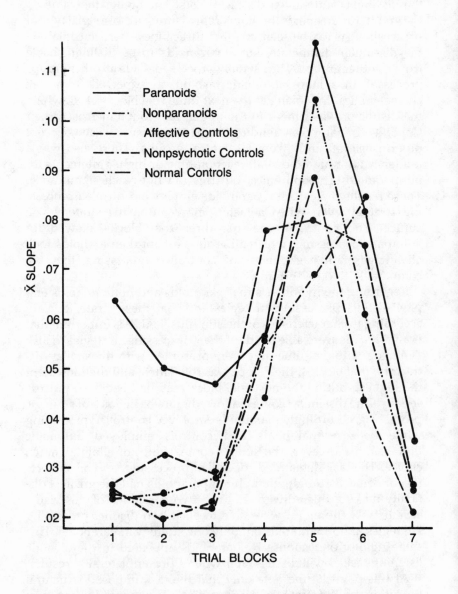

FIGURE 5. $\bar{X}$ slope on trial blocks 1–7, by groups. From Chamrad, 1982.

schizophrenic, they are not necessarily crazy; after some initial difficulties they employ the type of processing that the task demands of any information processor, namely controlled processing. I suspect that, were the situation reversed and the paranoids forced into a situation requiring automatic processing with no way to complete the task serially, the same adaptive process would occur after an initial period of adjustment.

We then repeated the initial study using dots (Magaro & Chamrad, 1983a) but divided the dot-enumeration task into versions using structured and unstructured dot arrays. Using two types of arrays increased the potential for using a parallel type of processing, since it was thought that structured patterns that formed a gestalt would encourage automatic processing. The unstructured dot arrays would demand more of a serial approach. The same acute subject groups were used, and the psychiatric controls again were mainly depressives. While the normal controls differed from the psychiatric groups on many dimensions, only educational level and vocabulary produced a difference between the psychiatric controls and the nonparanoid schizophrenics. Both subject variables correlated significantly with identification of letters in both hemispheres.

Again, as in the previous study (Pic'l et al., 1979), letters were recognized in the left hemisphere more often than the right. Letter position was also significant, as in the previous study, and the schizophrenic groups did not differ from the psychiatric control group when subject variables were controlled. So again, in both hemispheres letters are recognized by either schizophrenic group to the same degree as by other groups. In terms of dots, we replicated the previous results. All groups increased their errors as display size increased except the nonparanoid schizophrenics. However, there was an additional finding: the nonparanoids exhibited this performance only in the left hemisphere. In the right hemisphere they improved their performance with increased display size at least as well as other groups. This effect occurred with both dot arrays. Structured dot arrays only produced more accuracy than the unstructured ones. The results for the structured arrays are presented in Figure 6. As can be seen, the flat function for the nonparanoid group occurs only in the left hemisphere.

I interpret this work to mean there are processing styles that can characterize schizophrenics and paranoids. Much other work has come to this same conclusion and is reviewed elsewhere (Magaro, 1980). However, as seen in the information-processing model

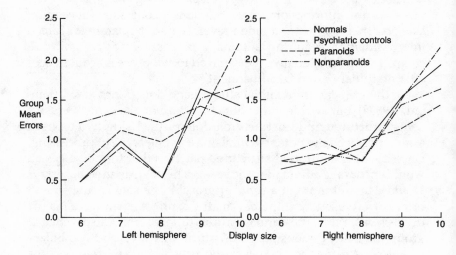

FIGURE 6. Structured dot enumeration by display size and left and right hemispheres.

presented in Figure 3, I do not believe encoding operates in a vacuum. The type and kind of other processes will relate to the type of processing employed to the same degree as to situational conditions. I shall now review the conceptual segments of the information-processing model.

Conceptual Organization

In explaining the relation between conceptual structure and the encoding process, I should first note that both encoding strategies require a representation in memory of the object being recognized. I have followed Hayes-Roth (1977) and labeled that single memory element a cogit—a single bit of information such as a letter, a number, or a word (Magaro, 1980). The encoding strategies are codes that explain how a stimulus representation on the icon or in the visual field is recognized. The exact nature of the code that transforms the physical field into a meaningful piece of information is a continued subject of investigation. I have applied two encoding strategies that explain the match in specific circumstances. In either controlled or automatic processing, however, a cogit is required to extract information from the stimulus field. As such, memory processes themselves become crucial to understanding the type of encoding employed by certain groups, because the strength of the cogit may influence the type of encoding strategy employed in the particular situation.

Schwartz-Place and Gilmore (1980) suggest that the encoding strategy of schizophrenics could be modified by the conceptual demands of an experimental task. In a detection task where number of lines were to be counted, process schizophrenics and controls performed equally. However, when the stimulus field consisted of both circles and lines and the subject had to report the number of lines, schizophrenics performed worse than controls. In effect, the task was to establish a category—lines—and ignore the other category, circles. A plot of the Schwartz-Place and Gilmore (1980) data suggests serial processing by both groups such that on the six-line condition, where there were no distractor circles, schizophrenics performed most differently from controls. This suggests a serial processing function, because the largest number of errors were at the larger display sizes irrespective of distractors. That is, as the display size (number of lines) increased, fewer lines were reported. Schizophrenics showed the same pattern but reported even fewer lines at each display size. This suggests that all groups serially processed the list and reported the number of lines processed during the stimulus exposure time and the duration of the icon. As the display size increased, fewer lines could be counted, so the number was underestimated. Presenting circles worsened the performance of schizophrenics relative to controls because schizophrenics did not divide objects into the categories I have labeled the cogit and, thus, processed each item in the field, including circles. Their underestimation therefore was greater than that of controls, who counted only the lines and disregarded the circles. Schizophrenics processed each character, distractor or not, and at a slower rate than the controls; hence, even without a distractor in the field the number of lines they reported followed the same function as when distractors were present in the smaller frame sizes. The more efficient processing strategy of "pigeonholing" (Broadbent, 1971) the stimuli into two categories and encoding only one category was not employed.

A test of this hypothesis was attempted in a second experiment in the same report (Schwartz-Place & Gilmore, 1980) by placing the line elements in gestalts that included vertical and horizontal lines arranged by degree of figural organization. The figural gestalts did not affect schizophrenics but did impair the performance of controls. The superior performance of schizophrenics was due to their not spending time switching between line gestalts and thus decreasing the time available for processing. They simply counted the lines in the display (Schwartz-Place & Gilmore, 1980).

These results suggest that schizophrenics serially process a small number of elements but do not organize them by conceptual grouping. However, from the encoding results presented above, we would expect schizophrenics to engage in less serial processing than controls. If task demands are such that serial processing is too difficult or automatic processing could be employed, we expect schizophrenics to engage in an automatic processing strategy more often than other groups. The Magaro and Chamrad (1983a) study, which used organized and unorganized dot patterns, found that nonparanoid schizophrenics serially processed only when the display had six or fewer dots. When the display size was more than six, they used an automatic processing strategy. In effect, when a large number of elements are presented, schizophrenics will not serially process but will attempt parallel processing, whereas paranoids still attempt to process serially. I believe the automatic processing strategy is preferred for nonparanoid schizophrenics, but it is still limited by situational demands. Paranoid schizophrenics prefer a serial type of encoding even when it is extremely difficult. If the Schwartz-Place and Gilmore (1980) study had used other schizophrenic subtypes instead of only process patients, we would have expected differential performance functions. That there was no control group of psychiatric patients also limits the generalizability of the results. However, these findings suggest that the serial processing strategy of nonparanoid schizophrenics is not deficient in itself but fails when confronted by certain task demands, especially those that require a cogit in their encoding.

We do not expect either schizophrenics or paranoids to have deviant cogits. If a word is presented, both groups should discriminate that stimulus into the same elements as others do and recognize it as the same word. Therefore we would not expect recognition-memory deficits. The usual recognition-memory paradigm measures the strength of the associated value of the cogit; encoding is not a primary factor, since stimuli are presented for long periods

and all groups recognize the same stimulus. Most recognition studies have not found schizophrenic subgroup differences or schizo-
phrenic/control differences in recognition. Nachmani and Cohen
(1969) found no difference between controls and a mixed patient
group of acute nonparanoid schizophrenics. Bauman and Murray
(1968) also reported no difference between a group of normals and a
mixed patient group of paranoid and nonparanoid schizophrenics,
even though the alternatives in the recognition list were semantically or acoustically similar to the correct words. Koh, Kayton, and
Berry (1973) presented words and high- and low-association nonsense syllables to young acute nonpsychotic nonparanoids in a
recognition task. Again the recognition memory of schizophrenics
in a signal detection analysis was found to be as good as that of
normals. The conclusion was that, regardless of frequency, conceptual categories, or association values, the recognition memory of
schizophrenics is as good as that of normals.

However, what of the case in which a number of associations
must be constructed in memory in order to complete a task such as
remembering words that have been presented? I believe nonparanoid schizophrenics would have difficulty with this. The problem
would be most obvious when they were required to recall material,
because recall is best performed when a number of associations are
organized into what I have termed an assembly.

Let me summarize what I consider the cognitive styles of paranoids and schizophrenics (Magaro, 1980). Paranoids rely on a rigid
conceptual process without adequate constraint from perceptual
data—stimulus features stripped of conceptual loading—while
schizophrenics rely primarily on perceptual data without adequate
categorization and classification from conceptual processes. Situations vary in the need to employ either process. The schizophrenic
or paranoid cognitive process will be found to be adaptive or maladaptive depending upon the demands of the situation and its
congruence with the dominant cognitive style.

Johnson (1982) offers a distinction between associational and
hierarchical memory organization that clarifies the difference in the
structure of the assemblies of paranoids and schizophrenics. Associational organization links terms on the basis of associations such
as black/white that occur through practice. The hierarchical form
considers not the degree of constraint between items, but the pattern of relation between them as related to superordinate categories.
An example would be the greater ease of recalling items in the same

conceptual category. That schizophrenics have no great difficulty with recognition tasks but usually exhibit a problem in recall, especially when there is a need to form categories, is evidence that nonparanoid schizophrenics do not use a hierarchical memory organization, although they may perform associative memory tasks adequately. That paranoids do not have a deficit in recall memory when psychosis is controlled (Magaro, 1980) is evidence that paranoids have adequate hierarchical memory organization. In fact, I will present some evidence that their memory organization is too hierarchical in that the superordinate categories contain too many associations.

An additional idea is that with little hierarchical coding there would be little "chunking" of information into larger units. In my formulation this would relate to the assemblies, where information is organized in a hierarchical fashion and the strength of the associations between elements is a function of the degree of use of a superordinate category. I would further expect that the serial coding required for memory storage, especially in creating a hierarchical organization, would also be applied to a detection problem. Hence the results on digit-span memory studies and the evoked potential that I shall discuss may all reflect a lesser memory organization for schizophrenics that would also be exhibited in decreased serial processing.

While nonparanoids have the greatest difficulty with the strength of configurations owing to associational memory structures, paranoids have strong idiosyncratic higher-order hierarchical memory structures that interfere with the formation of new assemblies. Differences in the recall memory of paranoid and nonparanoid schizophrenics suggest that nonparanoids have difficulty with memory tasks requiring hierarchical memory organization. This is not found with paranoids or normals. Koh and Kayton (1974) asked normals and acute nonparanoid schizophrenics to recall words varying in frequency, imagery, concreteness, meaningfulness, and affectivity under delay and no-delay conditions. Overall, the recall of normals was superior to that of nonparanoid schizophrenics. Schizophrenics made more intrusion errors, from both within and outside the memory list. Apparently schizophrenics were not able to generate an internal structure to aid them in recall. In the same study that found no differences in recognition memory, Koh, Kayton, and Berry (1973) used ordered and free recall to examine the subjective organization, categorical clustering, and hierarchical clustering schemata of acute nonparanoid schizophrenics. Schizophrenics did not show normative categorical clustering to the same extent as normals, nor did they show as much subjective organization to facilitate recall. Normals were superior on both uncategorized and categorized word lists. Whereas normals increased their categorical clustering (recalling items from the same conceptual category together) and subjective organization (grouping items together through trials) over trials, schizophrenics did not.

Another study not only demanded that schizophrenics form their own assemblies but provided a hint about why it is difficult for them to do so. Bauman and Kolisnyk (1976) studied interference effects in the short-term memory of acute schizophrenics. The task involved the recall of seven digits, but the order of recall was varied. The first analysis examined only the initial response of each subject in each serial position. Although normals exhibited superior recall over positions, schizophrenics followed the same recall pattern as normals, with greater recall at the beginning and end of the list. The next analysis examined the effect on recall of interpolation of the subjects' responses—that is, recall when subjects had to recite prior digits. Here schizophrenics had poorer recall when they had to recall more prior digits. They made more omissions and insertions but fewer reversals than normals. The conclusion was that as the schizophrenics responded they experienced greater difficulty with retrieval. The authors suggest that the problem was response interference owing to the lack of processing.

In other words, subjects needed to recreate the total list in order to present the digit at the expected position. One might say they had to "unitize" the list—that is, form the individual cogits into an assembly in order to form a single memory unit. I contend that the schizophrenics were not able to do this, since they do not usually engage in the serial activity necessary for such unitization. Possibly the results can be explained in terms of rehearsal, but from my analysis of the encoding results I suggest that schizophrenics do not serially process in any stage of information processing, including rehearsal, but prefer the more holistic automatic search. Bauman and Kolisnyk (1976) note that the task requires a serial processing in rehearsal. I postulate that, regardless of rehearsal, the task requires a strategy of serial processing—controlled processing—in memory. That strategy in itself is not a usual schizophrenic approach to discriminating a visual field or forming assemblies. Hence schizophrenics would be deficient in forming assemblies when not aided by experimental conditions. In short, nonparanoid schizophrenics do not maintain the associational structures that aid memory because there is little internal organization of elements. I have found no work that reports this deficit with paranoids.

A study by Harvey, Winters, Weintraub, and Neale (1981) is especially revealing when we consider this process as a vulnerability marker. With appropriate control groups for the parents of children at risk—unipolar and bipolar depressives—children at risk for schizophrenia produced deficits only on the initial segment of a digit-span task that contained distractors. The task, repeating five digits with a different-sex voice saying irrelevant digits in the two-second intervals between digits, required rehearsal of the initial digits while memorizing the latter digits. Schizophrenics did not perform this rehearsal, which the authors contend was because of the distracting digits interfering with a controlled processing into memory. They are thus proposing that the schizophrenics did not continue to serially process the initial list during retention but instead paid attention to the distractors. I agree with this interpretation, but I also think they could perform the rehearsal if the expectation was made explicit. Schizophrenics prefer not to serially code information, in terms of detection or memory, but this tendency is a strategy choice rather than a structural problem. In either case, however, it may be a vulnerability marker, though with different connotations in regard to reversibility.

While nonparanoid schizophrenics seem to perform memory tasks poorly because of weak cognitive structures, paranoids' assembly strength may be either helpful or a hindrance depending on task requirements. When paranoid and nonparanoid conceptual performance is examined in a recognition task where information regarding the target object is added slowly to an inadequate data base, paranoids tend to reach conclusions quickly rather than waiting for more information. McReynolds, Collins, and Acker (1964) found that delusional schizophrenics attempted to identify more pictures, and identified more pictures correctly, in the McGill Closure Test than nondelusional schizophrenics, supporting their view that the former have "a stronger tendency to organize ambiguous stimuli in a meaningful way" (pp. 211–212). In short, paranoids tend to assign specific meaning to stimuli in a stereotyped manner, a style that functions adaptively in situations where such expectations are justified. If the experimental situation is constructed so that expectations are not justified, however, we would expect paranoids to exhibit a deficit. On the other hand, nonparanoids' lack of conceptual control should permit a comparatively unbiased processing of complex perceptual material.

McDowell, Reynolds, and Magaro (1975) directly tested the effect of expectancy in paranoids and schizophrenics, using a signal detection task to demonstrate the interaction between task requirements and paranoid-nonparanoid adaptation. They predicted that where optimum performance should be improved by conceptual processes (expectation of a high-probability message), paranoids would perform better than nonparanoids, but that when the same task was altered so that such expectations would hinder performance (low probability message), nonparanoids would perform better. Generally, these predictions were supported. The effects of the paranoid conceptual emphasis and the schizophrenic perceptual emphasis were most clearly demonstrated in the medium-difficulty ranges, where paranoid performance was best on probable endings and nonparanoid performance was best on improbable endings. For the schizophrenics, lack of expectations permitted more accurate recognition of improbable words. Normals performed significantly better than either pathological group in the low-probability condition, suggesting that normals switch their processing strategies depending upon the situation.

Koh, Kayton, and Berry (1973) made the most direct attack on the question of associations and higher-order assemblies, what I term schemata. Following Miller's (1956) unitization theory, they hypothesize that schizophrenics cannot "chunk" input material into larger units to lessen the load of short-term memory. In my terms, they do not develop the associational strength between cogits to create strong hierarchical assemblies. Using a fixed and free recall procedure that explores the type and quality of the cogit assemblies, the authors were able to examine the subjective organization, degree of categorical clustering, and hierarchical clustering schemata used by young, acute nonparanoid, nonactively psychotic schizophrenics. As mentioned before, they found that schizophrenics do not use normative categorical clustering schemes to the same extent as normals, nor do they use as much subjective organization to facilitate recall. Normals were superior with both uncategorized and categorized word lists. While controls increased their categorical clustering (recalling items together through trials), schizophrenics did not. Since the recognition memory was the same for schizophrenics and controls in this study, the problem for nonparanoids was in the chunking process. Schizophrenics did not chunk to any great degree, nor did they organize by any common method; that is, the organizations developed by schizophrenics differed widely between individuals and from those of controls. The individualistic subjective organization suggests that schizophrenics have loose conceptual associations and that they do not form the assemblies common in the normal population. Poor recall, therefore, was due to the lack of strong assemblies, which were in turn due to a lack of strong associations. Hence, even though the cogit has the same strength as in normals, as evidenced in the lack of group differences in the recognition studies, the associations that form the assemblies are weak. Since the use of organizational schemes places the nonschizophrenic patient group between schizophrenics and normals, the authors conclude that the organization deficit in schizophrenics is a matter of degree, not quality (Koh, Kayton, & Berry, 1973).

Other studies have investigated complex information processing at the level of the schema. Task demands operated differentially for paranoids, nonparanoids, and controls. Hirt, Cuttler, and Genshaft (1977) designed a series of motor, perceptual, and symbolic tasks on a continuum of complexity. Generally, schizophrenics were found to be slower and paranoids faster than the other groups on symbolic tasks. The procedure was interesting in its approach to varying conceptual demands on subjects. As more conceptual demands were added, there was a concomitantly greater need to use assemblies. Accordingly, the deficit of nonparanoid schizophrenics increased while that of paranoids remained unchanged.

With tasks of increasing complexity, the different strategies or conceptual characteristics of the subgroups become clearer. Neufeld (1977) studied judgments of word similarity by paranoid and nonparanoid schizophrenics and by normals. A multidimensional scaling solution compared the three groups on dimensions used in judging verbal meaning. Paranoids used more dimensions than normals and nonparanoids, suggesting an emphasis on conceptual processing. Paranoids' judgments were also much less accurate than those of normals. Neufeld inferred that there was greater unpredictability in the judgments of paranoids. Apparently the assemblies of the paranoids were more idiosyncratic, with greater individual variability. In other words, the assemblies were more complex than those of normals, but the dimensions employed were more personal.

Encoding and Retrieval

It seems that the same serial and automatic processing strategies seen in the detection tasks also occur in memory retrieval tasks. Encoding and memory organization are related, because when there are strong assemblies the world is organized, so to speak, and expectancies are strong concerning what should exist in the physical external world. Therefore, in encoding a stimulus field there will be a naturalistic constant serial search for the cogit that is suggested by the conceptual order. This same process occurs in searching memory. Schizophrenics and paranoids seem to exhibit memory systems that vary in organization and are related to their styles of encoding.

In an excellent study Broga and Neufeld (1981) contend that the difference between paranoids and nonparanoids is in the response system. They note that paranoids produce inferior judgments of similarity among multidimensional stimuli (Neufeld, 1976), which may reflect a lower subjective criterion for a sufficient stimulus analysis, while nonparanoids evince a slowness in encoding stimuli, which may reflect guardedness against premature responding (Kietzman & Sutton, 1977). Their study was designed to separate response style from performance efficiency, and they conclude that paranoids are lowest in processing efficiency but high in the propensity to state the presence of stimuli, whereas nonparanoids are medium in processing efficiency and low in stating the presence of stimuli. Using a number of information-processing measures, they find that there is an interaction between the paranoid-nonparanoid dimension and task demands in that each group has a characteristic response style that could be facilitative or detrimental depending upon task requirements. For instance, paranoids would "draw certain inferences more liberally from present stimulation despite processing it less adequately. The nonparanoids tended to process more effectively than the paranoids but were more conservative in drawing certain inferences" (Broga & Neufeld, 1981, p. 506).

Of particular interest is a short-term memory task, the Sternberg (1975) choice reaction time procedure, which does not contain rehearsal but assesses speed of information retrieval in that one searches a memory list as one would search a detection list. On the trials when the target was present—positive memory sets—paranoids increased their reaction time as the size of the memory set increased. Nonparanoids, on the other hand, performed as though their memory set were equal to two elements—their reaction time on small sets was equal to that on larger sets. This is the same result I discussed in relation to the serial versus parallel processing of a detection task.

Of most interest is the unexpected finding that when the target was not present in the memory set—negative memory sets— nonparanoids' reaction-time slopes increased, even to being greater than those of controls. I interpret these results to mean that when the target is present nonparanoid schizophrenics process in an automatic manner so that slopes are low. When the target is absent, however, they have to repeat the search through the memory set, which they do in a serial manner, thus displaying the highest slope on negative traits. Paranoids, however, display the same slope as controls on positive trials even though they are slower, but they produce almost no slope on negative trials and have the highest intercept, which I interpret as indicating a repeated search of the memory set regardless of size.

On a short-term memory task where subjects memorize from one to five items, then are presented with a probe target and required to respond if the probe is in the set, therefore, nonparanoids do not exhibit a serial function if the probe occurs, indicating they have processed the memory set in an automatic fashion. Paranoids, on the other hand, exhibit a slope like that of normals, indicating a segmental search through the memory set. When the probe is not present in the memory set, opposite results occur. Schizophrenics produce a serial search function, while paranoids produce a flat function. The schizophrenics serial function follows from the results in a detection task. When the target is not present, they first engage in parallel processing and then sequentially check the list, providing an exaggerated serial search function (the highest of all groups in all conditions). For paranoids the new task of having no target is all the more perplexing, and they serially repeat the two-item set as long as the five-item set—their memory-set functions for all memory sets in the probe-absent condition are at the level of the large-item set in the probe-present condition. By contrast, the flat automatic processing function of nonparanoids in the probe-present condition is at the level of the two-item set of the serial function in the probe-absent condition. In summary, paranoids constantly recycle the list when the probe is not present, and they do this for any size of memory set. Schizophrenics, on the other hand, serially process the list when automatic strategy does not produce a target. Schizophrenics again are more flexible in that they change their strategy depending on the result of the initial preferred strategy.

The relevance of these results is twofold. First, they further indicate that the encoding strategies noted in a detection task for paranoid and nonparanoid schizophrenics also occur in memory retrieval. *Thus, when schizophrenics gather information either from the stimulus field or from memory, they prefer an automatic processing strategy. However, they will employ a controlled processing strategy when task conditions warrant such a procedure. Paranoids, on the other hand, gather information from the stimulus field or from memory in a serial manner. Moreover, they will persist in this strategy even when task conditions do not warrant such a procedure.*

The second conclusion relates to response strategies: nonparanoids are more conservative in stating the presence of a particular stimulus, while paranoids are more likely to attribute characteristics to stimulus events. I believe this is due to the conceptual organization of paranoids, which could be considered as containing tightly associated assemblies that impose conceptual order on a stimulus field. As in the study by McDowell et al. (1975), expectancies are more predominant in paranoids, resulting in easier attribution of the meaning of stimulus events. Such a strategy ensures a serial type of processing, a detailed looking for the features of the cogit, even when parallel processing could be sufficient. Such a condition becomes most obvious when the expected cogit is not present, as in the negative trials of the choice reaction time task used by Broga and Neufeld (1981).

Another way to demonstrate the effect of the assembly on encoding and thus emphasize the directional flow in information processing is to consider EEG results, especially those using an evoked-potential paradigm. Calloway and Naghdi (1982) use the terms automatic and controlled processing as theoretical constructs to explain a great many seemingly divergent data, especially various EEG and reaction-time measures. Their thinking parallels mine on many points; I shall note a few of the similarities to illustrate the theoretical and experimental design possibilities of considering schizophrenia in information-processing terms. It is of special importance that conclusions similar to mine have arisen independently, from the analysis of a completely different data base—that of EEG and reaction-time studies. First, these authors consistently raise the trait/state distinction to inquire whether controlled or automatic processing or an interaction of the two is related to schizophrenia as a trait or as a result of the psychosis. Second, they agree that the main deficit in schizophrenia is in the use of controlled processing. Automatic processing is more often employed and could account for deficits commonly observed on laboratory and psychophysiological measures. Third, they contend that the most reliable difference between schizophrenics and others can be observed at the encoding stage of information processing. Fourth, they believe that automatic and controlled processes can be modified, and thus that therapeutic manipulations directed at such processes can serve as a treatment for schizophrenia.

In effect both of our formulations recognize that the two cognition processes are interactive and subject to individual control; thus they would be sensitive to specific experimental manipulations, including the instructions or expectancy about an experiment. They note that the actual results in an experiment will depend upon the strategy of the schizophrenic. If a schizophrenic chooses not to use his deficit system—serial processing—he would make more use of the automatic system with little effect on some laboratory measures such as early components of the auditory evoked potential (AEP). That is, if schizophrenics attempt to use a serial processing system, they will appear like normals, or the P300 component of the AEP will be in the normal range. The point is that there are distinct information-processing strategies that are at least partially under subject control. I have spoken of this interaction between subject dimensions and task demands in an interpretation of the encoding literature, especially that requiring a conceptual distinction between elements, as in the study by Schwartz-Place and Gilmore (1980).

Of most interest is these authors' interpretation of the various components of the AEP, separated into those that can reflect automatic processing and controlled processing. For instance, they note that in the research paradigm where the AEP is elicited by the repetition of a single stimulus, the AEP of schizophrenics is smaller than that of normals. Also, whereas an AEP will recover after a long interstimulus interval, schizophrenics show less of this recovery. In each case it seems that schizophrenics have a greater inhibition of the AEP, which the authors interpret as indicating automatic processing. There is no task for subjects to perform, so the stimulus is processed in a parallel fashion. Callaway and Naghdi (1982) consider the P300 segment of the AEP to reflect the cognitive operations involved in serial processing. The interpretation of this measure is that the later wave activity is increased when expectancy is greater or stimuli are less task-relevant (Duncan-Johnson & Donchin, 1977). Supporting this view are the results with subject-produced AEPs, where subjects produce a response that is followed by the AEP stimulus. Here schizophrenics do not reduce their AEP relative to controls at the P300 stage (Braff, Callaway, & Naylor, 1977). In effect the cognitive expectancy or "thinking" about the stimulus-to-be is experimentally induced, and here the P300 is not reduced for schizophrenics. The proposition is that the reduced P300 reflects the operation of cognitive assemblies or the rehearsal of events, which could be past or present, and this does not customarily occur in schizophrenics. This process is reversed in the subject-produced AEP paradigm, where the P300 deficit disappears.

A strong confirmation of this position is found in a recent report by Baribeau-Braun, Picton, and Gosselin (1983). Examining only psychotic schizophrenics, those with clear evidence of thought disorder, they found that N1 potential was significantly larger for normals than for schizophrenics, but effects over stimulus conditions indicated that schizophrenics were able to focus selectively on different channels of auditory stimulation. However, when they examined the P300 component of the evoked potential, they found a larger amplitude for normals than for schizophrenics, indicating a "schizophrenic abnormality of the cerebral processes underlying the P3 component of the evoked potential" and suggesting that "the P300 abnormality is not secondary to any lack of stimulus-set attention or motivation on the part of the schizophrenic" (p. 875). In effect, disorganized schizophrenics have a thought disorder that could be characterized as not maintaining a selective processing strategy or not being organized conceptually to keep external stimuli ordered in a sequential manner.

There was no mention in this report of the performance of nondisorganized schizophrenics, although such a group was tested. Such a comparison would have been most helpful in clarifying whether the conceptual organization problem is a function of schizophrenia or of the psychosis. This study also did not control for psychosis, such as by comparing schizophrenics with other psychiatric patients. Therefore we cannot conclude that the P300 effect is due solely to the schizophrenic condition. However, the clear difference in the N1 and P300 effects across conditions supports the hypothesis that schizophrenia is a matter of not maintaining a strong conceptual organization or a serial processing strategy. Schizophrenics can selectively attend to relevant stimuli, but they do not process as much information as others, implying lack of a serial processing strategy, nor do they organize stimuli extensively relative to others. This study does not indicate which is the etiological deficit, the encoding or the conceptual organization. My formulation is more directional, and I consider schizophrenics to exhibit a serial encoding deficit because they lack the proper degree of conceptual organization.

Taking such hypotheses one step further into the high-risk literature, we find that late-wave activity (P350 and P400) elicited by infrequent relevant events is lower in children having a schizophrenic parent than in normal controls (Friedman, Vaughan, & Erlenmeyer-Kimling, 1982). These authors connect such measures to cognitive processes occurring after the discriminative decision and related to the thinking involved in the expectation of future events. This same result found with adult schizophrenics (Shagass, 1976; Pass, Klorman, Salzman, Klein, & Kaskey, 1980) suggests that the conceptual organization that can produce an expectancy of events is a vulnerability marker.

We can now return to our discussion of the Holzman (1974) study of smooth-pursuit eye movements. The question that remained was whether the response was a function of psychosis or a core marker of schizophrenia. The core marker interpretation was questioned because when conceptual elements were added to the target being followed the smooth-pursuit deficit decreased (Holzman, Levy, & Proctor, 1976). This result was linked to thought disorder, which could also be present in manics. The alternative interpretation stems from the current more-specific explanation of thought disorder. Here, I consider the thought disorder to be a minimal degree of association in the assemblies of nonparanoid schizophrenics. As such, any task condition that increases the strength of the associations or the directing of conceptual functions should improve performance. In effect, imposing a cogit on the eye-movement task would increase the use of conceptual categories that are normally not employed. This procedure would be similar to making a field more discernible, as in the Cox and Leventhal (1978) study or the subject-produced AEP. In effect, nonparanoid schizophrenics would exhibit a smooth-pursuit eye movement deficit in the natural state owing to their lack of serial processing involving a cogit.

However, this can be modified by experimental conditions or even conditions in the real world when conceptual order must be imposed upon events.

It may be that manics would also produce such a performance, though for a different reason. In the manic, psychosis would produce the same disorganization of associations in the assemblies that the schizophrenic exists within the nonpsychotic state. This is not to say the schizophrenic does not exhibit a thought disorder when psychotic, but it is an intensification of a usual style of information processing. The manic experiences disruption of a more organized assembly and schema. The different causes of the thought disorder are completely speculative, but one might expect that examining schizophrenics in the nonpsychotic state, as was done by the Chapmans (Chapman & Chapman, 1980), should produce greater differences between schizophrenics and manics than are found when both exhibit signs of psychosis. More specifically, one might expect that the conceptual condition employed by Holzman et al. (1976) would modify the smooth-pursuit eye movement of schizophrenics but not of manics.

To summarize briefly, paranoids perform the encoding function from iconic storage or memory in a particular manner—a serially controlled processing that is directed by a rigid assembly. The assembly defines the material that will be recognized, and a serial search of stimulus elements is enacted to find the specified elements. Because paranoids fail to consider the sensory context of stimuli, which is required to produce the information that allows a fluidity of conceptualization, they have difficulty in situations requiring flexible schemata. In the utilization of schemata, a conceptual process, schizophrenics show a deficit. They attend to the sensory aspects of stimuli in an automatic processing fashion and exhibit a deficit when conceptual organization would be helpful, in the form of searching for information either in the stimulus field or in memory. The dual hypotheses for paranoids and for schizophrenics suggest that the two groups experience distinctly different thought worlds. If my hypotheses are supported by further work, this will clarify the cognitive process underlying the "unshakable delusional system" of Kraepelin's (1976) paranoid and the "associative disturbance" of Bleuler's (1950) schizophrenic. I shall now explore the possibility that the characteristic cognitive style of each group resides in a specific neurological organization.

Hemisphere Specialization

Let me present the rationale for considering the hemispheres the basic structure underlying cognitive processes. Most of the early work on hemispheric activation indicated that the nature of the stimulus material determined which hemisphere would control processing and responding. Early studies focused on the verbal/spatial distinction. Later studies suggested that a distinction based on the requirement for analytic or holistic processing more adequately explained the differential competencies of the hemispheres. In either case, the general hypothesis is that, when stimuli are presented, both hemispheres will begin to process the material, but different types will be processed more competently and efficiently by one hemisphere or the other. To validate the potential correspondence of information-processing strategies and hemispheric specialization requires describing the role of each hemisphere. The right hemisphere, as the locus of visuospatial, nonlinguistic activity, could correspond to automatic processing. The left hemisphere, as the locus of abstract, linguistic activity, could correspond to controlled processing.

The automatic/controlled processing dichotomy is similar to the distinction between right and left hemisphere processing proposed by Kinsbourne (1974) and by Moskovitch (1979). Studies of brain-damaged patients suggest that automatic and controlled processing are emphasized by right and left hemispheres, respectively. For example, patients with right-posterior cerebral lesions behave as if preattentive structuring has not occurred (Hecaen & Angelergues, 1962). Similarly, patients with intact right hemispheres but with lesions in the left hemisphere draw pictures without detail but with good gestalt (Warrington, James, & Kinsbourne, 1966), suggesting that controlled processing is a left-hemisphere function.

The work I have just described generated the hypothesis that differences between paranoids and schizophrenics on various measures of performance could result from paranoids' preference for controlled processing and schizophrenics' preference for automatic processing—a left-hemisphere preference for paranoids and a right-hemisphere preference for nonparanoids. This hypothesis could also be couched in the more familiar deficit terms—that schizophrenics exhibit a deficit in the left hemisphere. I agree with the left-hemisphere deficit hypothesis but consider it due to a preference for a type of processing that cannot easily be performed in the left hemisphere (Magaro, 1981).

The hypothesis of a left-hemisphere deficit has been actively pursued (Flor-Henry, 1976; Flor-Henry, Koles, Howarth, & Burton 1979), and much evidence has accumulated to support the position (Gruzelier & Hammond, 1976). For example, Abrams, Redfield, and Taylor (1981) found that schizophrenics performed worse than affectives and similar to organics on some WAIS subtests that measure left-hemisphere function. They also found that schizophrenics performed worse than affectives on a set of left-hemisphere tasks but equally on right-hemisphere tasks. However, the simplicity of this formulation is being questioned and qualifications are being offered (Walker & McGuire, 1982). The qualifications I will pursue here involve who—paranoids or schizophrenics—exhibit the left-hemisphere deficit, and whether the deficit is a core process or a function of the psychosis.

Two recent studies using visual stimuli have attempted to examine the hemispheric preferences of schizophrenics and paranoids. The first (Magaro & Page, 1983) was a partial replication of the Beaumont and Diamond (1973) procedure where faces, letters, and shapes were presented tachistoscopically to one or both hemispheres. The letter task required the individual to examine two letters, one capital and one lower case. We required matching different letter forms to increase use of the left hemisphere by requiring a semantic match rather than template matching. The abstract shapes and faces were also different or the same and required just that judgment. The control groups and control subject variables were the same as in the previous studies.

As can be seen in Figure 7, when groups are compared on each task in each hemisphere, paranoid schizophrenics do not differ from controls in the right hemisphere, a finding contrary to our expectation that paranoids would exhibit a right-hemisphere deficit. As also shown in Figure 7, nonparanoid schizophrenics do exhibit a deficit when stimuli are presented to the left hemisphere. The deficit occurred with all stimuli, especially faces and letters. This group did not exhibit such a deficit in the right hemisphere, performing the same as controls.

When stimuli were presented to both hemispheres, nonparanoids differed from all other groups only on letter stimuli. That is, when one letter form, upper or lower case, was presented to one

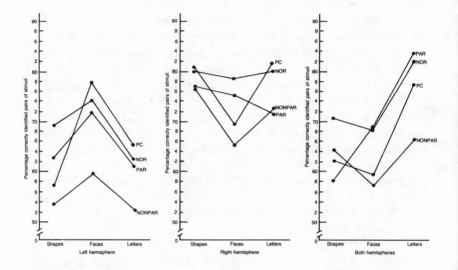

FIGURE 7. Hemispheric performance by tasks and psychiatric groups.

hemisphere and the other form was presented to the other hemisphere, nonparanoid schizophrenics performed more poorly than all other groups. I interpret this as due to the initial deficit in the left hemisphere mentioned above. In effect, if there is a left-hemisphere deficit, we would expect a problem in matching stimuli presented to the right and left hemispheres. However, since it was only the most intensely left-hemisphere task, letters, that created the deficit, it may be that the major difficulty also resides in the left hemisphere when subjects are required to match stimuli in both hemispheres. Incidentally, Beaumont and Diamond (1973) obtained essentially the same result and interpreted it as a difficulty in intercallosal transfer.

In brief, Magaro and Page (1983) found that paranoids could use both right and left hemispheres. We did predict a problem for paranoids in the right hemisphere or on the most intensely right-hemisphere task, the shapes, but this did not appear. Only nonparanoids exhibited the expected left-hemisphere deficit. The results from this study are therefore not surprising, in that they support most laterality work finding that schizophrenics perform worse than controls on tasks using the left hemisphere, while para-

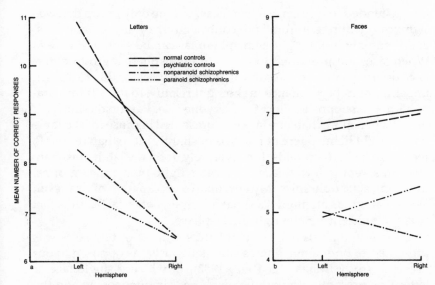

FIGURE 8. (*a*) Recognition of three letters presented unilaterally to left and right hemispheres. (*b*) Recognition of two faces presented unilaterally to left and right hemispheres.

noids perform like a comparable control group. However, we were not satisfied with the tasks used, because they did not allow the information-processing styles to be evidenced, since only one stimulus was presented to each hemisphere. It would require more than one stimulus to reveal the serial processing function we expected with paranoids. Here, without a serial processing opportunity, paranoids perform like controls.

To test this hypothesis in a more complex situation that could also involve a different type of information processing and decision making, Magaro and Chamrad (1983b) expanded upon the procedure above and presented (*a*) two faces or three capital letters to one hemisphere, (*b*) two faces to both hemispheres simultaneously, or (*c*) letters to both hemispheres simultaneously. The response to letters was spoken, whereas the faces were matched to an array of eight to ten faces placed on a card above the tachistoscope.

The first condition replicated our previous results. Letters were recognized more in the left hemisphere than the right. Nonparanoids tended to do worse than other groups in the left relative to the right hemisphere, but not significantly so. Both schizophrenic groups tended to recognize fewer faces, but the only group that was significantly different from both control groups was the paranoids, and then only in the right hemisphere, as can be seen in Figure 8. When faces are presented to the right hemisphere a group difference occurs relative to the control groups that seems due to a slight impairment in performance in the right relative to the left for paranoids and an opposite effect for everyone else. Paranoids showed a deficit when more than one face was presented because most people use the right hemisphere as much as or slightly more than the left to recognize faces. Paranoids, however, rely upon the left hemisphere and thus report fewer faces from the right than other groups, including schizophrenics. My speculative explanation of this result is that paranoids attempted a serial processing of facial features that was not efficient for the right hemisphere.

In the last analysis a set of two letters or a set of two faces was presented to both hemispheres simultaneously, as opposed to our previous study (Magaro & Page, 1982), in which a single face or letter was presented to both hemispheres simultaneously and the subject was to report whether they were the same or different. Here the person had to match what he saw with a field of faces. The only group difference in this condition was that nonparanoids recognized fewer letters in the left hemisphere. This result is presented in Figure 9. The trend is certainly for paranoids to identify fewer faces in the right hemisphere than the other groups, but this effect was not significant. Remember, however, that when faces were presented only to the right hemisphere with no stimulus presented to the left, paranoids differed from the control groups by recognizing fewer faces in the right. Also, when we collapsed data over all stimuli in terms of the hemisphere where stimuli were identified, paranoids differed from both control groups by recognizing fewer stimuli in the right hemisphere. Nonparanoids differed significantly in the left. To summarize, relative to appropriate controls, nonparanoids recognize fewer stimuli in the left hemisphere than the right, especially left-oriented stimuli, letters. Paranoids recognize fewer faces in the right. The strongest finding was for nonparanoids, but we are beginning to document a right-hemisphere deficit in paranoids.

This paranoid deficit in the right hemisphere did not occur in the earlier study (Magaro & Page, 1983), where a simple matching of faces was required, as opposed to the later task requirement to

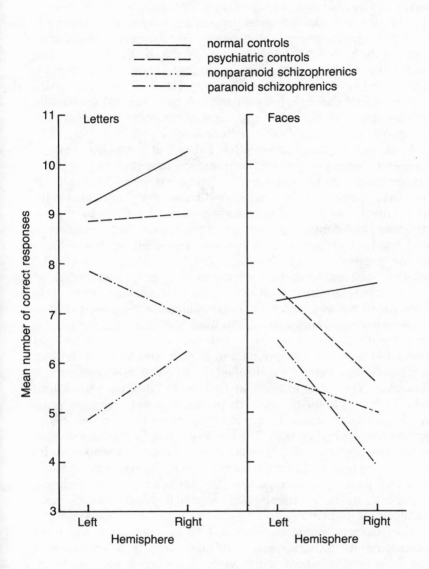

FIGURE 9. Recognition of two letters or two faces presented bilaterally to the left and right hemispheres.

identify more than one stimulus in both hemispheres simultaneously. This demand allows a serial processing process to be activated, but it also requires memory storage while searching the list and then forming the match. Certainly we can see that by the time a match occurred other faces in memory could be forgotten. This memory interpretation suggests that, relative to other groups, paranoids prefer the left hemisphere, owing to the recall nature of the task. We will see the importance of this task requirement, especially for paranoids, as we turn to the dichotic listening studies.

Some dichotic listening work has found that paranoids exhibit a left-hemisphere preference when recognizing linguistic stimuli. Lerner, Nachson, and Carmon (1977) required the recall of three or four digits presented dichotically and found that paranoids exhibited a much larger ear difference—greater laterality—than nonparanoids and controls. Although all groups recalled more words with right-ear presentation, paranoids utilized the left hemisphere to the greatest degree. Nachson (1980) noted that paranoids' left-hemisphere recognition of digits was about twice that of nonparanoids. Another finding was that when the number of shifts from ear to ear was tabulated, paranoids made the fewest shifts.

Gruzelier and Hammond (1980) used a similar design and also found that paranoids used the left hemisphere more than the right compared with control groups and shifted ears less readily than nonparanoids when they controlled for drug and psychosis effects. Gruzelier (1981) concluded that they were "dealing with a trait which pertains to the paranoid disposition—one which involved a rigid attentional stance in directing attention to favor left hemisphere processing" (p. 664). The authors noted that this disposition is increased by arousal, a state condition that could be modified by instructions to attend to the left ear. Of most interest is the manner in which paranoids distinguishes themselves by demonstrating a superiority in the left hemisphere, especially when the task has a memory component.

The memory demand, in effect, may bias left-hemisphere processing in dichotic tasks, in that there is a greater left-hemisphere dominance when verbal memory requirements increase (Bakker, 1970). This is especially so in a dichotic listening task, where the response seems to reflect a memory retrieval strategy rather than an auditory perceptual dominance (Friedes, 1977). As in the visual split-field studies discussed above, the right visual field advantage of verbal stimuli may be due to first reporting the right visual field—or, in the auditory task, the right ear input—and thus allowing a greater decay of left input, resulting in better left-hemisphere performance.

The idea that paranoids show left-hemisphere superiority in memory tasks relates to the encoding studies. I have said that paranoids possess sufficient memory retrieval capabilities but have rigid hierarchical associations that predispose them to a serial type of encoding. I am now suggesting that these processes are mainly left-hemisphere related (Bakker, 1970; Friedes, 1977; Hiscock & Kinsbourne, 1980), and that paranoids use the appropriate hemisphere for the processes they most employ. Schizophrenics are more automatic processors who do not employ serial processing or the same degree of memory organization and thus exhibit a left-hemisphere deficit or at times a right-hemisphere superiority, as shown in one of the hemiretinal studies cited above (Magaro & Page, 1983).

To summarize, in those studies that require a memory process, such as recalling digits presented to each ear or matching faces, there is a decided left-hemisphere advantage that is mainly related to the performance of paranoid schizophrenics (Gruzelier & Hammond, 1980; Lerner, Nachson, & Carmon, 1977). I interpret these findings as evidence for the paranoid disposition to rely on the strength of the cogit or the conceptual organization inherent in language, which is also shown in the preference for controlled processing in encoding. Others have noted that the right-ear advantage in dichotic listening is the result of an attentional strategy of biasing attention to the right ear owing to the left-hemisphere dominance for language (Broadbent, 1954). Also, such an orientation can produce a hemispheric preference that is a function of the expectancy of task demands, as in the "priming" effect discussed by Kinsbourne (1978) and Moscovitch (1979). In that case the ear asymmetries in schizophrenics may be seen as an exaggeration of normal hemispheric tendencies.

At first glance the idea of superior left-hemisphere performance in a schizophrenic group seems contrary to previous work (Flor-Henry, 1973, 1976; Gruzelier & Hammond, 1976), even though I am speaking only of paranoids on tasks that involve the operation of memory. However, even the hypothesis of a left-hemisphere deficit for schizophrenics does not have unanimous support. In a review of the laterality work requiring linguistic processing, six out of nine studies report greater ear differences—left hemisphere over right—

for at least a subset of schizophrenics than for controls (Walker & McGuire, 1982). These findings suggest that schizophrenics are more lateralized than controls, since in them the left hemisphere is even more dominant than the left hemisphere in others. When absolute accuracy scores for each ear are obtained rather than a laterality quotient, schizophrenics reveal a consistent tendency for greater absolute ear differences than normals, owing to a greater relative right-hemisphere decrement or left-hemisphere superiority (Walker & McGuire, 1982).

The reports of left-hemisphere preference for schizophrenics include tasks of word recognition (Caudrey & Kirk, 1979; Johnson & Crockett, 1982), reading comprehension not requiring memory (Green & Kotenko, 1980), and recognition of shapes (Schweitzer, 1982). Unfortunately these studies do not differentiate paranoid from nonparanoid schizophrenics, and when schizophrenics are compared with other psychotic groups the left-hemisphere superiority of schizophrenics disappears (Lishman, Toone, Colbourn, McMeekan, & Mance, 1978; Yozawitz, Bruder, Sutton, Sharpe, Gurland, Fleiss, & Costa, 1979). Also, Lishman et al. (1978) report that patients with the most symptoms produce the greatest laterality effects. In fact, all studies reporting a left-hemisphere advantage for schizophrenics failed to control for degree of psychosis or to separate schizophrenics into paranoid and nonparanoid groups (Green & Kotenko, 1980; Lerner, Nachson, & Carmon, 1977; Gruzelier & Hammond, 1980). I shall shortly discuss the results that indicate psychosis has some effect on laterality. Thus, even though some studies find that schizophrenics use the left hemisphere more in processing verbal stimuli than do normal controls, it is not clear whether this "overuse" of the left hemisphere is independent of the psychotic process. If schizophrenics were examined separately from paranoids, we would expect different hemisphere preferences for paranoids, but this discrimination would occur only when psychosis is controlled.

There are reports of right-hemisphere superiority in schizophrenics, especially on auditory tasks that require a minimum of conceptual processing, such as tone or syllable discrimination and measures of threshold (Gruzelier & Hammond, 1976; Colbourn & Lishman, 1979; Bazhin, Wasserman, & Tonkonogii, 1975; Wexler & Henninger, 1979). In these studies schizophrenics tend to exhibit greater left-ear superiority than do controls. Gur (1978) also found a right-hemisphere advantage for nonsense syllables in schizophrenics, whereas controls showed a left-hemisphere advantage. This suggests that schizophrenics used a holistic process that could be performed in the right hemisphere, whereas controls used the usual serial left-hemisphere strategy.

However, the idea that schizophrenics show right-hemisphere superiority relative to the left hemisphere or relative to the right hemisphere of other groups is not usually found in the literature. Probably this is because, as mentioned above, it is extremely difficult to construct a task that ensures automatic processing, where schizophrenics would be superior. A major problem is finding a "pure" right-hemisphere task—one that is performed with difficulty by the left hemisphere, thus demanding greater reliance on the left; in processing terms, a task that can be performed only by automatic processing. It is in this case that we would expect paranoids to exhibit an actual deficit. There is some indication from the studies done in our laboratory that paranoids do worse in the right hemisphere and that nonparanoids show a left-hemisphere deficit. However, we have never produced the right-hemisphere effects predicted. Possibly we have asked too much from the visual split-field technique, since it cannot escape interhemispheric transfer. Or possibly we have not looked closely enough at the schizophrenic subgroups and their level of psychosis.

HEMISPHERIC SPECIALIZATION AND PSYCHOSIS

Gruzelier (1981) made a fascinating study of the relation between symptom patterns and hemispheric dominance, relating the asymmetry of electrodermal responses to tones to symptom measures. Patients with a high left-hand response amplitude relative to that of the right hand exhibited syndromes characteristic of schizophrenics, while right-hand responders showed symptoms commonly described as characteristic of paranoids. Of most interest is that when we consider symptoms that indicate a high level of arousal, such as pressure of speech and situational anxiety, which are equivalent to the extent of the psychosis discussed earlier, a more complete clinical picture of the paranoid and nonparanoid schizophrenic emerges. In brief, electrodermal responses of the left or right hand to simple sensory stimuli reflecting an activation of the opposite hemisphere are directly related to degree of psychosis in the traditional paranoid and nonparanoid syndromes. The patient who responds more to sensory stimuli in the right hemisphere than in the left exhibits paranoid symptomatology, while the left-hemisphere-attending patient exhibits nonparanoid symptomatology.

Serafetinides, Coger, Martin, and Dymond (1981) chose items from the Brief Psychiatric Rating Scale (Overall & Gorham, 1962) that seemed most likely to reflect analytic processes and thus left-hemisphere activity. Examples of such symptoms are grandiosity, hostility, and suspiciousness. Spatial process reflecting right-hemisphere activity would be shown in such symptoms as anxiety, tension, and unusual mannerisms. The authors found that those patients with left-related symptoms produced higher-frequency evoked potential to light flashes in the left hemisphere than in the right. Patients with right-related symptoms showed the opposite effect. Left-hemisphere activation was mainly related to items reflecting thought disorder and to paranoid behavior, suggesting that in paranoids the left hemisphere is affected during psychosis. The right hemisphere is the site of the psychosis in schizophrenics.

In summary, in these two studies we find that schizophrenics, when psychotic, use the left hemisphere to attend to simple stimuli but exhibit greater EEG activity in the right hemisphere. Paranoids exhibit the opposite pattern. Taken together, these results could be interpreted to mean that psychosis "attacks" the right hemisphere in schizophrenics and the left hemisphere in paranoids. I interpret the Gruzelier (1981) results in "priming" terms, in that each group attends to sensory stimuli in the hemisphere opposite to the one that is most active (Kinsbourne & Hicks, 1978). It has been found that sensory orientation is contralateral to the more active hemisphere (Kinsbourne & Hicks, 1978). For instance, when normals are required to engage in a concurrent task during dichotic testing, they not only exhibit the generalized performance deficits found in schizophrenics, but also increase their left-hemisphere dominance (Wexler & Henninger, 1980). Put another way, left-hemisphere dominance may sometimes occur in psychotic schizophrenics because they attempt to avoid using the right hemisphere, which is occupied with a concurrent task, the psychotic activity. During psychosis, therefore, the schizophrenic's right hemisphere is perhaps being primed by psychotic material that will increase the orientation to the opposite hemisphere. We would thus expect left-hemisphere activity on some tasks for psychotic schizophrenics when task demands are simple. On the other hand, we should also find increased activation in the right hemisphere owing to the psychosis, as found by Serafetinides et al. (1981). In experiential terms, when schizophrenics are most psychotic they will "pull themselves together" by attempting to control their thinking, which involves ordering events in serial fashion to achieve greater constancy and less feeling of disorganization.

This hypothesis suggests that in paranoids the psychosis resides in the left hemisphere, their processing hemisphere, but that they can attend to the right for sensory stimuli. If the psychosis is seen as an exaggeration of usual processing strategies, it would not be unexpected for paranoids to exhibit signs of psychosis in the left hemisphere, but also to prefer the left hemisphere for most tasks. At the same time, the demands of the task must be considered, since when the paranoid is most psychotic there is the possibility of attending to the right hemisphere for simple sensory stimulation not requiring a great deal of conceptualization. Obviously, measuring hemispheric activation or dominance is crucial in determining hemispheric dominance and the site or presence of the psychosis.

I have said that the left hemisphere in paranoids is the functional site of the psychosis in terms of types of symptoms, possibly owing to an increased level of arousal (Gruzelier, 1981). The Wexler and Henninger (1979) results indicate that as the psychosis recedes the left hemisphere in paranoids becomes more dominant and the deficit in performance decreases. These results seem to follow my initial thinking that, as a controlled processing center, the left hemisphere is dominant in paranoids. Let me now add the corollary hypothesis that the left hemisphere is also the site of symptoms as the processing strategy becomes exaggerated into delusional thought.

Such a hypothesis leads to the prediction that paranoids will produce both less left-hemisphere dominance and poorer left-hemisphere performance when psychotic. The few studies that have tested paranoids and schizophrenics during the course of their illness do indicate a shift in laterality and decreased performance efficiency during psychosis. Wexler and Henninger (1979) used syllables in a dichotic listening task to compare schizophrenics with affective patients. All groups initially demonstrated the same degree of laterality, with the expected left-hemisphere advantage. The researchers then examined severity of pathology and found that a decrease in laterality is associated with greater psychosis as assessed by such signs as global illness, depressed mood, expressed anger, and paranoid behavior. As patients improved, there was greater laterality owing to left-hemisphere dominance, and this mainly related to two symptom scales, paranoid behavior and expressed anger, which are mainly characteristic of paranoids. Also, as the degree of laterality increased there was an improvement in performance. In effect these results might illustrate what happens to paranoids experiencing psychosis: performance suffers, with more dichotic listening errors, and as the use of the preferred hemisphere decreases there is less laterality. Psychosis thus seems to affect the processing style and, of course, the level of performance. In summary, the Wexler and Henninger (1979) results demonstrate that, in paranoids, with less psychosis, performance improves and the degree of laterality increases because of the increased efficiency of the left hemisphere.

I hope I have made it abundantly clear that I am speaking about processing preferences or dispositions, not about absolute or structural characteristics that are independent of situational determinants. In reviewing the information-processing literature, I took care to point out how task demands can override individual-difference dimensions, as with encoding below a set size of six. Thus, when I speak of a serial processing deficit or a left-hemisphere deficit in paranoids, I am not implying that schizophrenics will not engage in serial processing or use assemblies in understanding the world. The studies examining symptom patterns and laterality involved "priming" the contralateral hemisphere with concurrent tasks, and I predicted that schizophrenics would utilize the left hemisphere more than the preferred right during psychosis or when task demands are simple. In other words, though we expect schizophrenics to be right-hemisphere dominant and to experience the psychosis most directly in the right hemisphere in terms of the content and structure of symptoms, the left hemisphere is also affected by the psychosis. We would therefore expect the psychosis to diminish the controlled processing of schizophrenics in situations clearly calling for such a process. In other words, when I hypothesize that psychosis primarily affects the left hemisphere in paranoids, I do not mean that such effects are not experienced by schizophrenics. I am speaking not of split-brain patients but of individuals who use both hemispheres, so both are disrupted by stress. The psychosis diminishes overall performance because it affects both hemispheres, as I said earlier when I explained the generalized debilitating effect of psychosis in the usual finding that schizophrenics always appear deficient relative to normals.

A study by Johnson and Crockett (1982) illustrates the effect of the psychosis on the left hemisphere of patients, schizophrenics or others, and also the way schizophrenics exhibit right-hemisphere dominance. The authors tested patients upon admission and again when in remission, about to be discharged, and found that schizophrenics at admission did not differ from depressives but performed worse than normals in terms of recognizing words presented dichotically. The deficit of both groups was due to less left-hemisphere advantage. Of most interest, however, is that schizophrenics increased their left-hemisphere advantage from admission to discharge, as did depressives. This indicates that psychosis affects left-hemisphere performance in the recognition of dichotically presented words; as the psychosis recedes the left hemisphere becomes more dominant and performance improves. This applies to schizophrenics as well as depressives.

The results on dichotic recognition of musical chords indicate an effect specific to the schizophrenic sample. A group of schizophrenics switched from a right-hemisphere dominance on admission, which was also the preference of normals, to a left-hemisphere preference upon remission, mainly owing to decreased right-hemisphere recognition. From my prior hypothesis about the effect of psychosis on paranoids, we might expect paranoids to return to a preference for the left hemisphere in the nonpsychotic state. However, we would expect schizophrenics to become more right-hemisphere dominant upon recovery. This study did not separate paranoids from schizophrenics, but the authors do present data showing that at discharge 33% of the schizophrenic sample was still right-hemisphere dominant for chords. I suppose this was a subgroup of schizophrenics. The other 66%, whom I would consider to be the paranoids, switched from a right-hemisphere to a left-hemisphere dominance after recovering from the psychosis or were left-hemisphere dominant initially (approximately 33%) and remained in that state.

In regard to schizophrenia in general we can thus conclude that, as psychosis decreases, left-hemisphere functions return for verbal material and produce a laterality effect favoring the left hemisphere. The right hemisphere is not affected as much by the psychosis, since on the right-hemisphere chords test the average performance of the total schizophrenic sample at admission was equal to that of normals. However, for some schizophrenics the right hemisphere became less dominant than the left during recovery, while for another subgroup it remained dominant. In effect, it could be said that in some schizophrenics left-hemisphere dominance extends even to an attempt to analyze musical chords in a controlled manner, while another third of the schizophrenics, as well as normals, maintained the strategy of a more automatic processing in the right hemisphere.

Summarizing to this point, it seems that psychosis, as measured by degree of improvement, is certainly related to the performance of the left hemisphere. As the psychosis subsides, the left hemisphere performs more as in normals, implying that the left-hemisphere deficit so often found in schizophrenics is in fact a function of the active psychosis that in some research paradigms can be interpreted as an overactivation phenomenon (Gur, 1978). There is also some indication that psychosis has its greatest effect on the left hemisphere in paranoids. To create a principle from these results, the dominant hemisphere for interacting with the world seems to be the left in paranoids and the right in schizophrenics, but these also constitute the locus of the psychosis. Psychosis therefore may be seen as an exaggeration of the information-processing style dominant to the hemisphere preferred by each schizophrenic group. Thus, as symptoms increase, the left-hemisphere performance of paranoids suffers (Wexler & Henninger, 1979), which can be also seen as greater activity of the left hemisphere (Serafetinides et al., 1981) and lesser laterality (Wexler & Henninger, 1979). At the same time, since the left hemisphere is occupied with the psychosis, paranoids will attend to sensory input in the right hemisphere (Gruzelier, 1981). Schizophrenics when psychotic, however, will use the left hemisphere when attending to sensory stimuli and exhibit right-hemisphere disturbance, but they also will show a left-hemisphere deficit on tasks involving such processes.

As such, the original hypothesis on the hemispheric dominance of paranoids and schizophrenics (Magaro, 1980) is still viable and demonstrable if the effects of psychosis are considered. The left hemisphere in paranoids is the processor. When psychosis is greatest, this hemisphere is affected the most. Usually, paranoids maintain processing dominance in the left hemisphere and "shunt" attention to the right hemisphere for minimal discriminations when psychotic. This imbalance in hemispheric integration, however, produces the paranoid symptom picture aptly described by Gruzelier (1981). It is as if the left hemisphere has become autonomous, without any checks from the right, and thus exaggerates the normal left-hemisphere functions into a pathological thought process.

The reverse would be true for the schizophrenic, where increased psychosis leads to an exaggeration of the right-hemisphere function so it can exhibit task dominance (Bazhin et al., 1975) or a bias toward the right hemisphere that may be reflected in the often-reported left-hemisphere deficit (Gruzelier, 1981). The symptoms of psychosis, such as active hallucinations, may reflect a psychotic version of the automatic schizophrenic processing style. However, we must recognize that even though the psychosis exaggerates right-hemisphere processing, it also decreases left-hemisphere processing, as in all groups undergoing psychosis.

Structure and Strategy

The hemisphere results suggest strengths and weaknesses in structure—in this case, hemispheres. The encoding results suggested strength and weakness in types of processing. I prefer to consider the hemisphere results as due to modifiable cognitive strategies of information processing. Kinsbourne (1974) and others (Levy & Trevarthan, 1976) also speak of hemispheric dominance in this manner. Though there has been a recent renewal of interest in individual differences in the perceptual strategies of normals (Allen, 1975; Cooper, 1976; Hock, Gordon, and Marcus, 1974), little research in schizophrenia has investigated the possibility that the paranoid and nonparanoid are also capable of strategically manipulating their environments through the cognitive process.

Note that my use of the concept of strategy does not necessarily imply volitional control on the part of the individual (Underwood, 1978). I merely suggest that strategies may be developed and maintained by previous success with them or by a lack of awareness of alternative strategies, two situations that in themselves suggest future research in schizophrenia or therapeutic approaches aimed at the maladaptive cognitive style (Magaro, 1980). My emphasis on the importance of strategies in information processing stresses individual variability. Individuals behave differently in similar environmental situations, and the same individual might behave differently in the same situation at different times. However, I assume that individuals with particular cognitive styles that are comparable to personality traits (Mischel, 1976) may use particular strategies consistently and that these strategies for processing information may vary widely over a population of personalities or pathologies (Underwood, 1978). To fully account for variations in behavior at any level, from information processing to social interaction, we may find that individual strategies in cognitively structuring a situation assume a central role in our explanation. Whether the exact determination of this core process is at the level of the hemisphere or the psychological process or some integration of the two will be the subject of our future research.

Just as we have now begun to uncover the interaction between psychosis and schizophrenia, we are struggling with the interaction of processing and hemisphere. The question may not be what constitutes the core process or core processes in schizophrenia, but what factors produce dominance of core process. Of course, we have to separate elements before we can observe their interaction, and that is what I have attempted to do here. It is optimistic when thinking of schizophrenia to consider processing styles that influence the functioning of structure. Schizophrenic adjustment is then a matter of modifying a cognitive style. Most important, we seem to be speaking of core processes that can be modified but that are still unique to schizophrenia or paranoia and not psychosis. The next few years should see the field reap the rewards of a cognitive understanding of schizophrenia and explore the possibility that core processes, cognitive and neurological, are interrelated in purpose and possibly modifiable.

REFERENCES

Abrams, R., Redfield, J., & Taylor, M. A. Cognitive dysfunction in schizophrenia, affective disorder and organic brain disease. *British Journal of Psychiatry*, 1981, **139**, 190–194.

Abrams, R., & Taylor, M. Catatonia: Prediction of response to somatic treatments. *American Journal of Psychiatry*, 1977, **134**, 78–80.

Allen, L. Temporal order psychometric functions based on confidence rating data. *Perceptions and Psychophysics*, 1975, **18**, 369–372.

Asarnow, R., & Asarnow, J. Attention-information processing dysfunction and vulnerability to schizophrenia: Implications for preventive intervention. In M. S. Goldstein (Ed.), *Preventive intervention in schizophrenia: Are we ready?* Washington, D.C.: U.S. Department of Health and Human Services, Public Health Service, 1982.

Asarnow, R., & MacCrimmon, D. An attentional assessment of foster children at risk for schizophrenia. In L. Wynne, R. Cromwell, & S. Matthysse (Eds.), *The nature of schizophrenia*. New York: Wiley, 1978.

Bakker, D. Ear asymmetry with nonaural stimulation: Relations to lateral dominance and lateral awareness. *Neuropsychologia,* 1970, **8,** 103–117.

Baribeau-Braun, J., Picton, T. W., & Gosselin, J. Schizophrenia: A neurophysiological evaluation of abnormal information processing. *Science,* 1983, **219,** 874–876.

Bauman, E., & Kolisnyk, E. Interference effects in schizophrenic short-term memory. *Journal of Abnormal Psychology,* 1976, **85,** 303–308.

Bauman, E., & Murray, D. Recognition versus recall in schizophrenics. *Canadian Journal of Psychology,* 1968, **72,** 18–25.

Bazhin, E., Wasserman, L., & Tonkonogii, M. Auditory hallucinations and left temporal lobe pathology. *Neuropsychologia,* 1975, **13,** 481–487.

Beaumont, J., & Diamond, S. Brain disconnection and schizophrenia. *British Journal of Psychiatry,* 1973, **123,** 661–663.

Bleuler, E. *Dementia praecox or the group of schizophrenias.* New York: International Universities Press, 1950.

Bleuler, E. *The schizophrenic disorders: Long-term patient and family studies.* New Haven: Yale University Press, 1978.

Braff, D., Calloway, E., & Naylor, H. Very short term memory dysfunction in schizophrenia. *Archives of General Psychiatry,* 1977, **34,** 25–30.

Broadbent, D. E. The role of auditory localization in attention and memory span. *Journal of Experimental Psychology,* 1954, **47,** 191–196.

Broadbent, D. E. *Decision and stress.* New York: Academic Press, 1971.

Broga, M., & Neufeld, R. Multivariate cognitive performance levels and response styles among paranoid and nonparanoid schizophrenics. *Journal of Abnormal Psychology,* 1981, **90,** 495–509.

Burdock, E., & Hardesty, A. *A structured clinical interview manual.* New York: Springer, 1969.

Buss, A. H., & Lang, P. J. Psychological deficit in schizophrenia. I. Affect, reinforcement, and concept attainment. *Journal of Abnormal Psychology,* 1965, **70,** 2–24.

Calloway, E., & Naghdi, S. An information processing model for schizophrenia. *Archives of General Psychiatry,* 1982, **39,** 339–347.

Caudrey, D., & Kirk, K. The perception of speech in schizophrenia and affective disorders. In J. Gruzelier & P. Flor-Henry (Eds.), *Hemisphere asymmetries of functions on psychopathology.* New York: Elsevier/North-Holland, 1979.

Chamrad, D. Letter detection of paranoid and nonparanoid schizophrenics. Master's thesis, Ohio State University, 1982.

Chapman, C. J., & Chapman, J. P. *Disordered thought in schizophrenia.* New York: Appleton-Century-Crofts, 1973.

Chapman, L., & Chapman, J. Raulin scales for physical and social anhedonia. *Journal of Abnormal Psychology,* 1976, **85,** 374–382.

Chapman, L., & Chapman, J. Scales for rating psychotic and psychotic-like experiences as continual. *Schizophrenia Bulletin,* 1980, **6,** 476–489.

Colbourn, C., & Lishman, W. A lateralization of function and psychotic illness: A left hemisphere deficit? In J. Gruzelier & P. Flor-Henry (Eds.), *Hemisphere asymmetries of function in psychopathology.* New York: Elsevier/North-Holland, 1979.

Cooper, J. Individual differences in visual comparison processes. *Perception and Psychophysics,* 1976, **19,** 433–444.

Cox, P., & Leventhal, D. A multivariate analysis and modification of a preattentive perceptual dysfunction in schizophrenia. *Journal of Nervous and Mental Disease,* 1978, **166,** 709–718.

Cromwell, R., & Pithers, W. D. Schizophrenic/paranoid psychoses: Determining diagnostic divisions. *Schizophrenia Bulletin,* 1981, **7,** 674–688.

Cromwell, R., & Spaulding, W. How schizophrenics handle information. In W. E. Fann, I. Karacan, & A. Pokorny (Eds.), *Phenomenology and treatments of schizophrenia.* New York: Spectrum Publications, 1978.

Duncan-Johnson, L., & Donchin, E. On quantifying surprise: The variation in event-related potentials with subjective probability. *Psychophysiology,* 1977, **14,** 456–467.

Endicott, J., & Spitzer, R. A diagnostic interview: SAPS. *Archives of General Psychiatry,* 1978, **35,** 837–844.

Flor-Henry, P. Psychiatric syndromes considered as manifestations of lateralized temporal-limbic dysfunction. In L. V. Lartinen & K. E. Livingston (Eds.), *Surgical approaches in psychiatry.* Lancaster, England: Medical and Technical Publishing Company, 1973.

Flor-Henry, P. Lateralized temporal-limbic dysfunction and psychopathology. *Annals of the New York Academy of Science,* 1976, **280,** 777.

Flor-Henry, P., Koles, Z. J., Howarth, B. G., & Burton, L. Neurophysiology studies of schizophrenia, mania, and depression. In J. Gruzelier & P. Flor-Henry (Eds.), *Hemisphere asymmetries of function in psychopathology.* New York: Elsevier/North-Holland, 1979.

Friedes, D. Do dichotic listening procedures measure lateralization of information processing or retrieval strategy? *Perception and Psychophysics,* 1977, **21,** 254–263.

Friedman, M., Vaughan, L., & Erlenmeyer-Kimling, L. Cognitive brain potentials in children at risk for schizophrenia: Preliminary findings. *Schizophrenia Bulletin,* 1982, **8,** 514–531.

Garmezy, N. Old clues to new interventions in schizophrenia. In M. J. Goldstein (Ed.), *Prevention intervention in schizophrenia: Are we ready?* Washington, D.C.: U.S. Department of Health and Human Services, Public Health Service, 1982.

Goldstein, M., Held, J., & Cromwell, R. Premorbid adjustment and paranoid-nonparanoid status in schizophrenia. *Psychological Bulletin,* 1978, **70,** 382–386.

Green, P., & Kotenko, V. Superior speech comprehension under monaural versus biaural listening conditions. *Journal of Abnormal Psychology,* 1980, **89,** 399–408.

Gruzelier, J. Hemispheric imbalances masquerading as paranoid and non-paranoid syndromes? *Schizophrenia Bulletin*, 1981, **7**, 662–673.

Gruzelier, J., & Hammond, N. Schizophrenia: A dominant hemisphere temporal-limbic disorder. *Research Communications in Psychology, Psychiatry, and Behavior*, 1976, **1**, 33–72.

Gruzelier, J., & Hammond, N. Lateralized deficits and drug influences on the dichotic listening of schizophrenic patients. *Biological Psychiatry*, 1980, **15**, 759–779.

Gur, R. Left hemisphere dysfunction and left hemisphere overactivation in schizophrenia. *Journal of Abnormal Psychology*, 1978, **87**, 226–238.

Hamlin, P., & Lorr, N. Differentiation of normals, neurotics, paranoids, and nonparanoids. *Journal of Abnormal Psychology*, 1971, **77**, 90–96.

Harrow, M., Grinkle, R., Holzman, P., & Kayton, L. Anhedonia and schizophrenia. *American Journal of Psychiatry*, 1977, **134**, 794–797.

Harrow, M., & Quinlan, D. Is disordered thinking unique to schizophrenia? *Archives of General Psychiatry*, 1977, **34**, 15–21.

Harrow, M., & Silverstein, M. Psychotic symptoms in schizophrenia after the acute phase. *Schizophrenia Bulletin*, 1977, **4**, 608–615.

Harvey, P., Winters, K., Weintraub, S., & Neale, J. Distractibility in children vulnerable to psychopathology. *Journal of Abnormal Psychology*, 1981, **90**, 298–304.

Hayes-Roth, B. Evolution of cognitive structures and processes. *Psychological Review*, 1977, **84**, 260–278.

Hecaen, H., & Angelergues, R. Agnosia for faces (porsopagnosia). *Archives of Neurology*, 1962, **12**, 88–102.

Hirt, M., Cuttler, M., & Genshaft, J. Information processing by schizophrenics when task complexity increases. *Journal of Abnormal Psychology*, 1977, **86**, 256–260.

Hiscock, M., & Kinsbourne, M. Asymmetries of selective listening and attention switching in children. *Developmental Psychology*, 1980, **16**, 70–82.

Hock, H., Gordan, G., & Marcus, N. Individual differences in the detection of embedded figures. *Perception and Psychophysics*, 1974, **15**, 47–52.

Holzman, P. Eye tracking dysfunction in schizophrenic patients and their relatives. *Archives of General Psychiatry*, 1974, **31**, 143–151.

Holzman, P. The search for a biological marker of the functional psychoses. In M. J. Goldstein (Ed.), *Preventive intervention in schizophrenia: Are we ready?* Washington, D.C.: U.S. Department of Health and Human Services, Public Health Service, 1982.

Holzman, P., Levy, D., & Proctor, L. Smooth pursuit eye movements, attention, and schizophrenia. *Archives of General Psychiatry*, 1976, **33**, 1415–1420.

Holzman, P., Meltzer, H., Kringlen, E., Levy, D., Haberman, S., & Davis, J. Plasma CPK levels in monozygotic and dizygotic twins discordant for schizophrenia. *Journal of Psychiatric Research*, 1979, **15**, 127–131.

Iacono, W., Peloquin, L., Lumry, A., Valentine, R., & Tuason, V. Eye tracking in patients with unipolar and bipolar affective disorders in remission. *Journal of Abnormal Psychology*, 1982, **91**, 35–44.

Itil, T. M. Qualitative and quantitative EEG findings in schizophrenia. *Schizophrenia Bulletin*, 1977, **3**, 61–79.

Johnson, D. Coding processes in memory. In W. K. Estes (Ed.), *Handbook of learning and cognitive processes*, vol. 6. Hillsdale, N.J.: Lawrence Erlbaum, 1982.

Johnson, D. A. W. Studies of depressive symptoms in schizophrenia: The prevalence of depression and its possible causes. *British Journal of Psychiatry*, 1981, **139**, 89–101.

Johnson, O., & Crockett, D. Changes in perceptual asymmetries with clinical improvement of depression and schizophrenia. *Journal of Abnormal Psychology*, 1982, **91**, 45–54.

Kietzman, N., & Sutton, S. Reaction time as a psychophysical method in psychiatric research. *Schizophrenia Bulletin*, 1977, **3**, 429–436.

Kinsbourne, M. Direction of gaze and distribution of cerebral thought processes. *Neuropsychologia*, 1974, **12**, 279–281.

Kinsbourne, M. *Asymmetrical function of the brain*. Cambridge: Cambridge University Press, 1978.

Kinsbourne, M., & Hicks, R. Functional cerebral space: A model for overflow, transfer and interference effects in human performance. In J. Nequin (Ed.), *Attention and performance*, vol. 7. Hillsdale, N.J.: Lawrence Erlbaum, 1978.

Koh, S., & Kayton, L. Memorization of unrelated word strings by young nonpsychotic schizophrenics. *Journal of Abnormal Psychology*, 1974, **83**, 14–22.

Koh, S., Kayton, L., & Berry, R. Mnemonic organization in young nonpsychotic schizophrenics. *Journal of Abnormal Psychology*, 1973, **81**, 299–310.

Koh, S., Kayton, L., & Schwartz, C. The structure of word storage in permanent memory of nonpsychotic schizophrenics. *Journal of Consulting and Clinical Psychology*, 1974, **42**, 879–887.

Kopfstein, J., & Neale, J. Size estimation in schizophrenic and nonschizophrenic subjects. *Journal of Consulting and Clinical Psychology*, 1971, **36**, 430–435.

Kraepelin, E. *Manic-depressive insanity and paranoia*. New York: Arno Press, 1976.

Leff, J. Schizophrenia and sensitivity to the family environment. *Schizophrenia Bulletin*, 1976, **2**, 566–574.

Lerner, J., Nachson, I., & Carmon, A. Responses of paranoid and nonparanoid schizophrenics in a dichotic listening task. *Journal of Nervous and Mental Disease*, 1977, **164**, 247–252.

Levy, J., & Trevarthan, C. Meta control of hemispheric function in human split brain patients. *Journal of Experimental Psychology, Human Perception and Performance*, 1976, **2**, 299–312.

Lipton, R., Levin, S., & Holzman, P. Smooth-pursuit eye movements, schizophrenia, and distraction. *Perceptual and Motor Skills*, 1980, **59**, 159–167.

Lishman, W., Toone, B., Colbourn, C., McMeekan, E., & Mance, R. Dichotic listening in psychotic patients. *British Journal of Psychiatry*, 1978, **132**, 333–341.

Lorr, M. Multidimensional scale for rating psychiatric patients: Hospital form. *Veterans Administration Technical Bulletin*, 1953, November, 10–507.

Magaro, P. A. *Cognition in schizophrenia and paranoia: The integration of cognitive processes*. Hillsdale, N.J.: Lawrence Erlbaum, 1980.

Magaro, P. A. The paranoid and the schizophrenic: The case for distinct cognitive style. *Schizophrenia Bulletin*, 1981, **7**, 632–661.

Magaro, P. A., Abrams, L., & Cantrell, P. The Maine Scale of Paranoid and Nonparanoid Schizophrenia: Reliability and validity. *Journal of Consulting and Clinical Psychology*, 1981, **49**, 438–447.

Magaro, P. A., & Chamrad, D. L. Information processing and lateralization in schizophrenia. *Biological Psychiatry*, 1983, **18**, 29–44. (a)

Magaro, P. A., & Chamrad, D. L. Hemispheric preference of paranoid and nonparanoid schizophrenics. *Biological Psychiatry*, 1983, in press. (b)

Magaro, P. A., & Page, J. Icon thresholds in paranoid and nonparanoid schizophrenics. *British Journal of Clinical Psychology*, 1982, **21**, 213–219.

Magaro, P. A., & Page, J. Brain disconnection, schizophrenia, and paranoia. *Journal of Nervous and Mental Disease*, 1983, **171**, 133–140.

Magaro, P. A., & Vojtisek, J. Embedded figures performance of schizophrenics as a function of chronicity, premorbid adjustment, diagnosis, and medication. *Journal of Abnormal Psychology*, 1971, **77**, 184–191.

McDowell, D., Reynolds, B., & Magaro, P. The integration deficit in paranoid and nonparanoid schizophrenics. *Journal of Abnormal Psychology*, 1975, **84**, 629–636.

McReynolds, P., Collins, B., & Acker, M. Delusional thinking and cognitive organization in schizophrenia. *Journal of Abnormal and Social Psychology*, 1964, **69**, 210–212.

Meehl, P. *Psychodiagnosis—Selected papers*. Minneapolis: University of Minnesota Press, 1973.

Miller, G. A. The magic number seven plus or minus two: Some limits on our capacity for processing information. *Psychological Review*, 1956, **63**, 81–97.

Mischel, E. *Introduction to personality* (2nd ed.). New York: Holt, Rinehart, and Winston, 1976.

Moller, H. J., & Zerssen, D. Depressive states occurring during the neuroleptic treatment of schizophrenia. *Schizophrenia Bulletin*, 1982, **8**, 109–117.

Moscovitch, M. Information processing and the cerebral hemispheres. In M. Gazzangier (Ed.), *Handbook of behavioral neurobiology*. New York: Plenum, 1979.

Nachmani, G., & Cohen, B. Recall and recognition free learning in schizophrenics. *Journal of Abnormal Psychology*, 1969, **79**, 511–516.

Nachson, I. Hemispheric dysfunction in schizophrenia. *Journal of Nervous and Mental Disease*, 1980, **168**, 241–242.

Neale, J. Information processing and vulnerability: High risk research. In M. J. Goldstein (Ed.), *Preventive intervention in schizophrenia: Are we ready?* Washington, D.C.: U.S. Department of Health and Human Services, Public Health Service, 1982.

Neale, J., & Oltmanns, T. *Schizophrenia*. New York: John Wiley, 1980.

Neisser, U. Decision time without reaction time, experiments in visual scanning. *American Journal of Psychology*, 1963, **76**, 376–385.

Neisser, U. *Cognitive psychology*. New York: Appleton-Century-Crofts, 1967.

Neisser, U. *Cognition and reality*. San Francisco: Freeman Press, 1976.

Neuchterlein, K., Phillips-Yonas, S., Driscoll, R. M., & Garmezy, N. Attentional functioning among children vulnerable to adult schizophrenia. In E. Anthony, L. Wynne, & J. Rolf (Eds.), *High risk research in schizophrenia*. Washington, D.C.: U.S. Department of Health and Human Services, Public Health Service, 1982.

Neufeld, R. Simultaneous processing of multiple stimulus dimensions among paranoid and nonparanoid schizophrenics. *Multivariate Behavioral Research*, 1976, **4**, 425–442.

Neufeld, R. Components of processing deficit among paranoid and nonparanoid schizophrenics. *Journal of Abnormal Psychology*, 1977, **86**, 60–64.

Numbers, J., & Chapman, L. Social deficits in hypothetically psychosis-prone college women. *Journal of Abnormal Psychology*, 1982, **91**, 255–260.

Oltmanns, P. Selective attention in schizophrenic and manic psychosis: The effect of distraction on information processing. *Journal of Abnormal Psychology*, 1978, **87**, 212–225.

Otteson, J., & Holzman, P. Cognitive controls and psychopathology. *Journal of Abnormal Psychology*, 1976, **85**, 125–139.

Overall, J., & Gorham, D. The brief psychiatric rating scale. *Psychological Reports*, 1962, **10**, 799–812.

Pass, H., Klorman, R., Salzman, L., Klein, R., & Kaskey, G. The late component of the evoked response in acute schizophrenics during a test of sustained attention. *Biological Psychiatry*, 1980, **15**, 10–20.

Pic'l, A., Magaro, P., & Wade, E. Hemisphere functioning in paranoid and nonparanoid schizophrenics. *Biological Psychiatry*, 1979, **14**, 891–903.

Pope, H., & Lipinsky, J. Diagnosis in schizophrenia and manic depressive illness. *Archives of General Psychiatry*, 1978, **35**, 811–828.

Rabbitt, P. Some experiments and a model for changes in additional selectivity with old age. In F. Hoffmester and C. Mueller (Eds.), *Buyer symposium VII. Brain function in old age*. New York: Springer, 1979.

Rado, S. A schizotypical organization: Preliminary report on a clinical study of schizophrenia. In S. Rado & G. Daniels (Eds.), *Changing concepts of psychoanalytic medicine*. New York: Grune and Stratton, 1956.

Rado, S. Theory and therapy: The theory of schizotypal organization and its application to the treatment of decompensated schizotypal behavior. In S. Rado (Ed.), *Psychoanalysis of behavior*. New York: Grune and Stratton, 1962.

Ritzler, B. Proprioception and schizophrenia: A replication with nonschizophrenic psychiatric controls. *Journal of Abnormal Psychology*, 1977, **86**, 501–509.

Ritzler, B. Paranoia—Prognosis and treatment: A review. *Schizophrenia Bulletin*, 1981, **7**, 710–728.

Ritzler, B., & Rosenbaum, G. Proprioception in schizophrenics and normals: Effects of stimulus intensity and interstimulus interval. *Journal of Abnormal Psychology*, 1974, **83**, 106–111.

Rodnick, E., Goldstein, M., Doane, J., & Lewis, J. Association between parent-child transactions and risk for schizophrenia: Implications for early intervention. In M. S. Goldstein (Ed.), *Preventive intervention in schizophrenia: Are we ready?* Washington, D.C.: U.S. Department of Health and Human Services, Public Health Service, 1982.

Rosofsky, I., Levin, S., & Holzman, P. Psychomotility in the functional psychoses. *Journal of Abnormal Psychology*, 1982, **91**, 71–74.

Saletu, B. Central measures in schizophrenia. In H. Van Praag (Ed.), *Handbook of biological psychiatry. Part 2. Brain mechanisms and abnormal behavior—Psychophysiology*. New York: Marcel Dekker, 1980.

Saletu, B., Itil, T. M., Arat, M., & Akpinar, S. Long-term clinical and quantitative EEG effects of clopenthixal in schizophrenics: Clinical neurophysiological correlations. *International Pharmaco Psychiatry*, 1973, **8**, 193–207.

Schneider, K. *Clinical psychopathology*. New York: Grune and Stratton, 1959.

Schneider, W., & Shiffrin, R. M. Controlled and automatic human information processing. I. Detection, search and attention. *Psychological Review*, 1977, **84**, 1–66.

Schwartz-Place, E., & Gilmore, G. Perceptual organization in schizophrenia. *Journal of Abnormal Psychology*, 1980, **3**, 409–418.

Schweitzer, L. Evidence of right cerebral hemisphere dysfunction in schizophrenic patients with left hemisphere overactivation. *Biological Psychiatry*, 1982, **17**, 655–673.

Serafetinides, E., Coger, R., Martin, J., & Dymond, A. Schizophrenic symptomatology and cerebral dominance patterns: A comparison of EEG, AEK, & BPS measures. *Comprehensive Psychiatry*, 1981, **22**, 218–225.

Shagass, C. An electrophysiological view of schizophrenia. *Biological Psychiatry*, 1976, **11**, 3–30.

Shagass, C., Amadeo, M., & Overton, D. Eye tracking performance in schizophrenic patients. *Biological Psychiatry*, 1974, **9**, 295–360.
Shagass, C., Roemer, R., & Amadeo, M. Eye-tracking performance and engagement of attention. *Archives of General Psychiatry*, 1976, **33**, 121–125.
Shiffren, R., & Schneider, W. Controlled and automatic human information processing. II. Perceptual learning, automatic attending, and a general theory. *Psychological Review*, 1977, **84**, 127–190.
Silverman, J., Berg, P. D. S., & Kantor, R. Some perceptual correlates of institutionalization. *Journal of Nervous and Mental Disease*, 1965, **141**, 651–657.
Sollod, R., & Lapidus, L. Concrete operational thinking: Diagnosis and psychopathology in hospitalized schizophrenics. *Journal of Abnormal Psychology*, 1977, **86**, 199–202.
Spring, B., & Zubin, J. Attention and information processing as indicators of vulnerability to schizophrenic episodes. In L. C. Wynne, K. Cromwell, & J. Matthysse (Eds.), *The nature of schizophrenia: New approaches to research and treatment*. New York: Wiley, 1978.
Sternberg, S. Memory scanning: New findings and current controversies. *Quarterly Journal of Experimental Psychology*, 1975, **27**, 1–32.
Stone, M. Simple schizophrenia: Syndrome or shibboleth. *American Journal of Psychiatry*, 1968, **125**, 305–312.
Strauss, J., Kokes, R. F., Carpenter, W. T., & Ritzler, B. A. The course of schizophrenia as a developmental process. In L. C. Wynne, K. Cromwell, & J. Matthysse (Eds.), *The nature of schizophrenia: New approaches to research and treatment*. New York: Wiley, 1978.
Taylor, M., Redfield, J., & Abrams, R. Neuropsychological dysfunction in schizophrenics and affective disease. *Biological Psychiatry*, 1981, **16**, 467–478.
Underwood, G. *Strategies of information processing*. New York: Academic Press, 1978.
Vaughn, C., & Leff, J. The influence of family and social factors on the course of psychiatric illness: A comparison of schizophrenic and depressed neurotic patients. *British Journal of Psychiatry*, 1976, **129**, 125–137.
Walker, E., & McGuire, M. Intra and interhemispheric information processing in schizophrenia. *Psychological Bulletin*, 1982, **82**, 701–725.
Warrington, E., James, M., & Kinsbourne, M. Drawing disability in relation to laterality of cerebral lesion. *Brain*, 1966, **89**, 53–82.
Wexler, B., & Henninger, G. R. Alterations in cerebral laterality during acute psychotic illness. *Archives of General Psychiatry*, 1979, **36**, 278–284.
Wexler, B., & Henninger, G. R. Effects of concurrent administration of verbal and spatial visual tasks on a language related dichotic listening measure of perceptual asymmetry. *Neuropsychologia*, 1980, **18**, 379–382.
Wing, J., Cooper, J., & Sartorius, N. *Measurement and classification of psychiatric symptoms*. Cambridge: Cambridge University Press, 1974.

Yozawitz, A., Bruder, G., Sutton, S., Sharpe, L., Gurland, B., Fleiss, J., & Costa, L. Dichotic perception: Evidence for right hemisphere dysfunction in affective psychosis. *British Journal of Psychiatry*, 1979, **135**, 224–237.

Zubin, J. Problem of attention in schizophrenia. In M. L. Kietzman, S. Sutton, & J. Zubin (Eds.), *Experimental approaches to psychopathology*. New York: Academic Press, 1975.

Zubin, J., Magazines, J., & Steinhauer, S. *The metamorphosis of schizophrenia: From chronicle to vulnerability*. 1983. Forthcoming.

Zubin, J., & Spring, B. Vulnerability: A new view of schizophrenia. *Journal of Abnormal Psychology*, 1977, **86**, 103–126.

The Immediacy Hypothesis in a Theory of Schizophrenia

Kurt Salzinger

Polytechnic Institute of New York and the New York State Psychiatric Institute

The great advantage of being invited to present a paper is that one can discuss a topic of his own choosing and do so discursively. He can then use the opportunity to discover what it is he wishes to say and, after he has said it, what it all means. I found myself in this position as I returned to what I originally named the Immediacy Hypothesis. Having had this hypothesis included in books that discussed *theories* of schizophrenia, I finally asked myself to account for what in hindsight I can only describe as a fit of false modesty quite unbecoming to a resolute, not to say inflexible, scientist. This false modesty might well have been one reason for the view some have expressed that my hypothesis is "simplistic," a state far worse than "simple."

After further thought I decided that to label my behavior as springing from a fit would be unconscionable, given my view of the deleterious effects of labeling in general, and so I sought other explanations. The explanation I found was that the word "theory" had a certain aversiveness for me. After all, I do count myself among the radical behaviorists, and as such I am well aware of Skinner's famous paper (1950), "Are Theories of Learning Necessary?" Furthermore, I ended a paper of my own (Salzinger, 1973b) by asking whether theories of cognition were necessary. This has led me to realize that, though I am interested in generating theories related to schizophrenia, I am interested only in certain kinds of theory. What's more, now giving up all false modesty, I believe all others also ought to be interested in only that particular kind of theory, and so at the outset I will describe the theory we ought to accept to help us in the incredibly difficult task of learning what schizophrenia is all about.

After describing the requirements for a theory of schizophrenia, I will review what I believe to be the methodological pitfalls we must avoid if we are ever to test theories in valid ways. I will follow that with a description of the immediacy theory and the evidence, both experimental and clinical, that led me to espouse it. Finally, I will test its validity by determining how well it fits all the studies of schizophrenia reported in the *Journal of Abnormal Psychology* for the year 1981.

REQUIREMENTS FOR A THEORY OF SCHIZOPHRENIA

1. Given what we know about the seriousness of the behavior exhibited by people called schizophrenic and the recent spate of biochemical and genetic studies, the theory must leave room for a biological *Anlage*, or at least a biological involvement in accounting for the schizophrenic behavior.

2. Equally important, the theory must allow for an environmental basis or environmental influences in accounting for schizophrenic behavior, for two reasons: (*a*) because the person-varying but environment-consistent kinds of behaviors we see in schizophrenics cannot have arisen solely from the effect of a biological variable or variables, and (*b*) because "normal" biologically determined behavior also is modified when it meets its environment.

3. It follows from all of this that no theory of schizophrenia can be considered adequate that specifies a biological deficit apart from its interaction with the environment. Thus, being farsighted may save one's life when one is hunting and sees a charging animal from far enough away to protect oneself. On the other hand, being farsighted, without corrective lenses, would be very dangerous if one had to read dials to shut down a nuclear reactor.

What constitutes a deficit, then, is partly determined by the requirements of the environment. It is not at all clear how people learn that they are color-blind or tone-deaf or how much of a deficit this constitutes for them. Obviously these would be serious deficits only if discriminating colors or tones were essential to receiving some sort of significant reinforcement such as food, comradeship, or love. In this society brute strength, to take another example of a

The Immediacy Hypothesis in a Theory of Schizophrenia

VARIABLE SETS

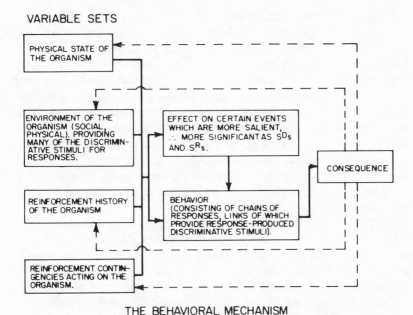

THE BEHAVIORAL MECHANISM

FIGURE 1. The behavioral mechanism explains the various ways behavior is controlled by variables that precede or follow it. From Salzinger (1980).

potential deficit, is no longer important because we have many devices to help us do heavy work. Memory for facts has also become considerably less important than in the days before writing; nevertheless, it is not difficult to think of situations where a good memory may indeed be critical—as, for example, remembering where the oxygen supply is in an emergency. On the other hand, one can think of situations where inability to discriminate color differences (deficit?) might constitute an advantage, as when shading differences among stimuli might provide the appropriate information for making a life-saving response. The argument here is best summarized by the word "interdependence."

4. When we decide that particular behaviors, sometimes referred to as symptoms, are caused by environmental factors, innate factors, or both, we still have the important task of specifying the behavioral mechanism (Salzinger, 1980) through which the sources of the abnormal behavior express themselves. Figure 1 demonstrates what I mean by the behavioral mechanism. Essentially this diagram shows that viewing behavior in the absence of controlling

variables provides an incomplete and often misleading picture. The box marked "behavior" indicates what investigators typically study. The rest of the diagram shows how the significance of the behavior must vary with the controlling conditions. Inspecting the "variable sets" shows that the behavior will vary, first of all, with the physical state of the organism (including such factors as fatigue, headache, sleep, drugs, and biochemical imbalance). The physical state affects both the stimuli to which the subject pays attention and/or which control his or her behavior, in the form of stimuli that precede (discriminative stimuli) and those that follow (reinforcing stimuli) the behavior, as well as the behavior itself. Behavior may thus be affected directly by the physical state or indirectly through the stimuli that control it.

Furthermore, the physical state of the organism interacts with the environment that provides the discriminative stimuli preceding the responses, with the reinforcement history, and with the current reinforcement contingencies acting on the organism. All of these variables then either affect the kinds of stimuli that precede and follow the behavior or affect the behavior directly. Finally, the consequences of the behavior, the box at the right end of the diagram, feed back to all of the variable sets, thus further complicating the picture. What does the diagram show us? It says that, whatever theory of schizophrenia we posit, we must trace its effects through the behavioral mechanism. I will therefore return to this diagram to explain the effect of the Immediacy Theory I intend to explicate here.

5. The symptoms of schizophrenia vary—from person to person as well as from time to time within a given person. The theory must concern itself with that variability and posit its source or sources. We must admit that the reasons for the variability might well be that diagnosis is not sufficiently precise (Salzinger, 1978) or that schizophrenia really consists of a conglomerate of disturbances, but it is important to make some comment on this matter.

I believe that a theory of schizophrenia, if it states the particulars precisely enough, ought eventually to produce an operational definition of a diagnostic category. Thus one strategy might be to have the *theory* produce the homogeneous groupings that the current diagnostic procedures cannot achieve. The theory-derived measure itself can then scale people by the degree to which they suffer from the posited disturbance or deficit. Sutton (1973) makes a similar suggestion when he speaks of the iterative method in diagnosis. He compares schizophrenics and normals on some objective measure and also conducts a structured interview with each of them. Those members of the two groups who differ from one another are then separated, and their responses on the interview are inspected to determine what aspect of the interview diagnosis relates to the difference on the objective measure, thus refining the interview procedure for future groups; naturally this must be replicated, and if it is, one then has the beginning of more homogeneous diagnostic categories. The difference between Sutton's strategy and mine is that his approach is empirical whereas mine uses a theory to direct the construction of techniques specifically designed to measure the theory-relevant parts of the patient's functioning without looking for confirmation in interview-elicited information.

6. The theory should be so stated that one can at least begin to relate it to a biochemical or physiological explanation or description of the "basic" fault in the schizophrenic patient. We must relate the behavioral mechanism to the internal state of the organism.

7. The theory must have a way of linking the functioning of the patient to successful intervention (even temporary success), for example, to such variables as drugs and behavior therapy.

8. The theory ought to explain both the complex, in vivo behavior we call symptoms and the more precise, controlled behavior evoked in experiments. The latter affords the opportunity for precise testing of the theory; the former is required to give intuitive understanding to the theory.

9. Since behavior varies over long periods—more dramatically during childhood and possibly during old age—the theory ought to say something about how behavior is acquired, maintained, and lost in the individuals with whom the theory deals. In some cases the way behavior changes characterizes the patient and his or her malady; in other cases the critical problem to be explained is not the way the behavior changes, but the way it remains the same over time and across different situations. In any case it is not enough to say that schizophrenics suffer from a deficit; one must also be able to say how this deficit interacts with the changing biology and environment of a growing or otherwise changing individual and whether that deficit manifests itself in the way the person changes.

10. A theory about schizophrenia must say something about social variables. Stress appears to be the simplest, most intuitively obvious, of all the variables in explaining why a particular person has broken down at a particular time (Zubin & Spring, 1977). In

recent years social class (Dohrenwend & Dohrenwend, 1969) and stressful life events (Dohrenwend & Dohrenwend, 1974, 1982) have been used to index social factors implicated in psychiatric disturbance. Liem and Liem (1982) discuss the interaction of social class and stressful life events. They conclude that there is a tendency for those with low social status to suffer from a larger number of life events, but that the critical effect is the moderating influence social class exerts on the life event when it occurs. Dohrenwend and Egri (1981) and Day (1981) recently examined the relationship of life events to schizophrenia. Neither review concluded that life events were powerful variables in schizophrenia, but neither felt they could be dismissed at this point. The implication is that a theory of schizophrenia ought to be able to comment on these effects, to show how the posited deficit might be implicated in such relationships.

When we speak of social factors in a theory of schizophrenia, however, we must also think of the patients in whom we see no stressful event triggering the schizophrenic episode. Here I would like to suggest that stress, anxiety, or arousal—all concepts that have at one time or another been favorites in theories of schizophrenia—seem not to explain how the environment acts with those factors to produce, or at least to exacerbate, schizophrenia. Theories using these concepts must be complemented by additional variables that specify how, say, higher arousal interacts with the environment to produce the deleterious interaction. Emotional response or greater arousal has to be considered a secondary factor rather than the primary one, I believe, because there is little evidence that it produces the problem. For one thing, lack of emotional response is often ascribed to schizophrenics, and for another not all or even a large enough number of stressful events produce difficulties we can call schizophrenia.

Knowing full well that God gave only ten commandments to his people, I hesitate to add an eleventh requirement for a theory of schizophrenia. But remembering the old saw about "he who hesitates," I will add one more.

11. Any theory must begin as simply as possible. The idea behind a theory is to use a minimum of concepts to explain a maximum of data. This is not to exclude the possibility of having later to add more concepts, but it is best to begin as simply as possible. A theory must allow a broader view—a look from a greater height that makes detection of detail impossible but brings to the fore the overarching

principle that explores the pattern formed by those obscured details.

These are the requirements—as I see them—for constructing a theory of schizophrenia. If they are satisfied, then we can test the resulting theory. Theory construction, however, is by no means the only problem facing a researcher in this area. The methods of testing are also fraught with problems, and I shall turn my attention to methodological problems before explicating my own theory of schizophrenia.

METHODOLOGICAL PROBLEMS

The study of abnormal individuals, beginning with the designation of membership in the class, is difficult. The road to valid experimental results is paved with loose cobblestones that trip up the best of investigators. The problems are so great, in fact, that had I omitted studies not plagued with methodological flaws, I would never have been able to construct any theory at all. This is not, however, an excuse to remain forever in the present methodological morass. I list the methodological problems here in the hope that investigators will pay greater attention to them so that our area of research may provide a better foundation for a theory.

1. The complexity of experimental situations often, if not always, requires a great deal of cooperation from subjects. Sometimes the cooperation consists of doing some particular task such as memorizing a list of words or more simply lifting a finger at the onset of a stimulus; at other times the cooperation required seems minimal, but it may be of equal importance to the validity of the data obtained. This can be true in cases of physiological measurement when, for example, all the subject has to do is sit still and look at a light. Failure to do so will reflect a lack of cooperativeness rather than poor psychophysiological functioning.

One way of dealing with these problems is to construct methods in which subjects do not know they are participating in an experiment. Some years ago we (Salzinger & Pisoni, 1958, 1960, 1961; Salzinger & Portnoy, 1964) successfully conditioned self-referred affect statements in schizophrenic patients who were ignorant not only that they were being conditioned, but even that they were participating in an experiment. This was so because, while the conditioning took place, they were engaged in an interview; since all had been interviewed before, they cooperated (or not) with what they believed were the requirements of an interview, not of conditioning. Cooperativeness was also excluded as an experimental artifact when we examined the patients' speech in monologues that we (Salzinger, Portnoy & Feldman, 1964a) obtained by simply asking them to talk about what had brought them to the hospital and otherwise to describe their life. We then prepared the resulting speech in the cloze procedure form for testing the communicability of the speech (Salzinger, Portnoy, & Feldman, 1964b, 1966), that is, the degree to which other people can understand it. Examining how understandable schizophrenic speech is clearly comes under the heading of a nonobtrusive observation technique and therefore obviates any problem of cooperativeness.

Other techniques that circumvent this problem compare baseline performance with performance under other conditions; this assumes that cooperativeness is equal during the two conditions and that the difference between conditions reflects the experimental variable. Still another technique to avoid the cooperativeness artifact is to search for behavior in which schizophrenic patients are better than normals; in that case less cooperativeness produces poorer performance as usual but serves to mitigate rather than exaggerate differences between schizophrenics and normals.

We can also deal with cooperativeness in our experiments by making it equal in the groups being compared, modifying the situation so that, though the topographical conditions are different, the functional conditions are the same. Thus we might use social reinforcement with a population of volunteer normal subjects but use cigarettes and coffee as reinforcement for patients on a ward. The point would be to match the reinforcement contingency on a task simple enough to reveal something exclusively about the reinforcer value, then employ those different reinforcers that equalize the groups in cooperativeness so as to reveal differences in other aspects.

In terms of motivation, it is startling that the consequences contingent on a patient's behavior while being tested have been left largely unexamined. Clearly some reinforcement is contingent on the patient's behavior, even if only avoidance of or escape from a negative reinforcement. Without knowing what reinforcement contingencies are acting, we have no way to ensure comparability between groups or between studies. Yet without paying attention to the reinforcement contingencies, mental health workers conduct interviews and quarrel about diagnostic differences. Structured interviews have become the rage, but the discriminative stimuli that function as questions are only half of what needs to be controlled; the other half is the reaction of the interviewer to the answers, the reactions that define the reinforcement contingencies. Although cooperativeness is important in interviews that determine who is to be called schizophrenic in the first place, it remains uncontrolled (Salzinger, 1978).

2. Cooperativeness is of course the degree to which subjects do what they are called upon to do. One endpoint of this dimension is doing nothing—that is, not cooperating at all. In looking over the literature in this area, it is appalling to see that investigators do not report how many subjects they cannot test on their tasks, that is, how many they discard from their samples. The problem is that as the cognitive approaches take over in the realm of testing schizophrenic patients, the complexity of tasks increases, with an undoubted increase in loss of subjects. The mere loss of subjects is of course not so important as losing certain kinds of subjects, with the consequence that one cannot know how generalizable any given sample is.

3. Along the same lines is the problem of the biased population we find in treatment centers. As has been demonstrated by Dohrenwend and Dohrenwend (1969), it is a biased population because not all those who are abnormal seek treatment. More than that, this population most likely is selected because these people have made a nuisance of themselves, which is hardly representative of any diagnostic category as a whole.

4. Once in the hospital, patients are subjected to different milieus, which undoubtedly influence the way they behave in experimental situations, no matter how well controlled. A study by Murray and Cohen (1959) is instructive in this context. They were able to show that different wards had different degrees of social organization as well as differences in severity of mental illness. Some wards, for whatever reason, seemed to foster isolation, while others encouraged social interaction among the patients. Responsiveness to the experiment might well reflect such a difference in ward atmosphere.

5. A problem that seems unsurmountable these days is drugs. Patients not only receive drugs wherever they are treated, but they have usually received drugs before they ever get to the mental

health agency that typically provides the patients we study. As a result most studies, if not all, use subjects who are schizophrenic *and* under the influence of one or more antipsychotic drugs. Comparing patients who receive drugs with those who do not provides no information at all on the effect of the drugs, no matter how many studies use this method. If the patients who receive a given drug do not differ from those who do, there are at least two possible explanations: either the drug does not affect the particular function being studied, or it improves the behavior of the presumably more agitated patients to the level of those who do not need the drug.

6. I have already spoken of the reinforcement variable with respect to cooperativeness. Now we need to take up behavior theory in general as a methodological problem that is largely ignored by most of those conducting research in schizophrenia. Ten years ago I outlined some of the ways the variables specified by behavior theory control the behavior of abnormal as well as normal individuals (Salzinger and Salzinger, 1973). I believe these are important enough to review here in the context of theories of schizophrenia.

The first point is that behavior is multiply determined. It is the final common pathway of a great many variables, and only some of these are characteristic of abnormality. I have already discussed the importance of the reinforcement contingency: $S^D \ldots R{\rightarrow}S^R$. According to this formulation, behavior (R) occurs on certain occasions (S^D = discriminative stimulus), and when it does it is reinforced (S^R = reinforcing stimulus) either through positive reinforcement or through escape from or avoidance of negative reinforcement.

Discriminative stimuli control behavior in the laboratory and also in the environment outside the laboratory. Zarlock (1966) demonstrated how even acutely disturbed schizophrenics who had been hospitalized at least once before, who were restricted to the ward, and who required tranquilizing drugs changed their behavior radically as a function of changing discriminative stimuli. For ten days a large room on the ward was modified to present four classes of discriminative stimuli: recreational, occupational, social, and medical. No differential verbal instructions were given as the conditions changed. Zarlock observed various classes of behavior under these different conditions. The number of pathological statements, such as hallucinations, delusions, somatic complaints, incoherent speech, and bizarre expressions, varied from three during the recreational situations to 12 in the occupational and social situation to 324 in the medical situation. Bizarre behavior such as praying out loud and gesturing occurred 33 times in the medical situation as opposed to twice in the recreational and occupational situations and four times in the social situation. It is interesting that the medical discriminative stimuli approximated the typical state hospital situation in which schizophrenics typically find themselves when hospitalized. This does not, of course, imply that the hospital produces schizophrenic psychopathology. On the other hand, it does clearly imply that the so-called symptomatology varies over different situations. Why is this important? Because the observations—whether clinical or experimental, whether for making a decision on treatment of a single patient or for testing a theory—must take into account the discriminative stimuli that are impinging on the patients being observed. The fact of the matter is that such specification of the environment in which the patient is observed is very infrequently achieved, never mind taken into account. There are many other examples of how the environment shapes the behavior of individuals, whether normal or schizophrenic. Unless we begin to specify these environments, we will fail to bring order to the patients' data.

The way patients respond to various discriminative stimuli of course depends on the current reinforcement contingency and on their reinforcement history. Braginsky, Grosse, and Ring (1966) and Braginsky, Braginsky, and Ring (1969) showed that by presenting a set of 30 items from the Minnesota Multiphasic Personality Inventory (MMPI) either as a "mental illness" test or as a "self-insight" test they could determine the extent to which patients admitted to mental symptoms. Patients who had been in the hospital longer (more than three years) checked off more symptoms in the "mental illness" test, which promised more hospitalization if they admitted to them, but fewer symptoms in the "self-insight" test, which related such admissions to briefer hospitalization because "it showed less mental illness." The reverse effect was found with patients who had been hospitalized less than three months. This study shows that the measurement of mental illness by items such as those found in the MMPI is sensitive to the reinforcement contingency specified. For the old-timers, being hospitalized apparently constituted a positive reinforcement, whereas for short-term patients it was a negative reinforcement to be escaped from.

As I said earlier, even physiological functions are influenced by behavioral factors, as demonstrated in the following study. Gaviria (1967) presented normal subjects with recordings that said, "May I have your attention, please?" These words were spoken by the listener himself, his spouse, an unfamiliar male voice, and an unfamiliar female voice. Using skin resistance and blood pressure as physiological measures, Gaviria found that habituation was slowest for the subject's own voice and his spouse's and faster for the unfamiliar voices. Thus the person who reads instructions to a subject would be expected to influence the outcome of an experiment even when the response is physiological. Discriminative stimuli, whether in experiments or in the natural world, exert important influences on people's behavior, and one has to take that into account when comparing the behavior of schizophrenics with that of normals or members of other diagnostic categories.

Reinforcement contingencies are critical in determining the behavior of patients and normals alike, although, to be sure, the groups' reactions may well vary as a function of the type of reinforcement, reinforcement history, and so on, they might have in common. I have already mentioned our reinforcement studies with the interview in which we (Salzinger & Pisoni, 1958, 1960, 1961; Salzinger & Portnoy, 1964; Salzinger, Portnoy, & Feldman, 1964a) showed that the degree to which schizophrenic patients emit speech in general, as well as self-referred affect statements in particular, varies with the delivery of reinforcement. We also showed that degree of conditionability related to the outcome of illness as defined by a follow-up at six months. Those that became conditioned to a greater degree in the course of the interview were released from the hospital earlier than those who were conditioned less. This suggests still another methodological complication in studying schizophrenic patients. Not only are schizophrenics affected by reinforcement, thus providing different information about themselves, but the degree to which they are influenced is partially determined by the severity of their illness.

One other general finding must be described here. Eisenberger (1970) reviewed a number of studies of social deprivation and satiation in normal subjects. The conditioning effect was greater when social reinforcement (the reinforcement most frequently in use with patients) was delivered after a period of social deprivation than when it was delivered after a period of social reinforcement.

Again we must point out differences—potential and actual—among diagnostic categories (schizophrenics apparently are socially isolated), reinforcement histories (e.g., living with a family or alone early in life), living quarters (e.g., different ward atmospheres in a hospital), waiting period before being examined, and so forth, all of which would contribute to different results because such people would respond differentially to the delivery of social reinforcement. To top all that off, we must remember that the delivery of reinforcement is not systematically controlled in most experiments.

The moral of this last methodological point is that we pay too little attention to the variables that control behavior but are not related to psychopathology; as a result we bring more variance to our already borderline reliable results. This suggests, about all the methodological points, that we must take these variables into account, at first perhaps only by taking note of the conditions under which we collect our data but eventually by standardizing those conditions for better comparability of studies.

7. Before leaving the methodological problems, I should note one very important development in psychiatry, the third edition of the *Diagnostic and Statistical Manual of Mental Disorders*—DSM-III (American Psychiatric Association, 1980). On the face of it, the use of the diagnostic criteria seems an improvement, since explicitness of definition always improves communication and possibly even the application of categories. That the definitions have become more explicit is, however, not enough, for these definitions continue to lack functional descriptions, including what I have just recounted in great detail—the occasions (the discriminative stimuli) when the particular behaviors occur that classify a patient as schizophrenic. Perhaps that will have to come from students of abnormal behavior other than psychiatrists, for the medical model that is at the root of psychiatric nomenclature is topographical in approach rather than functional. But we need such definitions.

One additional point. Whereas DSM-III has become much more specific in its diagnostic categories and therefore differentiates more finely, genetic studies of schizophrenia have gone in the opposite direction with a category of schizophrenic spectrum disorders much bigger and wider than what DSM-III recognizes as schizophrenia.

So much then for the general principles required to construct a theory of schizophrenia, and so much for the methodological pitfalls we must avoid in our studies. Let me now describe the Immediacy Theory of schizophrenia and the evidence on which its construction was based.

IMMEDIACY THEORY

In a recent "Sunday Observer" column in the *New York Times Magazine* (February 27, 1983, p. 22), Russell Baker reviewed what he had thought were the verities of life, at least as generally accepted. He lamented that many of them have turned out to be quite wrong. As he put it: "Life seemed to be an educator's practical joke in which you spent the first half learning and the second half learning that everything you learned in the first half was wrong." Thinking about the state of knowledge in schizophrenia, I concluded that we have not yet reached that lofty plane of knowing when we are definitely wrong. In this early era of theory building you might therefore consider this, at the very least, an attempt in that direction.

My entrance into schizophrenia research was marked by a study in which I applied no fewer than three theories to explain my data and used the data to shed light on the theories. The first of these theories came from Sandor Rado (1953), who felt there was a proprioceptive disorder at the root of what he called the schizotypal disorder. Since I was having my subjects judge the heaviness of weights as part of a larger experiment, I felt I could subject this theory to an exact test. I therefore compared my sample of acute schizophrenics with a sample of normals on accuracy in judging the weights (Salzinger, 1957). The results were quite clear: the schizophrenics and normals did not differ. I thus concluded it was unlikely a proprioceptive disorder could be basic in explaining the problems of the schizophrenic. Rosenbaum, Flenning, and Rosen (1965) retested this theory with weights lighter than those I had used. These investigators assumed—correctly, as it turned out—that the more intense stimuli I employed had obscured a proprioceptive deficit that might come to the fore when the stimuli to be discriminated were lighter, and they did find a deficit in proprioception. It is perhaps ironic that a theory stated by a psychodynamically oriented psychiatrist should be so testable, but that is how it went. In any case this is an interesting finding, but I hope you will agree, by the end of this chapter, that these findings are better subsumed under a more general theory of schizophrenia than this one.

The second theory I tested was the well-known one that schizo-phrenics have difficulty with abstraction. Goldstein (1944) has done as much as anyone to popularize the idea of this particular deficit in schizophrenia which holds that schizophrenics are unable to deal with any but concrete situations. To test that theory, I looked at the problem of shift in judgment. Subjects judged the heaviness of weights in a so-called unanchored condition where stimuli were presented one at a time and the subject simply had to say whether each weight was "very light," "light," "medium," "heavy," or "very heavy." In the "anchored" condition subjects had to perform the same task except that before judging each weight they were to lift an anchor weight (either an extremely heavy or an extremely light weight). Subjects were instructed to try to keep from shifting their judgments in response to the anchors, because in the course of pilot testing I had discovered that individual subjects instructed themselves differently—some told themselves to shift their judg-ments in response to the extreme values of the anchors, and others tried to keep their judgments constant. This also provided an oppor-tunity to determine whether subjects followed an abstract stimulus, the instruction, or a concrete one—the proprioceptive sensation produced by the weight. Since the schizophrenic subjects shifted more than the normal ones, I interpreted the results as confirming that schizophrenics respond less to the abstract stimulus than the concrete one.

Finally, I applied a third theoretical formulation to the data. The subjects' responses could be viewed as an example of stimulus constancy—the ability to keep a judgment constant in the presence of shifting stimuli. Everybody knows it is essential that we not shift our judgment in response to every change in stimulus. Take, for example, judging the height of people seen from a distance. Their retinal image is clearly smaller than that of a person close by; nevertheless, we all make approximately the same estimates of their heights. Failing to keep our judgment constant in these circum-stances would wreak havoc, and failing to keep constant one's judgment of the heaviness of objects might be expected to cause similar problems. Thus I found evidence for schizophrenics' inabil-ity to maintain constancy.

My first study in schizophrenia unhappily makes clear how easy it is to impose various theories on the same data with no hope of finding more evidence for one than for another. I hope the Immediacy Theory will offer as one of its advantages the possibility of being disconfirmed by data. Any theory that cannot be disproved is not scientific and is therefore not useful in understanding schizophrenia.

What is the basic tenet of the Immediacy Theory? The Immediacy Hypothesis states: The behavior of schizophrenic individuals is controlled primarily by stimuli immediate in their environment (Salzinger, Portnoy, & Feldman, 1966; Salzinger, 1971a, 1971b, 1972, 1973a; Salzinger, Portnoy, & Feldman, 1978). To understand the full implications of this hypothesis, one needs to examine the consequences for an individual whose behavior is controlled primarily by a subset of the stimuli that control the behavior of most other people. It is the contact with the environment of the person controlled by immediate stimuli that gives rise to immediacy theory.

Let us examine, by way of elucidation, the behavior of a blind man. Obviously such a person is not influenced by visual stimuli. That means (let us refer back to Figure 1) that a whole set of stimuli cannot and will not control his behavior as either discriminative or reinforcing stimuli (whether these visual stimuli are only physical or are acting as conditioned stimuli; that is, verbal or social ones). Figure 1 shows that an absence of input from visual discriminative stimuli will prevent the establishment of certain reinforcement contingencies—traffic lights for example—with potentially fatal consequences. It also implies the absence of information that is available to the rest of us in this society. Visual stimulation provides us with discriminative stimuli that prevent us from acting in embarrassing ways, as when we see someone's tearstained or smiling face. Being blind means missing the reinforcement history that allows one to act appropriately in such circumstances. Blindness is represented in Figure 1 by the box labeled "physical state of the organism." It follows from this that a man who is suddenly blinded might well have great difficulty getting around physically, responding to people, and so forth, because he has not built up the requisite reinforcement history that might allow him to act appropriately in his new circumstances. What do I mean by appropriately? To obtain the positive reinforcement and avoid or escape the negative reinforcement to which he had formerly been conditioned, the blind man would have to have his behavior reconditioned (brought under the control of other stimuli), and indeed that is what is done in such cases.

Following up the diagram, we find that the blind man's behavior would at first engender fewer consequences (receiving only nonvisual positive reinforcements and escaping only nonvisual negative ones) than before, and he would probably also receive more punishing stimuli than before, such as bumping into objects and people or missing appointments. Inspection of the feedback loops (Figure 1) shows us that a blind man might well have a less favorable reinforcement history and quite possibly experience changes in his physical state including such maladies as ulcers or at least heightened blood pressure; he might become emotional, emitting verbal and nonverbal behavior that removes him from contact with other people. I will not continue analyzing the blind man's interaction with the laws of behavior except to make one other point. In our society, blindness is a fairly obvious discriminative stimulus to others; since we are taught to be kind and helpful to blind people, this in some ways mitigates the aversive stimulation that might otherwise greet the blind person. This is often quite different for schizophrenic patients, since we do not recognize that they are controlled by only a subset of the stimuli that control the rest of us. This unrecognized condition no doubt contributes to the negative way we respond to them.

THE IMMEDIACY HYPOTHESIS AND THE BEHAVIORAL MECHANISM

Let us now trace the immediacy deficit through the behavioral mechanism diagram (Figure 1). If we look at the first column, we can try to specify where the schizophrenic's problem lies. The physical state of the organism box is involved because presumably the nervous system (either through some genetically mediated mechanism or because of some acquired fault) is responsible for the preponderance of immediate stimuli controlling the schizophrenic's behavior. It interacts with the environment box, which includes social, verbal, and physical stimuli. The reinforcement history would be expected to be different for such individuals, depending in part on how long immediate stimuli were the primary ones in control. A research question this model poses is: Has this individual been preponderantly controlled by immediate stimuli since birth and only recently been discovered to be different, or is this kind of control a more recent development? Note that responding to immediate stimuli is expected from children and is one of the bases of comedy or humor in adults. There are also occupations and activities where responding to immediate stimuli generally pays off, and so here we have a way of obscuring some of the immediacy effects. The "high risk" studies ought to be helpful in answering this question.

Whether the onset of this type of control is sudden or insidious, a mature person in whom most controlling reinforcement contingencies relate to immediate stimuli might well strike others as peculiar. In other words, the behaviors (see the box so marked in the second column) might be followed by punishing stimuli rather than positive reinforcers in the consequence box (the third column of Figure 1).

Having shown some of the effects of the limitation of immediate discriminative stimuli, let me now examine the effect of limiting reinforcers and punishers to immediate ones. First, behavior often, if not always, has both immediate and remote consequences; second, the immediate consequences of behavior are quite different from the more remote ones. If one is not controlled by remote reinforcers one cannot plan or work toward an end that takes time to achieve. This suggests why token economies, in contrast to other psychotherapeutic techniques, work so well with schizophrenic patients. What are some of the other effects immediate stimuli have on the behavior of the schizophrenic patient? Responding to immediate stimuli and not to the more remote ones we ordinarily consider context causes a great deal of misunderstanding or misconstruing of the behavior of others. For example, if one is pushed by someone, the stimulus alone might well be responded to as an assault rather than as an accident or playfulness. Although one of these "misunderstandings" might not be important, experiencing a number of them with the same person or in the same environment might well produce in the schizophrenic the kind of reaction we ordinarily call paranoia. A woman blinking because of a dust in her eye might be misconstrued by a male patient as attempting to flirt; if he acts on that misinterpretation, she might well be annoyed. In addition to misunderstandings, control by isolated stimuli (which is likely when the response is primarily to immediate stimuli) would be apt to result in lack of understanding and puzzlement. In either case—misunderstanding or lack of understanding—we might expect the patient to be suffering, which in turn might give rise to the kind of violent or socially isolating symptomatology we find in these patients.

In essence, Immediacy Theory starts with the Immediacy Hypothesis and traces its interaction with environmental conditions and the laws of behavior theory to present us with a picture of the schizophrenic. To determine the success of this process, we will take the DSM-III criteria for schizophrenia and evaluate the degree to which they can be derived from the interaction of the immediacy principle with the principles of behavior theory.

DSM-III Criteria for Schizophrenia and the Immediacy Hypothesis

DSM-III (American Psychiatric Association, 1980, p. 181) introduces its description of schizophrenia in the following way: "The limits of the concept of Schizophrenia are unclear." In addition to accepting this basic ambiguity, DSM-III uses a combination of criteria for inclusion in and exclusion from this category. The criteria are not along one dimension; that is, they are not restricted to describing the person's behavior. Behavior of certain types is expected, although as a criterion of schizophrenia it is stated in terms of at least one of a group of six behaviors. In addition, the diagnosis appeals to the concept of deterioration from a previous level of functioning and specifies a minimum of six months' duration. This manner of arriving at a classification has some objectionable characteristics, but since it is the only definition of schizophrenia generally accepted in this country I will use it. I do believe that sooner or later we ought to define schizophrenia, or whatever else we call it at that time, in terms of more specific behavioral mechanisms that can be more directly traced to a theoretical formulation, such as the Immediacy Hypothesis.

The first diagnostic criterion for schizophrenic disorder is "bizarre delusions (content is patently absurd and has no possible basis in fact), such as delusions of being controlled, thought broadcasting, thought insertion, or thought withdrawal." Keeping in mind that a delusion is a false personal belief not shared by a subgroup or culture (to exempt religious beliefs), we must now explain how a person who starts with a tendency to respond primarily to immediate stimuli might arrive at such strange beliefs. I have already commented that responding to immediate stimuli means responding to stimuli in isolation; typically it is the context—that is, the other stimuli present either at the same time or before—that gives accurate meaning (indicates precisely when a particular response will be reinforced) to stimuli impinging on a person. A delusion is almost an operational definition of responding to stimuli out of context; the schizophrenic accomplishes that through responding to the immediate stimulus. Even with all that, how can you arrive at the conclusion that you are broadcasting your thoughts? If you respond to immediate stimuli, you might well be incapable of discriminating what you think from what you say; if you do not differentiate the two, then you might in fact say things you thought you only thought about.

Additional criteria for schizophrenia are two other kinds of delusions: "somatic, grandiose, religious, nihilistic, or other delusions without persecutory or jealous content" and "delusions with persecutory or jealous content if accompanied by hallucination of any type" (DSM-III, p. 188). An example of a somatic delusion is thinking one's brain is rotting. What is interesting about these delusions, particularly when the patient merely states them verbally, is that they may constitute only *verbal* responses under the control of immediate stimuli; when these verbal responses become immediate stimuli for other responses, such as taking action against a person suspected of doing the patient harm, we find that immediate response-produced stimuli (talking or thinking to oneself) also can control behavior in these patients. Not all delusions are negative; some are benign, such as the delusions of grandeur. What holds these delusions together in one response class is that stimuli are responded to in isolation and therefore are misinterpreted. Which way they are misinterpreted is a matter of chance—of which particular stimulus evokes a response from the subject at that time. Thus, if the patient in question is told "You're terrific" that may elicit the response "I'm the greatest," which may in turn evoke the response "I am the president of the United States," and so forth.

The next two criteria for schizophrenia are different kinds of hallucinations. The first of these is described (DSM-III, p. 188) as "auditory hallucinations in which either a voice keeps up a running commentary on the individual's behavior or thoughts, or two or more voices converse with each other." The second is described (DSM-III, p. 188) as "auditory hallucinations on several occasions with content of more than one or two words, having no apparent relation to depression or elation." Both kinds of hallucinations are interesting. Some years ago Gould (1948, 1949, 1950) demonstrated that hallucinations are not auditory imagery but rather are subvocal speech, sometimes whispered and sometimes even shouted, by the patient who complains of hearing voices. He took physiological measurements and showed that 80% of the patients suspected of hallucinating showed increased muscle potential in the vocal apparatus, while only 10% of a group of patients without hallucinations showed such an increase. McGuigan (1966) had subjects who were hallucinating press a key whenever they heard a voice and found an increase of electrical activity in the larynx when that happened. In still another study, Mintz and Alpert (1972) gave schizophrenics two tasks. In the first, subjects were to imagine listening to "White Christmas" with both words and music and then rate the vividness of the image. Those who hallucinated reported achieving greater vividness than those who did not hallucinate. In the second task subjects were to listen to a series of sentences, repeat the sentences exactly as they heard them, then rate the confidence with which they gave the response. Hallucinating schizophrenics correlated + .54, whereas nonhallucinating schizophrenics correlated + .84, between the accuracy of their performances and the confidence with which they made their responses. This indicated that the hallucinators were less aware of their performance than were those who did not hallucinate. One can summarize these two experiments by saying that those who hallucinate have difficulty discriminating their response-produced stimuli from externally produced stimuli. Clearly this is the kind of problem that can arise if one is responding only to the immediate stimulus. In both response-produced and externally produced stimuli, an auditory stimulus impinges on the subject; discriminating between them requires responding to the other stimuli—that is, those that preceded the auditory one (whether produced by another person or by oneself).

The sixth and final criterion for schizophrenia is as follows: "incoherence, marked loosening of associations, markedly illogical thinking, or marked poverty of content of speech if associated with at least one of the following: (a) blunted, flat, or inappropriate affect, (b) delusions or hallucinations, (c) catatonic or other grossly disorganized behavior" (DSM-III, p. 188). Incoherence is, of course, very often the first behavior that calls a schizophrenic patient to the public's attention. Later on, when I review the experimental evidence for the Immediacy Hypothesis, I will present the various measures indicating that schizophrenics have a basic communication difficulty. Suffice it to say here that all forms of communication depend on responding to a large number of stimuli at the same time. Since many of these are response-produced, the cloze procedure, which I will explain later, is particularly suitable to making this particular deficit explicit. Restricting this criterion to incoherence associated with blunted affect and/or delusions and hallucinations and grossly disorganized behavior presumably screens out individuals suffering from such other diagnostic categories as mental retardation.

Any and all of these many and diverse symptoms could be caused by responding mainly to immediate stimuli. That deterioration is another criterion for schizophrenia suggests that responding primarily to immediate stimuli is not always a deficit or disadvantage, nor can its effect always be differentiated from other causes, such as in children, who respond to immediate stimuli because of developmental stage, or in humor, which makes such responding acceptable.

The requirement that the onset of the prodromal or active phase of the disorder occurs before age 45 can also be explained in forms of the Immediacy Hypothesis: it seems very unlikely that an individual could go through life with this deficit without getting into trouble by this time. It also suggests that such a debilitating disorder must be closely related to some biological foundation for the behavioral mechanism of control by immediate stimuli.

It remains for us to look at the symptoms listed as prodromal or residual—that is, the clear deterioration in functioning before the active phase of the disorder or the persistence of symptoms following the active phase. The symptoms include social isolation or withdrawal; they are not hard to explain considering that schizophrenics' response patterns cause alienation as other people get angry or avoid them. Impaired role functioning as wage earner, student, or homemaker or even neglect of personal hygiene and grooming might well constitute a combination of primary effects due to immediacy and secondary effects due to other people's reaction. The other symptoms of peculiar behavior, such as hoarding food, talking to oneself in public, digressive speech, magical thinking, and unusual perceptual experiences, are all very much like the active-phase symptoms and so have already been related to immediacy.

In general, we can conclude that the idea of control by immediate stimuli is consonant with the schizophrenic symptoms listed. This does not prove the validity of the concept, but it certainly meets an important requirement of any theory of schizophrenia—that it be capable of generating a plausible explanation for how the symptoms are produced.

Immediacy Theory: The Experimental Evidence

I would like to return now to experimental ways of investigating the role of immediate stimuli in the behavior of schizophrenics and trace the way I came to the idea of immediacy. In 1964 Dr. Portnoy, Dr. Feldman, and I decided to examine the speech of schizophrenic patients by means of an objective technique that would also be sensitive to social variables (Salzinger, Portnoy, & Feldman, 1964b). We decided to make use of a technique originated by Wilson Taylor (1953) to measure the readability of text materials. He found that such authors as Erskine Caldwell were much easier to understand than others like Gertrude Stein or James Joyce. The technique, which he called the "cloze" procedure, consists of the following: every fifth word of a given text is deleted and a blank is substituted for it. The resulting multilated text is then submitted to a group of subjects, who are asked to guess the deleted words. Scoring is simple and straightforward: one counts the words correctly guessed. Texts whose deleted words were more often guessed correctly were deemed more readable. In other words, high redundancy helps one to understand verbal material that is mutilated. It occurred to me that this technique would allow us to measure objectively the schizophrenic characteristic that is called thought disorder, tangential speech, or overly abstract or overly concrete thinking. All these characterizations stem from the difficulty of understanding people we call schizophrenic. We therefore took some speech samples collected in the course of our conditioning studies of verbal behavior (Salzinger, Portnoy, & Feldman, 1964a), typed them up exactly as the subjects had emitted them, deleted every fifth word, then had a group of normal subjects guess the missing words. When we compared the number of words correctly guessed in the schizophrenic speech and in speech from a matched group of normals, we found that normal subjects guessed the normal speech significantly better than the schizophrenic speech. What is more, guessing accuracy decreased from the first to the second 100 words of text for the schizophrenic speech but remained at the same level for the normal speech (See Figures 2, 3, and 4). Figure 2 shows the cumulative frequency of schizophrenics and normals whose proportion of correct guesses was at a given level or below. Thus seven out of 11 schizophrenics' speech (second 100 words) had 40% correct guesses or less while only one out of 11 normals (second 100 words) had 40% or less correct. Figures 3 and 4 show the proportion

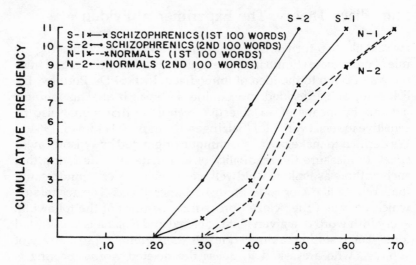

FIGURE 2. Cumulative frequency of schizophrenic and normal subjects as a function of proportion of correct guesses to total guesses (*C* score). S-1 and S-2 and N-1 and N-2 refer respectively to the first and second 100 words of the schizophrenic and normal passages. From Salzinger, Portnoy, & Feldman (1964*b*).

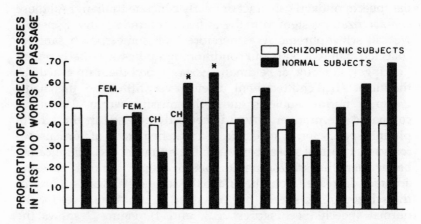

FIGURE 3. Proportion of correct guesses to total guesses (*C* score) in the first 100 words of the passages for each schizophrenic-normal matched pair. The two female pairs are indicated by *FEM*, the two chronic schizophrenics are indicated by *CH*, and the normal subject used in two pairs is indicated by an asterisk. From Salzinger, Portnoy, & Feldman (1964*b*).

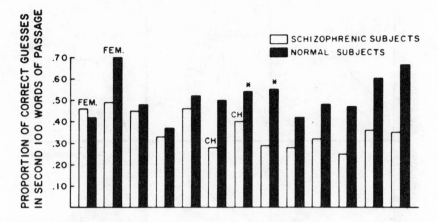

FIGURE 4. Proportion of correct guesses to total guesses (*C* score) in the first 100 words of the passages for each schizophrenic-normal matched pair. The two female pairs are indicated by *FEM,* the two chronic schizophrenics are indicated by *CH,* and the normal subject used in two pairs is indicated by an asterisk. From Salzinger, Portnoy, & Feldman (1964*b*).

correct for each of the matched patient-normal pairs, corroborating the differences between normals and schizophrenics and the increased difference farther into the speech sample.

What are the implications of this finding? It showed in a clear, quantitative way something we had known intuitively. Furthermore, despite the objectivity of the technique and its quantitative nature, it managed to provide information about something as complex as one person's ability to communicate with another. We checked its sensitivity to social variables by successfully relating communicability (how well one individual can predict the speech of another by means of the cloze procedure) to that person's position in a social network and to the length of time two people spent with one another (Hammer, Polgar, & Salzinger, 1969; Salzinger, Hammer, Portnoy, & Polgar, 1970). Although these findings were interesting, it was not obvious how we could relate them to other findings of difference between schizophrenics and normals. By that time I had already found that schizophrenics responded less to a verbal discriminative stimulus than did normals on a psychophysical task, the weight judgment task described earlier (Salzinger, 1957). I had also found that schizophrenics' verbal responses during

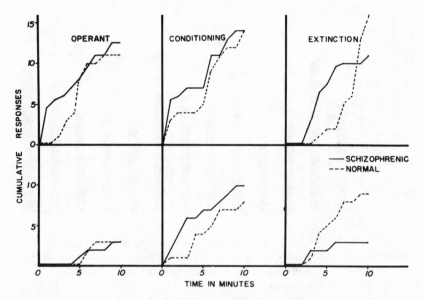

FIGURE 5. Individual cumulative self-referred affect response curves for two pairs of matched schizophrenic and normal subjects. The top pair shows two subjects with high operant levels, and the bottom pair shows two subjects with low operant levels. From Salzinger & Pisoni (1960). Copyright 1960 by the American Psychological Association.

an interview extinguished faster than did those of normals (fig. 5; Salzinger and Pisoni, 1960).

I will describe the more typical verbal conditioning task in some detail, for it was all the rage for simple and straightforward clinical Ph.D. dissertations in the fifties and sixties. In those tasks subjects were often asked to construct simple sentences out of one of three pronouns and one verb in the past tense, for example: "I [he, she] . . . called." Sentences with one particular pronoun were then reinforced, and conditioning was said to occur because subjects unfailingly eventually learned to use the proper pronoun. By contrast, the conditioning vehicle used in my laboratory was the interview. Subjects were asked a series of general questions, such as "Why are you here in the hospital?" "Tell me about your job." Questions were asked only when the subject had ceased speaking for at least two seconds. During the first ten minutes of the interview the experimenter only asked questions; during the second ten minutes verbal reinforcement consisting of the statements "yeah," "yes," "I see," "mmhm," and "I can understand that" followed each self-referred affect statement the patient emitted. Examples of the latter are "I hate," "I love," "I'm sad." Finally, the last ten minutes consisted of extinction, during which the experimenter reverted to the procedure employed in the first ten minutes. The interview was done face to face; it was recorded; the response class of self-referred affect was highly reliable, and the degree of conditioning in normals and schizophrenics, in contrast to extinction, was the same in the two groups (Salzinger & Pisoni, 1958, 1960, 1961; Salzinger & Portnoy, 1964; Salzinger, Portnoy & Feldman, 1964a). I need only add that the patients had received no drugs for at least one week before the experiment and that they did not know an experiment was being conducted, never mind that they were being conditioned.

To return to our question, what single concept can we find to explain the findings of a psychophysical experiment, a conditioning experiment, and a study in communication? The answer that occurred to me was the concept of immediacy. In the weight judgment experiment, the subjects were required to judge the heaviness of a series of stimuli; when they made those judgments without any special instructions to keep in mind, they did as well as the normals. But when they were required to lift an anchor weight before each weight to be judged and instructed to ignore the effect of that anchor (the most immediate stimulus of that stimulus configuration), they were controlled by the immediate stimulus and shifted their judgment. In the case of the difference in extinction, the faster decrease in the self-referred affect statements showed that the conditioning did not have as lasting an effect for schizophrenics as for normals. It became obvious that it was the lack of the immediate stimulus (the reinforcer) during extinction that made the schizophrenics' behavior shift back to the operant level so rapidly. In one case (weight judgment) the immediate stimulus caused the aberrant behavior; in the other case (extinction) the absence of the immediate stimulus caused it.

But what about speech communicability? An immediate external stimulus accounted for the greater ability to communicate in normals than in schizophrenics, particularly during the second 100 words.[1] The speech samples had been obtained by instructing sub-

1. A study by Rutter, Wishner, Kopytynska, and Button (1978) reported no significant difference between normals and schizophrenics. The schizo-

jects to talk about a number of topics listed at the beginning of the experiment; no further instructions were given later. As a consequence, the immediate stimulus of the instructions (as in the weight judgment experiment) became more remote with time, and the communicability of the second 100 words decreased because the speech began to wander from previous points in the monologue.

Language, however, contains within it a much more interesting kind of stimulus control, control by the response-produced stimulus, in which one verbal response governs another. Clearly, if such control were absent one could not understand any segments of speech. Phenomena such as word salad and tangential speech, both of which are attributed to schizophrenics, must in some way reflect the response-produced stimulus control as well as the external stimulus control. It has been fashionable to think of schizophrenic speech as disorganized, which suggests a loosening of stimulus control. The theory I offer says that the aberration relates to excessive control by immediate stimuli. Immediate response-produced stimulus control suggests that in schizophrenics longer segments of speech are less cohesive than in normals, reflected in the interesting way schizophrenic speech gives one the feeling one should understand it without providing the actual understanding. That feeling no doubt comes from the fact that in the short run the words are indeed connected; longer spans are the ones we find difficult to follow.

This kind of reasoning gave rise to the idea of testing the Immediacy Hypothesis directly (Salzinger, Portnoy, Pisoni, & Feldman, 1970). We took blanks from the cloze procedure studies described above, choosing them on the basis of high and low cloze scores and part of speech (lexical and function words). The passages of 10 normals and 10 schizophrenics who were matched on age, sex, education, and speech community, with their blanks matched on part of speech and cloze score, were presented to a group of normal subjects in the following way: each subject received each blank surrounded by two, four, eight, 16, or 28 words, half on each side of the blank. The results were as predicted (see Figure 6). As the

---

phrenics in that study, however, were receiving antipsychotic medication, which might well have improved their ability to communicate, thus making their study less than useful in evaluating the cloze procedure. Other critiques of that study are to be found in Salzinger, Portnoy, and Feldman (1979).

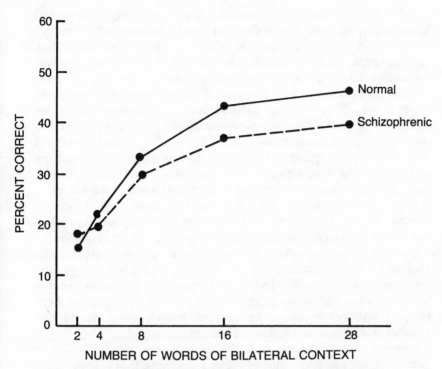

FIGURE 6. Percentage of correct words guessed from schizophrenic and normal speech segments as a function of the number of words of bilateral context. From Salzinger, Portnoy, & Feldman (1978).

amount of context increased for a given blank, so did the percentage of correct guesses; but the rate of increase of guessing the correct word for normal speech was greater than that for schizophrenic speech. In fact, with only two words surrounding the blank, schizophrenic speech appeared to be more accurately predicted than its normal counterpart.

Further analysis of these results showed that the difference was most profound in blanks that required function words as correct answers. This is to be expected, since function words depend almost entirely for their meaning on the surrounding words; if the schizophrenic is described as having difficulty in stimulus control, one would expect it to be most notable in words that depend in their emission on neighboring words. We have here a validation of the immediacy principle.

Other findings on the communicability of speech encouraged us in this interpretation. We developed a technique we called "reconstruction" (Salzinger, Portnoy, & Feldman, 1966), in which we took schizophrenic and normal speech samples, divided them up into successive 20-word segments, and put them on cards. We then randomized the cards and had normal subjects arrange them in the order in which they thought the speaker had emitted them. The results were clear. More errors were made in restoring the order of the segments for schizophrenic speech than for normal speech. A third technique applied to the speech samples was the unitization technique. The entire typed, unpunctuated speech sample was presented to normal subjects, who were instructed to mark it off in sentence units, crossing out any words they could not fit into the sentences. A comparison of normal and schizophrenic speech showed that a larger number of words had to be crossed out for the schizophrenic speech than for the normal speech. Substantially greater control by immediate stimuli in speech results in greater confusion for the listener. In schizophrenic speech a larger number of words do not fit in the larger context of sentences, nor are there enough linkages available to connect speech segments to one another in the reconstruction technique.

Communicability scores were also used to examine schizophrenic patients from another point of view. Reasoning that if these measures are significant—as we showed by relating them to schizophrenic-normal differences and to meaningful social distance measures (Hammer, Polgar, & Salzinger, 1969; Salzinger, Hammer, Portnoy, & Polgar, 1970)—we thought we ought to be able to relate them to outcome of illness as well. Using a six-month period of follow-up, we found that schizophrenic patients whose cloze scores were higher stayed in the hospital for a briefer period than those whose cloze scores were lower. Furthermore, we found that the second 100 words related to outcome better than the first 100 words, just as we found larger normal-schizophrenic differences for the second than for the first 100 words. The correlation between cloze score and outcome for the first 100 words was $-.29$, whereas the correlation for the second 100 words was $-.48$. Once more we find evidence for the validity of the immediacy concept: the degree to which immediacy controls the patient (as evidenced by the degree of communicability) appears to determine time to recovery. Finally, I should add some long-term follow-up data (15–19 years). Since these speech samples were collected in the sixties, we were able to determine total number of days spent in the hospital since the speech samples had been collected (Salzinger, Portnoy, Feldman, & Patenaude-Lane, 1980). When we related days spent in the hospital during those years to the cloze scores, we arrived at a correlation of −.39, which is statistically significant ($p < .05$). In other words, the more effective the communicability, the less time the patients spent in the hospital.

In 1977 we decided to compare the immediacy hypothesis with another theory of schizophrenia, what we called the lapse-of-attention hypothesis (Salzinger, Portnoy, & Feldman, 1977). McGhie (1969; McGhie and Chapman, 1961) hypothesized that the schizophrenic's basic problem consists of fluctuating attention; every once in a while the patient has a lapse of attention. We felt that our unitization technique (Salzinger, Portnoy, & Feldman, 1966) would allow us to locate intrusions—words that could not fit in the sentences into which the normal subjects had to divide the continuous speech. We took the unitized speech samples, eliminated the intrusions, and deleted every fifth word of the resulting texts for the cloze procedure. We did this for both schizophrenic and normal speech samples. Mean proportions of correct guesses for normal and schizophrenic samples with the intrusions were .57 and .45, respectively; for the samples with the intrusions excised the respective cloze scores were .56 and .46. Eliminating the intrusions did not affect communicability for either schizophrenic or normal speech, thus indicating that the difference in communicability cannot be attributed to momentary lapses of attention but rather must be attributed to a communicability deficit underlain by a continuous variable such as the effect of the immediacy of response-produced stimuli. If the lapses of attention explained the difference in communicability, then removing the intrusions should have raised communicability enough to eliminate the difference between normals and schizophrenics. Since it had no such effect, we can conclude that the lapse-of-attention hypothesis is not valid. It is also interesting that correlations between cloze scores and the number of intrusions approach significance only for schizophrenic speech, suggesting that the intrusions might be considered an extreme result of the communicability deficit of immediacy in schizophrenics, whereas the normal's intrusions are not related to general ability to communicate.

Two additional studies in recent years have employed the cloze procedure (Salzinger, Portnoy, Feldman, & Patenaude-Lane, 1980). Fourteen schizophrenic clinic patients gave us two monologues each, one about the reasons they were in the hospital, and one about things they enjoyed. When we compared communicability between the two kinds of speech samples, we found no difference. On the other hand, when we compared the two kinds of passages in terms of speech disturbance ratio based on Mahl's (1956) work, we found more disturbance in the "hospital" topic than the "enjoyable things" topic. This showed that the immediacy effect transcends emotional states.

In the second study we tested eight schizophrenic outpatients and eight nonschizophrenic psychiatric outpatients twice with a period of a week intervening. The correlation of the cloze scores between the two speech samples of the schizophrenics was $+.79$, $p < .05$; for the nonschizophrenics it was $-.16$ ($p < .05$). This showed that the immediacy effect was stable over time for the schizophrenics. For the nonschizophrenic patients, factors such as changes in emotionality might well influence ability to communicate.

Finally, one other study done in our laboratory relates to the immediacy concept. Hammer and Salzinger (1964) analyzed a small number of long speech samples from schizophrenics and normals. We found that schizophrenics used the same words repeatedly more often than normals. This finding also can be interpreted in terms of the Immediacy Hypothesis; normals usually avoid repeating the same words or series of words in an essay or conversation; assuming that schizophrenics also act under these restrictions, one can explain such repetition by assuming they use shorter spans to consider whether a word or series of words has been repeated.

EVIDENCE FROM OTHER LABORATORIES

Over the years I have found evidence for the immediacy effect in many studies done by others. These have been reviewed in some detail in a number of publications (Salzinger, 1971a, 1971b, 1973a; Salzinger, Portnoy, & Feldman, 1978), so I will go over these earlier studies only enough to give an idea of the outside support for the hypothesis.

I have already mentioned my first study in schizophrenia, in which I showed that schizophrenics are more likely than normals to respond to the immediate effect of lifting an anchor weight. Wurster (1965) replicated my study and added the following condition: he used the anchor weight merely as one of a series of weights; that is, it did not precede every weight to be judged. Under those conditions he found that the effect was less in schizophrenics than in normals. In other words, when the anchor was the immediate stimulus, its effect was greater than in normals; on the other hand, when the anchor weight was a remote stimulus (just one of the series of weights), it affected the normals more than the schizophrenics. The greater effectiveness of immediate anchors on the judgment of schizophrenics has also been demonstrated in the estimation of length of lines (Boardman, Goldstone, Reiner, & Fathauer, 1962).

Chapman (1956) found that schizophrenics were more distractible than normals in a card-sorting test, showing that the mere presence of stimuli, even when clearly irrelevant, controls schizophrenic responding enough of the time to cause deterioration of performance. A number of experiments can be cited to show that schizophrenics tend toward retinal image constancy rather than object constancy (Rausch, 1952; Boardman, Goldstone, Reiner, & Himmel, 1964; Weckowicz, 1964). We find that the schizophrenic has a tendency to respond to the proximal stimulus rather than to the more remote stimulus, which elicits the conditioned response that produces object constancy. A similar phenomenon was illustrated by Peastrel (1964), in which schizophrenics generalized more to homophones than to synonyms. The sound is the more immediate stimulus, whereas the meaning, which requires associations to the stimulus word, is the remote stimulus. Further along the lines of verbal stimuli, Chapman, Chapman, and Miller (1964) demonstrated that schizophrenics tended to respond with greater response biases—that is, to respond with the high-probability response regardless of context. That, of course, means they responded primarily to the more immediate stimulus.

Our finding of more rapid extinction in schizophrenics than in normals (Salzinger & Pisoni, 1960) was confirmed by Dinoff, Horner, Kurpiewski, and Timmons (1960). It also follows from this that token economies in which, at least in the beginning, every response is reinforced by delivery of tokens are more effective than conditions under which delivery of reinforcement is intermittent; furthermore, it is also clear why token economies must be introduced gradually, beginning with direct pairing of the tokens with primary reinforcers and then slowly increasing the time interval between presentation of the token and the primary, or more concrete, reinforcers. This suggests that control by immediate stimuli is not irremediable.

What is needed is a behavioral prosthesis to bridge the gap from control by immediate stimuli to control by more remote stimuli. Another means of accomplishing the same goal is to use higher-magnitude stimuli as was done by King (1962), who reduced the proverbially long schizophrenic reaction time by utilizing higher-magnitude stimuli. Immediacy of irrelevant stimuli would distract schizophrenics from responding as fast as possible under normal conditions; increasing the magnitude of the stimuli one wants schizophrenic patients to pay attention to is another way to get them to respond appropriately.[2]

An interesting experiment by Brengelmann (1958) consisted of having subjects reproduce the location of five different geometric objects around a central reference point. When schizophrenics and neurotics were given two seconds to inspect the stimulus, no difference was found between the two groups; but when the inspection time was increased to 30 seconds, schizophrenics' performance was worse than that of neurotics. Again we can cite the immediacy of the irrelevant versus the relevant stimuli as critical in governing the response of the schizophrenics; when schizophrenics have no opportunity to respond to other immediate stimuli (those not related to the stimulus the experiment requires them to respond to), their performance is fine. A brief inspection time gives less time for conflicting immediate stimuli.

Memory experiments also tend to verify the immediacy interpretation of the schizophrenic deficit. Nachmani and Cohen (1969) found that schizophrenics recall less verbal material than normals, but that their recognition ability is not significantly poorer than normals'. When many interfering immediate stimuli can be present, as is true in recall tasks, schizophrenics perform worse; on the other hand, when the immediate stimuli aid memory, as is true in recognition tasks, then schizophrenics do not perform worse than normals.

Finally, let us look at a recent experiment by Steinhauer and Zubin (1982). Using evoked potentials and dilation of the pupil as indices of information processing, they found that schizophrenics undergoing an episode do not respond to conditional probability of stimuli (which requires responding to a whole set of stimuli) but do

2. Chapman and Chapman (1973) interpreted the Immediacy Hypothesis as saying that magnitude of stimuli is another way of defining immediacy. This is not so. Higher magnitude of stimuli can be used to increase the smaller control usually exerted by more remote stimuli.

respond to changes in physical stimulus. That parallels exactly the effect I found some years ago in the weight judgment task when the immediate stimulus was the physical stimulus rather than the verbal instruction.

The fact of the matter is that finding studies consonant with the Immediacy Theory is not difficult. It seemed to me, therefore, that it might be more convincing to review a series of studies not selected by me to show that immediacy will explain the results. For that reason I have gone through all the articles published in the *Journal of Abnormal Psychology* for the year 1981 that deal with schizophrenia. I will review them and apply the immediacy concept. You can judge how well it fits the data. The studies, it happens, do not include any that set out to test my theory, and so one might surmise that they are either neutral or think so little of it that they do not believe it worth testing. In either case, one might expect these studies to betray no bias in favor of my theory.

STUDIES IN THE JOURNAL OF ABNORMAL PSYCHOLOGY, 1981

The year produced eleven studies ranging over almost the entire spectrum of research in schizophrenia. Let me begin by reviewing the four studies that have in common that they all look at early environmental influences in the production of schizophrenia.

The first study I will discuss comes from a research group known for its pioneering study of high risk children (Mednick & Schulsinger 1968, 1973). The study followed up a series of children born to known schizophrenic mothers and compared them with a group of matched children born to nonschizophrenic mothers. The differences turned out to be the following: on a continuous word association test in which the subject is supposed to continue to give associations to the stimulus word presented at the outset, the high risk children tended to associate not to the remote stimulus word but to the more immediate response word that they themselves had just emitted; and the electrodermal (GSR) response to the unconditional stimulus had a shorter latency for the high risk children and showed a greater degree of generalization, more resistance to extinction, and faster recovery.

These results are consonant with the Immediacy Theory, because GSR conditioning consists of eliciting a response by means of a stimulus. In other words, here we have an immediate stimulus continuing to elicit a response even after the unconditional stimulus (US) is no longer paired with it. Extinction would be expected to take longer in this case (contrary to the operant situation, where the critical stimulus or any stimulus like it is removed entirely) because the new context still has the conditional stimulus (CS) even though the unconditional stimulus is missing; since the schizophrenic responds to the immediate stimulus, the CS, before noting the absence of the US, extinction is slow. The same holds for the generalization stimuli, which control responding because at first they are like the CS; only longer consideration would make it clear that they are different. Recovery testing is done by pairing the conditional with the unconditional stimulus after a time interval of no stimulus presentation. Under these conditions, the schizophrenic response to the immediate stimulus, the CS, would make recovery rapid.

The paper now under discussion (Walker, Hoppes, Emory, Mednick, & Schulsinger, 1981) studied the boys who showed the above patterns of response and divided them into two groups: those who later became schizophrenic and those who did not. Comparison of the two groups showed that those who became schizophrenic suffered more paternal absence during their second year of life and experienced more childhood institutionalization during the first year of life and the sixth to tenth years. The investigators interpreted the results as showing that the father's presence ameliorated the disruptive effects of a schizophrenic mother in those children who did not become schizophrenic as adults. The father affects the vulnerable child directly by being there when the mother is absent and indirectly by preventing institutionalization because there is nobody to care for the child when the mother is institutionalized. This interpretation suggests that the immediacy tendency, as measured by electrodermal responsiveness, is a vulnerability indicator. The father acts to prevent the outbreak of schizophrenia. In terms of the behavior theory interpretation that I have given to the onset of schizophrenia, this means that the father continues to reinforce the child positively. In his absence (plus the diminished number of reinforcements an immediacy-prone child receives) the child experiences what must be a devastating drop in reinforcement, thus producing schizophrenic symptomatology that presumably was kept in check until then. Thus I conclude that this study is consonant with the Immediacy Theory.

The second study in this group, by Roff and Knight (1981), followed up the case records of some 43 male children from an average age of 11 years (in child guidance clinics) to an average age of 22 (at military service hospitals). The investigators followed them up further at age 44 years, when they were either hospitalized or claiming compensation. Using a rather complicated content analysis, they concluded that family disorganization, accompanied by maternal irresponsibility and indifference, was related to children's being more asocial and adults' having a less favorable outcome. This finding is not at variance with the preceding study, showing as it does the importance of the kind of reinforcement parents give to children. To the extent that the children studied in this paper were suffering from immediacy, we would expect the further reduction in reinforcement owing to such factors as mother neglect to be impinging on people who are particularly vulnerable because they initially have a relatively small number of reinforcements available.

The third study in this group examined family interaction in a more detailed way. Lewis, Rodnick, and Goldstein (1981) related communication deviance—a measure developed by Singer and Wynne (1965) and obtained from TAT (Thematic Apperception Test protocols of parents—to communication deviance in actual family interaction. Since previous studies (Jones, 1977) had shown that communication deviance in parents predicted the onset of schizophrenia-spectrum disorders, this group of investigators wanted to determine whether such individual communication deviance can also be found in actual family interaction. In general, high communication-deviant parents wandered from appropriate focus on the topic assigned for discussion as well as from the expression of feelings. With sons they focused on the topic too rigidly, and with daughters they frequently disregarded the assigned topic.

How does this relate to Immediacy Theory? In both cases the ultimate result is a reduction of positive reinforcement. In the case of rigid adherence, there must be many times when the parents withhold reinforcement because the adolescent is not staying strictly within the outlined topic. With the female adolescent, the problem is that no reinforcement can be obtained for the girl because the discussion does not stay with the point; furthermore, the girl fails to acquire the discussion skills appreciated by others that would ultimately result in positive reinforcement. To the extent that these children start out with the handicap of being able to respond only or primarily to immediate reinforcers, this further reduction in reinforcement would be expected to result in the kinds of stress that might precipitate full-blown schizophrenic symptoms (Zubin and Spring, 1977).

The fourth study in this series, by Zigler and Levine (1981), was based on the idea that the lower a person's developmental level (as measured by premorbid social competence in terms of education and marital status), the greater the probability that the person will become psychologically disordered, the earlier it will happen, and the poorer the prognosis. The results showed that paranoids had more social competence than nonparanoids, women more than men, and veterans hospital males more than state hospital males. Women in general were hospitalized later than men, which the authors explained not in terms of women's having less responsibility, since women who worked also were hospitalized later, but rather in terms of men's having responsibility earlier than women in our culture. The implications of this study are that all theories must pay attention to population differences between men and women, veterans hospital and state hospital patients, and to their variations in premorbid competence.

Immediacy tendencies must interact with premorbid competence and may in part also reflect degrees of competence. It is unlikely that somebody who is largely controlled by immediate stimuli (and we must assume some variation in degree of immediate stimulus control from person to person) would be able to achieve any significant level of social competence. On the other hand, those who have achieved such competence because of the large amount of social reinforcement and other kinds of positive reinforcement available in their particular environments, even though their behavior is primarily controlled by immediate stimuli, would become disordered in an obvious way when they are placed in a less supportive environment. This study, therefore, cannot directly validate the immediacy theory. What it does do is point out an area of study. It would be interesting to measure the amount of control by immediate stimuli during the premorbid time—perhaps in high risk children—to determine the empirical relation between amount of immediate stimulus control and their social and intellectual skills, for example, and later their likelihood of becoming symptomatic.

The remaining studies published in 1981 were more experimental. I will begin with experiments dealing with verbal material, then review psychomotor experiments, and conclude with psychophysical experiments. Kagan and Oltmanns (1981) used Cohen's (1976, 1978) referent communication task to compare schizophrenics, affectively disordered patients, and normals. The task consists of the following: The subject is given two words, one of which is underlined. That word is the referent. The subject is instructed to help another person, who has the same two words but without underlining, to guess which word is the referent by providing as a clue one of two associated words supplied for that purpose. For example, the subject may be given the words "drill" and "march," with the word "drill" underlined. The two clues are "dentist" and "parade." Although both clues are related to the referent word "drill," only the word "dentist" would allow the listener to tell that the referent is "drill." Cohen demonstrated that schizophrenics are adequate as listeners—that is, they are able to make use of the clue—but they are deficient in providing the clues.

This paper confirmed Cohen's finding. It is clearly consonant with the immediacy interpretation because when the schizophrenics receive a clue it is the immediate stimulus that is helpful to them; when the schizophrenic patient is the sender of information, however, he or she is confronted by two immediate stimuli for choosing the clue, and thus the performance deteriorates in the way that Cohen found earlier and Kagan and Oltmanns now found. The only fly in this ointment is that the schizophrenics did not differ significantly from the affective disorder patients, though it must be added that the affective disorder patients did not differ significantly from the normals either. They were midway between the schizophrenics and the normals. It seems to me that this finding is best interpreted by pointing out that the kinds of difficulty found in schizophrenics can well be found in others, although for different reasons, such as paying less attention when one is under stress than when one is relaxed. That affective disorder patients differed from neither the normals nor the schizophrenics gives credence to that kind of explanation. As to the immediacy interpretation, I would say that this experiment verifies it.

Pishkin and Bourne (1981) compared schizophrenic patients and normals on conceptual tasks requiring two kinds of processing. In one instance the subjects had to arrive at the attribute(s) that made a card sort correct in one pile or another. The cards bore geometric figures that varied in shape, color, size, and number of objects. Correct sorting was based on one attribute only (e.g., the color red) or on two attributes—in one case the presence of both attributes, in another, either one or both (e.g., red squares or red shapes, or squares of any color). In one condition subjects had to identify the attribute(s); in the other condition they had to extract the rules. Furthermore, in different conditions the subjects were able to see varying numbers of previous cards already sorted. The results showed that schizophrenics had no trouble sorting on the basis of one attribute only, but as the relation between attributes came into play they made more errors than normals. Furthermore, they were particularly ineffective when they themselves had to extract the rules for sorting the cards. Finally, they profited from seeing one previous instance of a card sort, but their performance deteriorated when they had to look at more than one example. All of this seems entirely consonant with the immediacy of the stimuli. In sorting based on one attribute only, the physical stimulus acting as the discriminative stimulus is right there and would enhance their performance; as the number of stimuli to be taken into account at the same time increases, however, having more than one stimulus either sets up a conflict about which one to respond to or makes one stimulus shut out the other(s) because it is more immediate. Finally, extraction of the rules requires responding to several immediate stimuli at the same time and in succession, a process that is very difficult if previous instances cannot continue to be part of the controlling stimuli. In essence, then, this experiment's results are in agreement with the immediacy interpretation.

A study by Harvey, Winters, Weintraub, and Neale (1981) constitutes the most direct evidence so far for the immediacy interpretation. Using the children of schizophrenics, unipolars, bipolars, and normals, these researchers compared performance on a digit-span task. The child had to listen without distraction to a female voice saying a series of six digits, then listen to a female voice saying five digits while a male voice said four irrelevant digits. There were no significant differences between the groups in the nondistraction condition; but in the distraction condition the children of unipolars and schizophrenics did worse than the children of normals, a finding not unlike that of the preceding study. However, this particular technique allowed for a more exact test of the implications of the immediacy interpretation. By analyzing the recall of the material in terms of the serial position of items, it became clear that only the schizophrenics' children did significantly worse than all the other groups on the first few items of the list of digits. Also of interest is that the finding for the children of schizophrenics confirms the finding for adult schizophrenics compared with normals and other

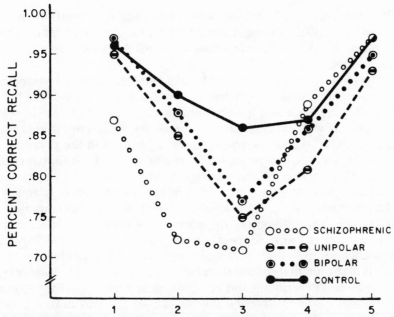

FIGURE 7. Serial position curves by group for items presented during distraction. From Harvey, Winters, Weintraub, & Neale (1981). Copyright 1981 by the American Psychological Association. Reprinted by permission of the authors.

psychiatric groups (Oltmanns, 1978). The authors suggest a deficit in controlled information processing as an explanation for their finding. A much more specific interpretation, however, is that the behavior of schizophrenics and their offspring is primarily controlled by immediate stimuli. Figure 7 shows that under the distraction condition not only is recall worst for the offspring of schizophrenics, but as the digit considered comes closer to the time of recall, schizophrenics' offspring abruptly rise to points higher than all the other groups. This study makes it clear that when more than one psychiatric group shows a deficit it does not imply that further detailed search would fail to produce a deficit specific to schizophrenia. Although these investigators did not use the immediacy hypothesis as a guide for this search, they might as well have. Finally, the reason this effect did not occur during the nondistraction condition is that in that condition the relatively small number of digits leaves most of the stimuli in the immediate stimulus condition. That the law of primacy still works must be attributed to the distinctiveness of the first item in any list of items to be recalled. A special discriminative stimulus always makes such an item easier to recall.

The next study, by Broga and Neufeld (1981), examined paranoid and nonparanoid schizophrenic patients and nonpatients on a battery of tests, including memory and stimulus coding tasks. Multivariate analysis extracted two dimensions to describe the three populations: (a) processing efficiency, which found the paranoids least efficient, the nonparanoids more efficient, and the nonpatients most efficient; and (b) response style, which found the paranoids with the greatest propensity to respond in the absence of adequate stimulus processing, the nonpatients next, and the nonparanoids with least. The differences in processing efficiency (even though this is a rather vague concept) can be related to the immediacy of stimulus control. Both schizophrenic groups are limited by the kinds of stimuli that control their behavior and would necessarily be less efficient in recalling and recognizing stimuli. As to the second dimension used to describe the patient groups and normals, we probably are finding different secondary reactions to their difficulties because of the tendency to respond to immediate stimuli. The difference may also lie in the tendency to respond to external immediate stimuli (in paranoids) and to private stimuli—that is, the response-produced immediate stimuli in nonparanoids that make them hesitate to respond because the response-produced stimuli send them off on tangents evoked by their responding primarily to close-by response-produced stimuli. But this is, of course, all speculation and should be verified by focused experiments.

The specific tasks used by Broga and Neufeld (1981) must be taken up in turn. Let us look first at the so-called selective attention and iconic memory decay procedure. The subject must report the presence of a particular letter in an array of eight. The array is exposed for 100 msec. The subject is told which letter to report by a bar marker placed in the position where the letter is. The bar marker appears at various times: 100 msec before the array is shown, at the same time, and 100, 200, 300, and 600 msec after the array is shown. The schizophrenic groups reported the correct letter significantly less often 100 msec before and 100 msec after seeing the array only. When the array and the bar marker were presented at the same time, the groups did not differ, since in this condition paying attention to immediate stimuli is helpful to schizophrenics. At the two time periods for which the schizophrenics showed a significantly worse performance than the normals, the normals were performing at considerably better than chance, and so one can see the deleterious effect on schizophrenics of a discrepancy in time between the marker and the array. At 200 + msec delays, however, schizophrenics and normals are both performing very close to chance. Here we find that even a 100 msec departure from immediacy causes deterioration in performance.

In the second task, based on letter matching, subjects had to indicate as fast as possible whether the two letters being shown had the same name. Schizophrenics had slower reaction times — certainly not surprising in view of the tremendous literature on reaction time. In responding as fast as possible, a tendency to respond to immediate stimuli can well interfere when subjects must attend to particular stimuli, for others may well catch their attention. In addition, since subjects must respond "the same" for stimuli physically different (upper and lower case letters), one would expect the immediate difference to slow down reaction time.

The next technique consisted of the short-term memory digit span from the Wechsler Adult Intelligence Scale. No significant difference was found, which agrees with the nondistraction condition of the Harvey et al. (1981) study reviewed above; in fact, it replicates the finding, since three to nine digits is the total number used for that test.

Another technique employed was the short-term memory and interference task. Consonant trigrams are exposed for 2 sec, and the subject is required to recall them after varying periods of time (3, 9, or 18 sec). The subject is prevented from rehearsing the trigram by having to subtract the number three cumulatively. The two schizophrenic groups forgot faster than the normals (clearly what the Immediacy Hypothesis would predict). Both groups had a larger proportion of omission errors than the normals, though the nonparanoids had a greater proportion than the paranoids. On the other hand, the percentage of intrusion errors was smaller for the nonparanoids than for either the normals or the paranoids, reinforcing the idea expressed above that the paranoids tended to respond without knowing what to say, whereas the nonparanoids tended to avoid responding if they were less than sure.

The short-term memory rehearsal process was essentially a choice reaction time task: subjects had to press a key as fast as possible to indicate whether they had seen that number before. Again the results were essentially the classic reaction time findings, with schizophrenics doing materially worse. The relation to the immediacy of stimuli has already been mentioned.

In the short-term memory rehearsal process, subjects were asked to say aloud the words they were thinking of as they looked at a list of new words to be recalled. Biserial correlations were computed between the number of times a given item was rehearsed and ability to recall that item, based on the first 16 of 20 items on the list. The correlations were higher for the normals than for the schizophrenics, suggesting that the mere rehearsal was less important for the schizophrenics than for the normals. Immediacy Theory would predict that the items rehearsed immediately before recall would be remembered best, but no relevant data were presented; nevertheless, since the last time the subject rehearsed the words would be more important than how many times they were rehearsed, one would expect the correlations to be less for the schizophrenics than for the normals, and that of course was the finding.

The final task in the battery tested long-term memory. Lists were presented either in random order or arranged in groups of related words; in both cases recall was significantly better for normals than for schizophrenics. In addition, clustering was greater for normals than for schizophrenics, a result that would be expected from the immediacy of stimulus control that takes place through propinquity in time rather than through closeness of meaning (cf. the Peastrel 1964 study cited above). All in all, the entire battery seems consonant with the effect of immediate stimuli on the behavior of schizophrenics.

The next study was done by Greiffenstein, Milberg, Lewis, and Rosenbaum (1981). A group of schizophrenic patients was compared with a group of normals and a group of neurological patients suffering from temporal-lobe epilepsy. The idea was to look for a common behavioral deficit in the two patient groups, since schizophrenia is supposed to involve the left temporal lobe. The technique used to compare them was simple reaction time with two schedules of preparatory intervals. In the case of regular preparatory intervals (time between the warning signal and the imperative stimulus) the intervals remained the same for ten trials, then shifted to the next preparatory interval for ten trials, and so on until all the intervals had been done; the irregular interval schedule consisted of 10 runs of six different preparatory intervals randomly distributed. Both the schizophrenics and the temporal-lobe epilepsy (TLE) patients failed to benefit from the regular preparatory interval presentation. For the normals, reaction time for the regular preparatory intervals was consistently shorter than for the irregular pattern of preparatory intervals. Clearly the normal person, unlike the schizophrenic and the TLE patient, is conditioned to respond within a certain time interval. The other groups showed the conditioning effect only for the short intervals; as the preparatory interval increases it becomes so long that control by immediate stimuli no longer helps the patient. That the behavior of TLE patients is similar to that of schizophrenics suggests that temporal lobe involvement may also be critical in the latter.

Manschreck, Maher, Rucklos, Vereen, and Ader (1981) had normals, schizophrenic patients, and affective disorder patients hit a telegraph key in time to various click rates. At slow click rates the accuracy of following did not vary among groups. At 80 beats per minute the difference among groups was greatest and also correlated with clinically rated thought disorder ($r = -.50$) and to type token ratio assessment of language disorganization. Although those with affective disorders did not show as much synchronization inaccuracy as the schizophrenics, they also seemed to suffer from it. As the rate of stimulation increased, all groups increased in accuracy in following the beat; when the beat was too slow, immediacy interfered. The authors explained the difficulty in terms of the patients' inability to take advantage of the redundancy of the information, which they said was similar to redundancy in language. Maybe so, but it seems more like a metaphor than a similarity.

The final experiment published in 1981 was performed by Saccuzzo and Schubert (1981), using three samples of adolescents. The first consisted of schizophrenics, the second of schizotypal personalities, and the third of nonschizophrenic spectrum controls (borderline personality disorder). Backward-masking procedures were used with a letter-detection task. The controls had the largest number of correct detections, the schizotypals the next largest, and the schizophrenic subjects the smallest. In all three cases an increase in the interval between the target stimulus and the masking stimulus caused an increase in number of correct detections. The authors interpret the results as showing that schizophrenics and those with schizophrenic spectrum disorders process information more slowly than others. If we assume that the immediate stimulus controls subjects' responses when the interval between stimuli is too short, then the second stimulus is the only one controlling their attention; as the interval between the target stimulus and the masking stimulus increases, subjects are able to make separate responses to each. Given enough time between target and mask, schizophrenics must be able to reach the same level of correct detection as controls. This experiment then seems to corroborate the immediacy control.

CONCLUSION

Either the experiments described above agree with the immediacy control of schizophrenic behavior, or else their results are not relevant to the theory.

As all scientists know, every good theory raises a number of further research questions. I will therefore conclude by listing some of the questions I would very much like to see investigated so as to shed further light on Immediacy Theory.

The first need is of course to determine more precisely the size of the time interval we should consider "immediate."

The second need is to determine the range of control by immediate stimuli. Are all behaviors potentially controllable in this manner in a schizophrenic? How variable is this kind of control over the life of the patient and also over shorter periods of time? It seems that patients do not always act aberrantly. If that is so, is there any lawfulness to the times when immediacy control reigns? That is, are there some times when that control is greater and others when it is less?

The third question to be raised concerning the Immediacy Theory is how much one can modify control by immediate stimuli. Can one transfer control to more remote stimuli by increasing the magnitude of those remote stimuli? Can one make the responses to remote stimuli more likely by preventing responses to immediate stimuli? Can one change the greater likelihood of responding to immediate stimuli by shaping ever closer approximations to responding to remote stimuli? Can one make use of behavioral prosthetic devices to get schizophrenics to respond to remote stimuli, such as tape recorders that would allow them to restore remote stimuli by replaying the tape?

The fourth question is a critical one about the theory of immediacy; it asks that we test directly whether a reduction in control by immediate stimuli will be accompanied by a reduction in such typical schizophrenic symptoms as delusions, hallucinations, and thought disorder.

The fifth question relates to the determination of which particular techniques or tests might be best for detecting and measuring control by immediate stimuli. The review of the *Journal of Abnormal Psychology* articles certainly has made it clear that some techniques are better than others for shedding light on degree of stimulus control.

In sum, there are a great many interesting questions one can ask about Immediacy Theory. I hope that many will join in trying to obtain answers.

REFERENCES

American Psychiatric Association. *Diagnostic and statistical manual of mental disorders* (3rd ed.). Washington, D.C.: American Psychiatric Association, 1980.

Boardman, W. K., Goldstone, S., Reiner, M. L., Fathauer, W. F. Anchor effects, spatial judgments, and schizophrenia. *Journal of Abnormal and Social Psychology*, 1962, **65**, 273–276.

Boardman, W. K., Goldstone, S., Reiner, M. L., & Himmel, S. Constancy of absolute judgments of size by normals and schizophrenics. *Journal of Abnormal and Social Psychology*, 1964, **68**, 346–349.

Braginsky, B. M., Braginsky, D. D., & Ring, K. *Methods of madness*. New York: Holt, Rinehart and Winston, 1969.

Braginsky, B. M., Grosse, M., & Ring, K. Controlling outcomes through impression-management. *Journal of Consulting Psychology*, 1966, **30**, 295–300.

Brengelmann, J. C. The effects of exposure time in immediate recall on abnormal and questionnaire criteria of personality. *Journal of Mental Science*, 1958, **104**, 665–680.

Broga, M. I., & Neufeld, W. J. Multivariate cognitive performance levels and response styles among paranoid and nonparanoid schizophrenics. *Journal of Abnormal Psychology*, 1981, **90**, 495–509.

Chapman, L. J. Distractibility in the conceptual performance of schizophrenics. *Journal of Abnormal and Social Psychology*, 1956, **53**, 286–291.

Chapman, L. J., & Chapman, J. P. *Disordered thought in schizophrenia*. New York: Appleton-Century-Crofts, 1973.

Chapman, L. J., Chapman, J. P., & Miller, G. A. A theory of verbal behavior in schizophrenia. In B. A. Maher (Ed.), *Progress in experimental personality research* (Vol. 1). New York: Academic Press, 1964.

Cohen, B. D. Referent communication in schizophrenia: The perseverative-chaining model. In K. Salzinger (Ed.), *Psychology in progress. Annals of the New York Academy of Sciences*, 1976, **270**, 124–140.

Cohen, B. D. Referent communication disturbances in schizophrenia. In S. Schwartz (Ed.), *Language and cognition in schizophrenia*. Hillsdale, N.J.: Lawrence Erlbaum Associates, 1978.

Day, R. Life events and schizophrenia: The "triggering" hypothesis. *Acta Psychiatrica Scandinavia*, 1981, **64**, 97–122.

Dinoff, M., Horner, R. F., Kurpiewski, B. S., & Timmons, E. D. Conditioning verbal behavior of schizophrenics in a group therapy-like situation. *Journal of Clinical Psychology*, 1960, **16**, 367–370.

Dohrenwend, B. P., & Dohrenwend, B. S. *Social status and psychological disorder: A causal inquiry*. New York: John Wiley, 1969.

Dohrenwend, B. P., & Egri, G. Recent stressful life events and episodes of schizophrenia. *Schizophrenia Bulletin*, 1981, **7**, 12–23.

Dohrenwend, B. S., & Dohrenwend, B. P. (Eds.). *Stressful life events*. New York: John Wiley, 1974.

Dohrenwend, B. S., & Dohrenwend, B. P. Life stress and illness: Formulation of the issues. In B. S. Dohrenwend & B. P. Dohrenwend (Eds.), *Stressful life events and their contexts*. New York: Neale Watson Academic Publications, 1982.

Eisenberger, R. Is there a deprivation-satiation function for social approval? *Psychological Bulletin*, 1970, **74**, 255–275.

Gaviria, B. Autonomic reaction magnitude and habituation to different voices. *Psychosomatic Medicine*, 1967, **29**, 598–605.

Goldstein, K. Methodological approach to the study of schizophrenic thought disorder. In J. S. Kasanin (Ed.), *Language and thought in schizophrenia*. Berkeley: University of California Press, 1944.

Gould, L. N. Verbal hallucinations and activity of vocal musculature: An electromyographic study. *American Journal of Psychiatry*, 1948, **105**, 367–372.

Gould, L. N. Auditory hallucinations and subvocal speech: Objective study in a case of schizophrenia. *Journal of Nervous and Mental Disease*, 1949, **109**, 418–427.

Gould, L. N. Verbal hallucinations as automatic speech: The reactivation of dormant speech habit. *American Journal of Psychiatry*, 1950, **107**, 110–119.

Greiffenstein, M., Milberg, W., Lewis, R., & Rosenbaum, G. Temporal lobe epilepsy and schizophrenia: Comparison of reaction time deficits. *Journal of Abnormal Psychology*, 1981, **90**, 105–112.

Hammer, M., Polgar, S., & Salzinger, K. Speech predictability and social contact patterns in an informal group. *Human Organization*, 1969, **28**, 235–242.

Hammer, M., & Salzinger, K. Some formal characteristics of schizophrenic speech as a measure of social deviance. *Annals of the New York Academy of Sciences*, 1964, **105**, 861–889.

Harvey, P., Winters, K., Weintraub, S., & Neale, J. M. Distractibility in children vulnerable to psychopathology. *Journal of Abnormal Psychology,* 1981, **90,** 298–304.

Jones, J. Patterns of transactional style deviance in the TAT's of parents of schizophrenics. *Family Process,* 1977, **16,** 327–337.

Kagan, D. L., & Oltmanns, T. F. Matched tasks for measuring single-word, referent communication: The performance of patients with schizophrenic and affective disorders. *Journal of Abnormal Psychology,* 1981, **90,** 204–212.

King, H. E. Reaction-time as a function of stimulus intensity among normal and psychotic subjects. *Journal of Psychology,* 1962, **54,** 299–307.

Lewis, J. M., Rodnick, E. H., & Goldstein, M. J. Intrafamilial interactive behavior, parental communication deviance, and risk for schizophrenia. *Journal of Abnormal Psychology,* 1981, **90,** 448–457.

Liem, R., & Liem, J. H. Relations among social class, life events, and mental illness: A comment on findings and methods. In B. S. Dohrenwend & B. P. Dohrenwend (Eds.), *Stressful life events and their contexts.* New York: Neale Watson Academic Publications, 1982.

Mahl, G. F. Disturbances and silences in the patient's speech in psychotherapy. *Journal of Abnormal and Social Psychology,* 1956, **53,** 1–15.

Manschreck, T. C., Maher, B. A., Rucklos, M. E., Vereen, D. R., Jr., & Ader, D. N. Deficient motor synchrony in schizophrenia. *Journal of Abnormal Psychology,* 1981, **90,** 321–328.

McGhie, A. *Pathology of attention.* Baltimore: Penguin Books, 1969.

McGhie, A., & Chapman, J. Disorders of attention and perception in early schizophrenia. *British Journal of Medical Psychology,* 1961, **34,** 103–116.

McGuigan, F. J. Covert oral behavior and auditory hallucinations. *Psychophysiology,* 1966, **3,** 421–428.

Mednick, S. A., & Schulsinger, F. A. Some premorbid characteristics related to breakdown in children with schizophrenic mothers. In D. Rosenthal & S. S. Kety (Eds.), *The transmission of schizophrenia.* New York: Pergamon Press, 1968.

Mednick, S. A., & Schulsinger, F. A. Learning theory of schizophrenia: Thirteen years later. In M. Hammer, K. Salzinger, & S. Sutton (Eds.), *Psychopathology.* New York: John Wiley, 1973.

Mintz, S., & Alpert, M. Imagery vividness, reality testing, and schizophrenic hallucinations. *Journal of Abnormal Psychology,* 1972, **79,** 310–316.

Murray, E. J., & Cohen, M. Mental illness, milieu therapy, and social organization in ward groups. *Journal of Abnormal and Social Psychology,* 1959, **58,** 48–54.

Nachmani, G., & Cohen, B. D. Recall and recognition free learning in schizophrenics. *Journal of Abnormal Psychology,* 1969, **74,** 511–516.

Oltmanns, T. F. Selective attention in schizophrenic and manic psychosis: The effect of distraction on information processing. *Journal of Abnormal Psychology,* 1978, **87,** 212–225.

Peastrel, A. L. Studies in efficiency: Semantic generalization in schizophrenia. *Journal of Abnormal and Social Psychology*, 1964, **69**, 444–449.

Pishkin, V., & Bourne, L. E., Jr. Abstraction and the use of available information by schizophrenic and normal individuals. *Journal of Abnormal Psychology*, 1981, **90**, 197–203.

Rado, S. Dynamics and classification of disordered behavior. *American Journal of Psychiatry*, 1953, **110**, 406–416.

Rausch, H. L. Perceptual constancy in schizophrenia. I. Size constancy. *Journal of Personality*, 1952, **21**, 176–187.

Roff, J. D., & Knight, R. Family characteristics, childhood symptoms, and adult outcome in schizophrenia. *Journal of Abnormal Psychology*, 1981, **90**, 510–520.

Rosenbaum, G., Flenning, F., & Rosen, H. Effects of weight intensity on discrimination thresholds of normals and schizophrenics. *Journal of Abnormal Psychology*, 1965, **70**, 446–450.

Rutter, D. R., Wishner, J., Kopytynska, H., & Button, M. The predictability of speech in schizophrenic patients. *British Journal of Psychiatry*, 1978, **132**, 228–232.

Saccuzzo, D. P., & Schubert, D. L. Backward masking as a measure of slow processing in schizophrenia spectrum disorders. *Journal of Abnormal Psychology*, 1981, **90**, 305–312.

Salzinger, K. Shift in judgment of weights as a function of anchoring stimuli and instructions in early schizophrenics and normals. *Journal of Abnormal and Social Psychology*, 1957, **55**, 43–49.

Salzinger, K. An hypothesis about schizophrenic behavior. *American Journal of Psychotherapy*, 1971, **25**, 601–614. (a)

Salzinger, K. The immediacy hypothesis of schizophrenia. In H. Yaker, H. Osmond, F. Cheek (Eds.), *The future of time*. Garden City, N.Y.: Doubleday, 1971. (b)

Salzinger, K. Schizophrenia and the immediacy hypothesis. *American Journal of Psychotherapy*, 1972, **26**, 567–570.

Salzinger, K. *Schizophrenia: Behavioral aspects*. New York: John Wiley, 1973. (a)

Salzinger, K. Inside the black box, with apologies to Pandora: A review of Ulric Neisser's *Cognitive Psychology*. *Journal of the Experimental Analysis of Behavior*, 1973, **19**, 369–378. (b)

Salzinger, K. A behavioral analysis of diagnosis. In R. L. Spitzer & D. F. Klein (Eds.), *Critical issues in psychiatric diagnosis*. New York: Raven Press, 1978.

Salzinger, K. The behavioral mechanism to explain abnormal behavior. *Annals of the New York Academy of Sciences*, 1980, **340**, 66–87.

Salzinger, K., Hammer, M., Portnoy, S., & Polgar, S. K. Verbal behavior and social distance. *Language and Speech*, 1970, **13**, 25–37.

Salzinger, K., & Pisoni, S. Reinforcement of affect responses of schizophrenics during the clinical interview. *Journal of Abnormal and Social Psychology*, 1958, **57**, 84–90.

Salzinger, K., & Pisoni, S. Reinforcement of verbal affect responses of normal subjects during the interview. *Journal of Abnormal and Social Psychology*, 1960, **60**, 127–130.

Salzinger, K., & Pisoni, S. Some parameters of the conditioning of verbal affect responses in schizophrenic subjects. *Journal of Abnormal and Social Psychology*, 1961, **63**, 511–516.

Salzinger, K., & Portnoy, S. Verbal conditioning in interviews: Application to chronic schizophrenics and relationship to prognosis for acute schizophrenics. *Journal of Psychiatric Research*, 1964, **2**, 1–9.

Salzinger, K., Portnoy, S., & Feldman, R. S. Experimental manipulation of continuous speech in schizophrenic patients. *Journal of Abnormal and Social Psychology*, 1964, **68**, 508–516. (a)

Salzinger, K., Portnoy, S., & Feldman, R. S. Verbal behavior of schizophrenic and normal subjects. *Annals of the New York Academy of Sciences*, 1964, **105**, 845–860. (b)

Salzinger, K., Portnoy, S., & Feldman, R. S. Verbal behavior in schizophrenics and some comments toward a theory of schizophrenia. In P. Hoch & J. Zubin (Eds.), *Psychopathology of schizophrenia*. New York: Grune and Stratton, 1966.

Salzinger, K., Portnoy, S., & Feldman, R. S. Intrusions in schizophrenic speech: The immediacy hypothesis vs. the lapse-of-attention hypothesis. *Comprehensive Psychiatry*, 1977, **18**, 255–261.

Salzinger, K., Portnoy, S., & Feldman, R. S. Communicability deficit in schizophrenics resulting from a more general deficit. In S. Schwartz (Ed.), *Language and cognition in schizophrenia*. Hillsdale, N.J.: Lawrence Erlbaum Associates, 1978.

Salzinger, K., Portnoy, S., & Feldman, R. S. Letter to the editor. *British Journal of Psychiatry*, 1979, **135**, 286–287.

Salzinger, K., Portnoy, S., Feldman, R. S., & Patenaude-Lane, J. From method to madness. In R. W. Rieber (Ed.), *Applied psycholinguistics and mental health*. New York: Plenum, 1980.

Salzinger, K., Portnoy, S., Pisoni, D., & Feldman, R. S. The immediacy hypothesis and response-produced stimuli in schizophrenic speech. *Journal of Abnormal Psychology*, 1970, **76**, 258–264.

Salzinger, K., & Salzinger, S. Behavior theory for the study of psychopathology. In M. Hammer, K. Salzinger, & S. Sutton (Eds.), *Psychopathology: Contributions from the social, behavioral, and biological sciences*. New York: John Wiley, 1973.

Singer, M., & Wynne, L. Thought disorder and family relations of schizophrenics. III. Methodology using projective techniques. *Archives of General Psychiatry*, 1965, **12**, 187–200.

282

Skinner, B. F. Are theories of learning necessary? *Psychological Review*, 1950, **57**, 193–216.

Steinhauer, S., & Zubin, J. Vulnerability to schizophrenia: Information processing in the pupil and event-related potential. In I. Hanin & E. Usdin (Eds.), *Biological markers in psychiatry and neurology*. Oxford: Pergamon Press, 1982.

Sutton, S. Fact and artifact in the psychology of schizophrenia. In M. Hammer, K. Salzinger, & S. Sutton (Eds.), *Psychopathology: Contributions from the social, behavioral, and biological sciences*. New York: John Wiley, 1973.

Taylor, W. L. Cloze procedure: A new tool for measuring readability. *Journalism Quarterly*, 1953, **30**, 415–433.

Walker, E., Hoppes, E., Emory, E., Mednick, S., & Schulsinger, F. Environmental factors related to schizophrenia in psychophysiologically labile high-risk males. *Journal of Abnormal Psychology*, 1981, **90**, 313–320.

Weckowicz, T. E. Shape constancy in schizophrenic patients. *Journal of Abnormal and Social Psychology*, 1964, **68**, 177–183.

Wurster, S. A. Effects of anchoring on weight judgments of normals and schizophrenics. *Journal of Personality and Social Psychology*, 1965, **1**, 274–278.

Zarlock, S. P. Social expectations, language, and schizophrenia. *Journal of Humanistic Psychology*, 1966, **6**, 68–74.

Zigler, E., & Levine, J. Age on first hospitalization of schizophrenics: A developmental approach. *Journal of Abnormal Psychology*, 1981, **90**, 458–467.

Zubin, J., & Spring, B. Vulnerability—A new view of schizophrenia. *Journal of Abnormal Psychology*, 1977, **86**, 103–126.

Cognitive Factors in the Social Skills of Schizophrenic Patients: Implications for Treatment

Charles J. Wallace and
Steven E. Boone

University of California at Los Angeles

*T*his chapter describes changes that have been made in a program of clinical research focused on designing and evaluating techniques for improving the social skills of chronic schizophrenics. These changes reflect a shift in the definition of "social skills" from one that initially emphasized observable motor behavior to one that includes not only motor behavior but also cognitive elements, conceptualized as components of a problem-solving process that is assumed to be an essential ingredient in producing a socially skilled response. This broadened definition suggests that a bridge might be built between some of the foci of experimental psychopathologists, such as dysfunctions in information processing, attention, and perception in schizophrenia, and the concerns of clinicians, such as improving the community and interpersonal functioning of their schizophrenic patients.

To illustrate these changes, we will review four studies. In the first study, conversation was increased using relatively traditional operant conditioning techniques. In the second study, basic interpersonal behaviors such as eye contact and voice volume were improved using an assertion-training format. In the third study, problem-solving skills such as generating and evaluating alternative responses were improved using a modified assertion-training format. In the fourth study, both community-living skills and problem-solving skills were taught by "modular" training techniques.

STUDY 1

Wallace and Davis (1974) compared the effectiveness of two interventions designed to increase the rate of conversation within dyads of chronic schizophrenic patients. The two interventions were providing information about possible topics of conversation and providing positive reinforcement in the form of tokens for conversing with one another. The study, conducted on the Clinical Research Unit at Camarillo (California) State Hospital, was prompted by the clinical concern that patients on the unit rarely talked to one another. Most of their free time, which was a considerable proportion of their day, seemed to be spent either looking at television or sleeping in the dayroom. It was felt that patients' quality of life both in and out of the hospital might be improved if they would converse and make friends with one another.

A number of studies that have systematically observed the activities of schizophrenic inpatients have verified these clinical observations. For example, Schooler and Spohn (1960) and Hunter, Schooler, and Spohn (1962) used the Location Activity Inventory to observe the behavior of a total of 150 chronic schizophrenic inpatients living on several treatment wards. During several weeks of observation only 2.7% of the observations were characterized by social activity, and the median number of observations of social activity per patient was zero. Recent data collected by Paul and Lentz (1978) indicated an almost identical rate of social interaction for the 56 chronic schizophrenic female patients they observed. Before implementation of an active treatment program, patients interacted at an average rate of 4% of observed opportunities, with a range per patient of 0 to 30%.

The objective of the Wallace and Davis (1974) study was to determine whether patients would begin conversing if they were given information about possible topics of conversation. The hypothesis was that patients did not have a sufficient "storehouse" of information to enable them to begin and sustain conversation. From a treatment perspective, immersing patients in an enriched social environment might provide enough information to lead to the desired increase in their interactions. If, on the other hand, more explicit reinforcement procedures were necessary to "prime the conversational pump," then a structured training program would be necessary to increase social interaction.

Single-subject research designs were used to compare the effects of the interventions with two dyads of chronic schizophrenic patients. Conversation was measured during daily sessions conducted in a small room on the unit. Three topics were included in each session: automobiles, sports, and movies. Conversation was measured by two observers who sat behind a one-way mirror, with the members of a dyad seated in front of the mirror at about a 45 degree angle to one another, approximately 3 feet apart. Each topic was introduced by one of the observers, who simply asked the two patients to converse about the topic. As the conversation proceeded, each observer pressed switches on a console whenever his assigned member of the dyad made eye contact with the other member of the dyad or spoke on the specified topic. The switches were connected to electromechanical programming equipment that recorded the number of seconds of eye contact, talk on the specified topic, and "conversation." To avoid reinforcing extended monologues directed to no one in particular, "conversation" was defined as talk on the specified topic with at least 1 second of eye contact for every 15 seconds of session time.

For three of the four patients who participated in the experiment, reinforcement consisted of tokens that could be exchanged for various items specially purchased to match each patient's preferences. The members of dyad 1 were given one token for every 10 seconds of conversation. One of the members of dyad 2 was given one token for every 2 seconds of conversation. For the second member of dyad 2, reinforcement consisted of the avoidance of extended interaction. If the patient did not converse long enough, he was required to repeat the interaction until his conversation met or exceeded the required duration.

To gain information about the three topics patients were required to read selected brief articles from that day's newspaper. To ensure that they comprehended the material, they were given a three-question multiple choice examination about each article and asked to reread the material until they answered all questions correctly.

The members of dyad 1, Brian and Mitch, had both been diagnosed as schizophrenic according to DSM-II criteria. They were in their early twenties and had been receiving primarily outpatient mental health services since their early teens. Neither was acutely ill when he participated in the experiment. The results of the single-subject, withdrawal design used with this dyad, presented in Figure 1, clearly indicate that the reinforcement contingency increased both patients' conversation. In contrast, information presented alone or in combination with the reinforcement contingency did not increase either patient's conversation.

The members of dyad 2, Nel and Jed, had both been diagnosed as schizophrenic according to DSM-II criteria. Nel had been continuously hospitalized for 23 years and was symptomatic when she participated in the experiment. Behaviors indicative of auditory hallucinations (e.g., looking away as if attending to verbal stimuli; speaking out loud with no observable stimulus) occurred primarily during periods of inactivity and were not apparent during her conversations with Jed. The same procedures were used with Nel as with Brian and Mitch except that Nel received one token for every 2 seconds of conversation. Jed was in his early twenties and had been continuously hospitalized for more than five years. The procedure used with Jed was the discriminated avoidance contingency, since he eschewed any potential reinforcers and his sole activity consisted of sitting in isolated locations on the unit.

The withdrawal design used with Nel and the combined changing criterion and withdrawal design used with Jed are presented in Figure 2. The results indicate that Jed's conversation was controlled by the avoidance contingency, while Nel's conversation was controlled by Jed. Jed's conversation increased as the duration required to avoid additional interaction was systematically increased from 2 to 10 seconds. His conversation immediately stopped when he was told that the contingency was withdrawn, and it immediately returned to its previous level when he was told that the contingency was reinstated. Nel's conversation, on the other hand, did not change when the contingency was withdrawn but did change concomitant with the changes in Jed's conversation. Information did not change the rate of either Nel's or Jed's conversation.

Thus the results indicated that explicit reinforcement procedures were necessary to increase the social interaction of chronic schizophrenic patients. Immersing patients in an enriched atmosphere that provided possible topics of conversation was not likely to increase social interaction. However, even though the experiment achieved its objective of evaluating the effects of the two interventions, several elements in the procedures and the outcomes were less than clinically satisfying. Anecdotal reports by members of the nursing staff indicated that there were no concomitant increases in the dyads' interactions on the ward, indicating that explicit programming would probably have to be implemented in many areas

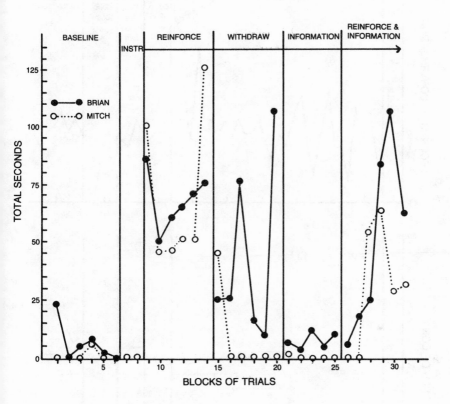

FIGURE 1. Total seconds of conversation per session, averaged across blocks of two sessions per block.

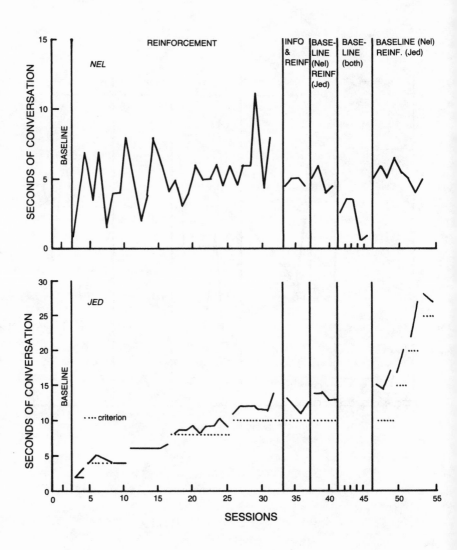

FIGURE 2. Average seconds of conversation per topic per session.

of patients' activities before there would be a substantial and clinically meaningful increase in social interaction. Additionally, the conversation that resulted barely approximated what might generally be considered "social interaction." The patients engaged in relatively long soliloquies that were only partially relevant to one another and did not include the exchange of information and feelings that seem an essential feature of social interaction. Finally, it was not at all clear that the patients perceived an increase in their social interactions as improving the quality of their lives. Although increased social interaction might have been desirable to clinicians, Nel and Jed in particular, who were more chronically and severely ill than Brian and Mitch, seemed to take little pleasure in interacting with one another.

Thus the second study in this series was designed to improve the basic interpersonal skills of less chronically ill patients who expressed a desire to feel more comfortable in social interactions. The procedures were designed to be relevant to each patient's social interactions, to take into account the attentional lapses characteristic of schizophrenic patients, and to help patients use these skills in social interactions outside the treatment setting.

STUDY 2

Finch and Wallace (1977) evaluated the effectiveness of modified assertion-training procedures designated to improve the basic interpersonal skills of 16 male schizophrenic inpatients, all living on the same treatment ward at the Sepulveda (California) Veterans Administration hospital. All 16 had been diagnosed as schizophrenic according to DSM-II criteria, were between the ages of 21 and 40 (mean of 29), had been hospitalized for a total of at least one year (mean of 3 years), reported themselves as being unassertive, and were willing to participate in procedures designed to improve their interpersonal skills. Interpersonal skills were defined in terms of six component behaviors: eye contact, loudness of speech, fluency of speech, affect, latency of response, and appropriate content. These skills were taught in one-hour sessions conducted by two advanced clinical psychology graduate students (a male and a female) three times a week for four consecutive weeks. The general format of each session consisted of the therapists' introducing and discussing a difficult interpersonal situation, then modeling appropriate and inappropriate behavior, and of patients' practicing appropriate responses with feedback given by both the therapists and the other patients. Frequently two or three practices were required to achieve a skillful performance, although a maximum of three rehearsals was set to keep the sessions as positive as possible.

To ensure that the skills learned in the sessions would be used in social interactions outside the treatment setting, patients were paired and each dyad was given "homework assignments" to complete between the sessions. During each session, patients discussed their successes and failures in completing the previous session's assignments. When appropriate, patients role played the assignments and received feedback from the group. As the assignments became more complex and patients were required to engage in social activities with each other, they suggested the assignments and extended invitations to members with similar interests.

In view of the day-to-day variability of symptoms in schizophrenia, each patient was asked to attend every session even if he was having a "bad" day. Only once was a patient absent from a session. All patients occasionally showed inattentiveness, and several procedural variations were made to reduce the effects of such lapses. As a first step in focusing attention, patients were trained to establish good eye contact. In addition, situations requiring skillful responses were purposely varied and of short duration. All instructions were simple and to the point. To further promote attending and group participation, each patient was responsible for giving performance feedback to the active participants.

If patients were not attending when another group member spoke to them, they were trained simply to say, "I'm sorry, I wasn't listening to what you were saying" rather than making some inappropriate response. If a patient began to drift off the topic, he was interrupted and his attention was redirected. If a patient gave a response that was irrelevant to the group topic, he was told so and asked to redirect his attention. Whenever a patient wanted to change the topic, he was trained to indicate his intention. This helped both the patient and other group members to differentiate between an intentional shift of attention and "drifting." As the group progressed, patients began to spontaneously correct each other's inattentiveness.

The training sessions used interpersonal situations that had been specifically chosen as relevant to these patients. Before the training, the 16 patients had responded to a questionnaire devised by the senior author to determine what they considered problematic interpersonal situations. Seven situations were identified: receiving a compliment, expressing an opinion, refusing an unreasonable request, accepting thanks, initiating a conversation, expressing an apology, and extending a social invitation. All these situations except expressing an opinion and expressing an apology were included in the training sessions. Additionally, patients suggested other problem situations during the training sessions.

To evaluate the effectiveness of the training procedures, the patients participated in special assessment sessions conducted before and after training by a female psychology graduate student. The assessment sessions consisted of seven interpersonal situations, four role played and three spontaneously enacted during the interchange between the assessor and the patient. Five of the seven situations were the same as those used in the training sessions: of the two not used, one was role played (expressing an apology) and one was spontaneously enacted (expressing an opinion). The entire session was recorded on audiotape and later rated independently by two psychology graduate students. Ratings were made of five of the six component behaviors: loudness of speech, fluency of speech, affect, latency of response, and appropriateness of content. All but latency of response were rated using the five-point scales (1 = poor to 5 = very good) and response definitions of Eisler, Miller, and Hersen (1973). Latency was measured with a stopwatch from the end of the assessor's prompt to the beginning of the patient's response. Eye contact was also rated by the assessor on a five-point scale (1 = poor to 5 = very good) at the end of each session. Unfortunately, eye contact could not be rated by the two raters, since there was no equipment available to record the session on videotape. Additionally, patients completed the Wolpe-Lazarus Assertiveness Test before and after training.

Eight of the 16 patients were assigned at random to receive the training, while the other eight participated in the standard treatment offered by the hospital. The assessor and the two raters were unaware of which patients were assigned to training or control conditions. The ratings were analyzed with a split-plot factorial ANOVA with one between-subjects variable (training vs. control) and two within-subject variables (spontaneous vs. role-played situations, trained vs. untrained situations). Since the small n precluded multivariate analysis, the results from each component behavior were analyzed separately. In each analysis, the dependent variable was the amount of change from pre- to post-assessment sessions

Table 1

Mean Changes for Experimental and Control Groups

Variable	Experimental Group	Control Group
Loudness	2.31	0.21
Fluency	2.34	0.01
Affect	2.11	0.10
Content	2.71	0.22
Eye contact	2.09	0.21
Latency	−2.62	0.05
Wolpe-Lazarus test	6.25	.25

averaged across the two raters and the three trained spontaneous and two trained role played situations. The Wolpe-Lazarus scores were analyzed using a split-plot factorial ANOVA with one between-subjects variable (training vs. control) and one within-subject variable (pre- vs. postassessments).

Table 1 presents the mean pre-post changes for the groups on the ratings of the six component behaviors and on the Wolpe-Lazarus test. The results of the ANOVA indicated that the treatment group significantly improved on all measures, and this improvement was consistent across both spontaneously enacted and role-played situations and across both trained and untrained situations. A split-plot factorial ANOVA conducted with the pretraining scores indicated that there were no significant differences between the groups at the start of the training.

Clinically, the results of the training were gratifying. Anecdotal comments by the nursing staff indicated that the trained patients improved their grooming and increased their social interactions. Furthermore, five of the trained patients were discharged compared with only one of the untrained patients. One of the five entered a vocational training program, two obtained full-time employment, one obtained part-time employment, and, although the fifth did not find a job, he was able to maintain himself in the community.

In spite of these encouraging results, several aspects of the procedures were not entirely satisfactory. Although the interpersonal situations used in the training were identified by patients as problematic, the relation of these situations to the clinical outcomes of improved quality of life and tenure in the community was not at all clear. Expressing a compliment, for example, may be difficult for patients but may occur so infrequently that skillful performance has little relation to achieving clinically meaningful outcomes. Furthermore, although the anecdotal comments of the nursing staff and the differences in the discharge rates pointed to the effectiveness of the procedures, no systematic data were collected about the effects of the treatment on variables such as psychopathology and general community functioning. Last but certainly not least in importance, it seemed that the training procedures were not systematically focused on the key behavioral component with which patients seemed to have great difficulty: developing the content of the response. Rather than focusing on the behaviors associated with the delivery of a response, it seemed necessary to focus on training patients to generate, evaluate, and select the correct responses for problem situations. Thus the next study in this series was designed to evaluate techniques for training chronic schizophrenics in problem-solving skills. The techniques, administered in a modified assertion-training format, included problem situations relevant to the patients' daily lives. The effects of the techniques were evaluated with a broad array of clinically meaningful outcome measures.

STUDY 3

Wallace (1982) evaluated the effects of an intensive regimen of training in social and problem-solving skills on the psychopathology and community adjustment of 28 male chronic schizophrenic inpatients. All patients had been diagnosed by the relatively stringent CATEGO criteria, and all had been hospitalized at least once before their participation in the project (mean of seven), though all had spent most of the time since the onset of their illnesses in community treatment facilities. Additionally, all but four of the patients had been living with relatives who were high in "expressed emotion" (EE). A series of studies conducted in England over the past 20 years (e.g., Vaughn & Leff, 1976) and now replicated in the United States have consistently indicated that a family environment in which one or more of the family members is high in EE exposes the patient to a significantly increased risk of rehospitalization,

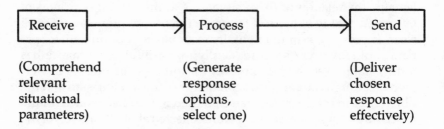

FIGURE 3. Problem-solving skills.

exacerbation of symptoms, or both. Thus most of the 28 patients were at risk for relapse based not only on their histories of multiple hospitalizations but also on their living with high EE relatives.

The training techniques were designed to improve patients' problem-solving skills, conceptualized as the major procedures required to elicit a socially skilled response in a problem situation. As indicated in Figure 3, these procedures consisted of "receiving" the parameters of the problem situation, "processing" these parameters to generate and evaluate possible response options, and "sending" the chosen option in a manner that would maximize the probability that the response would resolve the problem. Problem situations were differentiated into instrumental and friendship/dating situations. Instrumental situations were defined as those in which the interpersonal interaction was necessary to achieve a noninterpersonal goal such as having a Social Security check mailed or renting an apartment. Friendship/dating situations were defined as those in which the goal was maintenance or enhancement of the interpersonal interaction. Different skills within the receiving, processing, and sending procedures were defined for each type of situation.

As indicated in Table 2, the receiving skills for the instrumental problem situations were defined as identifying the interpersonal partner's status and emotion, comprehending the partner's messages, and recognizing one's own long- and short-term goals. The processing skills were defined as generating response options, predicting the effects of each on the partner's emotions and behaviors and on the achievement of the long- and short-term goals, and selecting the best option. The sending skills were defined as eye contact, voice volume and fluency, latency of response, body posture, hand gestures, and facial expressions.

Table 2
Receiving, Processing, and Sending Skills for Instrumental Problem Situations

Receiving Skills	Processing Skills	Sending Skills
1. Content of past and current messages	1. Determining own short- and long-term goals	1. Eye contact
2. Others' emotions	2. Generating response options	2. Voice volume
3. Others' status	3. Evaluating options in terms of goals	3. Fluency
4. Others' goals	4. Selecting best option	4. Latency
5. Others' identity		5. Body posture
		6. Hand gestures
		7. Facial expression

Table 3
Receiving, Processing, and Sending Skills for Friendship/Dating Situations

Receiving Skills	Processing Skills	Sending Skills
1. Content of past and current messages	1. Determining own goals	1. Eye contact
2. Others' emotions	2. Deciding level of self-disclosure	2. Voice volume
3. Topics of conversation	3. Continuing or terminating	3. Fluency
	4. Changing topics	4. Latency
		5. Nonverbal active listening skills
		6. Open- and closed-ended questions

As indicated in Table 3, the receiving skills for the friendship/dating situations were defined as identifying the interpersonal partner's status and emotions, comprehending the topic of the conversation, and recognizing other possible topics. The processing skills were defined as identifying the long- and short-term goals, recognizing the partner's wish to continue or terminate, identifying the appropriate level of self-disclosure, and determining when to relinquish or lead the conversation. The sending skills were defined as eye contact, voice volume, fluency, latency of response, hand gestures, facial expressions, other verbal and nonverbal active listening skills, and open-ended and closed-ended questions.

The techniques developed to teach these skills were a modification of those used in the earlier Finch and Wallace (1977) study. Training was conducted in a group format in which the trainer presented a problem situation as a scene to be role played by a selected patient. The role playing was recorded on videotape, and patients were asked a standard set of questions designed to assess their receiving and processing skills. When incorrect answers were given, the trainer applied specific procedures designed to elicit the correct answers. The number of incorrect answers was recorded, as well as the number of training trials required to elicit a correct response. The questions used with the instrumental situations were somewhat different from those used with the friendship/dating situations, reflecting the presumed differences in the skills required in each. However, within each type of problem situation all the questions were always asked in the same order after each instance of role playing. Sending skills were evaluated during the role playing and during playback of the videotape; if there was a deficiency, the trainer used instructions, coaching, modeling, and prompting as required.

To standardize the training and to ensure that relevant problem situations would be included, 88 selected instrumental problem situations were included in the training, 40 dealing with hospital problems and 48 dealing with community problems. The 88 situations had been chosen based on semistructured interviews with hospital staff members and community agencies. Additionally, 17 individualized situations were used with each patient, all of which addressed problems between the patient and members of his family. The scenes used in teaching friendship/dating skills were grouped into five sequentially arranged modules that began with selecting a topic to start a conversation, shifted to introducing new topics and using active listening skills to maintain the flow of conversation, and finished with "gracefully" exiting a conversation.

The effects of the problem-skills training were compared with those of a "control" treatment labeled "holistic health" treatment. Holistic health treatment was based upon the rationale, presented to the patients in great detail, that schizophrenia was a response to stress and that relapse could be forestalled or even prevented by increasing one's physical capacity to deal with stress and by using one of several stress-reduction techniques.

All of the 28 patients lived on the same inpatient unit during their participation in the project (the Clinical Research Unit at Camarillo State Hospital), and 14 were assigned at random to each of the two treatments. Because of limited bed space, patients were admitted to the project in cohorts of six. Five cohorts participated for a total sample size of 30, with two patients from the first cohort (one in each of the two treatments) withdrawing after three weeks of participation.

The two treatments were conducted for nine weeks with from two to six hours of daily therapy. The problem-solving skills training sessions included: (*a*) daily two-hour morning sessions designed to increase problem-solving skills; (*b*) thrice-weekly afternoon sessions designed to generalize training to new persons and places; (*c*) twice-weekly afternoon trips to the surrounding community to provide an opportunity to complete homework assignments; (*d*) twice-weekly evening sessions designed to enhance patients' community survival skills; (*e*) weekly meetings of patients and their families designed to increase family communication skills.

The holistic health treatment sessions included: (*a*) daily two-hour morning sessions of a standardized routine of yoga, jogging, and meditation; (*b*) thrice-weekly afternoon sessions designed to develop positive expectations about recovery and provide a rationale that schizophrenia is a response to stress and can be controlled by identifying and reducing stressors; (*c*) twice-weekly afternoon trips to the surrounding community; (*d*) twice-weekly evening sessions designed to increase self-esteem and provide a rationale for considering schizophrenia a growth experience; (*e*) weekly family therapy sessions. To control for differences among the trainers, each trainer rotated daily between the two treatments.

The effects of the two treatments were evaluated with the measures listed in Table 4. The confederate test of social skills was the same as that used by Goldsmith and McFall (1975). Each patient conversed with same- and opposite-sex partners separately for five minutes each. The patient was given four tasks to perform during the conversation (e.g., ask the confederate to join you socially for a cup of coffee) and was confronted with four demands made by the partner (e.g., forgot the patient's name). At the end of the conversation, the patient rated his own discomfort and skills on a nine-point scale; the confederate also rated the patient's discomfort

Table 4

Dependent Measures

Scale	Frequency	Staff
Brief Psychiatric Rating Scale (BPRS)	Biweekly and every follow-up	Psychiatrist
Psychiatric Assessment Scale (PAS)	Biweekly and every follow-up	Psychiatrist
Clinical Global Impressions (CGI)	Biweekly and every follow-up	Psychiatrist
Nurses' Observation Scale for Inpatient Evaluation (NOSIE-30)	Weekly during inpatient	Nursing staff
Nurses' Global Impressions (NGI)	Weekly during inpatient stay	Nursing staff
Interpersonal cognitive problem-solving skills (MEPS; Options; Consequences)	Pre and post and nine-month follow-up	Staff
Rathus Assertiveness Schedule	Pre and post and nine-month follow-up	Patient
Social Anxiety and Distress Scale	Pre and post and nine-month follow-up	Patient
Fear of Negative Evaluation Scale	Pre and post and nine-month follow-up	Patient

Note: Follow-ups were scheduled one, three, six, nine, 12, 18, and 24 months after therapy.

and skill and completed the Impact Message Inventory. Each conversation was videotaped.

The role-playing test of social skills used four instrumental scenes, two that had been used in the training and two that had not. The test format was much the same as the training format. The introduction and setting were read for each scene, and the role playing continued for only one exchange between confederate and patient. The patient was then asked six receiving and five processing questions, with no feedback given about the correctness of the answers. The role playing and answers were videotaped.

The aftercare information was collected every two weeks by the project social worker during one of the regularly scheduled contacts

Table 4 *continued*

Scale	Frequency	Staff
Minnesota Multiphasic Personality Inventory (MMPI-168)	Pre and post and every follow-up	Patient
Symptom Check List 90 (SCL-90)	Pre and post and every follow-up	Patient
Confederate Test of Social Skills	Pre and post and nine-month follow-up	Staff & patient
Roleplay Test of Social Competence	Pre and post and nine-month follow-up	Staff
Shipley-Hartford IQ Test	Pre and post and nine-month follow-up	Patient
Tennessee Self-Concept Test	Pre and post and nine-month follow-up	Patient
In-therapy process assessments	Daily during inpatient stay	Staff
Katz Social Adjustment (KAS)	Pre and nine-month follow-up	Patient and family
Present State Examination (PSE)	Pre and post and nine-month follow-up	Psychiatrist
Aftercare information	Biweekly after discharge	Staff

with each patient. A standardized interview was developed, with questions designed to elicit information about any changes since the last biweekly interview in the adequacy of self-care skills, the number of days of working, training, or schooling, the number of contacts with family members, the type and dosage of medication or illicit street drugs, the quality of life-style, and the quality and quantity of stressful life events.

The data were analyzed with two univariate statistical techniques. The first was a one-way analysis of covariance (ANCOVA) conducted separately with the data collected at each measurement point using the pretreatment scores as the covariate. The second was a split-plot factorial analysis of variance (ANOVA) with one between-subjects variable (holistic vs. problem-solving training) and one within-subject variable (pretraining measures vs. the specific measurement point selected for analysis) conducted separately for the data collected at each measurement point. Unfortunately, the small n precluded multivariate analyses. Additionally, not all data were collected for all subjects at each measurement point, since some subjects simply refused to participate in the procedures and others were hospitalized and unable to participate.

The results of the analyses of the in-therapy measures and the role-playing test indicated that patients not only learned the problem-solving skills but retained their learning nine months after discharge from the hospital. The average daily percentage of errors made in answering the receiving question dropped from 65% during the first three days of training to 19% during the last three days. Errors in answering the processing questions dropped from 76% to 14%. Summing across the receiving and processing questions used in the four scenes of the role-playing test, the results of the ANCOVA indicated that the problem-solving group scored significantly higher than the holistic group immediately after treatment ($F = 6.55, p < .01, df = 1, 23$) and at nine months after discharge ($F = 4.60, p < .05, df = 1, 16$).

The results of the confederate test indicated that the improvement noted in the training sessions and in the role-playing tests generalized to the 5-minute interaction with the confederate. The problem-solving group was described by the confederate on the Impact Message Inventory as significantly less hostile ($F = 5.46, p < .05, df = 1, 15$), less mistrusting, ($F = 9.22, p < .01, df = 1, 15$), less detached ($F = 9.47, p < .01, df = 1, 15$), less inhibited ($F = 10.12, p < .01, df = 1, 15$), and less submissive ($F = 10.38, p < .01, df = 1, 15$) at the nine-month testing than the holistic group. The additional ratings made by the confederate indicated that the problem-solving group significantly increased in ratings of appropriateness from pre- to posttreatment, whereas the holistic group did not improve ($F = 4.32, p < .05, df = 1, 25$). This differential pattern of improvement was maintained at the nine-month testing (interaction $F = 14.31, p < .01, df = 1, 17$). There were no differences on any other measure derived from the confederate test, including the number of tasks completed and the patients' ratings of their own skill and anxiety.

The results of the tests of interpersonal cognitive problem-solving skills (MEPS, Options, Causal, Consequences) indicated that there were no differences between the groups at any measurement point and no changes across time for either group on any scale. Interestingly, patients remarked that these tests were time consuming and extremely difficult to complete.

The results of the ANCOVA for the Katz Adjustment Scale indicated that the relatives reported greater improvement in functioning for the problem-solving group than for the holistic group. The problem-solving group was rated by relatives as significantly less negative ($F = 6.88, p < .05, df = 1, 15$), as less obstreperous ($F = 13.04, p < .01, df = 1, 15$), and as having less psychopathology ($F = 16.22, p < .01, df = 1, 15$) than the holistic group. The relatives of the problem-solving group were also significantly more satisfied than the holistic group's relatives with patients' performances of "socially expected" activities (e.g., working, going to church, visiting friends) and with patients' participation in recreational and leisure activities.

The analyses of the self-report and interview measures of psychopathology indicated that there were significant reductions in psychopathology for both groups from pre- to posttreatment, and these gains were maintained for all but the MMPI scales at the nine- and 24-month follow-ups. There were no significant differences between the groups at any measurement point on any scale.

During the two-year follow-up period, those in the problem-solving group were rehospitalized a total of 16 times, spending an average of 54.07 days in the hospital. In contrast, those in the holistic group were hospitalized a total of 38 times, spending an average of 87.43 days in the hospital. These differences, albeit substantial, were not significant because of marked patient heterogeneity.

Finally, a rating of relapse/no relapse was made by two psychiatrists based not only on the results of the Present State Examination and the Psychiatric Assessment Scale administered at the nine-month follow-up, but also on clinical outcome data obtained during the first year after discharge. The two psychiatrists rated the material blindly; their interrater agreement was 100%. Seven of the 14 problem-solving patients relapsed compared with 11 of the holistic patients; this difference was not statistically significant. It should be noted that the relapse rate of the problem-solving group was better than that generally found with patients living with high EE relatives.

Hence the results indicate that, at best, problem-solving training had a modest effect on patients' functioning. In comparison with the holistic group, the problem-solving group learned complex, cognitive problem-solving skills and maintained them over a nine-month period. There were improvements in some aspects of social skills noted by the confederate who conducted the five-minute interaction test, and patients themselves reported increases in their assertiveness. Patients' relatives also noted differential improvements favoring the problem-solving group in community functioning and psychopathology. However, these differential improvements did not result in different rates of rehospitalization or relapse, although members of the problem-solving group had substantially fewer rehospitalizations and were hospitalized for fewer days. Both treatments resulted in significant reductions in patients' psychopathology that were generally maintained over the two-year follow-up period.

Perhaps these rather modest differences are not surprising in view of the fact that all patients lived in the same highly structured, well-staffed (14 nursing staff members, full-time psychiatrist, psychologist, social worker, and recreation therapist for 12 beds) inpatient unit during their participation, and all took part in the unit's three-tier token economy. Thus all patients received additional behavioral treatment that could have blunted the differential effect of the two treatments.

It should be noted that the few differential improvements found in variables other than social skills cannot be unequivocally attributed to the problem-solving training. They can be attributed to the package of techniques, a component of which was family therapy. Considering that most of the differential improvements were noted in the measures based on relatives' reports, it is quite possible that family therapy was the effective ingredient in the package. Perhaps this indicates that a more efficient and effective approach to forestalling relapse is to modify patients' interpersonal environments to provide supportive networks that recognize environmental stressors and enhance their ability to cope with them.

Furthermore, anecdotal observations made during the course of training indicated that the nine weeks of training was relatively brief and that patients' deficits extended far beyond deficiencies in problem-solving skills. There also seemed to be a high degree of patient heterogeneity in response to the training in problem-solving skills. Some patients were relatively skilled and could have progressed through the training at a rapid pace that might have prevented the boredom they occasionally complained about. Other patients struggled to learn the procedures and could have benefited from even more intensive training conducted at a slower pace. What seemed to be needed was an individualized approach that integrated training in problem-solving with training in basic skills such as grooming, health care, shelter management, and job finding. Patients would then learn both the skills necessary to survive in the community and methods of solving the problems that occur when they use these skills.

Thus the training techniques to be described in the next section were designed to integrate training in community-living skills training and in problem-solving skills in a format that allowed patients to proceed through the program at their own pace. This individualization of training permitted a return to single-subject research designs used in the Wallace and Davis (1974) study. These would give a degree of flexibility in systematically introducing and rigorously evaluating variations in the basic training procedures that was not possible with the group designs used in the Finch and Wallace (1977) and Wallace (1982) studies.

STUDY 4

Wallace, Boone, Donahoe, and Foy (in press) evaluated the effects of techniques designed to train patients not only in the skills necessary to function adequately in the community but also in solving the problems they might encounter as they use these skills. The techniques are organized into "modules," each of which covers a major grouping of community survival skills such as self-care skills, apartment-finding and maintenance skills, and vocational skills. As indicated in Figure 4, each module consists of seven training components as follows:

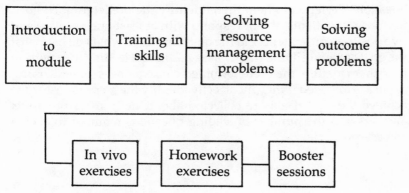

FIGURE 4. Seven training components of a module.

Introduction to the Module

This training component seeks to have patients actively identify the goal of a module, the consequences that will occur if the goal is achieved, and the steps necessary to achieve the goal. (Each of the steps is one of the skills that will be taught in the next training component.) After a module is briefly described, patients are asked the following set of questions.

1. What is the goal of this module?
2. What is the problem?
3. If you get [goal], what will happen?
4. Do you have time, money, skills, people to help?
5. What are the steps to get [goal]?

All questions and predetermined correct answers are written on a data sheet; the trainer compares patients' answers with those on the data sheet and institutes a correction procedure if any answer is incorrect. For example, the predetermined goal of the vocational module is to find and maintain a job. The predetermined positive consequences that would ensue from achieving this goal are a better standard of living, a more structured daily routine, a potentially more intellectually stimulating environment, and an opportunity for increased social contact. The predetermined negative consequences are a possible loss of pension benefits and the necessity of following a structured routine. The predetermined steps (skills) to obtain the goal are to explore job possibilities, obtain leads for possible jobs, and obtain an interview for a selected job. If patients do not respond correctly to the question about the goal of the module, the trainer asks an additional set of ever more leading questions designed to help them identify the predetermined goal. Similarly, if patients do not respond with at least one negative and two positive consequences to the question about what will happen if the goal is achieved, the trainer asks additional leading questions to help them identify the predetermined consequences. A similar procedure is followed if they incorrectly identify the steps necessary to achieve the goal. Data are collected about the number of correct answers and the number of leading questions required to elicit a correct answer.

Training in Skills

The skills that patients have just identified as necessary to achieve the goal of a module are taught using a combination of videotaped demonstrations and role-played practices. After reviewing the "place" of the skill in the sequence of steps necessary to achieve the goal, patients view a videotape that is periodically stopped to assess their attentiveness to and comprehension of the information conveyed in the demonstration. If they give incorrect answers, the trainer replays the videotape and highlights the information needed to correctly answer the questions. Data are collected about the number of correct and incorrect answers.

After they comprehend all the information, patients are asked to role play the skill. The enactment is observed for the presence/ absence of the behaviors demonstrated on the videotape. For example, the behaviors demonstrated during the videotaped presentation of a satisfactory job interview include being dressed appropriately, offering a pleasant greeting and a firm handshake, having good posture, adequately describing work history, indicating interest in the job and a willingness to work, gathering information about the outcome of the interview, and terminating the interview with a pleasant response and a firm handshake.

If a behavior has not been performed or has been performed incorrectly, corrective feedback is given, and the patient is asked to repeat the role playing. Data are collected about the presence/absence of each of the behaviors during role playing.

Resource Management Problems

After each skill has been correctly roleplayed, patients are taught to solve a set of "resource management" problems, conceptualized as the difficulties they might encounter when they attempt to marshal the resources necessary to perform each skill. The training procedures are based on a model of the steps necessary to successfully solve such problems (Figure 5). The trainer describes the skill and asks a series of questions designed to make patients actively consider each step outlined in the model:

1. What is your goal in using this skill?
2. What is the goal of this module?

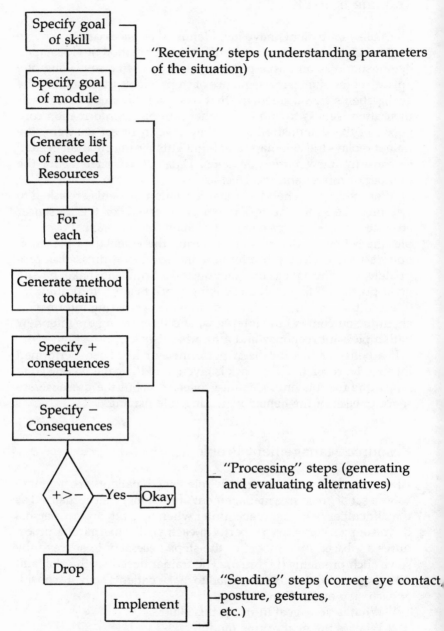

FIGURE 5. Steps in successfully solving a resource management problem.

3. What must you have to [*skill*]? (For each resource mentioned in 3)

4. How would you get [*resources*]?

5. If you were to get [*resource*] by [*method in 4*], what other positive consequences would happen?

6. If you were to get [*resource*] by [*method in 4*], what negative consequences might happen?

7. Do the positive consequences outweigh the negative consequences?

All questions and the corresponding correct answers are written on a data sheet; the trainer compares patients' answers with those on the data sheet and institutes a correction procedure if any answer is incorrect. For example, the predetermined resources necessary for a job interview are transportation to the interview, appropriate clothing, and a summary of personal information and vocational history. If patients do not respond with at least these resources to the question about what they must have to go on a job interview, they are asked a series of ever more leading questions until they do respond with these three resources. The predetermined alternatives to obtaining transportation to the interview are asking a friend or relative for a ride, taking the bus, using one's own car (if appropriate), and asking the trainer or "case manager" for a ride. If patients do not bring up each of these alternatives, they are asked leading questions until each has been mentioned and evaluated in terms of its positive and negative consequences. There are no predetermined answers to evaluating each alternative; the only criterion is that the consequences generated be realistic and be correctly evaluated in terms of their positive or negative value to each patient. At the trainer's option, an alternative such as asking a friend for a ride may be role played and evaluated for correct delivery in terms of eye contact, posture, fluency, and so forth. The trainer records on the data sheet the number of correct and incorrect answers.

Outcome Problems

After patients have been trained to solve the problems involved in marshaling the resources necessary to perform a skill, they are trained to solve the problems that might occur when they use the skill and the environment does not respond in an optimum manner. These are labeled "outcome" problems, and the training procedures

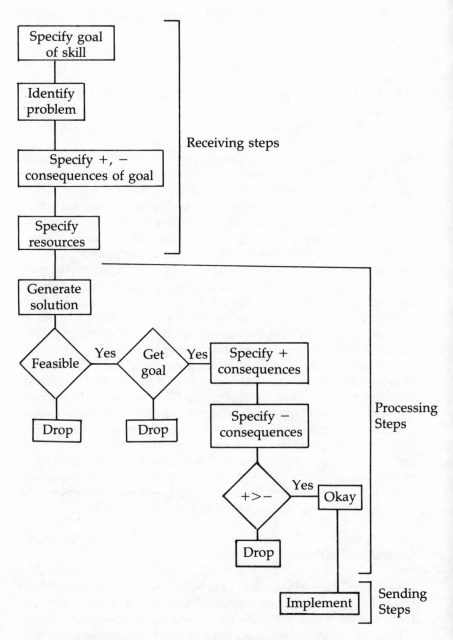

FIGURE 6. Steps in successfully solving an outcome problem.

are based on the model shown in Figure 6 of the steps necessary to solve the problems. The trainer begins by reading a description of the attempt to use the skill, the response made by the environment, and the resources available to solve the problem posed by the environment's response. Patients are then asked questions designed to make them actively consider the steps outlined in the model:

1. What is the problem?
2. Do you have time, money, skills, people to help?
3. What can you do to solve the problem?
4. Is [*method in 3*] feasible?
5. If you [*method in 3*], will you likely get your goal?
6. If you were to [*method in 3*], name as many positive consequences as you think would occur besides solving the problem.
7. If you were to [*method in 3*], name as many negative consequences as you can think of.
8. Do the positive consequences outweigh the negative consequences? The scoring of patients' answers, the teaching of correct answers, and the collection of data are all performed in the same manner as in teaching how to solve resource-management problems.

For example, a problem presented to all patients is that they arrive for a scheduled job interview but the interviewer has left and will return in an hour. The predetermined alternatives are to ask for another interviewer, wait the hour, come back another day, or simply leave. If patients do not generate all these alternatives in response to the question about what they can do to solve the problem, they are asked a series of leading questions until they identify all four alternatives. Similarly, there are predetermined answers to the questions about each alternative's feasibility and the likelihood of obtaining the goal. Incorrect answers again result in a series of leading questions designed to elicit the correct response. As in the resource management problems, there are no predetermined answers for generating the positive and negative consequences of each alternative. The trainer may ask patients to role play their solutions for evaluation and to practice delivery skills such as eye contact, fluency, and posture. Predetermined variations (e.g., the interviewer has left for the day, the patient has another job interview scheduled in an hour) are introduced, and the training procedures are repeated.

In Vivo Exercises

The in vivo exercises have patients perform in the "real world" the skills they have been taught in the training sessions. Patients are expected to marshal the resources necessary to perform the skill, and the trainer accompanies them on these performances to provide corrective feedback and to collect data about the quality of the performances.

Homework Exercises

The homework exercises are much the same as the in vivo exercises except that staff do not accompany patients. Rather, data are collected whenever possible about the permanent products of an exercise that verify its completion. If no permanent products result from an exercise, patients' self-report of completion is noted.

Booster Exercises

The "booster" exercises are designed to refresh patients' skills after a period of inactivity. The exercises consist of many of the same role-playing, problem-solving, in vivo, and homework exercises used in the original training.

Thus, the seven training components of each module, exemplified by the vocational skills module, fit together as indicated in Table 5 (p. 318). Of course many of the resources and the methods of obtaining them are the same from skill to skill. Once these methods have been learned, subsequent training sessions can be conducted rapidly, and certain segments (e.g., generating and evaluating the consequences of borrowing a resource) may be skipped at the trainer's discretion.

At this time, these techniques are being used as the major therapeutic component of a day treatment program conducted at the West Los Angeles Veterans Administration Medical Center (Brentwood Division). Patients are referred to the program from treatment units throughout the Center. Most of these patients have experienced repeated episodes of hospitalization–discharge–rehospitalization. Their interpersonal and community-living skills are initially assessed using a self-report instrument, confirmed whenever possible by significant others and by treatment personnel who are familiar with the patients. If deficits are reported, they are also confirmed by watching patients role play the skills, using the check-list of the appropriate modules. Based on the results of these assess-ments, an individualized treatment plan is written specifying the modules in which each patient will participate. Generally the mod-ules are administered to groups of three patients, although groups up to a maximum of six or seven can be accommodated.

The sequential teaching of the skills in each module and the use of groups of patients allow an evaluation of the effectiveness of the training procedures using two single-subject research designs: a multiple-baseline design across the skills being taught in each mod-ule, and a multiple-baseline design across groups of patients partici-pating in the training. Figure 7 presents the results of the multiple-baseline design across skills for one of the patient groups ($n = 3$) participating in the module on medication self-administration and symptom management. The module consists of four skills: knowl-edge of the effects of neuroleptic medication, self-administration of medication, monitoring the side effects of medication, and discuss-ing medication problems with a physician. Each skill consists of four to eight component behaviors. The graphs in Figure 6 present the average percentage of these behaviors the patients performed dur-ing each of ten assessment sessions. These sessions were conducted at different times and places than those of the training sessions and thus represent the generalization of the effects of training. Training was introduced for each skill at the point indicated by the dashed vertical line. Assessment sessions 9 and 10 were conducted two weeks and nine weeks after training. Training was always con-ducted until 100% of the component behaviors were performed during role playing. The results suggest that training was the effec-tive component in increasing the patients' skills, particularly for the first three skills.

Figure 8 presents the results of a multiple-baseline design evaluat-ing the effects of one part of the procedures for teaching problem-solving skills. Each graph in Figure 8 presents the average number of alternatives to three problems generated by two groups of two patients each. Training was initiated at the point indicated by the dashed vertical line. As in the multiple design used to evaluate the acquisition of the skills, the graphs present the results of assessment sessions conducted at different times and places than the training sessions. The training sessions were conducted until each patient

Group Skill Acquisition

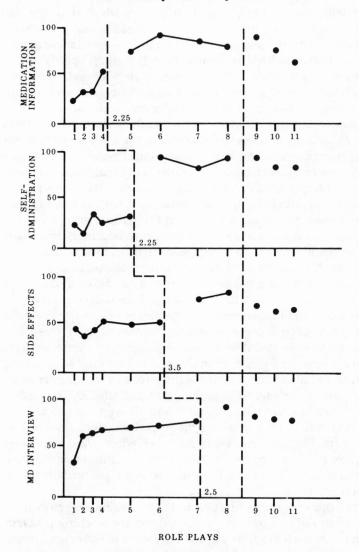

FIGURE 7. Average percentage of behaviors correctly performed by a group of three patients during acquisition of skills on the medication management module.

Cognitive Factors in the Social Skills of Schizophrenic Patients

Group Problem Solving Alternatives

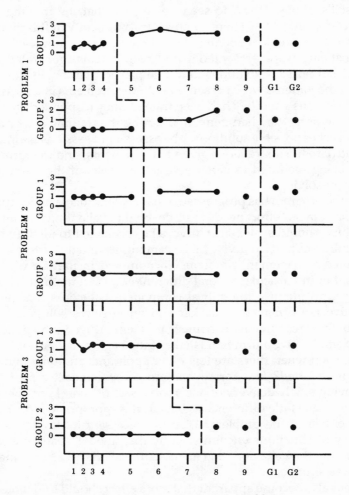

FIGURE 8. Average number of alternatives generated by two groups of two patients each to three problems presented on the medication management module.

had generated and evaluated three response alternatives. The results are certainly not as convincing as those for the acquisition of the skills, though they do seem to suggest that the training was moderately effective. There is, however, a difficulty in this method of assessing problem-solving skills. During the training sessions, the patients were presented with the problems, generated and evaluated possible solutions, and role played their final solutions. When the patients were presented with the problems in the assessment sessions after they had been trained, they responded with the final solutions they had generated during the training rather than with a list of possible solutions. The assessment sessions seem very sensitive to the instructions given to the patients, and the format is now being modified to better assess the effects of the training in problem-solving.

As the program has progressed, it has become increasingly apparent that a major effort needs to be devoted to validating its content. Not only should systematic surveys be conducted to identify both the skills required to survive in the community and the outcome and resource management problems encountered in the use of these skills, but in particular several different empirical methods should be used to identify the critical component behaviors that define effective performance of a skill and an effective solution to an outcome or resource-management problem. Must a job applicant, for example, give a firm handshake at the beginning of every interview, even when there are few other applicants and only minimal skill is required? Is a certain pattern of eye contact essential to achieving timely delivery of one's social security check, or does eye contact make little difference as long as the appropriate individuals are notified of the problem? It seems necessary to develop a taxonomy of situations encountered by the "modal" patient and to determine the behaviors that are essential to effective performance in these situations.

It has also become apparent that more effort should be devoted to developing effective methods of teaching community survival skills. Although the videotaped demonstrations and role-played practices do seem effective, even more effective methods may be suggested by a survey of the findings of experiments comparing different instructional technologies. For example, perhaps immersion in actual situations may be a better means of teaching community survival skills than the more "classroom" oriented approach currently used in the program. Similarly, much more effort should be devoted to validating the models of solving resource-management and outcome problems and the methods of teaching problem-solving skills. The data are equivocal about the effectiveness of the current teaching techniques, and further information about the problem-solving processes used by both schizophrenic and nonschizophrenic individuals would obviously be important for designing and implementing an effective program. It would be particularly helpful if such an effort could yield assessment instruments that would pinpoint patients' deficiencies in problem-solving skills and thus suggest focused remedial activities. There is evidence that schizophrenics are different from nonschizophrenics in several areas of interpersonal functioning (Wallace, in press), but the evidence is not thorough enough to construct a model of the problem-solving process or to suggest assessment instruments and treatment techniques.

SUMMARY

This chapter illustrates how changes have occurred in a clinical research program designed to develop and evaluate treatment techniques for improving the social skills of chronic schizophrenic patients. These changes have been primarily in the definition of a socially skilled response; rather than defining such responses solely in terms of motor behaviors, we have attempted to include several cognitive elements hypothesized to be critical aspects of the process of producing an effective social response. The inclusion of these cognitive elements suggests that the findings of experimental psychopathologists about the perceptual, attentional, and information-processing dysfunctions of schizophrenic individuals may be highly relevant to the development of more effective treatment techniques. For example, a patient may make an ineffective social response because of an attentional or perceptual dysfunction that results in inaccurate reception of critical social and situational stimuli. Similarly, an ineffective response may be produced because of an information-processing dysfunction that makes a patient generate a restricted number of alternatives and evaluate them incorrectly. If these attentional, perceptual, and information-processing dysfunctions are not simply linked to variations in symptomatology but represent enduring deficiencies, then an effective treatment strategy may require either that these dysfunctions be remedied (if at all possible) or that an environment be created that compensates for them.

Of course much more information is needed about the extent to which these dysfunctions might affect performance in the social situations patients commonly face. Certain situations may be relatively simple, requiring attention to only one or two critical stimuli and a response that is well within the social repertoires of most patients. Other situations may be far more complex, requiring a high degree of sustained attention and complex, "subtle" responses that are not within the social repertoires of most patients. For example, anecdotal observations made during the use of the techniques to teach friendship/dating skills suggest that ongoing conversations are particularly difficult for patients. These situations seem to require a high degree of sustained attention to keep track of shifts in topics, detect changes in the partner's emotions, and introduce planned changes in the stream of conversation. Other situations, such as asking for items from nurses, seem relatively simple and can be performed fairly well by patients, even those who are highly symptomatic. Thus, understanding the role of these basic attentional, perceptual, and information-processing procedures in social situations is essential to correctly incorporating the findings of experimental psychopathology into treatment techniques for the chronic schizophrenic patient. Nevertheless, the current conceptualization and direction of the program's treatment techniques suggest that such an incorporation may be useful.

REFERENCES

Eisler, R. M., Miller, P. M., & Hersen, M. Components of assertive behavior. *Journal of Clinical Psychology*, 1973, **29**, 295–299.

Finch, B. E., & Wallace, C. J. Successful interpersonal skills training with psychiatric inpatients. *Journal of Consulting and Clinical Psychology*, 1977, **45**, 485–490.

Goldsmith, J. R., & McFall, R. M. Development and evaluation of an interpersonal skills training program for psychiatric inpatients. *Journal of Abnormal Psychology*, 1975, **84**, 51–58.

Hunter, M., Schooler, C., & Spohn, H. E. The measurement of characteristic patterns of ward behavior in chronic schizophrenics. *Journal of Consulting Psychology*, 1962, **26**, 69–73.

Paul, G. L., & Lentz, R. J. *Psychosocial treatment of chronic mental patients.* Cambridge: Harvard University Press, 1978.

Schooler, C., & Spohn, H. E. Social interaction on a ward of chronic schizophrenics. *International Journal of Social Psychiatry*, 1960, **6**, 115–119.

Vaughn, C. E., & Leff, J. P. The influence of family and social factors in the course of psychiatric illness. *British Journal of Psychiatry*, 1976, **129,** 125–137.

Wallace, C. J. The social skills training project of the Mental Health Clinical Research Center for the Study of Schizophrenia. In J. P. Curran & P. M. Monti (Eds.), *Social skills training: A practical handbook for assessment and treatment.* New York: Guilford Press, 1982.

Wallace, C. J. The role of community and interpersonal functioning in the development course of schizophrenic disorders. *Schizophrenia Bulletin*, in press.

Wallace, C. J., Boone, S. E., Donahoe, C. P., & Foy, D. W. Treating the social and independent living skills of chronic mental patients. In D. H. Barlow (Ed.), *Behavioral treatment of adult disorders.* New York: Guilford Press, in press.

Wallace, C. J. & Davis, J. R. The effects of information and reinforcement on the conversational behavior of chronic psychiatric patient dyads. *Journal of Consulting and Clinical Psychology*, 1974, **42,** 656–666.

Table 5

Components of Vocational Rehabilitation Module

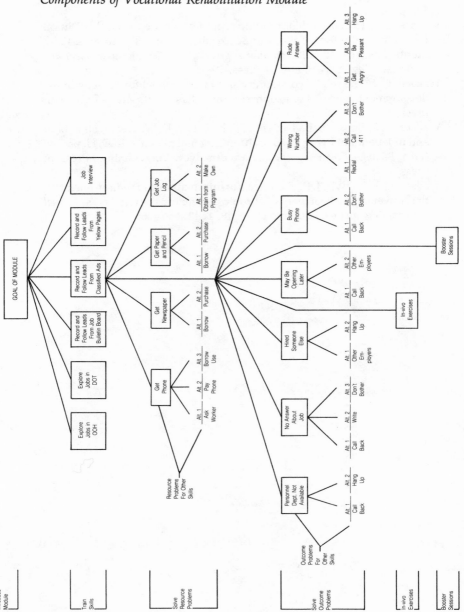

Discussion

Keith H. Nuechterlein

University of California at Los Angeles

*T*he view that human information processing is facilitated by the interaction of a
global, holistic processing mode and a detailed, analytic processing
mode is a common one in recent theories of cognition (Broadbent,
1977; Kinsbourne, 1982; Neisser, 1967). Variants of this theme play a
part in several of the theories of schizophrenia and psychosis that
are presented in this volume. Perhaps a similar separation of
comments into an initial overview of the terrain and a subsequent
detailed appraisal of certain critical features will facilitate an
evaluation of the contributions to this 31st annual Nebraska
Symposium on Motivation. Because a full analysis of the features of
this excellent series of papers would probably require a second
volume, I will focus on selected common and distinguishing
features as well as on particular strengths and weaknesses of the
contributions. Furthermore, because Dr. Spohn has provided an
analysis of the Spring 1983 session, I will restrict my detailed
comments to the contributions to the Fall 1982 session—those of
Drs. Cromwell, Magaro, and Venables.

GLOBAL, HOLISTIC FEATURES OF THE THEORIES
AND RESEARCH STRATEGIES

Certain themes are present in multiple contributions to this volume
and, from my perspective, can serve as guideposts to recent
developments in research on schizophrenic disorders. Many of
these common themes concern not the specific content of individual
contributions but rather improvements in research strategies or in
methodological conceptions. Furthermore, the combination of these
themes represented in each of the contributions varies.

1. Structural vs. Developmental Analysis

Several of the contributions reflect an increasing recognition that, for a full understanding of schizophrenia, studies of the cross-sectional structure of schizophrenic psychopathology need to be accompanied by studies of the development and course of schizophrenic disorders. The predominant research design that examines differences between actively symptomatic schizophrenic patients and normal subjects at a single point in time can shed light on the structure of schizophrenic psychopathological states. These cross-sectional comparisons may be particularly revealing if the measures are closely tied to theoretical constructs describing well-documented normal processes and if other psychopathological groups are included to evaluate the generality of anomalies in the schizophrenic patients. However, exclusive use of this research design implicitly assumes that schizophrenic disorders are static conditions that can be understood by evaluating abnormal characteristics at any single point in time during the psychotic period. The marked fluctuations in clinical symptomatology and impairment over time, as well as the fact that the initial onset of psychosis typically does not occur until adolescence or early adulthood, suggest that the static perspective available from cross-sectional studies of the psychotic period will be limited. Several of the contributors to the present volume emphasize studies of populations at risk for schizophrenic disorder or patients with remitted schizophrenic disorders as a means of clarifying developmental processes that contribute to schizophrenic symptomatology. A related emphasis in some recent research (Asarnow & MacCrimmon, 1982; Frame & Oltmanns, 1982; Laasi, Nuechterlein, & Edell, 1983) has involved evaluation of schizophrenic deficits across different points in time.

2. Trait vs. State Abnormalities

The increasing recognition that schizophrenic disorders need to be evaluated as developmental conditions has encouraged a distinction between abnormal traits associated with schizophrenia and abnormal states associated with schizophrenic psychotic episodes. Cromwell and Spaulding (1978) and Zubin and Spring (1977) have particularly emphasized a distinction between anomalies that are vulnerability-linked traits and those that are symptom-linked states. The former are abnormalities that are present before, during, and after schizophrenic psychotic periods and that are also present in first-degree relatives of schizophrenic patients at a rate higher than that of the general population. In Spring and Zubin's (1978) view, these vulnerability indicators are likely to be independent of symptomatology. Symptom-linked states, or episode indicators, are abnormalities that occur during the schizophrenic psychotic episode but are not present before or after this period.

A tripartite distinction that I, Michael Dawson, and our colleagues are employing in an ongoing longitudinal study of recent-onset schizophrenic patients at UCLA may be even more useful in examining abnormalities along a trait-state dimension. We distinguish stable vulnerability indicators, mediating vulnerability factors, and episode indicators. Stable vulnerability indicators are abnormalities that are present before, during, and after schizophrenic psychotic episodes and that do not change significantly across time. These anomalies, if relatively specific to schizophrenia, serve to identify vulnerability to schizophrenic disorder but may not contribute directly to symptom formation. Mediating vulnerability factors are abnormalities that are present before, during, and after schizophrenic psychotic episodes and that become more deviant during (or somewhat before) psychotic episodes. These variables may become increasingly deviant immediately before and during schizophrenic psychotic periods because they are contributors to processes of schizophrenic psychotic symptom formation. Thus, changes in these variables also may serve as short-term predictors of the emergence of psychotic symptoms. Episode indicators are abnormalities that are present during schizophrenic psychotic episodes but are absent in nonpsychotic periods. These anomalies may be integral parts of the psychotic state or secondary effects of the state.

This tripartite distinction remains an oversimplification of the different types of abnormalities associated with schizophrenic disorders, but serves to highlight some aspects of the trait-state issue introduced explicitly or implicitly by the contributors in their theoretical positions. In hypotheses about primary cognitive deficits in schizophrenic disorders, the contributors frequently imply that the hypothesized dysfunctions are mediating vulnerability factors in the development of schizophrenic psychotic symptomatology.

3. Continuity vs. Discontinuity over Time

A somewhat more complicated developmental issue that is introduced by some contributors is whether the abnormal processes that
lead to schizophrenic disorder are continuous or discontinuous over
time. The typical search for vulnerability-linked traits or processes
involves the assumption that an abnormality that contributes to the
predisposition to schizophrenia and to the early developmental
stages of the disorder will remain present after the schizophrenic
symptoms become clear. On the other hand, Venables introduces a
hypothesis that an earlier dysfunctional state may produce a shift in
development that increases the likelihood of later schizophrenia,
but he argues that this dysfunctional state might not continue to be
present during the schizophrenic period. Hypotheses that posit
such developmental shifts in the processes that lead to schizophrenic disorder will require particularly demanding longitudinal research designs to be tested adequately.

4. Etiological Factors vs. Determinants of
Course of Illness

An important difference in emphasis that distinguishes the contributors from each other concerns the degree to which their theories
and data focus on the factors that initially produce schizophrenic
disorder or the factors that determine the course of disorder. Although these factors may be identical for some substantive domains, a conception of schizophrenic disorder as a developmental
process could include shifts in the functional organization of the
individual or his social or biological environment during the
development of the disorder that would alter the nature of possible
subsequent influences. Most of the contributors to this volume
emphasize possible etiological factors in schizophrenic disorders,
but Wallace represents a group of researchers who have chosen the
course of the disorder as their major focus. An interesting corollary
of this distinction may be that theories and data about the etiology of
schizophrenic disorders may have the strongest practical implications for preventive intervention attempts, whereas theories and
data concerning the course of schizophrenic disorders may have
more direct application to the treatment of already disordered
individuals.

5. Functional Significance of Primary Deficits

A frequent theme among the contributors is that certain hypothesized primary deficits in cognitive or affective functioning are important causal factors in schizophrenic symptomatology or impaired social functioning. The contributions reflect an increasing current emphasis on seeking connections between fundamental deficits in elementary psychological or psychobiological processes and specific schizophrenic impairments. This attempt to document the functional significance of elementary deficits reaches its most sophisticated level in attempts to link an elementary cognitive or psychophysiological dysfunction to a specific type of schizophrenic symptom (e.g., Venables's association of electrodermal nonresponsivity to affective flattening and anhedonia). Some of the contributors attempt to make this fine-grained type of connection, whereas others appear to favor broader links between elementary cognitive or other psychological deficits and schizophrenic symptoms as a whole. In light of the diversity of schizophrenic symptom combinations (World Health Organization, 1973, 1979) and the multidimensional nature of schizophrenic outcome (Strauss & Carpenter, 1972, 1974), continued attempts to find relatively specific connections between fundamental psychological deficits and classes of schizophrenic symptoms and social impairments would be desirable.

6. Focus on Subgroups of Schizophrenic Patients

Another frequent feature of the contributions is an emphasis on subgrouping schizophrenic patients, although the subgrouping principles differ widely. Some contributors employ subgroups based on symptom clusters (e.g., paranoid/nonparanoid) or a combination of symptoms and course (e.g., continuous with negative symptoms), whereas others (particularly Cromwell) emphasize the usefulness of using laboratory cognitive and psychophysiological variables (e.g., reaction time crossover) as independent variables to achieve more homogeneous subgroups of schizophrenic patients. The inclusion of such a wide variety of subgrouping strategies within this set of contributions causes the reader to pause at times to wonder whether the differing theoretical concepts across authors refer to the same set of patients. The heterogeneity of schizophrenic disorders in terms of symptoms, outcome, and laboratory variables is frequently a very striking feature in systematic investigations, so the productivity of examining subgroups continues to seem high. However, it remains unclear whether any specific set of subgrouping principles will emerge as most useful across different applications. The familiar paranoid/nonparanoid and process/reactive distinctions still seem to serve many investigators well, but the use of laboratory measures as independent grouping variables is currently increasing.

7. Use of Modern Information-Processing, Attentional, and Neuropsychological Theories

Most of the contributors take advantage of the substantial advances that have been made in recent years in understanding normal human information processing and brain-behavior relationships. The theoretical positions of Knight, Venables, and Magaro draw heavily from contemporary information-processing and attentional theory for conceptions of possible abnormal processes in schizophrenic perception and cognition. Cromwell incorporates some aspects of attentional theory and genetic theory with an emphasis on tasks that have a history of fruitful application to schizophrenia, and Wallace introduces basic information-processing concepts into behavioral treatment research with schizophrenic patients. On the other hand, Salzinger prefers not to apply perspectives from attentional and information-processing theory to the examination of schizophrenic cognition and behavior.

Information-processing theory and related developments in cognitive psychology provide a much more differentiated set of constructs to describe processes that occur between stimulus and response than are available in traditional operant behavior theory (Lachman, Lachman, & Butterfield, 1979; Posner & McLeod, 1982). The impact of this difference in theoretical base is evident in the attempts of Knight, Venables, and Magaro to identify relatively specific stages, strategies, or modes of cognitive processing that are deviant in schizophrenic disorders, whereas Salzinger's immediacy construct is rather undifferentiated in comparison. Another result of the incorporation of contemporary information-processing concepts is an increasing emphasis on a process orientation rather than a structural orientation to descriptions of schizophrenic dysfunctions. The use of neuropsychological concepts of hemispheric specialization by Magaro and Venables (also mentioned by Knight) allows one possible bridge to biological bases of deviant cognition and affect, a link that will be vital for a theory of schizophrenic disorder if it is to account for evidence of genetic factors (Gottesman & Shields, 1976; Kety, 1983; Rosenthal, 1970). Thus, several of the contributors have used recent developments in information-processing and neuropsychological theory to frame their hypotheses, with the result that (a) the nature of the hypothesized deficits is more specific, (b) the deficits are phrased in terms of stages, strategies, or modes of processing, and in some cases (c) the deficits are tied to brain regions that normally specialize in the processing mode that is dysfunctional.

ANALYTIC PROCESSING OF THE INDIVIDUAL CONTRIBUTIONS

I will comment first on the contribution to this volume, by Dr. Cromwell, that evaluates and recommends certain methodological and conceptual approaches to current schizophrenia research. Then I will focus on the contributions of Drs. Magaro and Venables, which emphasize substantive theories of schizophrenic cognition and affect.

Rue Cromwell: Reevaluating the Theoretical Construct of Schizophrenia and the Methods by Which We Examine It

Dr. Cromwell presents us not with a theory of schizophrenia but rather with a way of approaching schizophrenia research. His initial emphasis is on limitations of several traditional approaches, after which he introduces different perspectives as guides to new research strategies.

Dr. Cromwell is particularly effective in demonstrating that premature closure in our conception of schizophrenic disorders may lead us to think that we understand more than we do about their nature and, even more important, may blind us to alternative constructs and research strategies that might be more productive than current ones. His emphasis of this theme is especially timely for American researchers and clinicians, because the recent publication of the *Diagnostic and Statistical Manual of Mental Disorders*, third edition, or *DSM-III* (American Psychiatric Association, 1980), offers a much more explicit and operational definition of schizophrenic disorders than has ever been available in the official nomenclature. The increased precision of definition of this group of disorders and their characteristic symptoms is a major achievement that should improve the reliability of this diagnosis and establish its official boundaries more clearly (Spitzer, Williams, & Skodol, 1980). At the same time, extra care must be taken to avoid the assumption that the *DSM-III* diagnostic criteria offer greater construct validity than any of the other recent sets of reliable diagnostic criteria for schizophrenic disorder (Fenton, Mosher, & Matthews, 1981).

Dr. Cromwell is very critical of the continued strong dependence on historical and cross-sectional clinical symptomatology for definitional criteria and advocates greater focus on criteria that allow prediction of treatment response and prognosis. The distinction between descriptive validity and predictive validity (Blashfield & Draguns, 1976a, 1976b) may help to capture his preference for diagnostic criteria. Descriptive validity, which refers to the degree of homogeneity in symptoms, personality characteristics, and historical factors used in making a diagnosis, is relatively deemphasized by Cromwell. In his view, the criteria for schizophrenic disorders should focus much more strongly on predictive validity, which indexes the extent to which a classification has pragmatic utility for treatment decisions and outcome prediction.

At the present stage in the development of the construct of schizophrenic disorder, increasing emphasis on predictive validity appears appropriate. Attempts to define these disorders and their subtypes on the basis of cross-sectional symptom clustering have already had some impact on our conceptions (e.g., Strauss, Bartko, & Carpenter, 1973; World Health Organization, 1973). Such strategies remain important, in my view, to obtain evidence of descriptive validity in early stages of constructing empirical classification systems, at which point factorial and clustering evidence for symptom-based syndromes is very helpful. For example, classification of childhood psychopathology is currently in this phase (Achenbach & Edelbrock, 1978; Edelbrock & Achenbach, 1980; Nuechterlein, Soli, Garmezy, Devine, & Schaefer, 1981; Soli, Nuechterlein, Garmezy, Devine, & Schaefer, 1981). Dr. Cromwell also appears to see some role for such approaches, as judged by his preference for factorial validity to clinical authority for construction of diagnostic criteria. Our conception of schizophrenic disorders could now benefit from increased focus on predictive utility.

As Dr. Cromwell notes, one of the difficulties in instituting criteria for classifying schizophrenic and related disorders into groupings with greater predictive validity is the relative paucity of research on the predictive value of nonsymptomatic variables. The recent trend to define schizophrenia primarily in terms of positive symptoms that can be reliably rated might have the ironic effect of reducing predictive validity to the extent that it lessens the role of negative symptoms that are predictive of prognosis but have traditionally been difficult to rate reliably (Knight, Roff, Barnett, & Moss, 1979; World Health Organization, 1973). The development of more reliable measures of negative symptoms, such as the scale developed by Andreasen (1982), will, one may hope, facilitate renewed emphasis on such symptoms in future diagnostic criteria. At the present time, one major factor influencing the validity of the operational definitions of schizophrenia for prediction of prognosis appears to be the inclusion of a time criterion for continuing symptoms in some diagnostic systems (Fenton, Mosher, & Matthews, 1981). Although this type of criterion is consistent with the dictum that "the best predictor of future behavior is past behavior," this "wait and see" strategy is of limited utility for clinical treatment decisions and reveals nothing about the factors that determine the course of illness.

I agree with Dr. Cromwell's suggestion that, even with increased emphasis on negative symptoms, adequate predictive validity for groupings of schizophrenic disorders is unlikely to be achieved without greater reliance on nonsymptomatic variables. Initial attempts to use some laboratory measures of electrodermal activity and simple reaction time to predict prognosis have been quite successful (Cancro, Sutton, Kerr, & Sugerman, 1971; Frith, Stevens, Johnstone, & Crow, 1979; Zahn & Carpenter, 1978; Zahn, Carpenter, & McGlashan, 1981). Furthermore, consideration of laboratory measures of possible intrapersonal vulnerability factors in combination with environmental stressors has heuristic value for development of vulnerability-stress interaction predictions (Dawson, Nuechterlein, & Liberman, 1983). In the ongoing prospective longitudinal study of schizophrenic patients in an early phase of illness that I am currently directing at UCLA, my colleagues Michael Dawson, Michael Gitlin,

David Lukoff, Peter Donahoe, Robert Liberman, Karen Snyder, Joseph Ventura, and I are examining the prediction of relapse and illness course that can be achieved through measurement of possible intrapersonal vulnerability factors as well as environmental stressors. Intrapersonal factors involve laboratory measures in attentional, electrodermal, and social skill domains, and social environmental measures include familial expressed emotion and stressful life events. This project is obviously consistent with Dr. Cromwell's emphasis on studying nonsymptomatic predictors and early phases of disorder.

In his fervor to promote new conceptions of schizophrenic disorder, Dr. Cromwell might exaggerate the limitations of our current definitional criteria to some extent. Thus, although I certainly agree with him that a retreat to clinical authority for further development of defining criteria is scientifically indefensible, clinical judgments regarding the presence of schizophrenia have been found to tap a disorder or group of disorders with a genetic component (Kety, 1983; Shields & Gottesman, 1972). Although the genetic predisposition is not specific to schizophrenic disorder as defined by *DSM-III* but appears to include at least the *DSM-III* category of schizotypal personality disorder (Kendler, Gruenberg, & Strauss, 1981), it does not appear to be completely nonspecific because the rates of many mental disorders are not increased significantly among the biological relatives of adopted schizophrenic individuals (Kety, Rosenthal, Wender, Schulsinger, & Jacobsen, 1978) or the adopted-away offspring of a schizophrenic parent (Rosenthal, Wender, Kety, Schulsinger, Welner, & Ostergaard, 1968).

The difficulty, as Dr. Cromwell notes, is that we do not know what form the genetic predisposition takes, nor do we have clear evidence that the genetic component is transmitted through a single major gene rather than through the cumulative effects of multiple genes. However, most current monogenic models include modifier genes and potentiating environmental variables to account for the lack of clear Mendelian transmission patterns, whereas polygenic models often assume that a few genes with unequal effects may account for a large proportion of the genetic variance in the predisposition to schizophrenia (Gottesman & Shields, 1982). Thus, proponents of these two types of genetic models share many assumptions, including the belief that it is not clinical schizophrenia per se that is genetically transmitted, but schizotaxia (Meehl, 1962), schizoidia (Heston, 1970), or certain endophenotypes (Gottesman & Shields, 1972). Furthermore, even some of those favoring multifactorial-polygenic models suggest a search for "partitionable facets of the syndrome . . . on the chance that ordinary twin, adoption, and family studies will reveal one or more of the high-value genes segregating in a clear Mendelian pattern" (Gottesman & Shields, 1982, p. 226). Gottesman & Shields (1982) include neurophysiological and brain scan variables among the suggested "partitionable facets of the syndrome," so their choices of plausible variables for genetic study are not far from the domain chosen by Dr. Cromwell and his colleagues as possible "schizophrenia-related variants." It seems that these genetic theorists share many of Dr. Cromwell's views and that the tendency toward the preemptive thinking that he criticizes is not universal.

A final issue is whether schizophrenia-related variants, once they are found, should be used as defining criteria for disorders that replace our current symptomatic grouping called schizophrenic disorders. The criteria for a schizophrenia-related variant are similar to those for vulnerability markers for schizophrenia as proposed by Spring and Zubin (1978), but allow more flexibility in the strength and the specificity of their relationship to clinically defined schizophrenia. Some flexibility in the relationship to current definitions of schizophrenia does seem critical, as Dr. Cromwell notes, if we are to avoid fruitless attempts to find variables that predict faulty symptomatic groupings with a very high degree of accuracy. Lack of specificity to schizophrenia as compared to other disordered states also need not eliminate a variable from consideration, Dr. Cromwell argues, because such a variable may nevertheless shed light on disordered processes that are common to several different clinical symptom patterns.

In my view, the usefulness of a schizophrenia-related variant as a new defining criterion for a reclassification of schizophrenic and related disorders does depend to some extent on its distribution and role in disorders other than clinical schizophrenia. It is true that abnormalities that occur across several disorders with quite different symptomatic patterns may be enormously useful in isolating similar disordered processes that contribute to each of the symptom patterns. However, this function of aiding understanding of common underlying processes may need clearer separation from utility as a diagnostic criterion.

Some variables may be related to factors that play a role in such a wide variety of clinical conditions that grouping the conditions together on this basis may underemphasize other critical etiological, symptomatic, and treatment considerations. To use an extreme example, we might find that low levels of general verbal intelligence predict poorer occupational adaptation among persons with various psychopathological conditions. If we used some current definitions of schizophrenia that include poor outcome (including work impairment) as a criterion, we might also find that schizophrenic patients were more likely to have low general verbal intelligence than normal individuals or persons with disorders that did not include poor work outcome as a defining criterion. This relationship with schizophrenia might be significant but not strong. By examining the families of these schizophrenic patients, we might discover that low verbal intelligence was more common in their first-degree relatives than in the general population. Moreover, low verbal intelligence might be found to be a relatively stable "abnormality" that was present before, during, and after the onset of psychotic symptoms in a subgroup of schizophrenic patients. However, despite the fact that this factor might meet the criteria for a schizophrenia-related variant and might predict work outcome, I think that Dr. Cromwell would agree that it should not be used as one of the defining criteria for schizophrenia or for a new diagnosis of low-verbal-intelligence schizophrenia.

General liability factors, such as the one in this fictitious but plausible example, might be more effectively incorporated into diagnostic systems through multiaxial approaches, as illustrated by *DSM-III*. Despite their weakness as defining criteria for a diagnosis, these relatively nonspecific factors may play a very important role in understanding the onset and course of a disorder and may be important considerations in treatment decisions.

By contrast with the example of low verbal intelligence, the possible schizophrenia-related variants that Dr. Cromwell has cited seem to have a much stronger relationship to clinical schizophrenia. Furthermore, to the extent that these abnormalities are not specific to clinical schizophrenia, their presence in a limited number of other disorders may indicate some common processes or end-products without reaching this same level of nonspecificity. The worthy challenge that Dr. Cromwell has placed before us, then, is to find those nonsymptomatic variables that are sufficiently related to our current conception of schizophrenic disorders to play a major role in their etiology, symptoms, treatment response, and prognosis. At the same time, we should not despair if our variables tap similar abnormalities in a few other syndromes, but should strive to understand the underlying common processes and their mode of familial transmission.

Peter Magaro: The Dimensions of Severe Psychopathology as a Cognitive Style Preference

Dr. Magaro presents a very interesting initial discussion of the relationship between psychosis and schizophrenia that emphasizes separation of dimensions of psychopathology. He then describes a theory of cognitive processes in paranoid and nonparanoid schizophrenia that is very creative synthesis of a large body of research on information processing and hemispheric specialization in these disorders. This theory posits that paranoid schizophrenia occurs in persons who prefer controlled processing, a mode that is associated with the left hemisphere, whereas nonparanoid schizophrenia occurs in persons who prefer automatic processing, which is associated with the right hemisphere. Finally, Dr. Magaro attempts to describe the effect of psychosis on information-processing performance and hemispheric bias for sensory input within the framework of preferences for controlled versus automatic processing strategies.

The initial discussion of the dimensions of psychopathology indicates the complexity of the phenomena that are under study. Dr. Magaro recognizes that psychosis is not unique to schizophrenia and that the characteristics and effects of psychosis need separation from any characteristics that are more specific to schizophrenic disorders. This emphasis is consistent with the increasing focus on trait/state issues and developmental approaches that I noted earlier as frequent themes in this volume. Dr. Magaro argues persuasively that we need to consider not only the extent of the symptomatology during psychotic episodes, but also the suddenness of onset (process-reactive dimension) and the duration of the illness to isolate any specific characteristics of schizophrenic disorders among individuals who already have a full-blown psychosis.

After reviewing several alternative procedures for separating the characteristics of psychosis from those of schizophrenia, Dr. Magaro suggests that the two major strategies to control for level of psychosis are (1) to measure the subject dimensions of level of thought disorder, process vs. reactive onset, and chronicity and to examine their relationships to the dependent variables and (2) to compare schizophrenic subjects with other groups that share the same level of psychosis as well as with nonpsychotic groups. Both strategies are useful in examining correlates of psychosis but certain limitations should be emphasized. First, the general effects of psychosis may be evident in correlations between measures of the level of psychosis and dependent variables in studies of psychotic populations, but one cannot appropriately control for these effects through use of the psychosis measure as a covariate in an analysis of covariance (e.g., Pic'l, Magaro, & Wade, 1979). Because the psychosis is an effect or an integral part of the schizophrenic disorder rather than an independent factor related to the dependent variable, the use of a psychosis measure as a covariate violates the assumptions of analysis of covariance (Huitema, 1980).

Second, the examination of actively psychotic schizophrenic patients, even in comparison with nonschizophrenic patients with an equivalent level of psychosis, cannot provide any direct evidence that certain characteristics of schizophrenia are trait-like vulnerability indicators. Studies of preschizophrenic individuals, patients with remitted schizophrenic disorder, and individuals with related but nonpsychotic conditions are necessary to shed light on possible fundamental characteristics that are associated with schizophrenic disorder outside of the psychotic period. Research on hemispheric dysfunctions, activation, and processing preferences within schizophrenia has thus far focused primarily on actively symptomatic schizophrenic patients. Therefore, the current data base is not sufficient to allow strong inferences about the role of such factors beyond these symptomatic periods. Promising recent attempts to extend the current data base by examining hemispheric effects across symptomatic and relatively nonsymptomatic states within the same patients (e.g., Johnson & Crockett, 1982) are noted by Dr. Magaro in one of his later sections.

Finally, as Dr. Magaro notes, we will need to be clearer about our conception of psychosis and its operational definitions if we hope to separate any general characteristics of psychosis from those of schizophrenic disorders. In DSM-III, psychosis refers to "gross impairment in reality testing" and includes delusions, hallucinations, and grossly bizarre behavior, including incoherence without awareness that one is not being understood (American Psychiatric Association, 1980). This conception corresponds rather well to the Thought Disturbance factor from the widely used Brief Psychiatric

Rating Scale (Guy, Cleary, & Bonato, 1975; Overall & Gorham, 1962) and to Dr. Magaro's use of the term "thought disorder" (assuming that he includes reality-distorting disorders in the form and content of thought). By this definition, only a subgroup of patients with major affective disorders manifest psychosis. Thus, simply comparing schizophrenic and affectively disordered groups does not ensure control for level of psychosis. I concur with Dr. Magaro's suggestion that an independent measure of the level of thought disturbance would be helpful in such designs to assess the equality of the level of current psychosis. In addition, a subset of affectively disordered patients might need to be selected to match the level of psychosis to that of the schizophrenic patients, if controlling for general level of psychosis was the major reason for inclusion of an affective disorder comparison group. This procedure, on the other hand, would result in the selection of a nonrepresentative affective disorder group, so findings from that group could not be generalized to a broader affective disorder population.

Dr. Magaro's emphasis on separate dimensions for levels of paranoid and schizophrenic pathology is an intriguing variation on the typical single dimension (usually treated as a dichotomy) from paranoid schizophrenia to nonparanoid schizophrenia. This conception is attractive because it allows various *DSM-III* diagnoses that share phenomenological features to be grouped along two dimensions of severity. However, whether the diagnoses on a dimension share a common etiology is quite unclear. Furthermore, although these separate dimensions have been retained in the subscales of the Maine Scale of Paranoid and Nonparanoid Schizophrenia (Magaro, Abrams, & Cantrell, 1981), Magaro's theory of preferred cognitive processing styles and associated hemispheric activity implies that paranoid and nonparanoid schizophrenia may be opposite poles of a single dimension. Thus, the existence of two symptomatic dimensions needs to be reconciled with the proposal that paranoid and nonparanoid schizophrenic patients are characterized by preferences for controlled, left hemisphere processing, and automatic, right hemispheric processing, respectively.

The theory of paranoid and nonparanoid schizophrenic cognition that Dr. Magaro presents is a highly creative and scholarly synthesis of several different human information-processing models and a wide range of experimental data from psychopathological groups. The extensive use of current information-processing and neuropsychological concepts as the underlying broad theoretical base allows the rapid progress in cognitive sciences to be applied to studies of schizophrenic cognition.

It is unfortunate for the study of psychopathological processes that the rapid growth of knowledge about normal human information processing has not yet been accompanied by general agreement among theorists on the most useful partitioning of specific stages, levels, or strategies of processing. Because Dr. Magaro has drawn from several different conceptions of information processing for his distinctions between paranoid and nonparanoid schizophrenic cognition, an examination of some differing assumptions of these information-processing models may help to highlight possible sources of confusion in their application to schizophrenic cognition.

Dr. Magaro draws the distinction between automatic and controlled processes most directly from Shiffrin and Schneider (1977), who emphasize the role played by practice with consistent associations between certain stimuli and certain categories (particularly distractor vs. target) in the development of automatic processes. Yet the experimental data to which he applies this distinction do not examine primarily the development of automatic processing over a training period, so one of the clearest procedures that was used by Shiffrin and Schneider (1977) to discriminate automatic and controlled processing is not emphasized. Instead, differences in the processing of number, letter, and dot arrays as a function of array size and presence of distractors, often averaged across blocks of trials at different stages of practice, become a major focus for distinctions between different models of information processing. In particular, Dr. Magaro uses the finding that performance declines as a function of the array size as evidence of controlled, serial processing. Following Schneider and Shiffrin (1977), he also uses a flat slope for performance as a function of array size as evidence of automatic, parallel processing.

The conditions under which Dr. Magaro examines performance as a function of array size differ from those employed by Schneider and Shiffrin (1977) in ways that make the correspondence of a flat slope to automatic processing less convincing. Pic'l, Magaro, & Wade (1979) used dot enumeration, a task that does not entail the search for target configurations (letters or numbers) among nontargets, and examined counting accuracy rather than reaction time as the performance index. Poorer than normal accuracy across array size, even for the smallest array (three dots), for the nonparanoid schizophrenic group, could easily reflect guessing or poor perceptual sensitivity for near-threshold dot stimuli rather than automatic, parallel processing. The fact that the dot enumeration task in this study did not show any trend toward a right hemisphere advantage among nonparanoid schizophrenics adds further doubt regarding the interpretation of their performance as reflective of automatic, parallel processing.

The conditions under which nonparanoid schizophrenic patients obtained a relatively flat reaction time slope as a function of memory set size in the Broga and Neufeld (1981) study also do not favor a clear distinction between automatic and controlled processing. The Sternberg choice reaction time task conditions involved changing the memory set across trials rather than using a fixed memory set. Automatic, parallel processing is very unlikely to be involved under these circumstances (Schneider & Shiffrin, 1977). Furthermore, because the paranoid-nonparanoid differences involved different types of stimulus displays (memory set item present vs. absent), I would agree with the interpretation by Broga and Neufeld (1981) that response decision aspects subsequent to the scanning of the memory set were the likely source of the flat reaction time function for nonparanoid schizophrenic patients.

Certain aspects of Dr. Magaro's position seem to be more consistent with information-processing distinctions other than that of Shiffrin and Schneider (1977). For example, the use of Neisser's visual search lists (Chamrad, 1982) sheds more light on differences in the usage of preattentive processes as compared to focal attention than on differences in automatic and controlled processing. Although the two distinctions have some common implications, Neisser's (1967) emphasis on the role of relatively crude physical differences among stimuli in preattentive discrimination is more closely connected to the experimental manipulation of target-distractor similarity. Thus, the fact that paranoid schizophrenics scan visual search lists slowly even when distractors are dissimilar from targets (Chamrad, 1982) is most relevant to a conclusion that they use focal attention in a situation in which most subjects rely more on preattentive processing to isolate targets.

The distinction between data-driven and conceptually driven processing (Norman & Bobrow, 1976) also seems more apt than that of automatic and controlled processing for Dr. Magaro's emphasis on the strong reliance of paranoid schizophrenic patients on a rigid conceptual guiding of information processing. In Shiffrin and Schneider's (1977) model, the initial encoding of all stimuli is an automatic, relatively passive process that can be supplemented by controlled processing under voluntary control. Thus, they argue against the role of active stimulus selection in the initial encoding of stimuli, in contrast to "early selection" positions such as that of Broadbent (1971).

These differing assumptions within models of normal information processing preclude a synthesis of views that retains all of the features of the original models. Dr. Magaro's extraction of aspects of several models is a creative attempt to retain the most useful features of each for interpretation of a wide range of experimental paradigms. Further clarification of the assumptions of his synthesized model of normal information processing will be useful in resolving apparent differences in basic assumptions and data interpretation that arise across the original models.

Peter Venables: Left Hemisphere Overactivity May Be a Result of Right Hemisphere Dysfunction

Dr. Venables presents a very scholarly and integrative developmental theory of schizophrenia that examines the areas of information processing and hemispheric dysfunction as well as certain aspects of emotional functioning. Because he examines many of the same topics that are explored by Dr. Magaro, the fact that he concludes that chronic, continuous schizophrenia may be characterized by a primary right hemisphere dysfunction is startling at first. Dr. Magaro, we recall, posits that the disorder that he considers to represent the central schizophrenic type (nonparanoid schizophrenia) is characterized by a preference for right hemisphere processing. Dr. Magaro argues that these nonparanoid schizophrenic patients are impaired primarily in tasks in which automatic, parallel right hemisphere processing is not adaptive. Although Dr. Venables agrees that schizophrenic patients show performance deficits in tasks that involve left hemisphere processing, he proposes that these may be due to overloading the left hemisphere to compensate for a primary right hemisphere dysfunction.

Dr. Venables's theory shares many of the basic virtues that were described in connection with Dr. Magaro's position. Dr. Venables shows a similar remarkable talent for synthesis of very diverse sources of data. His wide-ranging formulation provides bridges between sets of data that appeared previously to be quite unrelated or contradictory. Furthermore, Dr. Venables also presents his theory within the framework of current models of information processing and hemispheric functioning, thereby drawing on some of the same conceptual principles and distinctions that Dr. Magaro employs.

Although the reasoning that leads Drs. Venables and Magaro to different conclusions differs in several areas, their interpretation of perceptual organization studies appears crucial to a consideration of fundamental differences. Their divergent interpretation of the data of the second study of Schwartz-Place and Gilmore (1980) serves to illustrate their respective points of view. Schwartz-Place and Gilmore (1980) asked subjects to report the number of lines presented within brief presentations of arrays that varied in line orientation and grouping. The control subjects performed most accurately when lines were of identical orientation and were less accurate when lines differed in orientation and were nonadjacent. Process schizophrenic subjects, on the other hand, were unaffected by the manipulations of the stimulus organizational quality and were actually more accurate than the control subjects because of this. Dr. Magaro interprets these results to indicate that the schizophrenic patients did not organize the lines into a "conceptual grouping" according to orientation and proximity. Therefore, they had more time for counting due to "not spending the time switching between line gestalts." Dr. Magaro views the results as consistent with the reliance of nonparanoid schizophrenics on perceptual data with relatively little categorization from conceptual processes.

Dr. Venables interprets the same results as indicating a deficit in the initial preattentive, global analysis process among process schizophrenic patients. (This interpretation is also favored by Schwartz-Place and Gilmore [1980] and Dr. Knight.) Dr. Venables suggests later that the initial preattentive, global analysis deficit is associated with the right hemisphere. In contrast, Dr. Magaro views the weakness in use of conceptual grouping to guide controlled processing as associated with the left hemisphere. Thus, an important factor in the divergence of these theories concerns whether the perceptual organization of stimuli in such situations is considered an initial preattentive process or the application of a conceptual grouping to guide encoding. The issue of whether initial encoding of stimuli is a preattentive, relatively passive process or a conceptually driven, constructive process, or a combination is currently a matter of debate in cognitive psychology (Broadbent, 1977; Broadbent & Broadbent, 1980; Neisser, 1976; Norman &

Bobrow, 1976; Posner, 1978, 1982; Shiffrin & Schneider, 1977), so it is not surprising that this would be a source of theoretical divergence among experimental psychopathologists as well.

As Dr. Venables notes in his alternative interpretation of the Schwartz-Place and Gilmore (1980) results, some contemporary cognitive theorists view initial encoding and stimulus recognition as involving an early passive, holistic process that can be primed by a later active, analytic process through semantic context (e.g., Broadbent, 1977). His alternative interpretation of the Schwartz-Place and Gilmore (1980) results in terms of a failure in this priming process is compatible with Dr. Magaro's position. Additional research to tease apart these two possible interpretations of perceptual organization deficits in schizophrenia is clearly a difficult but important next step.

The basic idea that a dysfunction in processes that are usually completed in a preattentive, rapid, passive, automatic fashion would also lead to reduced performance in tasks that demand resources from a limited-capacity focal attention system is an appealing one. I have suggested elsewhere (Nuechterlein, 1982) that a dysfunction in the automaticity of the process of encoding very familiar stimuli (Posner, 1978; Schneider & Shiffrin, 1977) might help to reconcile indications that process schizophrenic patients are deficient not only in controlled, serial rehearsal processes (Oltmanns, 1978) but also in rapid recognition of single familiar letters (Braff & Saccuzzo, 1981; Saccuzzo & Braff, 1981). Completion of usually automatic functions through the use of attention-demanding processes would be less efficient and would reduce the processing resources that are available for serial comparisons, rehearsal, reasoning, and other analytic processes. Dr. Knight presents a very thoughtful consideration of the implications of possible deficits in automatic aspects of perceptual organization in his paper within this volume. The major limitation of these hypotheses regarding process schizophrenic deficits in preattentive or automatic processes at this time seems to be the lack of convincing direct evidence that these processes are faulty and that their functions are completed through the use of slower serial processes.

A few additional crucial points in the argument presented by Dr. Venables should also be highlighted. One concerns the use of verbal IQ as an index of central processing. Central-processing efficiency would certainly be a factor in verbal IQ scores, but these scores are a global final product of input, central-processing, and output capabilities and therefore may be impaired by deficits at any or all of these levels. Moreover, the data on verbal IQ impairments in the premorbid period for schizophrenic patients and among offspring of schizophrenic patients do not allow a determination of the direction of the causal arrow. It is as yet unclear whether low verbal IQ (or poor central processing) is a factor in predisposing some individuals to chronic, continuous schizophrenia or whether early subclinical processes leading toward schizophrenia produce impaired verbal IQ.

Another question concerns Dr. Venables's argument that impaired verbal IQ in preschizophrenic and high-risk populations may be due to processing both visuo-spatial and verbal material in the left hemisphere due to a primary dysfunction in the right hemisphere. If verbal IQ is impaired due to the increased competition for functional cerebral space (Kinsbourne & Hicks, 1978), why are the visual-spatial processes indexed by performance IQ not equally impaired? If anything, one might expect visual-spatial processes to be more impaired in this situation, because the left hemisphere would not be specialized in these functions.

In the development of the argument regarding the connection of electrodermal responsivity, anhedonia, and continuous schizophrenia, two links in particular require additional empirical examination. Dr. Venables suggests that electrodermal nonresponsivity among schizophrenic patients with prominent negative symptoms and among nonschizophrenic anhedonics selected by the Chapmans' Anhedonia Scale (Chapman, Chapman, & Raulin, 1976) may make this psychophysiological anomaly a promising screening tool for selection of children at elevated risk for schizophrenia. The first link that needs strengthening is whether persons from the general population selected on the basis of anhedonia do indeed have a substantially heightened risk of later schizophrenia. A second, related link concerns the specificity of electrodermal nonresponsivity to schizophrenia. A nonspecific relationship to schizophrenic and other severe psychopathological disorders may indicate important common processes in these disorders, but would move the electrodermal nonresponsivity from the status of a specific liability factor to that of a more general liability contributor. A review of the available evidence indicates that the specificity of the electrodermal nonresponsivity to schizophrenic disorders is not complete but the boundaries of its incidence in the other psychiatric disorders need additional examination (Dawson & Nuechterlein, in press).

These comments on certain weaker links in Dr. Venables's argument are not meant to diminish the recognition that he has presented a very creative, scholarly, and synthetic model of the development of chronic, continuous schizophrenia. Theoretical positions such as those presented by Drs. Venables and Magaro by necessity ignore a large amount of "noise" in their attempts to detect the "signals" in a large and diverse literature. Their formulations will have served their purpose if they generate appropriate, well-directed attempts to test their central hypotheses, which is all the more likely because of their disagreement at certain fundamental junctures. If a revised classification of the disorders that we now term schizophrenic is established during these efforts, I suspect that Dr. Cromwell will be pleased.

REFERENCES

Achenbach, T. M., & Edelbrock, C. S. The classification of child psychopathology: A review and analysis of empirical efforts. *Psychological Bulletin*, 1978, **85**, 1275–1301.

American Psychiatric Association. *Diagnostic and statistical manual of mental disorders* (3rd ed.) Washington, D.C.: Author, 1980.

Andreasen, N. C. Negative symptoms in schizophrenia: Definition and reliability. *Archives of General Psychiatry*, 1982, **39**, 784–788.

Asarnow, R. F., & MacCrimmon, D. J. Attention/information processing, neuropsychological functioning and thought disorder during the acute and partial recovery phases of schizophrenia: A longitudinal study. *Psychiatry Research*, 1982, **7**, 309–319.

Blashfield, R. K., & Draguns, J. G. Evaluative criteria for psychiatric classification. *Journal of Abnormal Psychology*, 1976, **85**, 140–150. (a)

Blashfield, R. K., & Draguns, J. G. Toward a taxonomy of psychopathology: The purpose of psychiatric classification. *British Journal of Psychiatry*, 1976, **129**, 574–583. (b)

Braff, D. L., & Saccuzzo, D. P. Information processing dysfunction in paranoid schizophrenia: A two-factor deficit. *American Journal of Psychiatry*, 1981, **138**, 1051–1056.

Broadbent, D. E. *Decision and stress*. London: Academic Press, 1971.

Broadbent, D. E. The hidden pre-attentive process. *American Psychologist*, 1977, **32**, 109–118.

Broadbent, D. E., & Broadbent, M. H. P. Priming and the passive/active model of word recognition. In R. S. Nickerson (Ed.), *Attention and performance VIII*. Hillsdale, N.J.: Lawrence Erlbaum Associates, 1980.

Broga, M., & Neufeld, R. Multivariate cognitive performance levels and response styles among paranoid and nonparanoid schizophrenics. *Journal of Abnormal Psychology*, 1981, **90**, 495–509.

341
Discussion

Cancro, R., Sutton, S., Kerr, J. B., & Sugerman, A. A. Reaction time and prognosis in acute schizophrenia. *Journal of Nervous and Mental Disease,* 1971, **153,** 351–359.

Chamrad, D. Letter detection of paranoid and nonparanoid schizophrenics. Unpublished master's thesis, Ohio State University, 1982.

Chapman, L. J., Chapman, J. P., & Raulin, M. L. Scales for physical and social anhedonia. *Journal of Abnormal Psychology,* 1976, **85,** 374–382.

Cromwell, R. L., & Spaulding, W. How schizophrenics handle information. In W. E. Fann, I. Karacan, A. D. Pokorny, & R. L. Williams (Eds.), *Phenomenology and treatment of schizophrenia.* New York: Spectrum Publications, 1978.

Dawson, M. E., & Nuechterlein, K. H. Electrodermal and other psychophysiological dysfunctions in the developmental course of schizophrenic disorders. *Schizophrenia Bulletin,* in press.

Dawson, M. E., Nuechterlein, K. H., & Liberman, R. P. Relapse in schizophrenic disorders: Possible contributing factors and implications for behavior therapy. In M. Rosenbaum, C. M. Franks, & Y. Jaffe (Eds.), *Perspectives on behavior therapy in the eighties.* New York: Springer, 1983.

Edelbrock, C., & Achenbach, T. M. A typology of child behavior profile patterns: Distribution and correlates for disturbed children aged 6–16. *Journal of Abnormal Child Psychology,* 1980, **8,** 441–470.

Fenton, W. S., Mosher, L. R., & Matthews, S. M. Diagnosis of schizophrenia: A critical review of current diagnostic systems. *Schizophrenia Bulletin,* 1981, **7,** 452–476.

Frame, C. L., & Oltmanns, T. F. Serial recall by schizophrenic and affective patients during and after psychotic episodes. *Journal of Abnormal Psychology,* 1982, **91,** 311–318.

Frith, C. D., Stevens, M., Johnstone, E. C., & Crow, T. J. Skin conductance responsivity during acute episodes of schizophrenia as a predictor of symptomatic improvement. *Psychological Medicine,* 1979, **9,** 101–106.

Gottesman, I. I., & Shields, J. *Schizophrenia and genetics: A twin study vantage point.* New York: Academic Press, 1972.

Gottesman, I. I., & Shields, J. A critical review of recent adoption, twin and family studies of schizophrenia: Behavioral genetics perspectives. *Schizophrenia Bulletin,* 1976, **2,** 360–398.

Gottesman, I. I., & Shields, J. *Schizophrenia: The epigenetic puzzle.* Cambridge: Cambridge University Press, 1982.

Guy, W., Cleary, P., & Bonato, R. R. Methodological implications of a large central data system. In *Proceedings of IXth Congress, CINP.* Amsterdam: Excerpta Medica, 1975.

Heston, L. L. The genetics of schizophrenia and schizoid disease. *Science,* 1970, **167,** 249–256.

Huitema, B. E. *The analysis of covariance and alternatives.* New York: Wiley, 1980.

Johnson, O., & Crockett, D. Changes in perceptual assymetries with clinical improvement of depression and schizophrenia. *Journal of Abnormal Psychology*, 1982, **91**, 45–54.

Kendler, K. S., Gruenberg, A. M., & Strauss, J. S. An independent analysis of the Copenhagen sample of the Danish Adoption Study of Schizophrenia: I. The relationship between schizotypal personality disorder and schizophrenia. *Archives of General Psychiatry*, 1981, **38**, 982–984.

Kety, S. S. Mental illness in the biological and adoptive relatives of schizophrenic adoptees: Findings relevant to genetic and environmental factors in etiology. *American Journal of Psychiatry*, 1983, **140**, 720–727.

Kety, S. S. Rosenthal, D., Wender, P. H., Schulsinger, F., & Jacobsen, B. The biologic and adoptive families of adoptive individuals who become schizophrenic: Prevalence of mental illness and other characteristics. In L. C. Wynne, R. L. Cromwell, & S. Matthysse (Eds.), *The nature of schizophrenia: New approaches to research and treatment.* New York: Wiley, 1978.

Kinsbourne, M. Hemispheric specialization and the growth of human understanding. *American Psychologist*, 1982, **37**, 411–420.

Kinsbourne, M., & Hicks, R. E. Functional cerebral space: A model for overflow, transfer and interference effects in human performance. In J. Requin (Ed.), *Attention and performance VII.* Hillsdale, N.J.: Lawrence Erlbaum Associates, 1978.

Knight, R. A., Roff, J. D., Barnett, J. & Moss, J. L. Concurrent and predictive validity of thought disorder and affectivity: A 22-year follow-up of acute schizophrenics. *Journal of Abnormal Psychology*, 1979, **88**, 1–12.

Laasi, N., Nuechterlein, K. H., & Edell, W. S. Serial recall deficit in schizophrenia: State or trait? Paper presented at the meeting of the Western Psychological Association, San Francisco, April 1983.

Lachman, R., Lachman, J. L., & Butterfield, E. *Cognitive psychology and information processing.* Hillsdale, N.J.: Lawrence Erlbaum Associates, 1979.

Magaro, P. A., Abrams, L., & Cantrell, P. The Maine Scale of Paranoid and Nonparanoid Schizophrenia: Reliability and validity. *Journal of Clinical and Consulting Psychology*, 1981, **49**, 438–447.

Meehl, P. E. Schizotaxia, schizotypy, schizophrenia. *American Psychologist*, 1962, **17**, 827–838.

Neisser, U. *Cognitive psychology.* New York: Appleton-Century-Crofts, 1967.

Neisser, U. *Cognition and reality: Principles and implications of cognitive psychology.* San Francisco: Freeman, 1976.

Norman, D. A., & Bobrow, D. G. On the role of active memory processes in perception and cognition. In C. N. Cofer (Ed.), *The structure of human memory.* San Francisco: Freeman, 1976.

Nuechterlein, K. H. Schizophrenic information-processing deficit: What type or level of processing is disordered? *The Behavioral and Brain Sciences*, 1982, **5**, 609–610.

Nuechterlein, K. H., Soli, S. D., Garmezy, N., Devine, V. T., & Schaefer, S. M. A classification system for research in childhood psychopathology: Part II. Validation research examining converging descriptions from the parent and from the child. In B. A. Maher and W. B. Maher (Eds.), *Progress in experimental personality research* (Vol. 10). New York: Academic Press, 1981.

Oltmanns, T. F. Selective attention in schizophrenic and manic psychosis: The effect of distraction on information processing. *Journal of Abnormal Psychology*, 1978, **81**, 212–225.

Overall, J. E., & Gorham, D. R. The brief psychiatric rating scale. *Psychological Reports*, 1962, **10**, 799–812.

Pic'l, A. K., Magaro, P. A., & Wade, E. A. Hemispheric functioning in paranoid and nonparanoid schizophrenia. *Biological Psychiatry*, 1979, **14**, 891–903.

Posner, M. I. *Chronometric explorations of mind: The third Paul M. Fitts lectures.* Hillsdale, N.J.: Lawrence Erlbaum Associates, 1978.

Posner, M. I. Cumulative development of attentional theory. *American Psychologist*, 1982, **37**, 168–179.

Posner, M. I., & McLeod, P. Information processing models—In search of elementary operations. *Annual Review of Psychology*, 1982, **33**, 477–514.

Rosenthal, D. *Genetic theory and abnormal behavior.* New York: McGraw-Hill, 1970.

Rosenthal, D., Wender, P. H., Kety S. S., Schulsinger, F., Welner, J., & Ostergaard, L. Schizophrenics' offspring reared in adoptive homes. In D. Rosenthal & S. S. Kety (Eds.), *The transmission of schizophrenia.* London: Pergamon, 1968.

Saccuzzo, D. P., & Braff, D. L. Early information processing deficit in schizophrenia: New findings using schizophrenic subgroups and manic control subjects. *Archives of General Psychiatry*, 1981, **38**, 174–179.

Schneider, W., & Shiffrin, R. M. Controlled and automatic human information processing: I. Detection, search, and attention. *Psychological Review*, 1977, **84**, 1–66.

Schwartz-Place, E. J., & Gilmore, G. C. Perceptual organization in schizophrenia. *Journal of Abnormal Psychology*, 1980, **89**, 409–418.

Shields, J., & Gottesman, I. I. Cross-national diagnosis of schizophrenia in twins. *Archives of General Psychiatry*, 1972, **27**, 725–780.

Shiffrin, R. M., & Schneider, W. Controlled and automatic human information processing: II. Perceptual learning, automatic attending, and a general theory. *Psychological Review*, 1977, **84**, 127–190.

Soli, S. D., Nuechterlein, K. H., Garmezy, N., Devine, V. T., & Schaefer, S. M. A classification system for research in childhood psychopathology: Part I. An empirical approach using factor and cluster analyses and conjunctive decision rules. In B. A. Maher & W. B. Maher (Eds.), *Progress in experimental personality research* (Vol. 10). New York: Academic Press, 1981.

Spitzer, R. L., Williams, J. B. W., & Skodol, A. E. DSM-III: The major achievements and an overview. *American Journal of Psychiatry*, 1980, **137**, 151–164.

Spring, B. J., & Zubin, J. Attention and information processing as indicators of vulnerability to schizophrenic episodes. *Journal of Psychiatric Research*, 1978, **14**, 289–302.

Strauss, J. S., Bartko, J. J., & Carpenter, W. T. The use of clustering techniques for the classification of psychiatric patients. *British Journal of Psychiatry*, 1973, **122**, 531–540.

Strauss, J. S., & Carpenter, W. T. The prediction of outcome in schizophrenia I. Characteristics of outcome. *Archives of General Psychiatry*, 1972, **27**, 739–746.

Strauss, J. S., & Carpenter, W. T. The prediction of outcome in schizophrenia II. Relationships between predictor and outcome variables. *Archives of General Psychiatry*. 1974, **31**, 37–42.

World Health Organization. *The International Pilot Study of Schizophrenia*. Geneva: Author, 1973.

World Health Organization. *Schizophrenia: An international follow-up study*. New York: Wiley, 1979.

Zahn, T. P., & Carpenter, W. T. Effects of short-term outcome and clinical improvement on reaction time in acute schizophrenia. *Journal of Psychiatric Research*, 1978, **14**, 59–68.

Zahn, T. P., Carpenter, W. T., & McGlashan, T. H. Autonomic nervous system activity in acute schizophrenia II. Relationships to short term prognosis and clinical state. *Archives of General Psychiatry*, 1981, **38**, 260–266.

Zubin, J., & Spring, B. Vulnerability—A new view of schizophrenia. *Journal of Abnormal Psychology*, 1977, **86**, 103–126.

Discussion

Herbert E. Spohn

The Menninger Foundation

INTRODUCTION

*B*efore launching into my commentary, I think it behooves me to present my credentials as a discussant of the excellent chapters by Dr. Knight, Dr. Salzinger, and Dr. Wallace. Having performed extensive experimental psychopathological studies of attention dysfunction in schizophrenia, albeit from a task-oriented perspective, provides me with some qualifications to comment knowledgeably on both Knight's and Salzinger's chapters. Earlier in my career I was concerned with the effects of social structure in mental hospitals on the behavior and course of illness in chronic schizophrenic patients. Insofar as my work during that period entailed the development and evaluation of social skills training programs, I can bring a modest degree of expertise to bear on Wallace's chapter.

More recently I have been occupied with a series of methodological studies whose aim was and continues to be to determine the degree and direction of effects of antipsychotic medication on cognitive and psychophysiological dysfunction, predominantly in chronic schizophrenics. The data and knowledge base I have acquired in the course of these studies constitutes the major contextual framework for my comments on Knight's and Wallace's chapters.

COMMENTS ON R. G. KNIGHT'S CHAPTER

In the past fifteen years several significant, innovative trends have emerged in schizophrenia research. As evidence for a genetic loading in schizophrenic spectrum disorders gained widespread credibility, the search for markers of vulnerability attained considerable momentum. Experimental tests of classical and modern theories of formal thought disorder have given way to scale-building efforts designed to describe thought disorder by psychometrically sound instruments. An explosion of new knowledge of brain functioning has found its way into schizophrenia research concerned with cognitive dysfunction via neurophysiological concepts and electrophysiological measurement techniques. And finally, information-processing models and methods derived from cognitive science have rather gradually gained favor with experimental psychopathologists. Investigators in this area, however, have displayed some uncertainty, even discomfort, about such models and methods, typically reflected in the ambivalent phrase "attention/information-processing dysfunction." It was this phrase that designated a section of presentations at the Second International Rochester Conference on Schizophrenia in 1978. Such uncertainty derives in part from a lack of thoroughgoing familiarity with the complex and voluminous empirical and theoretical literature in this area. Moreover, until now no one has systematically thought through the conceptual and methodological implications of the utilization of information-processing models and methodology in the study of cognitive dysfunction in schizophrenia. In his chapter, Knight has undertaken this task in a most creditable fashion.

He makes a cogently argued, persuasively reasoned, comprehensive case for the application of the "process-oriented" strategy to the elucidation of cognitive dysfunction in schizophrenia. Through examples from his own research and through an apt appraisal of the applicability of converging contemporary information-processing models to the understanding of early visual-processing deficit, he demonstrates the explanatory power of information-processing models and the efficiency of process-oriented methodology. He calls for the abandonment of atheoretical approaches to cognitive dysfunction in favor of guidance by theoretical models and provides ingenious strategic solutions to the general deficit problem, thus legitimizing the process-oriented approach and setting the stage for a new departure in programmatic schizophrenia research.

The bulk of my additional comments on Knight's chapter will concern the proposition that in both task-oriented and process-oriented approaches the effect of antipsychotic drug treatment on cognitive function is a methodological problem as serious as the general cognitive deficit problem in its consequences for the interpretation of experimental findings. But first I shall set forth some mildly critical concerns about the process-oriented approach.

As an investigator who came of age professionally in a task-oriented era, I do want to set straight the historical record of task-oriented strategies. I think in his polemic zeal Knight over-states the atheoretical nature of task-oriented research. The classical simple reaction time paradigm (Rodnick & Shakow, 1940) has generated several theoretical models (e.g., Shakow, 1962; Bellissimo & Steffy, 1972) and will in all likelihood generate more. Similarly, the size-estimation task has played a central role in Rodnick and Garmezy's censure-deficit model (1957)[1] and in Silverman's attention theory (1964). I think the task-oriented approach is more deserving of the criticism that the models it has generated are narrowly confined to the parameters of a particular task than of the criticism that it is entirely devoid of theoretical concerns. In turn, a major virtue of the process-oriented approach is not so much that it brings theory to bear on the study of cognitive dysfunction as that theory determines the nature of the tasks and methods to be employed in testing dysfunction hypotheses.

Ironically enough, I think a case can be made that the process-oriented models thus far employed in schizophrenia research are also at some risk of being confined to a narrow data base, particularly insofar as they seem to be focused on primarily visual-spatial configural processing and much less on auditory-temporal verbal processing.

In a similar connection, I consider it of some importance that information-processing deficits such as Knight's "perceptual organization deficit" be shown to be related to more complex forms of psychopathology in schizophrenia, as a means for validating the deficit and demonstrating that it is not trivial. I am not referring here to the desirability of showing that there are rough analogies between deficit and phenomenology or that particular deficits are confined to particular subgroups. I am recommending that relations between deficits and symptoms be predicted and tested. These observations lead me to a more general consideration of the problem of model validity in the process-oriented approach.

A major virtue of this approach—the availability of a plethora of information-processing models—is, as Knight himself points out, also one of its major embarrassments. Experimental psychopathologists who elect the process-oriented approach will be aware of a history of changing fashions in models and will confront contemporary

---

1. It is of some historical interest in the present context that a full-scale version of the "censure-deficit model" was first published in the 1957 volume of the *Nebraska Symposium on Motivation*.

arrays not only of converging models, but also of competing models. Knight requires that experimental psychopathologists master this array of models and place their empirical bets on the most probable winner in a validity competition. To be sure, this is a dilemma inherent in the scientific method itself, but for Knight's experimental psychopathologists it is double-pronged. The process-oriented investigator who can claim no special expertise in cognitive science may typically be in the situation of having invested heavily in a model he or she may not fully understand and whose validity is problematic, to study a deficit in schizophrenics the existence and nature of which is speculative. I have perhaps overstated the dilemma. Nonetheless, my example dramatizes the validity problem and suggests that experimental psychopathologists' discomfort may lead them to cling to their chosen models even in the face of disconfirmation, inventing auxiliary theories to protect this "poor thing but my own." Worse yet, this dilemma sets the stage for the evolution of rival camps among information-processing models. Indeed, we may already be witnessing the formation of contending factions, as between Saccuzzo and Braff on the one hand and Knight and Spaulding on the other. No one can lay responsibility for this at Knight's door. Indeed, he deals effectively and extensively with the problem of auxiliary theories in the disconfirmation of models and confronts the validity problem in a forthright and creative fashion.

There is a contemporary research trend in experimental psychopathology to which, in my view, Knight has given insufficient attention and which may also be of some help in the solution of the validity problem. The electrophysiological study of cortical activity has made substantial progress in the past ten years in relating cortical events to cognitive processes and in identifying cortical correlates of cognitive dysfunction in schizophrenia. Electrophysiological brain study methods such as the evoked cortical response paradigms, with their attention to time-locked sequences of brain wave forms, seem to interface particularly well with stage-type information-processing models. A combination or merging of process-oriented and electrophysiological study methods may amplify the explanatory power of either approach and provide the linkage of psychopathology in schizophrenia to pathology at the level of neurophysiology and neurochemistry. Moreover, if in a given experimental situation entailing both information-processing and electrophysiological methods, parallel or complementary predictions derived from both an information-processing model and a neurophysiological functions domain are confirmed (or not disconfirmed), the credibility of the information-processing model may thereby be strengthened. I hope it will be evident that in the formulation above I am *not* claiming that an information-processing model acquires credibility because it can be readily "translated" into neurophysiological terms or because to a given pattern of information-processing data a neurophysiological "explanation" can be readily fitted.

I shall turn now away from the validity problem entailed by the process-oriented approach and take up the methodological issues engendered by the fact that the great majority of schizophrenic patients involved in the information-processing studies Knight cites in the early sections of his chapter were receiving antipsychotic medication. In so doing I must acknowledge that Knight's creative and extensive treatment of the general cognitive deficit problem has encouraged me to systematize here my thinking and experience in the study of the effects of antipsychotic drugs on psychological and psychophysiological dysfunction in medicated schizophrenic patients. Moreover, much of what I say will be seen to be broadly applicable to both process- and task-oriented research.

To begin with, it is instructive to characterize as polar opposites Salzinger's view that data derived from medicated patients can have no valid bearing on the dysfunction characteristic of schizophrenia and Knight's view that drug effects are merely nuisance variables. I believe both are overstatements.

It reflects a lack of familiarity with an extensive drug evaluation research literature to suggest that antipsychotic drugs are nuisance variables, on a par, perhaps, with the effects of sedatives or analgesics. Antipsychotic medications reduce or remove a fairly broad range of schizophrenic symptoms and, though not rehabilitative, do permit most schizophrenic patients to function more efficiently and realistically in interpersonal environments. In some patients, though certainly not in all, antipsychotics produce total symptomatic remission. Indeed, this is why such medication is aptly designated antipsychotic.

When drug effects on cognitive dysfunctions are examined in placebo-controlled studies they are characteristically found to be in the direction of normalization. Patients behave more like normal individuals on-drug than off-drug and function at a higher level on-drug relative to their own level before drug treatment, although schizophrenics rarely achieve full normality. On the other hand, I know of no instances in which the antipsychotic action of drugs has been found to introduce compensatory dysfunction, such as narrowing the span of attention in distraction-prone patients. The drugs do, however, produce short-term reversible and long-term irreversible side effects that are clearly, and in some cases grossly, dysfunctional. I shall seek to show below that both the normalizing target actions and the dysfunctional side effects of drug treatment represent methodological concerns for experimental psychopathology research.

The effects of drugs on a variety of dysfunctions in schizophrenic patients have been examined in independent-group-design studies that entailed drug withdrawal or washout and used placebo controls. The following exemplifies, but does not describe exhaustively, the findings of such studies. Reaction time in regular order of preparatory interval presentation is reduced by medication (Spohn, Lacoursiere, Thompson, & Coyne, 1977) and the crossover effect is compressed (Spohn, Note 1). Improved performance on the Continuous Performance Test (CPT) suggests that drugs normalize concentration or vigilance (Orzack, Kornetsky, & Freeman, 1967; Spohn et al., 1977). Accuracy in size estimation is enhanced and excessive visual scanning is reduced by drugs (Spohn et al., 1977). Short-term memory span is increased, and a Rorschach-based index of thought disorder (Johnston & Holzman, 1979) is reduced (Spohn, Note 1). There is also some evidence (Spohn, Note 1) that Knight's "perceptual organization deficit" is normalized. I shall present these findings in detail at a later point. Such electrodermal variables as basal skin conductance level and amplitude of specific responses are reduced, and the frequency of nonspecific responses is decreased in schizophrenic patients on drugs (Tecce & Cole, 1972; Spohn et al., 1977). Finally, in data from medicated chronic schizophrenics that I have recently analyzed, there is evidence that elevated indexes of tardive dyskinesia are associated with increased latencies in reaction time and with poor eye tracking (Spohn, Note 2).

I should point out that my phrasing in this catalog of drug effects may be misleading insofar as it suggests that the antipsychotic drugs act directly on cognitive and psychophysiological dysfunction. There is virtually no evidence to substantiate such an interpretation. In all likelihood, effects on particular dysfunctions are mediated in some fashion that we do not yet fully understand. Hypotheses that some dysfunction effects are mediated by effects on electrodermal variables and others by effects on general cognitive deficit are currently under study in my laboratory.

By no means all forms of dysfunction examined thus far have been found to be modified or normalized by antipsychotic drugs. Indeed, it is of particular interest that drug effects are selective or disjunctive even with respect to different aspects of performance on the same task or on similar tasks as well as with respect to differing indexes within the same functional sphere. Thus, for example, while short-term memory (STM) span at a short exposure duration (250 msec) is increased in medicated patients, short-term memory span at a longer exposure duration (750 msec) is unaffected (Spohn et al., 1977; Spohn, Note 1). Eye tracking when "cognitive focusing" is possible is improved by drugs, while baseline performance is unaffected (Spohn, Note 1). As already noted above, several electrodermal indexes including basal skin conductance level and nonspecific responses are reduced, but the skin conductance orienting response (SCOR) is unmodified (Spohn, Note. 1).

Antipsychotic drug effects are also complexly related to classification dimensions such as chronicity and premorbid social-sexual adjustment. Among recent-onset schizophrenics, good premorbid patients appear to be substantially more susceptible to normalization than poor premorbid subjects (Goldstein, Judd, Rodnick, & LaPolla, 1969). In chronic schizophrenics drugs do not respect the premorbidity dimension—they normalize dysfunctions in good and poor patients alike (Spohn et al., 1977).

Having adduced a substantial amount of evidence bearing on the effects of antipsychotic drugs, I now want to develop systematically its methodological implications for both task- and process-oriented studies of cognitive dysfunction in medicated schizophrenic subjects. Generally speaking, the most prudent methodological expectation on the part of experimental psychopathologists has to be a conservative one—that any form of dysfunction under study in medicated schizophrenics is likely to be reduced in magnitude or severity. Let me dramatize this point in relation to Knight's identification of a perceptual organization deficit in poor premorbid schizophrenics. In my current work, imposing a cognitive mask 150 msec after onset of a target stimulus of a six-letter array reduced STM span in drug-withdrawn chronic schizophrenics to a greater extent than in on-drug control patients. Under the same conditions, STM span returned to prewithdrawal levels when the patients were remedicated.

In some circumstances, however, the drug-effect data permit somewhat more specific cautions. Response latencies in schizophrenic patients without abnormal involuntary movements are likely to be shorter on-drug than off-drug. This methodological caution seems particularly relevant to process-oriented investigators employing response latencies to discriminate between parallel and sequential processing. On the other hand, when the response is motoric and signs of tardive dyskinesia are present in medicated *or* unmedicated schizophrenics, reaction time can be expected to be elevated. Similarly, smooth-pursuit eye movements and possibly saccadic eye movements as well are likely to manifest signs of dysfunction in the presence of tardive dyskinesia beyond such dysfunction as has already been shown to be related to psychopathology per se in functional psychoses (Holzman and Levy, 1977).

Within-task selective or disjunctive effects pose special methodological problems, particularly in relation to strategies to finesse the general cognitive deficit problem. They may mimic a pattern of adequate and deficit performance predicted from a hypothesis that assumes the presence of a specific form of dysfunction or differential deficit. Similarly, disjunctive effects may attenuate performance differences when task difficulty is manipulated.

Let me say, to conclude my comments on Knight's chapter, that there are no simple solutions to the methodological problem represented by the mostly normalizing effects of antipsychotic drugs. Correlating medication dosage levels in medicated subjects within a given study with test performance or behavior in an effort to determine direction and magnitude of drug effects is likely to be misleading because the relation between drug dosage level and therapeutic response is not linear. Comparisons of test performance or behavior between medicated patients and patients who are drug-free because for a variety of reasons drug treatment is not indicated for them are flawed because such drug-free patients are atypical. Drug withdrawal is, in most circumstances, practically unfeasible and ethically unacceptable. In sum, when experimental psychopathologists who are either task- or process-oriented are concerned with the drug-effect problem, they may have no recourse other than to look to the rather specialized research literature, some of which I have cited above, for clues on whether and to what extent the dysfunction under study is masked by antipsychotic drugs.

COMMENTS ON K. SALZINGER'S CHAPTER

I think it is felicitous that in his contribution to this volume Salzinger has been moved to establish his widely known and most heuristic immediacy hypothesis as a theory of schizophrenia. His many creative and ingenious experimental contributions on behalf of the hypothesis that schizophrenics are more prone than normal individuals to respond to immediate stimuli in their environment clearly provide an ample empirical base for theory building. But Salzinger has achieved more in his chapter than a conceptualization of this largely self-generated data base. He has boldly undertaken something rather rare in the experimental study of schizophrenic psychopathology— the formulation of a systematic theory that aims at encompassing all psychopathological phenomena in schizophrenia. Moreover, he has permitted us to witness the theory-building process itself. It seems only fitting, therefore, that I as discussant depart from the security of my own area of expertise in the psychopharmacology of schizophrenia and undertake a critical appraisal of immediacy theory. In so doing I shall confine myself to three tasks: a critique of its structure and internal consistency, a determination of its susceptibility to falsification, and an assessment of its heuristic value.

I think the way Salzinger goes about preparing the ground for theory building is particularly valuable. The criteria he sets forth as minimum requirements for a meaningful theory of schizophrenia reflect his extensive experience in the empirical study of schizophrenic dysfunction and are likely to be welcomed by most investigators in this field. What is perhaps less likely to be greeted with general enthusiasm is his binding the immediacy hypothesis to the conceptual foundations of radical behaviorism. This should come as no surprise, however, to anyone who has followed Salzinger's work, and indeed it affords the theory its systematic structure.

His methodological critique of experimental psychopathological studies in schizophrenia seems to me both appropriate and illuminating. Again, the author's long empirical experience stands him in good stead here. I resonate particularly with his comments on the antipsychotic drug problem. As I have noted elsewhere, however, there is a practical and realistic middle ground between his radical position that behavioral data from medicated schizophrenic patients are largely invalid and Knight's characterization of drug effects as nuisance variables.

I find one of the two empirical "tests" to which Salzinger puts the immediacy theory—its applicability or consistency with his own body of work, conceptualized in terms of the immediacy hypothesis—largely convincing. He is less persuasive, however, in his ingenious efforts to demonstrate its "validity" by reinterpreting in immediacy terms a set of more or less randomly chosen experimental studies informed by hypotheses deriving from other theoretical contexts. I shall have more to say about this later on. For now I want to assess both the virtues and the failings of immediacy theory.

I consider it one of its principal virtues that the theory is built on the solid foundations of a general theory of human development and behavior. While the theory is not synthetic, since it draws on a limited and circumscribed data base, it appears, nonetheless, to be capable of accounting for a broad range of psychopathological phenomena in schizophrenia as well as etiological processes. Moreover, it appears to do so in terms of a single general principle. Accordingly, it merits praise as being elegantly simple, a characteristic highly desirable in a general theory and one that in the present instance lends immediacy theory considerable heuristic appeal. Finally, on the plus side, the theory is internally consistent and eminently operationalizable.

With respect to its weaknesses, I regard as a serious problem, in Salzinger's present formulation, his failure to state an explicit and clear definition of the immediacy principle independent of particular experimental arrangements and results, a definition that would permit unambiguous predictions in any experimental or behavioral situation. His present formulation forces a critic to infer the principle from numerous exemplifications of it. However, in an effort to infer a definition of an immediate stimulus from numerous applications of the concept to experimental arrangements and results, I was forced to conclude that an immediate stimulus may be one that is temporally proximal, spatially proximal, isolated, or more intense than other stimuli; it may be an experimentally defined anchor, a stimulus defined as irrelevant in particular cognitive context, or the presence or absence of reinforcement. This lack of consistency in the definition of the central principle of immediacy theory has some very serious consequences. It renders the theory vulnerable to the charge that it is inherently not susceptible to falsification by experimental test. Inconsistent definitions of the immediate stimulus give rise to the possibility that any given experimental result may be subject to multiple interpretations and even to the interpretation that an immediate stimulus is whatever schizophrenic patients respond to.

I feel certain that as experienced an investigator and as learned a scholar as Salzinger does not need to have these consequences of ambiguous definitions of the immediacy principle pointed out to him. I suspect that in his effort to demonstrate the universal applicability of the immediacy hypothesis it became stretched out of shape. Ironically, in this stretching process Salzinger identified linkages of the immediacy hypothesis to other task- and process-oriented cognitive dysfunction hypotheses.

COMMENTS ON C. R. WALLACE'S CHAPTER

In my comments on Wallace's chapter I want to begin with the acknowledgment that Wallace's work and that of his associates is serving an important public policy aim. In the early years of deinstitutionalization of large numbers of chronic schizophrenic patients in precarious symptomatic remission related to drug treatment, it was simply not realized that symptom remission is not the equivalent of social rehabilitation. Thus many chronic schizophrenics were forced into marginal, unproductive, lonely lives in communities that feared and shunned them. The systematic and painstaking assessment of social skills deficiencies in chronic mental patients and the thoughtful training procedures now being afforded such patients by Wallace and his associates greatly improve their chances of achieving a satisfying and enduring adjustment in the community.

I am a relative stranger to the technology for teaching social skills described in Wallace's chapter. I am most impressed by the sophistication and imaginativeness he brings to bear on the challenging tasks he has undertaken. In light of my own research interests, I have been intrigued by that behaviorist social skills trainers such as Wallace, as well as behavior therapists and directors of token economy programs for chronic schizophrenics, commonly report that their training procedures are successful only when their patients are receiving antipsychotic medication. I think this insight derives from clinical experience and has not been systematically investigated. Therefore I believe that the most constructive contribution I can make in my discussion of Wallace's chapter is to use my specialized experience and knowledge of psychopharmacological research in schizophrenia to examine the interaction of anti-psychotic drug treatment and social-skills training efforts.

In a recent article (Schooler & Spohn, 1982) we reported the evaluation of a socioenvironmental treatment program applied to fifty chronic schizophrenic patients in a Veterans Administration hospital ward well over twenty years ago. Although our program lacked the sophistication and sensitivity of Wallace's approach, it was intended as a social-skills retraining program for patients presumably deskilled by years of institutionalization. Our re-socialization program, implemented by a large, well-trained nursing staff, sought to create a sense of community and in a variety of ways urged and even forced patients to increase their social interaction with each other and with staff. We did not employ an explicit reinforcement program, although in regularly scheduled, frequent group meetings we provided snacks.

Our results after two years of program operation indicated that while we had indeed succeeded in increasing the level of both active and passive social interaction among most patients, we had also increased the level of anxiety on the ward, which led in turn to significant symptom exacerbation not found in patients on a control ward. Of particular relevance in the present context, however, was the finding that a subgroup of patients medicated throughout the program, who did not display increased anxiety or symptoms, also did *not* manifest the increased social interaction characteristic of most of the patients.

Before venturing an interpretation, let me call attention to rather similar findings reported in a series of studies by a group of British investigators (Brown, Birley, & Wing, 1972; Leff, Kuipers, Berkowitz, Eberlein-Vries, & Sturgeon, 1982). These investigators have been concerned with interventions designed to protect against relapse and rehospitalization of chronic schizophrenic patients who are in close contact with "high expressed emotion" relatives. ("High expressed emotion" is characterized by a high level of critical comment directed toward the patient—hostility, frequent expression of dissatisfaction, and emotional overinvolvement.)

In an early study Brown et al. (1972) found that chronic schizophrenic patients discharged to high expressed emotion families relapsed significantly more often than did patients returning to families practicing a policy of benign neglect. But there was a subgroup among the patients exposed to high expressed emotion families who were on antipsychotic medication and who did not relapse, or whose relapse occurred significantly later than in drug-free patients. Brown and associates interpreted the main findings of the study as implying that chronic schizophrenics who are not afforded the opportunity for social withdrawal are at greater risk for relapse than patients who can withdraw as needed. Furthermore, the authors concluded that antipsychotic medication provided some degree of prophylaxis to patients in high expressed emotion homes against the intrusive behavior of other family members.

This group of investigators has since gone on to develop a social intervention program explicitly coupled with antipsychotic drug treatment for patients in high expressed emotion families. This program was evaluated in the recent study by Leff et al. (1982) and found to be highly effective.

In my view, the findings by Schooler and Spohn (1982) and by Brown et al. (1972) converge on the interpretation that antipsychotic drug treatment promotes learning of *social withdrawal* when such learning is adaptive and protects symptom remission. I propose the following post hoc hypothesis to account for what I think can reasonably be regarded as a form of social skills learning. Normalization of cognitive dysfunction by drug treatment provided the efficiency required to plan behavioral strategies needed to achieve privacy and safety from intrusion. As these strategies succeeded, reduction in anxiety (or arousal) played a reinforcing role.

A study by Hogarty and Goldberg (1973) throws further light on this interpretation. These investigators conducted a large-scale placebo-controlled study in which the aim was to determine whether a combination of antipsychotic drug treatment and major role therapy for discharged chronic schizophrenics was superior to drug treatment alone or major role therapy alone. The latter consisted of intensive social casework and vocational counseling. Generally speaking their findings were positive. Drug treatment combined with major role therapy achieved the best and most enduring community adjustment. There was, however, in their drug and major role-treated sample a subgroup of patients who not only did not benefit from the combined treatment, but relapsed and required rehospitalization. On close examination it was found that these patients, though drug-treated, were not largely asymptomatic; that is, their symptoms had not been reduced to the same extent as in patients who responded positively to the combined treatment. Hogarty and Goldberg concluded, on the basis of this finding, that the cognitive complexity of the training program overburdened the information-processing capacity of the only partially remitted patients, leading to exacerbation and thus to rehospitalization.

In conclusion, the evidence I have brought to bear on the antipsychotic drug treatment/social skills training interaction issue suggests that the reduction or normalization of cognitive dysfunction by medication in chronic schizophrenics is a necessary precondition for the successful application of social skills training. Cognitively impaired patients may not be able to respond to the appropriate, in Salzinger's terms, discriminative stimuli or to perceive as such reinforcement scheduled by the trainer. Moreover, it appears that social skills training in cognitively impaired chronic schizophrenics may actually be toxic in its effects. I strongly suspect that sophisticated social skills trainers like Wallace are already intuitively or explicitly aware of these preconditions and requirements. For less experienced and sophisticated investigators, there may be some value in developing a checklist or inventory to assess the "cognitive readiness" of social skills training candidates.

REFERENCE NOTES

1. Spohn, H. E. *Attention, thought disorder and drug action in schizophrenia.* Progress Report, Continuation Grant Application, United States Public Health Service Grant MH32220-04, 1981.

2. Spohn, H. E. Attentional and psychophysiological correlates of eye tracking and thought disorder in chronic schizophrenics and affective disorder patients. Manuscript in preparation for publication, 1983.

REFERENCES

Bellissimo, A., & Steffy, R. A. Redundancy-associated deficit in schizophrenic reaction time performance. *Journal of Abnormal Psychology*, 1972, **80**, 299–307.

Brown, G. W., Birley, J. L., & Wing, J. K. Influence of family life on the course of schizophrenic disorders. *British Journal of Psychiatry*, 1972, **121**, 241–258.

Goldstein, M. J., Judd, L. L., Rodnick, E. H., & LaPolla, A. Psychophysiological and behavioral effects of phenothiazine administration in acute schizophrenics as a function of premorbid status. *Journal of Psychiatric Research*, 1969, **6**, 271–287.

Hogarty, G. E., & Goldberg, S. C. Drug and sociotherapy in the aftercare of schizophrenic patients. *Archives of General Psychiatry*, 1973, **28**, 54–64.

Holzman, P. S., & Levy, D. L. Smooth pursuit eye movements and functional psychoses: A review. *Schizophrenia Bulletin*, 1977, **3**, 15–27.

Johnston, M. H., & Holzman, P. S. *Assessing schizophrenic thinking: A clinical and research instrument*. San Francisco: Jossey-Bass, 1979.

Leff, J., Kuipers, L., Berkowitz, R., Eberlein-Vries, R., & Sturgeon, D. A controlled trial of social intervention in the families of schizophrenic patients. *British Journal of Psychiatry*, 1982, **141**, 121–134.

Orzack, M. H., Kornetsky, C., & Freeman, H. The effects of daily administrations of carphenazine on attention in schizophrenic patients. *Psychopharmacologia*, 1967, **11**, 31–38.

Rodnick, E. H., & Garmezy, N. An experimental approach to the study of motivation in schizophrenia. In M. R. Jones (Ed.), *Nebraska Symposium on Motivation, 1957*. Lincoln: University of Nebraska Press, 1957.

Rodnick, E. H., & Shakow, D. Set in the schizophrenic as measured by a composite reaction time index. *American Journal of Psychiatry*, 1940, **97**, 214–225.

Schooler, C., & Spohn, H. E. Social dysfunction and treatment failure in schizophrenia. *Schizophrenia Bulletin*, 1982, **8**, 85–98.

Shakow, D. Segmental set: A theory of psychological deficit in schizophrenia. *Archives of General Psychiatry*, 1962, **6**, 1–17.

Silverman, J. The problem of attention in research and theory in schizophrenia. *Psychological Review*, 1964, **71**, 352–379.

Spohn, H. E., Lacoursiere, R. B., Thompson, K., & Coyne, L. Phenothiazine effects on psychological and psychophysiological dysfunction in chronic schizophrenics. *Archives of General Psychiatry*, 1977, **34**, 633–644.

Tecce, J. J., & Cole, J. O. Psychophysiological responses of schizophrenics to drugs. *Psychopharmacologia*, 1972, **24**, 159–200.

Subject Index

Author Index